GROUP CARE AND EDUCATION OF INFANTS AND TODDLERS

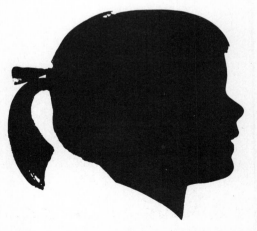

In every child there is something precious that is in no other.

GROUP CARE AND EDUCATION OF INFANTS AND TODDLERS

MARGARET G. WEISER, Ed.D.

Associate Professor, Division of Early Childhood
and Elementary Education, University of Iowa,
Iowa City, Iowa

with **61** illustrations

The C. V. Mosby Company

ST. LOUIS • TORONTO • LONDON   1982

MOSBY

A TRADITION OF PUBLISHING EXCELLENCE

Editor: Julia Allen Jacobs
Manuscript editor: Nelle Garrecht
Design: Susan Trail
Production: Kathleen Teal

Cover photo by **Randall Hyman**

The C.V. Mosby Company
11830 Westline Industrial Drive, St. Louis, Missouri 63141

Library of Congress Cataloging in Publication Data

Weiser, Margaret G., 1922-
    Group care and education of infants and toddlers.

    Bibliography: p.
    Includes index.
    1. Child development. 2. Day care centers.
3. Children—Care and hygiene. 4. Motor ability
in children. 5. Socialization. I. Title.
HQ774.5.W44   305.2′3   81-14142
ISBN 0-8016-5538-2   AACR2

AC/VH/VH 9 8 7 6 5 4 3 2 1   02/B/283

To two persons whom I hold dear and who have been
most influential in my growth as an early childhood educator:

Sarah Lou Hammond Leeper,

formerly at Florida State University and the University of Maryland,

and

Gladys Gardner Jenkins

at the University of Iowa.

PREFACE

The group care and education of very young children is a comparatively recent but rapidly growing phenomenon throughout the world. The rising demand for infant and child group day care, irrespective of its setting (center based or home based) is emerging from a variety of factors: a growing consciousness of the lasting effects of deprivation, an increasing number of women employed outside the home, the isolation of the nuclear family in urbanized societies, and a growing body of knowledge and theory concerning the importance of the early years as it relates to future attitudes, values, and achievement in and out of school.

Because of the recency of the professionalization of the care and education of young children, there exists a serious lack of persons who are qualified and competent in the new profession of early childhood education and development. Although universities, colleges, and other agencies have provided laboratory schools for young children since the early 1920s, they usually have served as centers for research and training and typically have drawn children from upper-middle class families. They have been on a partial day basis and on an academic year schedule. In spite of the quality of these endeavors, the number of teachers who were trained in these centers was far less than the number of early childhood teachers needed to meet the sudden national mandate for preschool classes designed to give poor children a "head start" on their schooling. Following the expression of federal interest in the 1960s, state departments of education issued new teaching endorsements for the years below public school, and state departments of social welfare updated their licensing standards, which had previously focused on foster homes, boarding institutions, and the like. A new profession, that of the Child Development Associate, was called for by Edward Zigler, then Director of the Office of Child Development (HEW), and the Child Development Associate Consortium was formed to devise a procedure to assess those competencies deemed valuable in the delivery of early childhood group programs. There is now a national credential signifying the meeting of these competencies for teachers of groups of children ages 3 to 5 years. Early childhood education has become a visible facet of our society. The number of research studies and textbooks has proliferated; workshops and minicourses and one-year, two-year, and four-year programs have been established and are being attended by an ever-increasing number of persons desiring to enter, or to become more qualified in, early childhood education.

Why, then, this textbook? The need for qualified teachers of children ages 3, 4, and 5 still exists, but provisions have been and are being made to meet this need. The need for qualified teachers and caregivers of very young children, of children from the very first months of life, has been virtually ignored in teacher education programs. Therefore, this text has been designed to be used in courses that offer the theory and practice of the care and education of very young children to prospective teachers and caregivers.

As is true of most worthwhile endeavors, we need to know where we have been in order to know where we are and where we are going. This maxim is particularly appropriate for the topic at hand, because without the acknowledgement of the importance of the early years, there is no reason to pursue the issue beyond the usual instructions given in the typical "babysitter" manual. Unlike many methods textbooks, this one concerns itself first with the evolution of the recognition of the importance and significance of the very early years; from there the emphasis is placed on the current state of the art and on recommendations for current and future programs. The knowledge gained from the information contained herein, and the involvement in a related practicum situation, should enable the student to be a competent beginning teacher and caregiver of very young children.

Because both the adults and the children involved in early care and education are male or female, the two genders are used interchangeably throughout the text. Also, each involved adult has two interchangeable roles, those of caregiver and teacher. The involved adults are referred to as either caregiver or teacher, or caregiver/teacher. Neither role can be divorced from the other.

A completed textbook is the result of the efforts of many persons. I am especially indebted to Bettye Caldwell, for the use of the AID developmental objectives. I am grateful to Jane Dunlap Petersen, for the descriptions of "typical days" in the lives of very young children in a center-based day care and education program, and to Jane Kaplow Rosenthal, for the explanation of the system of primary caregiving. Both have served as head teachers of the infant and toddler rooms at the Early Childhood Education Center, University of Iowa.

Special acknowledgement is also given to Dr. Alfred Healy, who reviewed the Care and Protection Curriculum, and to Dr. Gerald Solomons, Director, Region VII Child Abuse and Neglect Resource Center; to Annemarie Shelness, Physicians for Automotive Safety; to Sandra Zimmerman, Insurance Institute for Highway Safety; and to Dr. Susan Aronson, whose endeavors in advocating health and safety for children in day care have been recognized nationwide.

Any book about children needs photographs of children to make it come alive. I take this opportunity to express my appreciation to Sally Antes, University Infant and Toddler Center of Western Illinois University, Richard Elardo and Jan Cronin of the Early Childhood Education Center, University of Iowa, and to the many parents of the children.

I am grateful to my typist, Connie Barthelman, not only for the typing, but the re- and re-retyping of the manuscript.

It is my hope that the text will be helpful to persons who are giving, or will give, care and education to our youngest citizens.

Margaret G. Weiser

CONTENTS

The importance of the early years

There can be no better way to begin a text on the care and education of our youngest children than with the statement of the Declaration of the Rights of the Child, a declaration that was unanimously adopted by the representatives of the 78 countries in the General Assembly of the United Nations on November 20, 1959.

The preamble states that the child, because of his physical and mental immaturity, needs special safe-guards and care, both before and after birth, and that indviduals and groups should strive to achieve children's rights by legislative and other means. Mankind, it says, owes the child the best it has to give.

In ten carefully worded Principles, the Declaration affirms that all children are entitled to:

1. The enjoyment of the rights mentioned, without any exception whatsoever, regardless of race, color, sex, religion or nationality
2. Special protection, opportunities, and facilities to enable them to develop in a healthy and normal manner, in freedom and dignity
3. A name and nationality
4. Social security, including adequate nutrition, housing, recreation and medical services
5. Special treatment, education and care if handicapped
6. Love and understanding and an atmosphere of affection and security, in the care and under the responsibility of their parents whenever possible
7. Free education and recreation and equal opportunity to develop their individual abilities
8. Prompt protection and relief in times of disaster
9. Protection against all forms of neglect, cruelty and exploitation
10. Protection from any form of racial, religious, or other discrimination, and an upbringing in a spirit of peace and universal brotherhood (UNICEF, 1974, p. 9)

This text offers suggestions and guidelines for efforts toward the realization of these rights for very young children in group care. A paraphrase of the introductory comments frequently found in nineteenth century children's books is just as appropriate for us.

Attend! We are now beginning.
When we get to the end of the
story we shall know more than
we do now.

1

Chapters 1 and 2 lay the foundation for the following chapters by tracing how the first few years of life have been regarded by philosophers and educators throughout history. It is not our purpose to attribute prime importance to any one stage of development, but rather to establish the fact that the beginning years are important, just as are the following years.

Chapter 2 presents an overview of selected child development theories and a general sequence of the development of behavioral characteristics from birth to age 36 months. Goals for the care and education of all children should be derived, in part, from knowledge of child development, and the chapter concludes with a discusion of goals and objectives for the group care and education of children from birth to age 36 months.

CHAPTER 1

THE IMPORTANCE OF THE VERY EARLY YEARS: HISTORICAL PERSPECTIVE

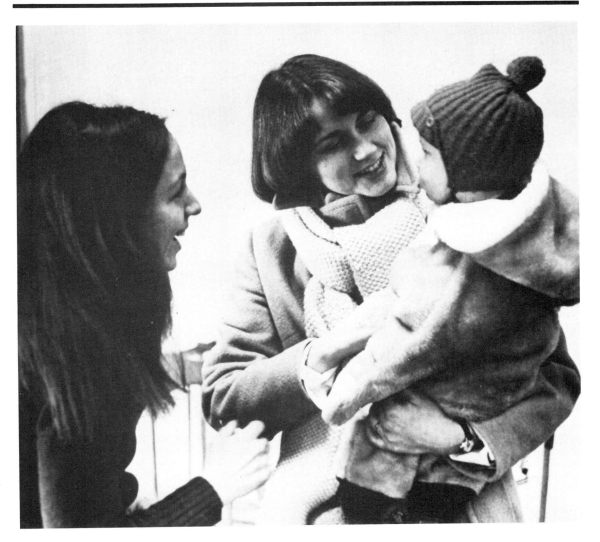

All the flowers of all the tomorrows are in the seeds of today.
Chinese proverb

What is a baby worth? In some parts of the United States a healthy newborn can be purchased for $25,000 on the black market. The price may be as little as $5,000 if the baby is obtained through a legitimate adoption agency. The cost in money may be even less through a public agency, but the waiting period may be as long as 5 years. Babies apparently have a high value today, at least for some adults.

We have reason to believe that babies and young children have been treasured by society even from the very beginnings of human history. Archeologists have found numerous artifacts representing pregnant women (but not children), and anthropologists have concluded that the legal and religious sanctions of marriage came into being solely for the protection of children. Children assured the continuation of the race.

Written history reveals that recognition of the importance of the early years of life has been sporadic. It has taken many forms and has frequently been selective rather than universal. The values, attitudes, and goals of societies determine the place of the young child in their midst. Depending on their time and place in history, some children have been valued as future soldiers, some as future philosophers and kings, and many as potential wage earners; others have been viewed as liabilities, even disasters. Almost always, boys have been more highly valued than girls. Until the nineteenth century all children were viewed as miniature or incomplete adults, and their importance was determined solely by their anticipated adult roles. Childhood was brief and of little account—a period of marking time.

In spite of the various views about young children, the popular assumption is that throughout history young children have been cared for and nurtured within the family at least until they were old enough to join the work force—which may have been as young as 5 years of age. However, this was not the case. The coming of civilization meant that upper-class women, at least, assigned the role of nurse and caregiver to servants or to slaves. Old Testament prophets felt the need to tell mothers it was their duty to nurse their children; in the second century AD Plutarch strongly admonished mothers to nurse their young. In 1633, Comenius (the "father" of early childhood education in Czechoslovakia) maintained that babies received not only alien milk, but alien morals from the wet nurse. In the 1700s Rousseau stated that there would be a reform in morals and no lack of citizens for the state if mothers would nurse their own children. At that time, it was estimated that of the 21,000 children born in Paris each year, 1400 were nursed by their mothers or wet nurses in their homes; 2600 were placed in suburban nursery care, and the remaining 17,000 were sent into the country to be cared for by professional wet nurses. The children sometimes stayed as long as 12 years!

In the United States the owners of Southern plantations customarily assigned the nursing and rearing of their young children to their slaves. During the same time period, the apprentice system was based on families rearing and training children other than their own, while sending their own children to other families.

In twentieth century America, especially during times of national stress, very young children have been cared for by others either in the home or outside the home while mothers work or receive job training. It might be assumed that voluntarily assigning the nursing and care of very young children to persons outside the immediate family implies an unawareness of the importance of these beginning months and years. It is also evident that, despite the hue and cry about the sanctity of the home for the rearing of its young, such has never existed as a universal phenomenon.

To a very large degree, any historical review of attitudes involves the drawing of inferences from happenings and writings and is always subject to some misinterpretation. The story of the evolution of the recognition of the importance of the very early years presents two additional difficulties: First, very young children have been only occasionally viewed as important enough to write about. Second, the word *infant* has been used to refer to varying age ranges, from the first 7 years of life—"in this age it cannot talk well or form its words perfectly, for its teeth are not yet well arranged or firmly implanted" (Le Grand Proprietaire, 1556, cited in Aries, 1962, p. 21)—to the entire span of years preceding adulthood. There was no term to distinguish between child and adolescent in seventeenth century France; *enfant* was used for both. As recently as 1824, a father wrote of his "infant" daughter, about 10 years old. Today the first years of compulsory schooling in Britain are

housed in the "infant school," which serves children aged 5 through 7 years. However, within these limitations, a selected review of history does reveal the evolution of the importance accorded the very early years.

BEFORE THE MIDDLE AGES
Greece

Greece was the site of the beginnings of Western civilization, and some note was made of young children even in the days of antiquity. In the eighth century BC, Spartan children were less the offspring of their parents than the property of the state, and immediately after birth were inspected for physical fitness by a citizens' committee. Those deemed not fit were tested by being exposed to the elements of the mountains in northern Greece—a test that would probably have killed even a healthy baby. Those infants who were deemed fit were almost immediately immersed in the life we now call Spartan, a life away from home, with no tenderness or nurturing, a life designed from the start to teach obedience, military prowess, and stamina. Healthy children did have value, but only as future soldiers or as mothers of future soldiers.

The peak of Sparta's civilization was the military crushing of Athens, about 404 BC. Out of Athenian shame and turmoil came the first educational theorists, Plato and Aristotle, both of whom recognized the importance of the early years in the formation of good persons and good citizens. Plato's *Republic* contains guidelines for the leadership training of the future guardians of the political state, including provisions for the regulation of marriage and procreation. All children of free men were to be removed at birth from their parents and reared by state-supported nurses, but all other adult citizens were also charged with the protection and education of all the children. Plato's major concern for the very young child was the formation of character, and he admonished the nurses to tell stories that

Pottery vases from the Early Iron Age (750-500 B.C.). Baby feeding bottle in middle.

Courtesy Metropolitan Museum of Art, the Cesnola Collection. Purchased by subscription, 1874-76.

presented only the human virtues and to ignore the ancient myths and legends that contained violence, lust, and passion. Historically, Plato is the first known writer to acknowledge the critical period of infancy. In the *Dialogues* he quotes Socrates as saying: "The beginning is the most important part of any work, especially in the case of a young and tender thing; for that is the time at which the character is being formed and the desired impression is more readily taken. . . . Anything that he receives into his mind at that age is likely to become indelible and unalterable."

Plato's goals were twofold: (1) to train a wise ruling class, and (2) to free parents from the demands of child care so that they might actively meet their civic responsibilities. The motivating force was obviously not good child care. (We have not made much progress. When it exists at all, government interest in child care is still for the benefit of adults who need to be employed or to be trained for future employment.)

Plato (428–348 BC) concerned himself with the ideal; his recommendations were far removed from the customs of his time and were never put into practice; however, the *Republic* is the first great educational classic in historical time. Aristotle (384–322 BC) dealt with the real and based his guidelines for the upbringing of small children on direct observation of children and "other young animals." He recommended a regime of more milk and less wine; physical movement exercises; exposure to cold temperatures (with a view to future military service); minimal association with slaves; and censored tales and stories. Children up to the age of 7 years were to be reared at home by their mothers or nurses, under the guidance of a children's tutor who made certain that the stories told, the language used, and the games played were moral and appropriate for future citizens. Until the age of 5 there were no prescribed studies or tasks, because the necessary physical exercise would occur naturally during periods of

Animal-shaped pull toy (and vase) from the Early Iron Age (1200-1800 B.C.).

Courtesy Metropolitan Museum of Art, the Cesnola Collection. Purchased by subscription, 1874-76.

free play. Unlike Plato's proposal, Aristotle's educational system was designed only for the male children of free citizens.

Plutarch (46-120 AD), although best known for *Parallel Lives*, also recommended appropriate methods of childrearing. Like Plato, he was concerned with parenting, warning against cohabitation with courtesans and concubines, and urging the husband's abstinence from wine when he approached his wife. Mothers of newborns were advised to feed their infants and nurse them themselves. Immediately after birth, they were to manipulate the child's limbs so that they would grow straight. This advice was in direct opposition to the customs of the times, when not only the Greeks but also the Romans and the Jews wrapped their infants

tightly in swaddling bands. Frequently even the infant's head was protected by a pointed, close-fitted cap that also covered the ears and the back of the neck. Swaddling is an ancient practice that has continued throughout the centuries in many parts of the world. It is simply the wrapping of the child with strips or bands of cloth, in some cases so tightly that little or no movement is possible. Swaddling as such is not practiced in the United States, but our babies are often wrapped snugly in hospital nurseries and are "tucked in" tightly in their cribs at home. The modern Chinese swaddle their babies tightly for the first month but leave legs and feet free.

Plutarch further admonished parents to be very selective in choosing the foster mothers, nursemaids, or young slaves who would be nurses and servants or companions of young children. They were to be Greeks who were moral and distinct in their speech.

Plutarch was a firm believer in the virtues of early habit training (behavior modification!) and described the first recorded animal research study on learning. Apparently, Lycurgus took two puppies and reared them in different ways in an attempt to show the positive effects of habit training on future performance. At a gathering of the Spartan lawgivers, he demonstrated the results by putting the two dogs down in front of a dish of food and a live rabbit. One dog immediately ran after the hare; the other gobbled up the food. When the lawgivers did not understand, Lycurgus explained, "These dogs are both of the same litter, but they have received a different bringing-up, with the result that one has turned out a glutton and the other a hunter. In regard to habits and manners of life, let this suffice" (Moralia, cited in Ulich, 1954, p. 92).

The Roman Empire

While the early Greeks were concerned with lofty ideals and philosophy, the Romans were bound to the practical matters of daily living and the governing of an ever-growing number of conquered peoples of diverse cultures and races. Unlike the Greeks, the early Romans depended upon the power of the home as the site of learning to honor the gods, the family, and the country. We know little beyond this, although Quintilian (35–95 AD) offered some very specific suggestions about the education of very young children. No doubt, the great empire fell before the suggestions were put into practice. He believed that most, if not all, children of free men were quick to reason and ready to learn, and therefore the father should plan his son's education from the moment of birth. Once again, the custom of assigning the direct care of little children to other than the natural mother becomes apparent: "Above all see that the child's nurse speaks correctly. . . . It is the nurse

that the child first hears, and her words that he will first attempt to imitate. And we are by nature most tenacious of childish impressions. . . . It is the worst impressions that are most durable" (Institute of Oratory, cited in Ulich, 1954, p. 104).

Quintilian also expressed dissatisfaction with the common practice of teaching the names and order of the letters before teaching their shapes, and suggested that young children be given sets of ivory letters to play with. After the children could recognize and differentiate the shapes, they were to be supplied with wooden boards on which the letters had been cut out so that the mistakes that occurred with wax tablets could not happen. After the child had progressed to syllables and words, he would then copy lines containing sound moral lessons, which would contribute to character formation.

Similar advice about an infant's training and education was offered by Jerome in 403 AD, who also recommended boxwood or ivory letters as playthings, and the letter shapes supplied so that there would be no mislearning. Jerome's concern was to nurture souls for a future world. Christianity had begun to supplant the concerns for military strength and political administration, and the names of the apostles and the patriarchs from Adam downward were to be the first learned words. A glimpse of the customs of the day is contained in the following exerpt from a letter addressed to a Roman matron who wished to raise her infant daughter as a virgin dedicated to Christ: "Let her very dress and garb remind her to whom she is promised. Do not pierce her ears or paint her face dedicated to Christ with white lead or rouge. Do not hang gold or pearls about her neck or load her head with jewels, or by reddening her hair make it suggest the fires of ghenna" (Principal Works of St. Jerome, cited in Braun and Edwards, 1972, p. 23).

The only other indication we have of the value of very young children in these centuries, an indication much more direct than the advice and various guidelines previously referred to, is the passing of the Roman law in 318 AD proclaiming infanticide a criminal act. Nonetheless, infanticide continued to be practiced without much condemnation until the eighteenth century, and it continues today in one form or another.

MIDDLE AGES (400–1400 AD)
AND THE RENAISSANCE (1400–1700 AD)

The idea of childhood completely disappeared during the Middle Ages—although of course there were children! As soon as the swaddling bands were removed (at 9 to 12 months), infants were dressed just like the men or women of their social class. Because of superstition and lack of medical knowledge or hygiene, only one child of every two or three lived to adulthood, and the Church began the immediate baptism of all infants to save them from eternal damnation before they died.

The Middle Ages were indeed the Dark Ages. Europe was torn by wars and hunger, leaving little time or inclination for tenderness, individuals, or grandiose plans concerning education and childrearing. The major contribution of the period was the safekeeping of the ancient literary works, preserved and copied by the monks in the monasteries, and it was to these writings that the noblemen of the Renaissance turned for guidance. Because Plato and Aristotle had planned education for the elite of their societies, the education of the Renaissance was directed toward the male children of noble parentage. The young male child of rank was considered precious, because he promised the continuation of the family, but even he was not allowed childhood. Swaddling was discarded at 4 to 6 weeks of age; both girls and boys were then dressed in lace-edged petticoats, full-skirted frocks with full real sleeves (as well as false sleeves to be used as leading strings to control the child's efforts to walk), aprons, bibs, and lace-edged bonnets. This was the mode of dress (minus the leading strings) for the remainder of a girl's life.

The boys were "breeched" at age 5 or 6 years, but over the breeches was worn a floor-length doublet with added false hanging sleeves. Under the doublet were a matching petticoat and decorative underpetticoats. With minor changes, this, too, became the lifetime mode of dress.

Chivalry came into being near the close of the Middle Ages (1200–1400 AD). Knighthood was in flower and involved a new gentleness, an esteem for women and young children, and an intense interest in the childhood of Jesus, who until then had been pictured as a stern, child-sized adult with little compassion. (Neither artists nor anyone else had any interest in studying children.)

By the end of the fifteenth century the Christ child began to appear likelife. By this time artists had begun to study the anatomy of children, and both body proportions and facial features became more realistic. From this religious interest in the baby Jesus evolved an interest in all young children, which unfortunately went to extremes. In many cases children became objects of amusement.

As was formerly the case, as soon as they left the infant stage, children were immediately immersed in all facets of adult life. An account of the beginning years in the life of Louis XII of France highlights this total immersion. The Dauphin was born in 1601, and the royal physician kept detailed records of his charge's activities and development. Before 17 months of age, the Dauphin played with the "usual toys": a hobbyhorse, a windmill, a top; at 17 months of age Louis could play the violin and sing at the same time, as well as play mall (similar to our game of golf). By the age of 2 years, Louis started to talk, and his tutors made him pronounce the syllables separately. He was also taken to the King's apartments where he danced and sang with the adults, although he still played his childish games. When he was 2 years, 7 months he was given a doll collection; and at 2 years and 9 months, he was moved from his cradle to his own bed. At age 3 years, 4 months, he could dance all the adult dances and was taught to read. At age 4, he was taught to write, and started to learn Latin, but still played with dolls. By age 5 or 6 he practiced archery and played cards, chess, and countless parlour games (cited in Aries, 1962, pp. 62-65).

Not only was young Louis a source of amusement, but precocious as well! Few children, of course, were heirs to thrones. For most, childhood was brief, with even the small toddlers joining their families in weeding, planting, and harvesting.

These were the conditions into which Comenius (1592-1670) was born—a time when parents were nonsolicitous of little ones, or so they appeared, because the fate of the infant could just as easily be death as life, and one could not allow oneself to become too emotionally attached. Comenius dared to suggest that not only was there an identifiable stage of growth from infancy until 6 years of age, but also that there was an appropriate educational curriculum for this stage. Such a startling proposal was too revolutionary and too removed from everyday life to be accepted during his lifetime. However, some 300 years later he was acclaimed as the father of early childhood education, at least by his native Czechoslovakia. Today his recommendations for teaching very young children are put into practice in home intervention programs, day care centers, nursery schools, and kindergartens in Western Europe and the United States. Comenius proposed an educational ladder, beginning with a school "at the mother's knee," not an actual school, but one that should exist in every household. He even outlined a detailed curriculum for mothers, including the training of the senses, rudimentary facts, and vocabulary development. Comenius was the first advocate for very early childhood education since Plato and Aristotle. However, he recommended education for boys *and* girls from *all* economic classes.

John Locke (1632-1704), a contemporary of Comenius, was concerned with the education of upper-class boys. Locke's view of the newborn's mind as an empty slate, a blank sheet of paper, led him to the conclusion that very early experiences made impressions of lasting importance. Unfortunately, he considered mothers too soft with their children, and recommended a tutor from the earliest months. Locke, although unmarried and childless, was colonial America's favorite philosopher. He counseled, "Would you have your son obedient to you, when past a child? Be sure then to establish the authority of a father, as soon as he is capable of submission, and can understand in whose power he is. If you would have him stand in awe of you, imprint it in his infancy" (cited in Bremner, Vol. 1, 1970, p. 132).

Locke described a baby of his time as:

. . . rolled and swathed, ten or a dozen times round; then blanket upon blanket, mantle upon that; its little neck pinned down to one posture; its head more than it frequently needs, triple-crowned like a young page, with covering upon covering; its legs and arms as if to prevent that kindly stretching which we rather ought to promote . . . the former bundled up, the latter pinned down; and how the poor thing lies on the nurses lap, a miserable little pinioned captive (cited in Cunnington and Buck, 1965, p. 103).

Although historians call this period the Renaissance, the reawakening of scientific thought and mathematical and astronomical knowledge included no consideration whatsoever of child development. At the end of the 1600s, early childhood was an almost nonexistent stage of life, and the voices of Comenius and Locke were not even heard, let alone heeded. The young child was considered either innately bad or morally asleep. Comenius totally rejected the idea of innate badness and attributed morality to education and firm (not harsh) discipline; Locke maintained that the infant was born with no predisposition toward anything.

One bright note: the first published edition of the Mother Goose tales appeared in 1697.

WESTERN EUROPE IN THE EIGHTEENTH AND NINETEENTH CENTURIES

It is essential to keep in mind the vast differences between the writings and recommendations about childrearing in any period in history and the harsh realities. The first half of the eighteenth century found one out of every three infants abandoned, and the foundling homes were so crowded that the infant mortality rate reached as high as 80%.

It was also in the eighteenth century that an idea was reintroduced that toppled the European world—and is still creating reverberations. First hinted at in Greece and Rome, then set forth in Locke's writings in the seventeeth century, it appeared full bloom in Rousseau's *Social Contract* first published in 1762: the people are more important than their rulers. Not only that, but "everything is good as it comes from the hands of the Author of Nature (p. 1). "Our instruction begins when we begin to live; our education begins with our birth (p. 9). Should not the education of a child begin before he speaks and understands" (p. 27)?

The very young child has at last appeared, and is naturally good, no longer tainted by original sin. The child no longer requires punishment to be rid of the evil one, but rather is good, at least until society and education introduce their artificial ways. Both the *Social Contract* and *Emile or Treatise on Education* were published in 1762, and both had a tremendous impact. The French Revolution erupted the year after Rousseau died; harsh discipline has virtually disappeared from the schools of the world.

Rousseau dignified the first 5 years of life as a recognizable and important stage of development, proclaiming that children should be treated as children, not as irrational animals or miniature adults. He argued that children had

their own ways of seeing, thinking, and feeling, and that their appropriate education was natural growth in a natural environment. His ideas constituted the beginnings of child study as a discipline and incorporated the concept of the young child as an active, searching organism who learned through play and living, with minimal interference from adults. Perhaps most important is Rousseau's fundamental concept, developed partially by Comenius, that childhood is a time important in and of itself, during which childlike behavior is appropriate.

Fortunately for the children, Rousseau advocated breast-feeding by the natural mother, fresh air, and loose clothing. As the result of his writings many mothers discarded the swaddling bands and nursed their infants instead of immediately sending them to a wet nurse. Even the paintings of this period depict the ideal nature of the child. The painting shown in Fig. 1-1 was originally named "Nature," a direct reference to Rousseau's writings.

This concept was further reinforced by Pestalozzi (1746–1827). Not only did he agree with the natural unfolding of childhood, but also he re-emphasized the role of the home and the "mother's knee" in the early education of the child. According to Pestalozzi, if education in the schools was to have real value, it should imitate the methods in the home. In *How Gertrude Teaches Her Children* (1801) he outlined his educational premise: sense impressions lead to awareness, and awareness forms the foundations of language and academic skills. He stated that "very great harm is done to the child by taking it away from home too soon and submitting it to artificial school methods. The time is drawing near when methods of teaching will be so simplified that each mother will be able not only to teach her children without help, but continue her own education at the same time" (cited in Braun and Edwards, 1972, p. 56).

Within a span of only 40 years we not only have the young child as an identifiable, whole

FIG. 1-1   The Calmady Children, Sir Thomas Lawrence.

Courtesy Metropolitan Museum of Art. Bequest of Collis P. Huntington, 1925.

human being, but we also have the blueprint for modern early childhood education and for the home-based education of very young children. The educational innovations of Comenius, Rousseau, and Pestalozzi made the child interesting as a focus for educational attention, but scientific study of the child itself was necessary in order to formulate a theory of child development based on empirical analysis. We owe the introduction of the child as subject for such study to Darwin's *On the Origin of the Species* (1859). Almost all of American child psychology is derived from the comparative studies of Dar-

win, whose observations of the infant and child led him to his theory of the descent of man. Darwinian theories are biological. Some 50 years later Sigmund Freud introduced the notion that stages of development are sequential and occur in a biologically predetermined order.

However, prior to Darwin and Freud, Froebel had pulled together the previous thinking and added some of his own in his major work published in 1826 (*The Education of Man: the Art of Education, Instruction, and Training*), which he put into practice in his kindergarten in

1837. His first school was attended by some 50 children who ranged in age from 1 to 7 years. (Even today in Europe "kindergarten" designates group education for children from 3 to 6 or 7 years of age, unlike our own adaptation for 5-year-olds only.) The first volume of the *Education of Man* gives specific information about the very early years:

Disregard about the value of earlier, and particularly the earliest, stages of development with reference to later ones, prepares for the future teacher and educator of the boy difficulties which it will be scarcely possible to overcome. . . . The child, the boy, man, indeed, should know no other endeavor but to be at every stage of development wholly what this stage calls for (pp. 29-30). . . . From a very early period . . . children should never be left too long to themselves on beds or in cradles without some external object to occupy them. . . . It is advisable to suspend in a line with the child's natural vision, a swinging cage with a lively bird. This secures occupation for the sense, and the mind, profitable in many directions (p. 49). . . . Even very small children, in moments of quiet, and particularly when going to sleep, will hum little strains of songs they have heard; this, too, . . . should be heeded and developed even more in melody and song. Undoubtedly this will soon lead in children to a self-activity similar to that attained in speech, and children whose faculty of speech has been thus developed and trained, find, seemingly without effort, the words for new ideas, peculiar associations and relations among newly discovered qualities (p. 71). . . . Let us live with our children; then shall we begin to grow wise, to be wise. . . . Living with our children implies on our part sympathy with childhood, adaptability to children, and knowledge and appreciation of child-nature; it implies genuine interest in all that interests them, . . . it implies seeing ourselves with the eyes of a child, hearing ourselves with the ears of a child, judging ourselves with the keen intuition of a child (p. 89).

Froebel added to the growing number of books for mothers: *Mother-Play and Nursery Songs* is the source of many of the finger plays, action songs, and stories used in early childhood classes throughout the world (Fig. 1-2). Also, many of the toys and manipulatives used by young children today are closely related to the wooden building blocks and different colored balls of yarn that he devised as playthings. (Froebel advised teachers to wash the yarn balls at least once a year!) To Froebel, also, we owe the introduction of women, instead of men, as teachers of young children.

Apparently Froebel's philosophy had few immediate followers in the educational system of the late 1890s. A female principal of a New York City school was evaluated in 1893 as excellent for her 25 years of service. She believed "that what the child knows and is able to do on coming to school should be entirely disregarded, that he should not be allowed to waste time, either in thinking or in finding his own words to express his thoughts, but that he should be supplied with ready-made thoughts as given in a ready-made vocabulary" (Rice, cited in Braun and Edwards, 1972, p. 97).

This happy thought leads us to the United States.

UNITED STATES

From the earliest colonial days to the twentieth century young children were taught the alphabet and the rudiments of reading and writing in the home. Childhood, as a unique part of human life, had no advocate and no protection against the railings of religious leaders such as Jonathan Edwards, who wrote in 1740: "All are by nature the children of wrath, and heirs of hell. . . . As innocent as children seem to be to us, [yet they] are young vipers, and are infinitely more hateful than vipers, and are in a most miserable condition . . . and they are naturally very senseless and stupid, being born as the wild asses colt, and need much to awaken them" (cited in Bremner, Vol. 1, 1970, p. 139).

Such a violent opinion of very young children had definite overtones for early childrearing. In addition, the prevailing belief that original sin caused illness delayed serious attempts at the prevention and treatment of both childhood and

FIG. 1-2   Pat-a-cake, in S.E. Blow: The songs and music of Friedrich Froebel's Mother Play, New York, 1895, D. Appleton & Co., p. 35.

adult maladies. The most important medical advance in the early nineteenth century was the smallpox vaccination. It was not until 1880 that the American Medical Association established its pediatric section. In 1881 silver nitrate prophylaxis was placed in the eyes of the newborn for the first time as blindness preventative.

Fortunately, not all early Americans agreed with Jonathan Edwards. We have been told that "one of the most precious flowers of Puritanism" was a girl born in 1708 in Boston. At the age of 2 she knew her letters, spoke distinctly, and told many stories from the Scriptures. At age 3 she recited the catechism and many psalms, and read "distinctly"; at age 4 she "asked many astonishing questions about divine mysteries. As her father was president of Harvard College, it may be inferred she had an extended reading course" (Glubok, 1969, p. 112).

Until the beginning of this century young children of affluent white parents were treasured and educated. Other young children were valued also, but as economic assets to their families or owners. Adam Smith reported on child power as the nation's wealth: "A numerous family of children, instead of being a burden, is a source of opulence and prosperity to the parents. . . . A young widow, with four or five young children, who, among the middling or inferior ranks of people in Europe would have so little chance for a second husband, is there [North America] frequently counted as a sort of fortune. The value of children is the greatest of all encouragement to marriage" (cited in Bremner, Vol. 1, 1970, pp. 169-170).

In the South slave children were economic assets. They were legally equated with the off-spring of tame and domestic animals, and as objects of property; they were administered by the owner.

What about the children of the "savages" of America? A Belgian Jesuit missionary described the childrearing practices of Plains Indians in a letter to his niece written in 1851. In the mid-

1800s the only "school" for the Indian children was the example of their elders. The father had charge of the boys; the girls were the mother's responsibility. These native Americans paid great attention to the children's physical development, and plunged the newborn several times into water to build up the child's resistance, regardless of the season of the year. Someone other than the mother cared for the baby for the first week. When the child was returned home, she was fastened securely onto a cradle-board, which was used until she was able to walk. The cradle was hung inside the lodge or outside on the branch of a tree, close by the other family members. When the family traveled, the baby went right along in the cradle hung from the saddle-bow, out of the rider's way but with no danger (Bremner, Vol. 1, 1970). It might appear that "savage" childrearing was more humane than that espoused by Jonathan Edwards.

Not all "nonsavage" mothers in the eighteenth and nineteenth centuries had the time or inclination to rear and teach their young children. Many sent their infants and toddlers to a neighbor, usually a poor widow or dame, for their "day care." The "dame schools" thrived in New England, where their quality was as varied as the widows or dames who ran them. Lucy Larcom (1889) was one of the more fortunate children; she described her dame school as follows:

Aunt Hannah used her kitchen or her sitting room for a schoolroom, as best suited her convenience. We were delighted observers of her culinary operations and other employments. If a baby's head nodded, a little bed was made for it on a soft comforter in the corner, where it had its nap hour undisturbed. But this did not often happen; there were so many interesting things going on that we seldom became sleepy. Aunt Hannah was very kind and motherly, but she kept us in fear of her ferule, which indicated to us a possibility of smarting palms. The ferule was shaped much like the stick with which she stirred her hasty pudding for dinner,—I thought it was the same,—

and I found myself caught in a whirlwind of family laughter by reporting at home that 'Aunt Hannah punished the scholars with a pudding-stick'. There was one colored boy in school, who did not sit on a bench like the rest, but on a block of wood that looked like a backlog turned endwise. Aunt Hannah often called him a 'blockhead', and I supposed it was because he sat on that block. Sometimes, in his absence, a boy was made to sit in his place for punishment for being a 'blockhead' too, as I imagined. I hoped I should never be put there. Stupid little girls received a different treatment,—an occasional rap on the head with the teacher's thimble; accompanied with a half-whispered, impatient ejaculation, which sounded very much like "Numskull!' . . . I began to go to school when I was about two years old. . . . But I learned my letters in a few days, standing at Aunt Hannah's knee, while she pointed them out in the spelling-book with a pin, skipping over the 'a b abs' into words of one and two syllables, thence taking a flying leap into the New Testament, in which there is concurrent family testimony that I was reading at the age of two and a half years (pp. 42-44).

Apparently young future kings had no corner on precocity.

During the nineteenth century, many manuals on the proper methods of childrearing appeared, and the stage of early childhood was firmly acknowledged in the New World. Another change of importance: judges began to override the traditional rights of fathers in custody cases, placing the welfare of the child as top priority. At that time it was universally assumed that a child's future welfare depended on a mother's care.

How far have we progressed in the recognition of the importance of the early years? With due appreciation for the thoughts and writings of theorists and educators from England, France, Switzerland, Czechoslovakia, and Germany, we have accorded the young child status as a subject for scientific inquiry and the early childhood period as a stage in human development with age-specific behaviors and needs. At the beginning of the twentieth century, the American debt to Europe was considerable.

Twentieth century

During the twentieth century the United States has faced disastrous wars, periods of depression and inflation, baby booms, and zero population growth. We have also accumulated a diverse collection of social welfare and health programs, which contain minimal focus on the very young child per se. The longest lived democratic experiment is still suffering from growing pains, but one of the positive facets of the experiment is our growing acknowledgement of the significance of the very early years of human life.

Changes in all aspects of child study were discernible by 1910. The first revolutionary factor was the measurement of intelligence and the assessment of human variability. Galton was convinced that the major differences in babies were hereditary, but Binet maintained that the intelligence of children (that is, their capacity to learn) could be increased by stimulation. His original scale contained 55 tests arranged according to the year in which the majority of normal children acquired each skill or ability. According to his findings, most children by the age of 3 years could (1) point to facial features; (2) repeat two digits; (3) enumerate objects in a picture; (4) give their last name; and (5) repeat a sentence of six syllables.

In the 1920s and 1930s the issue of infant and young child development was being debated, but only in the halls of academia. At Yale, Gesell was maintaining that environment had very little effect; it was the child's individual biological characteristics that made the difference. Watson of Clark University argued that environment and education made a great deal of difference.

Skeels and his colleagues at the University of Iowa were working in an overcrowded orphanage where they discovered two little girls (aged 13 and 16 months old chronologically) who showed considerable retardation. It was decided that the girls should be moved to a less crowded institution, since "nothing" could be done for them. They were moved into a home

for "feebleminded" adolescent girls and older
women. A few months later, Skeels returned to
the home for the feebleminded and found two
bright, alert little girls, not at all mentally retarded as they had seemed months before. They
even tested in the normal range of intelligence.
What had happened? The toddlers had been
"adopted" by the older girls on the ward, who
rocked them, played with them, and talked to
them; in other words, they showered them with
attention and stimulation. As a result, Skeels
then purposely transferred an experimental
group of 13 orphanage children, all under 3
years of age, and all considered "unsuited for
adoption" (the current term is mentally retarded
or disabled), to the same institution for older
girls and women. The ten girls and three boys
had no gross physical handicaps, but their mental development was seriously retarded. One or
two children were placed in each ward, and
again the women and ward attendants became
attached to "their" children, and gave them almost constant attention and encouragement.
This personal interest was the unique feature of
the experimental setting. The thirteen children
were observed until they were 4½ years of
age; final tests of mental development showed
an IQ score change from +7 to +58 points; none
had failed to show some gain. In the contrast
group still in the orphanage only one child had
any gain in IQ points (+2); negative change
ranged from −8 to −45 points. But the best was
yet to come. Skeels conducted a follow-up study
some 30 years later; his findings are summarized
in Table 1-1. The contrast in outcomes highlights
the first significant indication of the effect of
very early environmental experience. What
happens before the age of 3 can make a difference!

Unfortunately, the original study received
much criticism. Critics claimed that the study
was not well done, that tests were not given
correctly, and that the statistical analysis was
wrong. Such criticisms were not justified. The
academic world apparently was not yet ready to

TABLE 1-1   Adult status of Skeels' subjects

Experimental (N=13)	Contrast (N=12)
All reached adulthood, 11 in adoptive homes.	One subject died in the institution. None had been adopted.
All were self-supportive; none showed need for psychiatric or economic support.	Four were without occupation; others worked as dish-washers, part-time food service helpers; one as a typesetter.
Mean grade completed: 12.0	Median grade completed: 2.75

accept new ways of thinking about the early
years, early experiences, and the nature of intelligence.

During World War II the whole issue of the
importance of the early years received little attention, but in the late 1940s and into the 1950s,
researchers began to discover that the infant
had a number of capabilities that could be
studied. It was learned that very young infants
could discriminate among visual stimuli, visually track a slowly moving object, and react to
tactile experiences. Infants were found to listen
to a soft rattle or a caregiver's voice, and to have
different reactions to female and male voices. As
a result, it was conjectured that the infant constantly received and reacted to stimuli, and with
each stimulus reaction, the infant's brain stored
experience for future learning.

More studies followed in the next two decades, all of which added to the documentation
of the significance of the very early months and
years of life. It has been conjectured by some
researchers that foundations of behavior, personality, and cognitive structures are established by the age of 3 years, and that these basic
structures regulate the child's current and future views of himself and of his encounters with
the world. If the child has been discouraged
from exploration or deprived of consistent care
and affection during the first 3 years, he or she
apparently constructs a defensive shield against
the world that is difficult to penetrate. This pro-

tective mechanism does not seem to form if the young child has engaged in consistent reciprocal human relationships. Therefore the maturational view of development has been revised because it does not include reciprocal relationships; the "blank slate" view has been replaced, because it ignores the child's own predispositions and readinesses for relationships and interactions.

The findings of these more current researchers might have remained in the psychological journals had not two major publications appeared in the 1960s. Hunt (1961) conclusively ended the contention that the development of intelligence was predetermined by genes and therefore fixed. He suggested that we discover ways to "govern the encounters that children have with their environment, especially during the early years of their development" (p. 363). In 1964 Bloom reported his analysis of over 1,000 longitudinal studies of the development of human characteristics. He concluded that "in terms of intelligence measured at 17, about 50% of the development takes place between conception and age 4" (p. 88).

In the last decade, numerous studies have shown a consistent finding of no relationship between socioeconomic status and IQ test scores at 15 months, and significant correlations between socioeconomic status and IQ test scores by 3 years of age. Kagan (1971) has reported on discernible differences in patterns of attention and reaction to visual and auditory stimuli as early as 8 months of age. White and Watts (1973) classified 1- and 2-year-olds as "competent" or "not competent," using a list of psychological characteristics. They followed the development of the two groups of children, and their original classification proved accurate at the end of a year. Teachers of 3- and 4-year-old children from less advantaged backgrounds have become increasingly aware that many of these children have already suffered a decrease in both motivation to learn and expectations for success, apparently never to be regained. One of the oft-cited reasons for the mixed success of the

federally funded compensatory programs is that probably they did not start soon enough. Newspapers recently reported a study of Israeli nursery school children indicating that even the most intense educational effort starting at age 3 failed to achieve effective integration of the disadvantaged children with their peers, intellectually or socially. The results of the study indicate that deprivation has measurable effects during the first 3 years of life.

TODAY

Today the concern about very early training and development is reflected in studies and programs involving thousands of children all over the world. In spite of the recent explosion of reseach, we still do not know very much; we do not know if the child does outside the laboratory what she does inside the laboratory. We do not know the specific effects of specific environments or the extent of the role of individual differences in determining these effects. We do not know how the socialization process occurs and what agents are the most effective socializers. There is much we do not know, but we do know enough from observational material, theories, and experimental data to make educated guesses.

Have the American policy makers and the educators kept pace with the implications of research? Just where are we nationally with respect to our very young children and their families?

We have not yet recovered from the 1971 veto of child development legislation, which would have initiated the application of what we know about the very early years. In his message to Congress in 1971, President Nixon stated, "For the Federal Government to plunge headlong into supporting child development would commit the vast moral authority of the National Government to the side of communal approaches to child rearing over against the family-centered approach" (p. 1636).

The celebration of our country's bicentennial

elicited some summary statements about "where we are" nationally:

1. Families: "We seem to see individuals creating or dissolving families for their individual needs rather than a family organization responding to terms of its total membership" (Sudia, in Grotberg, n.d., p. 57).

2. Child health: "Contrary to what most Americans believe, our infant mortality rates are now higher than sixteen other countries, and dropping more slowly than a number of other countries. Compared to the mortality rates of other countries, that of white American infants ranks 8th, that of non-white Americans, 31st" (National Council of Organizations for Children and Youth, 1976, p. 32).

3. Education: "Tomorrow's education will begin early in the child's life. Self-motivation, attitudes towards others, the length of time that immediate gratification is postponed for more distant rewards, perceptions of complex phenomena, the ability to focus attention—all these are markedly influenced in the period from birth to age five" (Tyler, in Grotberg, n.d., pp. 212-13).

4. Child welfare: "There is much unfinished business" (Datta, in Grotberg, n.d., p. 221).

5. Child development: "Findings from many of the studies of the 1960's suggested the need to know more about infant development in order to help parents function more effectively, to provide intervention programs at earlier ages, and to recognize the increasing demand for services for very young children" (Grotberg, n.d., p. 418).

The questions "Where have we been?" and "Where are we now?" have been partially answered. Now we must ask, "Where are we going?" It has been estimated by Clarke-Stewart that over 23 million books on childrearing have been sold over the last 5 years, running the gamut from the ever-popular *Baby and Child Care* editions by Spock to *Toilet Training in Less than a Day* by Azrin and Foxx. Parents, early childhood educators, and child advocates are working hard to gain societal recognition of the importance of the early years. Part of the future is in our hands because of our commitment to the care and education of very young children.

■ CHAPTER SUMMARY ■

The position of very young children in society has slowly evolved from having virtually no special value to valuing selected healthy children in the pre-Christian era and valuing all children as souls for a future world in the early Christian period. Then the young child "disappeared" until the early seventeenth century when Comenius and John Locke proclaimed the importance of the very early years, although little attention was given to their admonitions. Rousseau, in the eighteenth century, dignified the first 5 years of life and introduced the idea of *childhood* as opposed to small-sized adulthood. Pestalozzi and Froebel in the nineteenth century were the first notable practitioners in early childhood education, and actually taught very young children with methods much more appropriate than the traditional rote teaching in Latin and Greek. The theories of Comenius, Pestalozzi, and Froebel have had considerable impact on pedagogical methods in both Europe and the United States. Today, the importance of the early childhood years is recognized and accepted by professional persons in the fields of psychology, medicine, social welfare, and education, but societal commitment in Western countries is yet to come.

SUGGESTED ACTIVITIES/POINTS TO PONDER

1. Compulsory beginning school age ranges from 5 to 7 years of age. Do you agree with beginning school at these ages? Why or why not? What should be the compulsory beginning school age in this country?

2. Should provisions for education be available to children below compulsory school age? If so, under what sponsorship (state departments of education, state departments of social services, state departments of health, the federal government, other)? Explain your choice of sponsor.

3. The very early years are now recognized as influential in

the development of the child. Should public funds be used to subsidize a parent so that he or she might stay home with a young child? Should public funds be used to subsidize child care for children of parents who are employed out of the home?

REFERENCES AND SUGGESTED READINGS

Aries, P.: Centuries of childhood, New York, 1962, Random House, Inc.

Bloom, B.S.: Stability and change in human characteristics, New York, 1964, John Wiley & Sons, Inc.

Blow, S.E.: The songs and music of Friedrich Froebel's mother play, New York, 1895, D. Appleton and Co.

Braun, S.J., and Edwards, E.P.: History and theory of early childhood education, Belmont, Cal., 1972, Wadsworth Publishing Co., Inc.

Bremner, R.H., editor: Children and youth in America: a documentary history, Vols. 1-3, Cambridge, Mass., 1970–1974, Harvard University Press.

Clarke-Stewart, A: Popular primers for parents, American Psychologist 33:359, 1978.

Cole, L.: A history of education, New York, 1950, Rinehart & Co.

Cunnington, P., and Buck, A: Children's costume in England, New York, 1965, Barnes & Noble, Inc.

Downer, M.: Children in the world's art, New York, Lothrop, Lee & Shepard Co., 1970.

Froebel, F.: The education of man: the art of education, instruction, and training, New York, 1887, D. Appleton and Co. (Illustrated by W.N. Hailman; originally published in 1826).

Glubok, S. editor: Home and child life in colonial days, New York, 1969, Macmillan Publishing Co., Inc.

Greenleaf, B.: Children through the ages: a history of childhood, New York, 1978, McGraw-Hill Book Co.

Grotberg, E., editor: 200 years of children, Washington, D.C., n.d., Department of Health, Education and Welfare.

Hunt, J.: Intelligence and experience, New York, 1961, Ronald Press.

Kagan, J.: Change and continuity in infants, New York, 1971, John Wiley & Sons, Inc.

Kessen, W., editor: The child, New York, 1965, John Wiley & Sons, Inc.

Larcom, L.: A New England girlhood, Boston, 1889, Houghton Mifflin Co.

McGraw, M.: The child in painting, New York, 1941, The Greystone Press.

National Council of Organizations for Children and Youth: America's children 1976, Washington, D.C., 1976, The Council.

Nixon, R.: The President's message to the Senate returning S. 20007 without his approval, December 9, 1971, Weekly compilation of Presidential documents, VII, 1971.

Osborn, D.K.: Early childhood education in historical perspective, Athens, Ga., 1980, Education Associates.

Rasmussen, M., editor: Dauntless women in childhood education, Washington, D.C., 1972, Association for Childhood Education International.

The Rights of Children, Reprint Series No. 9, Harvard Educational Review, Cambridge, Mass., 1974.

Rousseau, J.J.: Emile or treatise on education, New York, 1893, D. Appleton and Co. (Translated by W.H. Payne.)

Skeels, H.M.: Adult status of children with contrasting early life experiences: a follow-up study, Serial No. 105, 31, No. 3, Monographs of the Society for Research in Child Development, 1966.

Ulich, R.: Three thousand years of educational wisdom, Cambridge, Mass., 1954, Harvard University Press.

UNICEF and the rights of the child, UNICEF/6601 #5203, New York, 1974, United Nations Children's Fund.

White, B.L., and Watts, J.C.: Experience and environment, vol. 1, Englewood Cliffs, N.J., 1973, Prentice-Hall, Inc.

CHAPTER 2

EARLY CHILD DEVELOPMENT AND RELATED GOALS FOR THE GROUP CARE AND EDUCATION OF INFANTS AND TODDLERS

PART I: Principles of early child development

**Before I got married I had six theories about bringing up children;
now I have six children and no theories.**

Lord Rochester (1647-1680)

EARLY CHILD DEVELOPMENT: OVERVIEW

Child development is easily defined as the study of how children develop, yet the experts in the field maintain that "child development" defies precise definition. We might therefore suspect that our simple answer is not so simple after all. Like most simple answers to questions about human beings, the definition involves an in-depth investigation of which fundamental questions need to be asked. It is important not only to ask the questions but also to find the answers. It is essential for all persons in any responsible relationship with young children to know how and why children develop the way they do. They can then plan experiences and environments, both in and out of the home, that are relevant and appropriate for maximizing the potential of young children.

There is also a need for widespread understanding about the normal range in the date of onset of certain developmental landmarks. For example, there are reliable reports of children learning to walk at 7 or 8 months of age, but a large number of perfectly normal children do not learn to walk before they are 15 or even 18 months of age. We therefore need to ask and answer the following: What characteristics result because of membership in the human race? In a specific family? Under all or just some environmental conditions? Are there individual differences? Why? How do these determinants of growth and development interact and modify one another?

The first part of this chapter is designed to offer clues to some of the answers, but will no doubt lead to more questions. It serves two functions, depending on the background knowledge of the reader. It will serve either as an introduction to theories of child development or as a review of selected developmental theories. In either case, it is necessary background information for planning the care and education of very young children.

The newborn appears totally helpless and dependent, and frequently has a physical appearance only a mother could love! This new person many times protests entrance to the world loudly and vigorously, but apparently the inevitable is soon accepted. Within 5 or 6 days the infant is able to respond to visual, auditory, and tactile stimulation with strong preferences and dislikes. This new baby is *capable* of selecting stimuli to which to respond or ignore, to physically withdraw from an external cause of pain, or to react with total body movement to internal distress. Almost immediately, an infant can lift or turn his head in order to avoid suffocation, reflexly grasp objects with hands and feet, visually track a slowly moving object, locate a small object with the mouth when touched near the mouth, and suck. All physiological systems of a human being are in working order at the time of a normal birth; not only does the newborn have potential for humanness, the newborn *is* human. Very soon after birth (some say while still in the womb) the baby's education begins.

Burton White (1975), a leader in child development, maintains that "the period that starts at eight months and ends at three years is a period of primary importance in the development of a human being. To begin to look at a child's educational development when he is two years of age is already much too late" (p. 4). White is attempting to break new ground, because no society in Western civilization has accorded educational importance to the earliest years.

White and his colleagues have presented evidence to show that many skills and abilities of the "competent" 6-year-old are also part of the behavioral repertoire of advanced 3-year-olds. Such abilities include: (1) using adults as resources for information, food, and assistance; (2) leading and following age-peers; (3) expressing emotions of affection, hostility, and pride; (4) using expressed language extensively and meaningfully; (5) recognizing discrepant happenings or appearances; (6) anticipating consequences; and (7) attending to more than one thing simultaneously or in rapid succession. "The 10- to 18-month period of life is in effect a critical period for the development of the foundations of competence" (White and Watts, 1973, p. 245). It is a temptation for casual readers to interpret White's many writings as saying "all is over" by 3 years of age, and, indeed, the implication is there. My inclination is to agree that the early years are important—as are other years.

Competence (or its absence) is directly attributable to a unique composite of influential agents at work in the child's development. This uniqueness holds true not only in differentiating the competent from the not-so-competent, but also in differentiating individuals within each of these categories. The first and primary principle of child development is just this: *Each child is unique because of a unique biological inheritance (excepting monozygotic multiple births) in combination with a unique life experience from the time of conception.*

We are all so matter-of-fact about children (they are born and they seem to grow without much effort) that we overlook the miracle that takes place each time a child is conceived, born, and reaches adulthood. A sense of wonder comes from increased knowledge about the many-sided components of child development, and should be enhanced by each personal contact with a child.

NORMATIVE-MATURATIONAL THEORIES
Stages and ages

Historically, when the young child was even considered, it was usually in the guise of a miniature adult, and little or no concern or thought was given beyond that. We might attribute William Shakespeare the honor of being the first "ages and stages" theorist. The following is from *As You Like It:*

> All the world's a stage,
> And all the men and women merely players:
> They have their exits and their entrances;
> And one man in his time plays many parts,
> His acts being seven ages. At first the infant,
> Mewling and puking in the nurse's arms.
> And then the whining school-boy, with his satchel
> And shining morning face, creeping like snail
> Unwillingly to school . . .

Shakespeare apparently did not view infants or young children with much pleasure! The real breakthrough in the consciousness of the evolution of human growth and development came with the publication of Darwin's *On the Origin of the Species* (1859) and *Expression of the Emotions in Man and Animals* (1877). As noted by Kessen (1965), for at least 50 years "the developing human being was seen as a natural museum of human phylogeny and history; by careful observation of the infant and the child, one could see the descent of men" (p. 115). Interestingly enough, Darwin never intended that his theory of survival of the fittest be applied socially—and probably not even biologically—to humans. Nevertheless, the impact of Darwinian theory led to the totally new field of child observation and inquiry.

Personality development

Sigmund Freud, a doctor of medicine, applied the theories of evolution to stages of human development, maintaining that stages were sequential and biologically determined. He assigned stages of personality development to the ages of human life: (1) the first year, the oral stage, with pleasure as the motivation; (2) the second and third years, the anal stage, encompassing a growing awareness of self and a beginning awareness of societal demands; (3) the third and fourth years, the phallic stage, with its concern with sexual identity, approval from others, and the testing of aggressive behavior. Freud's influence is still alive and well in the United States, particularly in psychoanalytic fields.

The issue of the emergence of all types of identity (not just sexual) has never been felt more keenly. Identity is a uniquely human characteristic, a natural by-product of human experience. In its Report to the President, the U.S. Commission on the International Year of the Child points out that there are "many types of identity—family, ethnic and cultural, religious, political, economic, physical, sexual, and intellectual. Identity involves aspects of a person's being. Research during the past decades has firmly established the validity of the concept of the uniqueness of each individual. And more recent evidence strongly indicates that the foundation for this individual unique identity is established in the early years" (1980, p. 19). Each human being has an identifiable sense of identity, but not every human being has a favorable and realistic sense of identity.

Erikson's theory of personality development

Erik Erikson's theory of personality development outlines the maturational sequence involved in the emergence of identity. The knowledge he has given to child development theory is somewhat unique in that it is a rational presentation rather than a systematic developmental theory, and it deserves attention. Erikson presented his theory at the Midcentury White House Conference on Children and

Youth in 1950, and since then his theory has been accepted by virtually all persons involved in the care and education of children, as well as by researchers and theoreticians. According to Erikson, in each stage of child development there is a central problem that has to be solved, at least temporarily, if the child is to proceed positively to the next stage. Some central problems may never be totally resolved. Each conflict appears in its purest form at a particular stage.

Trust vs. distrust. The first component of a healthy personality is a sense of trust, which develops from the child's satisfying experiences during the first 18 months of life. Having biological needs anticipated and met by others with consistency and continuity, gaining control over one's body movements, and experiencing pleasurable encounters with objects and persons all assure the baby that the world is a dependable place. The baby's trust-mistrust problem is symbolized in the game of peek-a-boo. In this game, which infants begin to like at about 4 months of age, an object disappears and then reappears. There is a slightly tense expression on the infant's face when the object "goes away"; its reappearance is greeted by wiggles and smiles. Only gradually does a baby learn that things continue to exist even when out of sight, and only gradually does a baby learn that there is order and stability in the universe. Studies of mentally ill individuals and observations of infants who have been grossly deprived of affection and attention suggest that trust is an early-formed and important element. It is a common finding of psychological and social investigations that individuals having a "psychopathic personality" were so unloved in infancy that they had no reason to trust the world or humanity.

For most infants in our society a sense of trust is not difficult to come by. Psychologists tell us that primary caregivers (usually mothers) create a sense of trust in a child not by the particular techniques they employ, but by the sensitiveness with which they respond to the child's needs. A sense of trust is the most important building block in a healthy personality, and it emerges at the most vulnerable period of a child's life (birth to about 18 months).

Autonomy vs. doubt and shame. Much of the child's energy during the next 2 years will be focused on the need to establish autonomy. The positive outcome is self-control without loss of self-esteem; the unfavorable outcome is doubt and shame. This is the period of muscle system maturation and the resulting ability to coordinate a number of action patterns, such as walking, talking, manipulating objects, holding on, and letting go. Although some psychologists have concentrated particularly on bladder and bowel control during this period, the ramifications of developing and establishing autonomy cover a much wider area. The child needs to develop a sense of adequacy and self-reliance. The child must experience over and over again that he is a person who is permitted to make choices. At the same time the child must learn some of the boundaries of self-determination. Not only are some objects out of reach, but also there are some adult commands that are strongly enforced.

The independence of the individual, or personal autonomy, is an outstanding feature of the American way of life, but is neither encouraged nor permitted in societies that value conformity and universal obedience to authoritarian figures. In our society, we maintain that everyone has the right to have and express opinions and to be in control of one's affairs. The conflict of autonomy vs. doubt and shame is forcefully met for the first time between 18 months and 3 years of age, although much of the normal life span involves a continuing resolution of the problem.

Initiative vs. guilt. By the ages of 4 and 5 years, having established a trust in the world and the persons and objects in it, and having asserted one's sense of personhood, the young child looks beyond present reality to future possibilities. This is the time for all kinds of learning—about the various roles and functions of adults, about social relationships with age-mates and others, and about the usefulness and pleasure of imagination, particularly when projects dreamed up are either physically impossible or not permitted. Children at this age are beginning to feel guilty even for mere thoughts (the beginnings of conscience are in evidence).

These first three stages—developing a sense of trust, a sense of autonomy, and a sense of initiative—are probably the most important for personality development. The following stages are *accomplishment (or industry) vs. inferiority* (5 years to puberty); *identity role vs. role confusion* (adolescence); *intimacy vs. isolation* (adulthood and relationships); *generativity vs. stagnation* (parenthood and/or creativity and productivity); and *ego identity vs. despair* (old age and a sense of satisfaction with one's accomplishments). The first three stages are also the most important for the emergence of a sense of identity.

The beginnings of a sense of self originate in the infant's body through countless experiences involving touch, sight, hearing, smelling, and movement. The knowledge that things exist outside oneself is gradually achieved, and the infant's sense of separateness continues to emerge as certain actions elicit response from the environment. Another aspect of identity emerges with a change in the infant's attachment to the significant person(s) from one based on need and need gratification (during the first 6 months) to one based on love (second 6 months). Attaining the physical skills of locomotion firmly establishes the sense of separateness, and by the time the child is 2½ years old there is no remaining question of personhood and identity. The various identities relevant to each person (family, ethnic, religious, economic, physical, and intellectual) are quite firmly established by the age of 6 years.

The drive toward and the pleasure in achieving a sense of one's identity is well illustrated by the following description of a momentous event in the life of young Tommy.

THE PLAYERS: Tommy, age 3½
         Older sister
         Mother
SCENE: A restaurant, where all three are seated at a table. Mother and big sister have just given their orders for lunch to the waitress.
ACTION: Waitress to Tommy, "And what would you like?"
   Mother to waitress, "Oh, I'll order for him."
   Waitress, ignoring mother, repeats her question to Tommy, looking squarely at him.
   Big sister to waitress, "He's too little, I'll order for him," and then to Tommy, "What do you want?"
   Waitress, ignoring big sister, repeats her question to Tommy.
   Tommy to waitress: "A hamburger."
   Waitress to Tommy: "Do you want everything on it—lettuce, | tomato, | pickle, | onion, | mustard, ketchup?"
   Tommy to waitress: "Everything."
   Waitress leaves, Tommy turns to mother, and exclaims, "Hey Mommy, she thinks I'm real!"

Every child is "real," and must be so recognized and treated.

Physical-behavioral development

Many of the major tests of early development currently in use are drawn from the work of Dr. Arnold Gesell, who founded the Yale Clinic for Child Development in 1911, and who was the first to study children over a period of time using scientific procedures. He agreed with Freud in his biological and behavioral approach to child development. His studies describe age-related behaviors by years, and emphasize the divergent and convergent aspects of development. Groterg (n.d.) explains Gesell's theory as follows:

The various aspects of human growth and development, i.e., physical, intellectual, social and emotional, are divergent in terms of rate and harmony, and are periodically convergent into nodal stages, when the different aspects are in harmony. Gesell saw the divergent stages and ages as causes for conflict and disorder in the child's behavior, and the convergent or nodal stages and ages as sources of order and harmony in the child's behavior (p. 398).

On the basis of his early research on 109 middle-class families in Connecticut, Gesell and his colleagues produced an instrument for use in screening children for gross normality, and revised editions of the test have been in wide use ever since. The normative data of Gesell and Amatruda are still considered appropriate in terms of testing. According to Healy (1980), Chairperson of the Division of Developmental Disabilities, University of Iowa, the Gesell and Amatruda Developmental Screening Inventory is one of the major tools used by pediatricians to identify very young children who are physically or mentally handicapped. The Bayley Test of Infant Development, the Cattell Test, and the Denver Developmental Screening Test all depend largely on the work of Gesell.

Although Gesell's interpretation of the basic determinant of development (i.e., maturation) has been substantially revised by more recent studies, his age norms have stood the test of time. In very condensed form, the following sequence of development exemplifies Gesell's approach to child development.

By the end of the first 28 weeks, the infant has eye control, holds her head erect and steady, and reaches out for, grasps, transfers, and manipulates things.

By age 52 weeks, the child uses his fingers with adult precision, and stands and walks with support. In the second year the child learns to walk and run, articulate words, control bowel and bladder functions, and has a rudimentary sense of personal identity. Between 2 and 3 years of age the child can speak in sentences to articulate thoughts. He tries to understand the environment and to obey cultural demands; he is no longer an infant (Knoblock and Pasamanick, 1974).

The notion of normal development is based on the fact that certain patterns of behavior appear at certain ages (or age ranges), and when a behavior or ability does not emerge "on time" or emerges ahead of time, it is a significant exception. Many developmental changes do occur in predictable sequences. Physical development proceeds from head to foot, illustrated in the relatively early accomplishment of head movements and visual fixation (the first week); eye-hand coordination (3 months), and the relatively late appearance of standing and walking (8 to 13 months). Progress in the development of motor responses during the first year also moves from the central to the peripheral segments of the body (the upper arm and leg are brought under control before the hands and feet). Also observable is the trend from large to small muscles: for example, the 1-year-old has progressed from awkward movements, to grasping and walking, to more precise and refined movement.

Knowing when new behaviors and abilities can be expected is necessary in the care and education of young children for the setting of expectations and for program planning, whether it be in the home or elsewhere. At best, developmental charts and schemes contain lists of behaviors normally present at given chronological ages for 50% of the children. The other 50% are either ahead or behind the norm. It necessarily follows that the setting of realistic expectations and the provision of appropriate stimulation can be accomplished only when each child is viewed as an individual with unique characteristics, including a unique developmental time table. Children at any given age can vary in height and weight and still be considered normal, but a dwarf will differ in height and weight to an extent that is considered atypical.

In the normative-maturational approach, each stage is a direct reflection of the individual's maturational level at the time. The stages form an invariant sequence through the maturational unfolding of a series of innate biological patterns. Illustrative of the educational implications of this approach is the "hands-off" theory of instruction, particularly in the teaching of reading. Teachers who follow the maturational theory wait until the child is "ready" according to a developmental time schedule, and ignore the possible influential agents of the child's previous experiences and interests, the methods of instruction, and the types of materials used. For the teacher or caregiver of the infant, the maturational theory might lead to leaving the child in the crib because the ability to crawl or walk is not yet specified on the timetable.

The influence of the Gesell findings is widespread, and norms have been glibly memorized with little or no understanding of the range of normal variation. If "the book" says a certain behavioral item appears on the average of 15 months but with a range of 12 to 18 months, parents are disappointed if their child does not exhibit the behavior at the stroke of 12 months and are alarmed if such behavior does not appear by 15 months. Gesell's infant schedules are still used by many professional persons for the evaluation of a child's progress, particularly during the first year of life.

Over the last 25 years an impressive body of research data and knowledge has been accumulated that indicates wide differences in various aspects of development in children. We now know that the inner laws of physical development are considerably influenced by amount of sleep, habits of elimination, amount and character of food intake, amount of fluid intake, and degree and kind of physical activity. Attitudes, fatigue reactions, stability of personality, and changes in mental development play important roles as well. The results of this research leads to the second child development principle: *Heredity and environment never operate as separate entities; neither can exert an influence without the other.*

Cognitive and mental development

The major breakthrough on age-related intellectual functioning was the Binet method of age scaling developed in 1907. His approach resulted in widely accepted age norms for the development of mental abilities, although Binet's prime concern was to identify retarded children for placement in institutions. He did not theorize about mental development, but he did help expand our understanding of age-related intellectual functioning. We turn to the writings of Jean Piaget for the most fully developed theory of the development of mature cognitive thought to date.

Piaget's stages of development of logical thinking

Piaget was less interested in precise ages than in sequential stages, which are qualitatively discrete. He saw mental growth as an extension of biological growth, governed by the same principles and laws. He emphasized the normative aspects and attempted to identify those mental structures that hold true for individuals and for the human species. Like Gesell, Piaget maintained that an understanding of normal development is a prerequisite for an understanding of differences between individuals, but his concept of development stressed the role of the child's experience, as opposed to Gesell's concept of maturation. Piaget assumed that developmental change is based both on biological processes of maturation, and on the experiences of an active subject who gains knowledge by acting on the world and by utilizing the feedback from his actions to construct increasingly complex schemata, or mental structures.

If we accept the definition of intelligence as the ability to adapt to and make sense out of the environment (there are other equally correct definitions), it is logical to accept the theory that the development of this ability passes through a series of maturational stages.

Piaget's taxonomy of developmental periods of major developmental epochs includes many so-called stages, substages, and subperiods, and his writings are inconsistent to both numbers and names of stages, substages, etc., from one publication to the next. However, he has consistently designated three major periods of intellectual development from birth to maturity.

Period of sensorimotor intelligence (birth to 2 years). There are six major stages in this period, with a few substages scattered throughout. Essentially, each child begins as a totally egocentric, uncoordinated neonate who engages only in reflexlike activities (from which Piaget says intelligence begins) to a child who acts intentionally and who can solve problems through actions that indicate some remembrance of past actions and new combinations of past experiences. At the culmination of the sensorimotor period, the child can: (1) imitate quite complex actions of persons and objects, whether visibly perceptible or remembered; (2) truly pretend or make-believe; (3) remember and think about actions, rather than simply perform them; (4) infer a cause, given only its effect, and forsee an effect, given its cause; and (5) recognize that an object is a thing (or person) apart, subject to its own laws of displacement and action. The child has progressed from total egocentrism (a consideration of the world from only a personal point of view) to an awareness of separateness and both self-identity and "other-identity." As the child moves toward an ability to symbolize, the next period is entered.

Period of preoperational thought (2 to 7 years). In Piagetian terms, an *operation* is the mental manipulation of an object or event. It necessitates the use of logic. The very young child does not yet seem capable of applying logic in conclusions or explanations of happenings. This child might be described as: (1) completely egocentric, but very curious; (2) able to use language as a social tool and for communicating needs or desires; and (3) ready with an explanation for everything. The characteristics of a child's pre-operational thinking during these years are of particular importance in planning educational programs.

1. The child is unable to think from any point of view except her own, and is unable to imagine how it would be (or look) from another point of view or perspective.
2. The child is greatly influenced by what is perceived at a given moment, and will pass judgments on what is perceived, rather than on past experiences. The child concentrates on one variable only, usually the variable that stands out visually.
3. The child cannot understand that an object can have more than one attribute or quality and consequently belong in more than one classification.
4. The child pays little or no attention to another person's thoughts or language.

Period of concrete operations (7 to 11 or 12 years). During the major portion of the elementary school years, the child appears to have a fairly stable and systematic mental framework with which to understand the world of objects and events. Piaget describes objects or events that are seen and experienced as *concrete*. The child's mental operations, therefore, are tied to reality.

Period of formal operations and abstract thought (11 or 12 years into maturity). The young person can deal effectively both with reality and the abstract world.

•   •   •

It should be noted that Piaget's material on sensorimotor development is scattered through a number of books and articles: primary sources are *The Origins of Intelligence in Children* (1952) and *Play, Dreams and Imitation in Children* (1962). It should also be noted that while Gesell obtained his data from groups of highly

advantaged children, and therefore has received criticism, Piaget's data on sensorimotor development was obtained almost exclusively from his own three children. He has also received criticism for this. With the exception of the specificity of ages for particular accomplishments, however, Piaget's theory has held firm since it was first introduced in the United States, in spite of numerous attempts to upset the invariance of the stages. Nonetheless, Piaget's theory is not in itself adequate to explain human development and behavior.

"Ages and stages" re-evaluated

Most modern theorists have concluded that age per se is not a good criterion for establishing developmental stages. Even Piaget admits that, although his stages always succeed one another, accelerations or delays will occur with differences in social environment and past experiences. With the current evidence that discredits the concepts of predetermined development and fixed intelligence, and the proposals that the early years are the most influential for intellectual growth, the traditional faith in maturational theory is in serious question. Developmental theory based on maturation is useful, but incomplete. The related assessment instruments and scales are of help in stating sequences of development and will reveal gross handicaps. In individual cases the scales seem to underestimate abilities of some and are of little help in predicting later intellectual abilities of others. A poignant reminder of the recent change of direction in developmental theories may be inferred from the obvious omission of any reference to the maturational-normative point of view in the most recent edition of *Carmichael's Manual of Child Psychology* (Mussen, 1970).

INDIVIDUAL UNIQUENESS

The prevailing thought about individual differences before the 1960s was essentially that of predetermination by genetic and hereditary influences. As McClearn (1964) noted, however, even limiting the theory "to genetic homogeneity has pitfalls beyond count; the number of possible genotypes far exceeds the number of persons now living, plus those who have ever lived, in all human history. Excepting identical twins and other identical multiple births, each human being is a unique and unrepeatable event" (p. 472). It should not be surprising, therefore, that each baby even from the same parents is a surprising individual. Parents often remark on the differences between their own children; a second child may well have a very different temperament from the firstborn.

Empirically established information about the individuality among young children is scarce, but significant data have been collected that demonstrate that children can be identified by styles of functioning at very early ages. Birth or near-birth differences have been categorized as follows: (1) activity level; (2) rhythmicity or regularity of biological functions; (3) approach or withdrawal as the initial reaction to a new stimulus; (4) adaptability or modification of the initial reaction; (5) intensity of reaction regardless of its direction; (6) intensity level of stimulation necessary to evoke a discernible response; (7) quality of mood, ranging from pleasant and friendly to unpleasant or hostile; (8) distractibility; (9) attention span and persistence.

These nine categories of components of behavioral activity were used in a longitudinal analysis of the first 2 years of the lives of 80 children. The findings "contributed evidence that initially identifiable characteristics of reactivity are persistent features of the child's behavior throughout the first 2 years of life" (Thomas et al, 1963, p. 71). Succeeding studies, reported in 1968 and 1970, gave data on 141 children from birth to preadolescence, with the finding that about 65% of the children could be reliably categorized soon after birth, with their ratings remaining relatively stable throughout the study.

The etiology of differences in behavioral style has not yet been ascertained, although evidence is constantly accumulating. There is good reason to believe that racial and cultural backgrounds may cause remarkable differences in temperament and behavior among newborns. The prediction that individual differences will be found in any group of children is probably the safest prediction that can be made, and the implications of the existence of such initial differences are of particular importance to parents, caregivers, and teachers. Not only will individual children respond in individual ways to the same environmental influence, but also the child's response will frequently determine the related behavior of the significant persons in the child's life. A simple example will illustrate this profound concept.

Imagine two infants in a day care center or home, one of whom appears active and alert, and also seeks adult attention by babbling and smiling and wiggling all over when an adult approaches. The other is less active and less vocal, and apparently needs (or wishes) less attention. These infants might be described as "active" and "reflective," and the adult will almost automatically be drawn to the active child, engaging in mutual vocalizations and movements, which give pleasure to both. Adults, too, seek reinforcement and will respond to the child who is both active and responsive. The reflective child has perhaps even more need for attention but she will receive less, thus starting a cycle that may result in the child's withdrawal or apathy in extreme cases.

The same rules and approaches cannot be applied to all children, and each child's primary reaction pattern must be understood and respected. A generally accepted sequence of the behavioral characteristics of children from birth to 36 months of age is presented in Table 2-1.

Formerly, such personality variables as motivation, anticipation, curiosity, and expectations of success or failure were considered part of the

TABLE 2-1   Sequence of behavioral characteristics*

	Birth to 6 months	6 to 9 months	9 to 18 months	18 to 24 months	24 to 36 months
Thinking	Baby discriminates mother from others, is more responsive to her Baby acts curious, explores through looking, grasping, mouthing Recognizes adults, discriminates between strangers and familiar persons Shows he's learning by anticipating situations, responding to unfamiliarity, and reacting to disappearance of things Uses materials in play such as crumpling and waving paper Looks a long time at objects he's inspecting	Baby shows persistence in doing things Becomes aware of missing objects Makes connections between objects—pulls string to secure ring on the other end, uncovers a hidden toy Increases his ability to zero in on sights or sounds he's interested in Baby's attention span is prolonged Baby shifts his attention appropriately, resists distraction	Baby unwraps an object, takes lids from boxes Recognizes shapes in a puzzle board Names familiar objects Baby becomes increasingly curious about surroundings, sets off on his own to explore further than ever before Becomes more purposeful and persistent in accomplishing a task	Child says the names of familiar objects in pictures Explores cabinets and drawers Begins to play pretend games	Child can name many objects Begins to grasp the meaning of numbers Child's memory span is longer Child's ability to reason, solve problems, make comparisons develops Child grasps the concepts of color, form and space Begins to respect and obey rules Shows strong interest in investigating the functions and details of household objects
Language	Baby coos expressively, vocalizes spontaneously Baby vocalizes over a sustained period of time to someone who is imitating his sounds Baby babbles in wordsounds of two syllables	Baby babbles to people Says "da-da" or equivalent Notices familiar words and turns toward person or thing speaker is referring to Shows he understands some commonly used words	Baby jabbers expressively Imitates words Says two words together	Child uses two-word sentences Has vocabulary of 20 to 50 words Begins to use "me," "I," and "you" Follows verbal instructions Listens to simple stories	Child uses language as a way of communicating his thoughts, representing his ideas, and developing social relationships Child enjoys using language, gains satisfaction from expressing himself and being understood Understands and uses abstract words such as "up," "down," "now," "later"

Continued.

*From Huntington, D.S., and others: Day care, 2 serving infants, DHEW Pub. No. (OCD) 73-14, Washington, D.C., 1973, U.S. Government Printing Office.

TABLE 2-1   Sequence of behavioral characteristics—cont'd

	Birth to 6 months	6 to 9 months	9 to 18 months	18 to 24 months	24 to 36 months
Body expression and control	Baby develops own rhythm in feeding, eliminating, sleeping and being awake—a rhythm which can be approximately predicted Baby quiets himself through rocking, sucking, or touching Adjusts his posture in anticipation of being fed or held (in crib, on lap, at shoulder) Head balances Baby turns to see or hear better Baby pulls self to sitting position, sits alone momentarily Eye and hand coordinate in reaching. Baby reaches persistently, touches, manipulates Retains objects in hands, manipulates objects, transfers from hand to hand Baby engages in social exchange and self-expression through facial action, gestures, and play	Baby sits alone with good coordination Manipulates objects with interest, understands the use of objects—rings a bell on purpose Practices motor skills, crawls, stands up by holding on to furniture Uses fingers in pincer-type grasp of small objects Increases his fine-motor coordination of eye, hand, and mouth	Baby stands alone, sits down, walks with help Is gradually gaining control of bodily functioning Throws ball Becomes more aware of his body, identifies body parts Stands on one foot with help Walks up and down stairs with help Needs adult as a stable base for operations during his growing mobility and curiosity	Hand coordination is increasingly steady—child can build tower of many blocks Climbs into adult chair Runs with good coordination Climbs stairs, using rail Uses body actively in mastering and exploring surroundings—an active age	Child can jump and hop on one foot Child walks up and down-stairs, alternates his feet at each stair Begins to notice the differences between safe and unsafe activities Expands his large muscle interests and activities Tries hard to dress and undress himself
Social play and responsiveness	Baby imitates movements Gazes at faces and reaches toward them, reacts to disappearance of a face, tracks face movements Responds to sounds Smiles to be friendly Mouth opens in imitation of adult	Baby cooperates in games Takes the initiative in establishing social exchanges with adults Understands and adapts to social signals Shows ability to learn by demonstration	Baby plays pat-a-cake, peek-a-boo Responds to verbal request Imitates actions Stops his own actions on command from an adult Uses gestures and words to make his wants known	Child scribbles with crayon in imitation of adults' strokes on paper Likes parents' possessions and play that mimics parents' behavior and activities Follows simple directions Controls others, orders them around	Child tests his limits in situations involving other people Says "no" but submits anyway Shows trust and love Enjoys wider range of relationships and experiences, enjoys meeting many people other than parents

	Baby likes to be tickled, jostled, frolicked with. Makes social contact with others by smiling or vocalizing. Quiets when someone approaches, smiles. A mutual exchange goes on between adult and child through smiling, play, voice, bodily movement	Focuses on mother as the only person he'll permit to meet needs		Tests, fights, resists adults when they oppose or force him to do something. Child is able to differentiate more and more between people	Likes to try out adult activities, especially around the house, runs errands, does small household chores
Self-awareness	Baby smiles at his own reflection in the mirror. Looks at and plays with his hands and toes. Feels things about himself through such actions as banging	Baby listens and notices his own name. Makes a playful response to his own image in mirror. Begins to assert himself	Baby becomes aware of his ability to say "no" and of the consequences of this. Shows shoes or other clothing. Asserts himself by "getting into everything," "getting into mischief." Wants to decide for himself	Child recognizes body parts on a doll. Identifies parts of own body. Child takes a more self-sufficient attitude, challenges parents' desires, wants to "do it myself." Child's sense of self-importance is intense—protests, wants to make own choices	Child becomes aware of himself as a separate person, can contrast himself with another. Expresses preferences strongly. Expresses confidence in own activities. Expresses pride in achievement. Values his own property
Emotions	Baby shows excitement through waving arms, kicking, moving whole body, face lighting up. Shows pleasure as he anticipates something, such as his bottle. Cries in different ways to say he's cold, wet, hungry, etc. Makes noises to voice pleasure, displeasure, satisfactions. Baby laughs	Baby expresses some fear toward strangers in new situations. Pushes away something he does not want. Shows pleasure when someone responds to his self-assertion. Shows pleasure in getting someone to react to him	Baby shows preference for one toy over another. Expresses many emotions and recognizes feelings in other people. Gives affection—returns a kiss or hug. Expresses fear of strangers. Shows anxiety at separation from mother, gradually masters this	Child desires to be independent, feed self, put on articles of own clothing. Shows intense positive or negative reactions. Likes to please others, is affectionate. Shows some aggressive tendencies—slaps, bites, hits—which must be dealt with. Shows greater desire to engage in problem-solving and more persistence in doing so. Develops triumphant delight and pride in his own actions. Becomes frustrated easily	Child strives for mastery over objects. Child can tolerate more frustration, more willing to accept a substitute for what he can't have. Shows strong desire for independence in his actions. Gradually channels his aggressive tendencies into more constructive activities. Uses language to express his wishes and his feelings toward others. Shows a developing sense of humor at surprises, unusual actions, etc.

inherited characteristics of any one person. It has now been almost conclusively shown that these variables are learned, and that they are learned from the very first days and weeks of life. The medium for learning is the reciprocal interaction between child and environment. Therefore, our third child development principle is: *Growth and development occur when a child is engaged in mutually fulfilling actions with other persons.*

In our efforts to learn and put into practice our knowledge of child development, let us not lose our sense of wonder, so ably expressed by Pablo Casals.

Do you know what you are?
You are a marvel.
You are unique.
In all the world there is no other child exactly like you.
In the millions of years that have passed there has never been a child like you.

And look at your body—what a wonder it is! Your legs, your arms, your cunning fingers, the way you move!

You may become a Shakespeare, a Michelangelo, a Beethoven
You may have the capacity for anything.
Yes, you are a marvel.

PART II: Goals and objectives for the care and education of infants and toddlers

The beginning is the most important part of the work.

Plato, *The Republic,* Book 11377B

APPROACHES TO GOALS

A baby is born in the United States every 9 seconds. That means that almost 3.5 million babies join us yearly. Each one depends on adults for nurturance, encouragement, and unqualified love, and every adult, at some time or other, has had or will have the opportunity to influence at least one baby's growth and development, either directly or indirectly. Those adults who are not part of the human services professions (medicine, education, or social welfare) and who are not parents themselves still have direct input to issues related to child care and education by virtue of their voting (or not voting) for the local and national politicians who write the legislation.

Of those babies born in the early 1980s, one of every three has a mother who will work out of the home sometime during that baby's first 3 years of life. If predictions are correct, one of every *two* babies before the age of 3 will soon have a mother working out of the home. The traditional family, in which the husband worked out of the home and the wife stayed in the home with the children, is a part of the historical past, and now describes less than one tenth of the families with young children. The one unchanging aspect of our society is the young child's continuing need for nurturance, encouragement, and unqualified love.

Recognition of this immutable fact has led to this and many other publications suggesting guidelines, methods, and concerns involved in the care and education of infants and toddlers who are out of their homes for a substantial part of their day on a regular basis. The location may

be a large or small group center or a family day care home. It may serve children up to 3 years of age, or children from infancy to public school age, or even through the elementary years. The emphasis of this book is on the infants and toddlers, up to age 3 years.

Until very recently, out-of-home care for young children was custodial with the goals of care and protection; the caregiver was a glorified babysitter. Even today, many persons, including some educators, still are convinced that babies need no more than food, rest, and a little rocking and holding. When the baby starts to "toddle," just remove the breakables and let her go! And when the *adult* has had enough, plop her into the crib or playpen!

Today we have an abundance of information about children's needs and characteristics, about the importance of the early years, and about the disastrous effects of custodial care. Today there is no excuse for having care and protection as the *primary* goals for out-of-home services for children.

Whatever child development information has been offered to parents of very young children is equally appropriate for teachers and caregivers of young children. Childrearing advice is equally applicable to parents and to teachers/caregivers. However, some modifications are necessitated by the logistics of having more children and more adults in child care centers. Centers may be homelike, but they are not home.

It is hoped that parents and teachers of very young children agree on the goals and objectives for their children. We all have glibly verbalized "the growth and development of the total child" as a goal many times, but have recognized and acted upon the phrase's total meaning in too few instances. The very nature of the goal is too global to enable us to plan the specific encounters of specific children that will encourage and enhance the growth and development of the total child in a group situation.

Goals for the care and education of very young children may be expressed in global terms or in varying degrees of specificity. They may come from various points of reference: universal goals of the society, goals of parents as a total group, goals determined by the characteristics and needs of the children. Goals are also stated in terms of the hoped-for accomplishments of the centers themselves, which go beyond the confines of the daily program and setting for the children.

UNIVERSAL GOALS

Goals for authoritarian societies are stated in simple, direct terms: "the new Soviet man" (the Soviet Union) or "a good party member" (People's Republic of China). Definitions of these terms are relatively straightforward, and therefore it is relatively easy to plan and program the care and education of their children. However, universal success in meeting these goals is open to question. It is considerably more complex to plan child care and education in democratic societies because of emphasis on the individual and respect for cultural pluralism. In spite of societal and cultural differences, however, there seem to be universal goals of parents for their children regardless of their geopolitical location or culture.

1. The physical survival and health of the child. . . .
2. The development of the child's behavioral capacity for economic self-maintenance in maturity.
3. The development of the child's behavioral capacities for maximizing other cultural values—e.g., morality, prestige, wealth, religious piety, intel-

lectual achievement, personal satisfaction, self-realization—as formulated and symbolically elaborated in culturally distinctive beliefs, norms, and ideologies (Levine, 1974, p. 56).

Can these be helpful in formulating goals for infant-toddler care and education? Certainly there is no disagreement with the goal for the physical survival and health of the children, nor should there be disagreement about the development of the child's behavioral capacities for economic self-maintenance or for the other cultural values. The foundations of achieving all these goals are laid in the first few years of life: attitudes toward exploring, questioning, and learning; expectations of success or failure; defense mechanisms for physical or psychological abuse. These universal goals contain some indication of our responsibilities toward young children, but again they are too global for specific planning.

GOALS TO MEET CHILDREN'S NEEDS

Although professional persons and children's centers express their goals and objectives in different words and with different emphases, they all speak to at least some of the needs of the young child. A quality center attempts to meet all of them. A custodial center stops at meeting the physical needs—care and protection—reminiscent of the institutional environments of former years, which are still being referred to in arguments against infant-toddler day care.

Ira Gordon (1975) addressed the issue of goals for very young children by stating, "Homes or institutions must not only meet physical needs, but also attend to intellectual needs through stimulation, reasoning, rewards for attainment, direct face-to-face language interaction, and to emotional needs through a single, consistent mothering one who is affectionate and responsive, and sees the child as a unique individual" (p. 45).

The needs of children that must be met to

reach the goal of growth and development of the total child might be stated as follows. All children need:

1. An environment that is
   a. Physically safe, clean, and healthful (including nutritious food)
   b. Emotionally warm and supportive; trust-supporting
   c. Comfortable and functional
   d. Rich in sensorimotor and social experiences
   e. Available for extensive exploration, manipulation, and discovery of objects
   f. Available for social relationships with adults and other children
   g. Consistent and predictable
2. Primary (or significant) attachment(s) to one or a few loving adults who:
   a. Respect uniqueness in temperament, state, and developmental stage
   b. Meet dependency needs, both social and physical, as well as encourage increasing independence
   c. Frequently initiate physical, social, and verbal contacts with the child
   d. Respond to and reinforce the child's physical, social, and verbal behavior most of the time (always would be ideal)
   e. "Program" experiences, interactions, and materials appropriate to children's individual current levels of functioning
   f. Are consistent and predictable
3. Stimulation that is
   a. Self-initiated
   b. Other-initiated
   c. Object- or environment-initiated
4. Self-determined cycles of activity, rest, and relaxation
5. A sense of trust and security, leading to a sense of autonomy, effectiveness, and competence
6. Freedom and opportunity to develop at

one's own pace, accompanied by adult and environmental support and guidance toward self-control, responsibility, and mastery

These are innate needs of all young children, whether in or out of a group setting. Living in a group imposes additional ones:

7. Learning to live happily away from the family group and home setting for part of the day
8. Learning to modify personal needs or desires, or at least delay their gratification, upon occasion
9. Learning to establish and enjoy personal relationships with nonfamily members

GOALS TO MEET SOCIETAL NEEDS

When we think in terms of what children need to learn, instead of what children need, we introduce an element of society- and culture-related values, expectations, and realities.

The pioneer of group day care and education for very young children was Harriet Johnson, whose report of the Nursery School in New York City describes the very beginnings of the developmental-interaction approach to early childhood education for which Bank Street College and Barbara Biber are now well-known. The written report contains no goals per se; however, Johnson did offer various children's accomplishments at the end of the experiment, which have been reworded into the goals listed below. They are both far-sighted and near-sighted. They reflect the view toward child development that prevailed in the early decades of the twentieth century, and therefore do not give sufficient emphasis to cognitive or intellectual abilities. Nevertheless, they are of value in this review, as well as being historically important. The implied goals are the following:

1. To learn to live happily away from the intimate contact with the family
2. To establish enough motor control so that

the approach to the physical environment is with "readiness and confidence"

3. To go through a day with the least possible amount of direction and dictation
4. To establish interests and explore them independently
5. To share in the life of a social group and to modify demands in relation to their peers

More current statements of the goals of early care and education are offered in many reports of theory, research, and model programs. Gewirtz (n.d.) offers the global goal "to stimulate and enhance development of the child's behavior systems in socially desirable ways" (p. 173) and also offers a more specific list of generally valued behaviors: "(1) bodily skills, gross and fine movements; (2) social responsiveness; (3) speech and language skill; (4) self-reliance; (5) freedom from fear or anxiety; (6) emotional independence; (7) perseverance; (8) ability to acquire information about the environment; and (9) tolerance for delay of reinforcement" (p. 203).

Appleton and colleagues (1975) have categorized necessary skills as cognitive, behavioral, and social, and their examples of each give implications for program planning. For instance, cognitive skills include attention (or attending), perception, and conceptualization. Behavioral skills include the self-care skills, and motor abilities and their inhibition. Social skills include the use of language, the appropriate use of adults as resources, and the development of various personal attributes (self-esteem, independence, cooperation, warmth, and flexibility).

Honig (1976) lists the following developmental tasks for children in their very first years:

increasing the variety and sophistication of pre-hension skills; intercoordinating information received; developing the concept of object permanence; increasing the degree of intentionality and the understanding of causal relationships; learning to imitate; improving cognitive skills involving classification, polar concepts, and seriation; learning language; developing large muscle skills; learning ever finer sensory discriminations and skills; and internalizing first a sense of trust, then a sense of autonomy and initiative.

Huntington et al. (1973) summarize the developmental goals of a child from birth to 3 years in the following manner:

1. Gaining increasing control of his body systems; development of regulatory physiologic mechanisms; gross and fine motor development and coordination.
2. Increasing awareness of self as a separate identity; a sense of self involving who and what he is.
3. A sense of effectiveness and competence; a sense of controlling his destiny at least to a limited extent—the opposite of powerlessness and sense that no matter what he does it makes no difference.
4. The ability to communicate needs, wants, feelings and ideas; the use of verbal and non-verbal methods of communication; the development of a sense of being understood.
5. The ability to take initiative, to be curious and exploratory, the ability to act.
6. To have hope and faith and a belief that the world is, by and large, a good place.
7. The ability to trust others and be trustworthy; to develop a sense of responsibility.
8. The ability to give and receive from other people; to be appropriately dependent and appropriately independent; to cooperate with others and to respect others.
9. The ability to be flexible and open to new ideas, new feelings and new people.
10. The ability to think, to remember, to order, to perceive, to categorize, to learn, to be creative in intellectual processes, to attend, to observe, to inspect and investigate, to reflect.

11. The development of skills, and techniques for gaining skills.
12. To be motivated to broaden knowledge of self, others, the inanimate world and the world of ideas; to explore and to discover.
13. The ability to control impulses when appropriate or to express them when appropriate; to be able to affirm and to negate; to exclude, to postpone; to hold on and let go; to follow rules and to believe in their importance. (p. 16).

Admittedly, these are expressed in more or less global terms, but they are a direct reflection of the body of knowledge known as "child development."

Very specific developmental objectives for young children have been listed by Caldwell in the AID (Advances in Development) Chart. These objectives have been incorporated in Section Three of this text, which presents the de-

---

GOALS FOR YOUNG CHILDREN IN A GROUP SETTING

A. Positive feelings about self
   1. I *am.*
   2. I *can.*
B. Positive feelings about others
   1. About adults
      a. They love me.
      b. They enjoy me.
      c. They take care of me when I need care.
      d. They help me when I need help, but they also encourage me to do things by and for myself.
      e. I like "big people."
   2. About other children
      1. I like to be near or with them.
      2. They like to be near or with me.
C. Positive feelings about the world
   1. The world is full of interesting things to see, hear, touch, and find out about.
   2. The world is full of interesting people to see, hear, touch, and find out about.
   3. I *can learn* about the world and the things and people in it.

velopmental-educational curriculum for infants and toddlers in group settings.

Another approach to goals and/or objectives for young children is to use their feelings and attitudes as a frame of reference. The goals in the boxed outline were written with this perspective.

GOALS FOR CENTERS

The last point of reference for the determination of goals is that of the center itself. Center goals may focus on the needs and characteristics of infants and toddlers, that is, to meet physiological needs, to provide for optimal development, or to create an environment that provides security, safety, and happiness. The Learning Center in Philadelphia operates under the primary goal of creating a familylike atmosphere with a secure relationship between each child and the caregivers, and attempts to meet this goal by providing a male and female caregiver for each group of 10 children, aged from infancy to 4 years.

Many programs reported in the literature have been established as demonstration or research centers, and their goals reflect these broader purposes. The Children's Center at Syracuse University (SUNY) was established in the 1960s as a demonstration day care program for infants and toddlers, and one of its main goals was the evaluation of group day care for very young children on an objective rather than a clinical basis. The profession owes much to this endeavor, because one of their evaluations showed that, at least for their population of children and families, there were no negative effects resulting from maternal separation for many hours during each day. Apparently, mother-child attachments were not disrupted or minimized by the child's regular attendance at an all-day center-based program. Needless to say—but necessary to point out—the Children's Center was an example of a very high quality program; therefore a generalization of this finding to many centers in existence today is not valid. Many so-called developmental day care settings seem to stress *either* warm interpersonal relations *or* encouragement of curiosity and beginning cognitive and language skills, but rarely both.

Because of the discouraging long-range results of many of the early education models designed for 3- and 4-year-old economically or culturally disadvantaged children in the late 1960s and early 1970s, some infant-toddler programs were established to remediate "deficits." Most of these have been part-day programs, designed specifically for developing readiness for the academic content of the primary grades, but a few have attempted to educate parents as teachers of their own children, with excellent results. National attention is now being focused on handicapped or "at risk" infants and toddlers. The major goals of these programs are the early identification and remediation of the handicapping condition(s), and the programs are either part-day, whole-day, or in the child's own home.

One essential goal of any quality program is to meet the needs of parents and to involve them in all aspects of the program. Goals presented by Evans and Saia (1972) not only include the parents, but also propose a down-to-earth reminder about goals and outcomes.

All day care centers should:
1. attempt to meet the needs of each individual child for maximum physical, intellectual, psychological, and social growth;
2. develop a program which will best meet the desires and needs of the parents and the community it serves;
3. make the best possible use of all available resources;
4. realize that perfection is unobtainable, but that progress is achieved by doing the best possible job with the resources available (1972, p. 49).

TABLE 2-2 Children's needs and characteristics with related implications for caregiver/teacher behaviors and attitudes

	Child	Teacher
Social-emotional	Needs to feel sense of belonging	Establishes a close relationship that is caring and nurturing
		Is alert to child's needs for people and social experiences
		Includes child in group activities, either as spectator or as actual participant
	Likes to be with or near other children (sociocentric)	Provides opportunities to watch or join other children
	Is self-centered (egocentric)	Does not insist on group involvement, sharing behaviors, etc., that are beyond child's level of functioning
	Likes to be independent	Offers opportunities for child to do things for and by self; provides chances for child to assume responsibilities
		Provides materials and experiences that require initiative or problem-solving by child
	Needs adult guidance and support	Is accepting and appreciative of child's efforts
	Needs affection and praise	Gives child unlimited affection and appropriate praise; helps child learn socially acceptable ways of showing interest or affection.
	Has a good sense of humor	Plays with child; offers appropriate discrepancies in actions and words; laughs with child
	Is easily stimulated	Recognizes the fine line between enough and too much
	Is easily frustrated	Recognizes that a young child will persist only when successful, and may be able to handle only one or two failures with a task before giving up
		Provides challenges that match child's level of functioning
	Needs to experience success	Plans cumulative program of new experiences based on previous ones, so as to provide an appropriate match for the child's current level of functioning
	May have "unreasonable" fears of strangers or changes in environment or routine or activities	Understands that fearful children usually regress in their behavior; is soothing and supportive; shows love with body contact and quieting language
		Introduces changes slowly, one step at a time
	Is dependent upon all adults, but very dependent upon significant adults for social-emotional development	Is a "significant" adult by forming a close, nurturing, consistent relationship
Physical-behavioral	Is very active	Provides opportunities and space for free and vigorous movement
	Has developing control of large muscles; beginning control of fine muscles	Provides large muscle activities and equipment; gradually adds such activities as self-feeding, drawing, painting
	Tires easily	Adapts schedule to individual child's physiological needs

Continued.

TABLE 2-2   Children's needs and characteristics with related implications for caregiver/teacher behaviors and attitudes—cont'd

	Child	Teacher
Physical-behavioral —cont'd	Is highly susceptible to communicable diseases	Is alert to any change in child's usual behavior or appearance; is able to recognize early symptoms of child diseases; instills and enforces habits of cleanliness
		Expects irregular attendance at the center
	Has a small tummy	Provides meals on schedule, but snacks should always be available
	Is establishing handedness and eyedness	Provides activities and materials that require use of either or both hands
	Is far-sighted	Does not force near-vision activities; should let the child determine closeness
	Is progressing from nonverbal cry to verbal communication	Listens, responds, imitates; initiates "conversations"
	Is very dependent upon adults for satisfying physical needs	Responds to needs with appropriate actions immediately or as soon as possible
Cognitive	Is intensely curious and eager to learn; learns by doing	Provides a wide variety of materials and experiences in an interesting environment; provides opportunities to explore, manipulate, and discover
		Eliminates safety hazards in the environment
		Allows time and space for individual explorations with only the necessary restrictions for the sake of safety
		Is alert for new signs of interest
		Knows progression of mental development and provide opportunities that match and stretch the child's behavior and thinking
	Has a very short attention span for other-initiated tasks	Allows time and freedom for self-initiated tasks that tend to encourage greater persistence
	Understands through sensorimotor experiences	Provides time and opportunity to experience many kinds of things and activities
	Enjoys "playful" experiences with language and activities	Smiles, laughs, enjoys, and adopts "playful" attitude toward routines and interactions
	Is dependent upon all adults, but very dependent upon significant adults for learning	Is a "significant" adult by forming a close, nurturing, consistent relationship; reinforces and encourages child's behaviors in all areas of functioning

How can we conclude? Have we come full circle, back to "the growth and development of the total child"? Perhaps. A somewhat more definitive general goal might be "to maximize the potential of children and to reinforce their families." Many teachers and other staff members in infant-toddler day care centers spend long hours discussing how to state their goals, perhaps for licensing purposes, advertising, or as a set of guidelines for their daily experiences with children. As is too often the case in educational endeavors for students of all ages, there is frequently an observable gap between stated goals and the actual programs.

To some extent, the preceding discussion has been theoretical—we should work toward this or that goal. To help bridge some gaps and as an illustration of the principle that any statement of goals has practical implications, Table 2-2 presents child needs and characteristics and the related caregiver/teacher behaviors and attitudes.

■ CHAPTER SUMMARY ■

Three major child development principles have been presented:

1. Each child is unique because of a unique biological inheritance in combination with a unique life experience from the time of conception.
2. Heredity and environment never operate as separate entities; neither can exert an influence without the other.
3. Growth and development occur when a child is engaged in mutually fulfilling actions with other persons.

There is sufficient evidence to mandate intentional efforts for both the socialization and the education of very young children. Infants must learn there is order and predictability in their world. This sense of trust is accomplished through interactions with sensitive and responsive caregivers. Toddlers must achieve a sense of identity and of autonomy. Both can be achieved when the environment, including persons, permits and encourages them to explore, manipulate, and solve toddler-sized problems.

Children will not effectively learn skills that are inappropriate for their stages of development, but learning can be enhanced by practicing the skills typically exhibited at the child's particular stage of development. Learning is enhanced by the knowledgeable arrangement of the physical environment, and by the behaviors and attitudes of knowledgeable caregivers.

Any child, even the youngest, can benefit from supplementary care and education outside the home delivered by nonfamily members, if there is a positive integration of physical setting, caring and knowledgeable adults, appropriate activities and experiences, and home-center coordination. A definitive statement of long-term goals and short-term objectives is the first step in the establishment and continued functioning of this integration for infant-toddler care and education.

SUGGESTED ACTIVITIES/POINTS TO PONDER

1. Observe a child at any or all of the following ages: 6 months, 9 months, 18 months, 24 months, 36 months. Do the child's behavioral characteristics agree with those stated in Table 2-1?
2. Observe a group of children of the same chronological age. In what ways are they similar? In what ways do they differ?
3. In what ways are the sense of identity and the sense of autonomy similar? In what ways do they differ?

REFERENCES AND SUGGESTED READINGS

Appleton, T., Clifton, R., and Goldberg, L.: The development of behavioral competency in infancy. In Horowitz, F.D., editor: Review of child development research, vol. 4, Chicago, 1975, University of Chicago Press.

Bloom, B.S.: Stability and change in human characteristics, New York, 1965, John Wiley & Sons, Inc.

Bower, T.G.R.: Human development, San Francisco, 1979, W.H. Freeman & Co.

Brazelton, T.B.: Infants and mothers: differences in development, New York, 1969, Dell Publishing Co., Inc.

Brazelton, T.B.: Toddlers and parents: a declaration of independence, New York, 1974, Delacorte Press.

Bronfenbrenner, U., editor: Influences on human development, Hinsdale, Ill., 1972, Dryden Press.

Caplan, F., editor: The parenting advisor, Garden City, N.Y., 1977, Anchor Press.

Church, J.: Understanding your child from birth to three: a guide to your child's psychological development, New York, 1973, Random House.

Caldwell, B.M., Wright, C.M., Honig, A.S., and Tannenbaum, J.: Infant day care and attachment, American Journal of Ortho-Psychiatry **40**:397-412, 1970.

Erikson, E.H.: Childhood and society, rev. ed., New York, 1964, W.W. Norton & Co., Inc.

Evans, E.B., and Saia, G.E.: Daycare for infants, Boston, 1972, Beacon Press.

Fowler, W.: Curriculum and assessment guides for infant and child care, Boston, 1980, Allyn & Bacon, Inc.

Galinsky, E., and Hooks, W.H.: The new extended family, Boston, 1977, Houghton Mifflin Co.

Gewirtz, J.L.: Stimulation, learning, and motivation principles for daycare settings. In Grotberg, E.H., editor: Day care: resources for decisions, Washington, D.C., n.d., Office of Economic Opportunity.

Gordon, I.J.: Success and accountability, Childhood Education **43**:338-347, 1972.

Gordon, I.J.: The infant experience, Columbus, Ohio, 1975, Charles E. Merrill Publishing Co.

Granger, R.H.: Your child from one to six, DHEW Publication No. (OHDS) 77-30026, Washington, D.C., 1977, U.S. Government Printing Office.

Grotberg, E.H., editor: 200 years of children, Washington, D.C., n.d., U.S. Department of Health, Education and Welfare.

Healy, A.: Personal communication, June 3, 1980.

Highberger, R., and Schramm, C.: Child development for day care workers, Boston, 1976, Houghton Mifflin Co.

Honig, A.S.: The training of infant care providers, Voice for Children 9(1):12-17, 1976.

Hunt, J.M.: Intelligence and experience, New York, 1961, Ronald Press.

Huntington, D.S., Provence, S., and Parker, R.K.: Day care, 2 serving infants, DHEW Publication No. (OCD) 73-14, Washington, D.C., 1973, U.S. Government Printing Office.

Ilg, F.L., and Ames, L.B.: Gesell Institute's child behavior, New York, 1972, Barnes & Noble Books.

Johnson, H.M.: Children in "the nursery school," New York, 1972, Agathon Press, Inc. (Originally published in 1928.)

Kagan, J., Kearsley, R.B., and Zelazo, P.R.: Infancy: its place in human development, Cambridge, Mass., 1978, Harvard University Press.

Kessen, W.: The child, New York, 1965, John Wiley & Sons, Inc.

Knobloch, H., and Pasamanick, B.: Gesell and Amatruda's developmental diagnosis, ed 3, New York, 1974, Harper & Row, Publishers, Inc.

Langenbach, M., and Neskora, T.: Day care: curriculum considerations, Columbus, Ohio, 1977, Charles E. Merrill Publishing Co.

Levine, R.A.: Parental goals: a cross-cultural view. In Leichter, H.J., editor: The family as educator, New York, 1974, Teachers College Press.

Lichtenberg, P., and Norton, D.G.: Cognitive and mental development in the first five years of life, Public Health Service Pub. No. 2057, Washington, D.C., 1970, National Institute of Mental Health, U.S. Government Printing Office.

McCall, R.B.: Infants: the new knowledge, Cambridge, Mass., 1979, Harvard University Press.

McClearn, G.E.: Genetics and behavior development. In Hoffman, M.L., and Hoffman, L.W., editors: Review of child development research, vol. 1, New York, 1964, Russell Sage Foundation.

Mussen, P.H., editor: Carmichael's manual of child psychology, ed 3, New York, 1970, John Wiley & Sons, Inc.

Mussen, P.H., Conger, J.J., and Kagan, J.: Child development and personality, New York, 1979, Harper & Row, Publishers, Inc.

North, A.F.: Infant care, Washington, D.C., 1980, U.S. Government Printing Office.

Osofsky, J.D., editor: Handbook of infant development, New York, 1979, John Wiley & Sons, Inc.

Painter, G.: Teach your baby, New York, 1971, Simon & Schuster, Inc.

Piaget, J.: The origins of intelligence in children, New York, 1952, International University Press.

Piaget, J.: Play, dreams, and imitation in childhood, New York, 1962, W.W. Norton & Co., Inc.

Piaget, J.: Science of education and the psychology of the child, New York, 1970, Orion Press.

U.S. National Commission on the International Year of the Child: Report to the President, Washington, D.C., 1980.

Scarfe, N.V.: The importance of security in the education of young children, International Journal of Early Childhood 4:27-30, 1972.

Smart, M.S., and Smart, R.C.: Infants: development and relationships, New York, 1973, Macmillan Publishing Co., Inc.

Smart, M.S., and Smart, R.C.: Infants: development and relationships, ed 2, New York, 1978, Macmillan Publishing Co., Inc.

Spock, B.: Baby and child care, New York, 1977, Pocket Books, Inc.

Stone, L.J., Smith, H.T., and Murphy, L.B.: The competent infant series, vols. 1–3, New York, 1978, Basic Books, Inc.

Streepey, S.: Today he can't. Tomorrow he can! Your child from birth to two years, vol 1, New York, 1971, The Learning Child.

Thomas, A., and others: Behavioral individuality in early childhood, New York, 1963, New York University Press.

Thomas, A., Chess, S., and Birch, H.G.: Temperament and behavior disorders in children, New York, 1968, New York University Press.

Thomas, A., Chess, S., and Birch, H.G.: The origins of personality, Scientific American **223**:102-109, 1970.

White, B.L.: The first three years of life, Englewood Cliffs, N.J., 1975, Prentice-Hall, Inc.

White, B.L., and Watts, J.C.: Experience and environment: major influences on the development of the young child, vol. 1, Englewood Cliffs, N.J., 1973, Prentice Hall, Inc.

White, B.L., and others: Experience and environment: major influences on the development of the young child, vol 2, Englewood Cliffs, N.J., 1978, Prentice-Hall, Inc.

White, B.L., Kaban, B.T., and Attanucci, J.S.: The origins of human competence: the final report of the Harvard Preschool Project, Lexington, Mass., 1979, Lexington Books.

SECTION TWO

The care and protection curriculum

One of the ironies of the current emphasis on the developmental care and education of very young children is an apparently decreasing emphasis on the health and safety components in any child care setting, whether in a group center or in a family day care home. For instance, many center goal statements are prefaced in the following manner: "Assuming health and safety provisions have been made, our goals are . . .", and the stated goals are directed toward the encouragement of the cognitive and social-emotional development of the children. We cannot assume anything so vital; we just might be throwing out the baby with the bath water!

The care and protection curriculum includes the safety, health, and nutrition of children (and their caregivers and teachers) and merits as detailed attention as the developmental or educational curriculum in the behavioral, social-emotional, and cognitive domains. Ideally, the health and safety components should be so well known and internalized that the adults' conscious attention is freed to focus on the developmental aspects of the program.

Just as we cannot assume that the health and safety needs will be met by the adults, even conscientious, loving adults, we should not assume that group living for very young children automatically increases the risks of accidents or illness. It is very possible that such risks can be minimized in a quality center.

The chapters in Section Two present the essential components of the care and protection curriculum designed for the group care of very young children.

CHAPTER 3

SAFETY AND THE VERY YOUNG CHILD

PART I: Safety components of infant-toddler care

An ounce of prevention is worth a pound of cure.

Benjamin Franklin

All young children get their share of cuts, bruises, and even sprains in the course of growing up. Minor injuries, although upsetting at the moment, can usually be treated with a gentle swab of antiseptic, a bandage, and a soothing hug and kiss. Serious accidents, however, are another matter. No child should experience even one such accident. Serious accidents are avoidable; they occur because adults underestimate the child.

Current statistics show that the majority of accidents during the first few years of life occur in the home, but this finding may change as more and more young children are served by out-of-home care during the daytime hours. In addition, it has been impossible to get valid data about incidents and types of accidents and injuries in many day care centers or homes, except on an individual basis, because of their independence and diversity. The usual sources of such statistics are the accident and liability insurance companies, but the issuance of such coverage for children (and staff) in noninstitutionalized child care centers and homes is a relatively new phenomenon.

Countries with national health insurance plans have such records, and are justly proud of the statistics. In Sweden, for example, there are significantly fewer accidents at day care centers than in the children's homes for the same children. This statement is particularly meaningful when we consider the long daytime hours children spend at the centers. The Swedish attention to safety is immediately evident to the visitor. Many pieces of equipment are made of large, multishaped, multicolored chunks of foam rubber that can be combined or folded into child-sized tables, chairs, or room dividers.

Small items such as crayons and little toys and blocks are stored in natural woven baskets on uncluttered shelves. Tempered glass insets in the lower half of Dutch doors leading from the children's rooms to the adult kitchen and staff rooms enable children to watch but not be underfoot. To provide additional elements of safety, door hinges are covered with smooth, vertical sheaths of molded plastic, so that little fingers cannot be smashed.

It may not be possible to design a completely accident-proof center or home, but it is possible to either remove or prevent access to sources of injury. As a result, breakables and poisons will be virtually eliminated. The goal is accident prevention through risk reduction.

Accidents will still happen in any group of children, but will be the result of a child's actions (falling, bumping) rather than adult carelessness or lack of information.

MOTOR VEHICLE ACCIDENTS*

Are the following statements true or false?
1. After the critical neonatal period, motor vehicle accidents rank second as the cause of death in childhood.
2. Most parents use child restraint devices in the proper manner when very young children are riding in a motor vehicle.
3. In order to meet the government standard, any car seat or restraint device manufactured after April 1, 1971, had to pass a crash test.

---

*The information provided about motor vehicle accidents has been approved by the Physicians for Automotive Safety and by the U.S. Department of Transportation, National Highway Traffic Safety Administration.

4. The safest place for an infant or toddler riding in an automobile is on the lap of a belted passenger.
5. All child safety devices bearing the tag "Meets or exceeds Federal Motor Vehicle Standard 213" are considered safe.
6. It is dangerous for young children to wear safety belts.
7. A seat belt that encloses both adult and a young child provides adequate protection against injury in case of collision or near-collision.
8. Restraint devices for children who are unable to sit up by themselves are designed so that the child faces forward in a semireclining position.
9. Children receive less severe injuries in the event of a collision when they are thrown clear of the vehicle.
10. A large percentage of childhood fatalities and injuries resulting from motor vehicle collisions or near-collisions could be eliminated by appropriate precautions by adults.

How did you rate the above statements? Most adults do not get a perfect score. The correct responses are included in the following discussion.

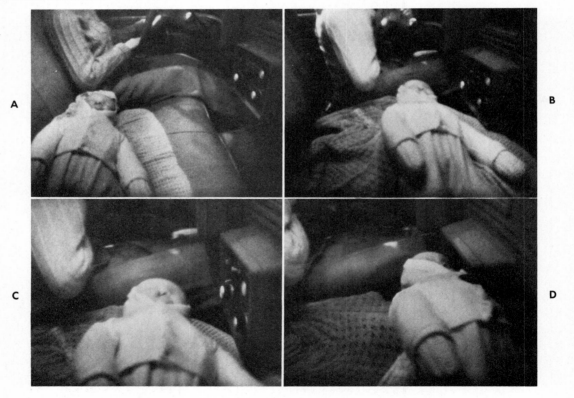

FIG. 3-1 Crash sequence for an unrestrained infant.

Courtesy Insurance Institute for Highway Safety: Children in crashes, Washington, D.C., 1980, p. 6.

Child passenger accidents

The vast majority of young children riding in motor vehicles are either unprotected or inadequately protected from serious injury or death in the event of an accident. After the early critical period, the leading killer of young children is the automobile accident. The cause and effect relationship contained in the above statements is a direct one.

According to the United States Department of Transportation, in 1978, 669 children below the age of 5 years were killed while riding in cars, and tens of thousands more were seriously injured. The highest death rate in this 5-year

span was for children under 1 year of age. Figs. 3-1 and 3-2, give clear indications of two main causes of this high death rate. The photographs are from slow motion films of the Insurance Institute for Highway Safety (1980). They show crash tests of dummy figures in a late model automobile impacting a solid barrier at 24 to 25 miles per hour. Fig 3-1, *A*, shows the precrash position of an infant lying unrestrained on the front seat next to an adult; *B* and *C* show first forward movement of the baby in a wide angle and a close-up shot less than 0.1 second after impact—just before the baby's face contacts the instrument panel. There is no time whatsoever

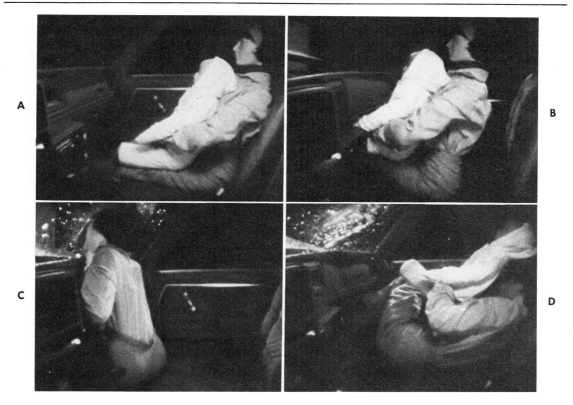

FIG. 3-2   Crash sequence for an infant in lap of unbelted adult.

Courtesy Insurance Institute for Highway Safety: Children in crashes, Washington, D.C., 1980, p. 4.

for the adult to save the baby from smashing into the protruding knobs of the instrument panel only 0.25 second after impact (*D*).

An adult's arms are usually a very safe place for an infant, but *not when riding in a car*. The Highway Safety Research Institute at the University of Michigan ran a series of tests simulating the effects of 15 mph and 30 mph impacts on 17 lb. dummy infants who were held in the arms of adult volunteers who were anchored with lap-shoulder belts. Not one volunteer could hold on to the "baby," even knowing when the impact would occur. Other crash tests have shown that a 10 lb. infant dummy is thrown forward with a thrust of 300 lbs. in a 30 mph impact.

The results of a similar test are vividly shown in Fig. 3-2. Fig. 3-2, *A*, shows the precrash position of an unbelted adult sitting in the right front passenger seat holding baby on her lap; *B* shows the forward movement of the adult and baby 0.1 of a second after impact—just before they smash into the instrument panel and windshield; *C*, the adult's body becomes a battering ram—crushing the infant into the instrument panel and shattering the windshield, only 3/20 of a second after impact; *D* shows the adult and infant as they rebound from the windshield and instrument panel, only half a second after the initial impact.

The serious problem of unrestrained children in motor vehicles is not limited to infants. Fig. 3-3, also from the Insurance Institute for High-

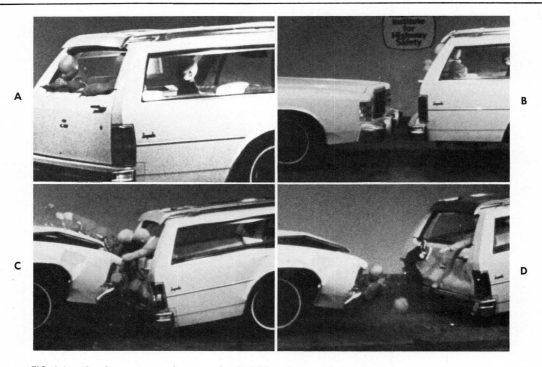

FIG. 3-3   Crash sequence of unrestrained children in a station wagon.

Courtesy Insurance Institute for Highway Safety: Children in crashes, Washington, D.C., 1980, p. 5.

way Safety, shows a crash test of a 6-year-old and two 3-year-old children in the rear cargo area of a parked station wagon being hit from the rear by another vehicle traveling at about 30 mph. Fig. 3-3, *A*, shows the precrash position of the children; *B* shows the two cars 0.02 seconds before impact; *C* the children are catapulted through the rear window, only 0.42 seconds after the impact; *D* shows the children's position 0.865 seconds after impact. One child's head is smashing against the pavement.

The photographs leave no doubt as to the necessity of proper restraint systems for all young children riding in motor vehicles. However, both casual observations on our streets and highways and research studies reveal that the majority of children in cars are either unprotected or inadequately protected in case of a collision or near-collision. Recent surveys have shown that a very low percentage of young children involved in motor vehicle accidents were using child restraints properly.

The anatomical structure of a young child is different from that of an adult. Therefore young children need specially designed restraint systems that distribute crash forces over a large

area of the body. However, if a proper restraint is not available, it is infinitely safer to use a regular automobile seat belt rather than leaving the child unrestrained. Fastening the child and an adult with the same seat belt will not provide adequate protection against injury. In fact, such dual fastening may greatly compound the child's injuries. Car beds and household booster seats have no place in an automobile. There are specially designed car booster seats that elevate the child and enable the use of a combination lap-shoulder belt in the front seat, or a lap belt and a specially installed harness in the back seat.

An appropriate restraint system will do more than minimize the extent of injury in the case of a collision or near-collision. It will keep the child inside the vehicle. When a child is thrown clear of the vehicle, injuries can be fatal.

Crash-tested devices and how to use them

Federal safety standards for child restraint devices have been in effect since 1971. The devices that met the standards were tagged or labeled "Meets or exceeds Federal Motor Vehicle Safety Standard 213." However, these devices do not necessarily offer the protection needed.

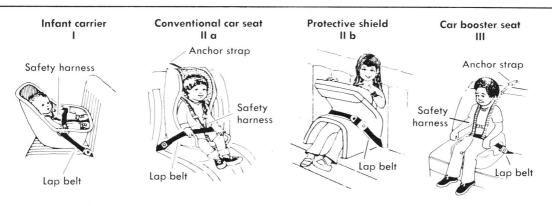

FIG. 3-4   Don't risk your child's life.

Courtesy Physicians for Automotive Safety.

The standards were not based on actual crash (or dynamic) tests. Ten years of hard work on the part of citizens and professionals resulted in revised standards, effective January 1, 1981. The new standard applies to all restraint devices manufactured since that date and is based on crash-test data.

The Physicians for Automotive Safety (September, 1980) have provided sketches of restraints that illustrate the approved design concept. Many seats combine the features shown in Fig. 3-4.

Detailed instructions for the correct use of these approved types of restraints are taken from the same brochure *Don't Risk Your Child's Life!*

I. *Infant Carriers*, suitable from birth up to 17 or 20 pounds, are designed to face rearward (never forward). The infant rides in a semireclining position, secured with a harness. The carrier is strapped to the seat of the vehicle with a lap belt.

Rolled up receiving blankets placed around the baby's head and shoulders will provide support during the early weeks of life.

IIa. *Conventional Car Seats* are suitable for children who are able to sit up by themselves [up to age 4 or 5 years]. The child is held in by a harness; the seat is anchored to the vehicle with a lap belt.

Some devices require the belt to be threaded through the back where it can remain permanently buckled. Others must be anchored with the belt around the front as shown in the illustration.

Many seats require the use of a top anchor strap to prevent them from pitching forward in a crash. If the seat is to be used in the front, this does not present a problem: the strap is simply hooked into the lap belt in the seat behind. (It does, however, make one set of rear belts unusable).

If the seat will be used in the back, an anchor bracket has to be installed. In a sedan this involves drilling a hole through solid metal in the rear window ledge. In a station wagon or hatchback, the anchor plate has to be installed well back in the cargo area or truck space. A strap that is secured to the rear of the seat back or straight down to the floor will not hold the seat upright in a severe crash. Follow manufacturer's instruction.

Anchor brackets are obtainable separately for installation in a second car. (Note: Seats offering a "reclining" feature should be used in the fully upright position when facing forward.)

IIb. *Shield-type Devices* distribute crash forces by cushioning the child's body on a padded surface.

Some of these seats require only the use of a lap belt which can remain permanently fastened. As children get older, they manage to climb in and out by themselves; this can be a great convenience so long as the child can be trusted to stay inside while the car is moving. (Note: Shield-type seats are not suitable for children who wear eye-glasses.)

III. *Booster Seats* are particularly suitable for children who have outgrown conventional car seats. The booster is sold with a harness which requires permanent installation [for use in the back seat] (see above for instructions on how to secure a top anchor strap). (Note: The midpoint of the child's head must not exceed the height of the seat back). (Physicians for Automotive Safety, Sept. 1980, unpaged)

Why is this detailed information included in a publication describing the group care and education of infants and toddlers? There are four major reasons. First, adults are notorious for piling children into cars and station wagons and taking off for the grocery store or the day care center or on a trip. Second, parents· of very young children in day care frequently may be in a stress condition when delivering or picking up their children. They are either in a rush to get to work, or in a rush to get home again. Accidents are more frequent under stress conditions. Third, the caregivers in the day care center or home are in a unique position to share information about the restraint devices necessary to decrease the likelihood of injury or fatality. Fourth, an increasing number of centers are providing pick-up and delivery service in their own vans or station wagons, as well as using them for an occasional field trip. Therefore specific information about dynamically tested restraint devices must be readily available and put into practice by all adults who transport young children. Brochures giving even more detailed information may be obtained from Physicians for Automotive Safety, 50 Union Avenue, Irvington, NJ 07111,* and U.S. Department of Transportation, National Highway Traffic Safety Administration, Washington, DC 20590.

According to the American Academy of Pediatrics, "reasonably priced automobile seat restraints are widely available and have been shown to reduce deaths in auto accidents by over 90 percent and serious injuries by almost 80 percent" (U.S. Commission on the International Year of the Child, 1980, p. 94). Unfortunately, not all child care providers are willing to invest in approved restraint devices because of the expense involved. These devices are to motor vehicle safety what immunizations are to health. They should be required just as stringently as are immunizations (see Chapter 5).

Child restraint loan programs have been established in several states with the help of government funding. The programs are administered by insurance companies, Chambers of Commerce, the Jaycettes, hospital auxiliaries, or other groups of concerned persons. The state of Michigan has taken the lead, followed by South Dakota, Connecticut, Ohio, and Iowa, among others.

One last word of caution. The instructions for correct installation and use are specific to each brand of safety device. Even the information and ratings supplied by consumer organizations are based on correct usage only.

The true-false statements at the beginning of this section are all false, with one exception. A large percentage of childhood fatalities and injuries resulting from motor vehicle collisions or near-collisions *can be eliminated* by appropriate precautions by adults.

---

*Send 35 cents and a self-addressed, stamped, long white envelope.

Basic "rules of the road" for children in motor vehicles

In addition to the proper use of child restraints, a few basic "rules of the road" are necessary:

1. Adult supervision for children getting in and out, always away from the street side
2. All children securely and correctly fastened in before starting the motor
3. All car doors locked before starting the motor (the best locking devices can be controlled from the driver's seat)
4. Children never left alone in a motorized vehicle, whether the engine is running or not
5. At least one adult in addition to the driver when more than two children are in the vehicle

Pedestrian accidents

Automobiles and other motor vehicles are also instrumental in the deaths and injuries of child pedestrians. Of course, precautions are in order for pick-up and delivery: an adult other than the driver should always be in attendance, and the children should always get out of the vehicle on the curb side. The local police department or traffic authorities are helpful in placing restrictions on through traffic at or near the pick-up and delivery area. Such measures as cross-walks, stop signs, "loading area" signs, and "children crossing" signs can alert the drivers in the vicinity. When possible, the loading area should be off the street. Parents and staff members should agree on a specific location and should not deviate from the established pattern. Wherever the area, efforts should be made to encourage parents or other drivers to personally accompany the child(ren) inside the center or home and transfer each child to the appropriate caregiver, as well as remove the child's wraps. Not only is this procedure effective as a safety measure, but it frees staff members from loading duty. It also ensures parent-caregiver communication at the beginning and end of the day.

There are logical precautions for walking field trips, also. Walks close to traffic should be on the wide shoulders of highways or the sidewalks of streets. Streets, highways, or country lanes should be crossed at points protected with traffic lights or at points with maximum visibility. Children should be kept in a group, led and followed by adults. Various methods of grouping for safety include hand-holding pairs of children (not particularly reliable for toddlers); a long knotted rope with each child holding onto a knot (also not very reliable); or every two children holding the hands of an adult. In Western European countries young children wear harnesses with an attached leash; this is both safe and logical, but the use of harnesses and leashes has not been adopted in the United States.

Walking trips provide excellent opportunities for involving parents or volunteers to achieve a safe adult/child ratio. Unfortunately, most infants and toddlers in group settings do not have parents available for such outings. Ideally, walks in the immediate neighborhood of the center or home will include no more than four children and two adults, thereby providing many opportunities for the investigation of ant hills and the like. Such discovery or exploration walks should far outnumber walks with a specific destination, such as the grocery store or the library. The pleasures of these walking trips should not be lessened by constant admonitions by adults as to behavior. Adults who are knowledgeable in child development theory know two related facts: (1) very young children lack impulse control, and (2) verbal directions or commands directed to young children are unreliable. The only guarantee of an accident-free experience is the optimal adult child ratio.

FALLS AND RELATED INJURIES
Incidence

Deaths from falls in the toddler age group far exceed the number of the more sensational accidents by drowning or poisoning. Fortunately, although no child can be protected from all falls, most spills are fairly minor. Children fall from beds, cribs, and highchairs, on newly waxed or wet floors, on skidding throw rugs, and out of windows. Some caregivers move cribs next to open windows for the "stimulation" of watching the fascinating world outside and apparently place total reliance on a screen latch that is not childproof. Children do not bounce when they fall. They may suffer skull fractures, brain damage, or dislocation or fractures of the extremities in addition to internal injuries. Remember that babies can climb on large toys left in a crib or playpen and fall over the railing. As soon as the baby can stand, the crib mattress should be put at its lowest position and the side rail locked at the highest position.

Almost half of the traumatic injuries of early childhood involve head injuries; the peak age is the second year of life. In addition to the potential for serious related physical or mental injury, emotional damage is very possible. The various hospital procedures—stitching up lacerations, taking radiographs, setting fractures and broken bones—are distress situations for little ones.

Children do not fall because caregivers are "bad" caregivers. They fall because caregivers are not aware of or do not heed emerging patterns of development. New behaviors emerge rapidly during infancy and toddlerhood. Yesterday the baby lay on her back on the table, today she rolled over, *and off!* The peak age of incidence for all falls is between 12 and 36 months.

Recommendations

Selected recommendations for the prevention of falls (and related accidents) in an infant-toddler center follow:

- Furniture and equipment should be sturdy and without sharp or splintered edges, loose parts, or toxic paint.
- Old equipment should be modified to meet the recommendations of the U.S. Consumer Product Safety Commission; new equip-

ment (cribs, highchairs, baby walkers) should bear a label stating it meets the U.S. CPSC safety standards. All such equipment should be tip-proof.

- Floors should not be highly waxed; rugs should be skidproof. Floors and rugs should be easy to clean and cleaned daily.
- Stairs with more than three steps should have safety gates that open toward the exits. Stairways should have toddler-height hand rails on each side and should be well lighted and clear of any extraneous material.
- Cribs and playpens should not be placed by open windows; all openable windows should have sturdy screens or guards that have safety locks.
- Glass panels in doors should be made of tempered glass and clearly marked. Solid doors should have a lengthwise vertical inset of tempered glass. Dutch doors (or half-doors) are less likely than one-piece solid doors to cause accidents.
- The outdoor area should be fenced, and gates should have childproof locks (natural barriers such as dense shrubbery are not childproof); all parts of the area should be visible for supervision; there should be no holes in the ground (ditches, wells, etc.) into which children might fall.
- Outdoor equipment such as swings and climbing apparatus should be rigid, permanently anchored in the ground, and in good repair. Portable wading pools should be drained and upended when not in use.
- Concrete or asphalt surfaces should not be under climbing structures or swings. The most desirable surfaces for outdoor play areas are grass, artificial turf, and perhaps bark chips, with strips of hard surface for riding or pulling wheel toys.
- The outdoor area must be "policed" each time for broken glass or other hazards before children are allowed in the area.
- Very young children should be supervised

by adults at all times, both indoors and outdoors.

CHOKING, SUFFOCATION, AND STRANGULATION
Choking

The sixth ranking cause of accidental death in the United States is foreign body obstruction of the airway or breathing passages. It ranks first as a cause of accidental death for infants below the age of 1 year.

This should come as no surprise. Again, child development information shows that curiosity is a driving force in infants and is satisfied by mouthing the many small objects found on or near the floor or on reachable low tables. Babies choke on food or food-related objects such as bones, egg shells, and peanut shells, as well as on peanuts, beans, corn, carrots, fruit skins or pits, and hard candies, all of which are high-risk foods for infants and toddlers. Foreign bodies such as balloons (particularly lethal), beads, bobby pins, safety pins, coins, screws, and tacks are all potentially dangerous objects for infants. A good rule of thumb is that objects with a diameter less than 1½ inches or with removable parts less than 1½ inches in diameter should not be accessible to children under 2 years of age, or to children who are still mouthing objects. A second rule of thumb is to restrict children from walking, running, or playing while they have food or anything else in their mouth.

If, in spite of precautions, an infant is choking and forcefully coughing, encourage the coughing and breathing but *do not* interfere. If the coughing is weak and the child has difficulty in breathing, prompt action is urgent. The American Red Cross recommends three maneuvers for relieving airway obstruction: back blows, manual thrusts, and manual removal of the object. These maneuvers are described here in brief form, but specific directions should be obtained from the local Red Cross chapter and should be part of the reference library of every care center.

1. If the child is breathing adequately, keep

him/her in an upright position, and verbally encourage coughing.

2. If the child is having difficulty breathing, hold her head down and against your forearm, and deliver back blows.

3. If the object is not dislodged by the back blows, use a chest thrust. Previously, the abdominal (Heimlich Maneuver) thrust was used. According to the American Red Cross (1980), abdominal thrusts are not recommended in infants and children up to 8 years of age, because they may cause injury to the abdominal organs, especially the liver. The combination of back blows and chest thrusts is superior to either technique used alone.

4. If still unsuccessful and the object is *visible*, attempt to remove the object with your fingers. Blind finger sweeps are to be avoided in infants and children since the object can easily be pushed back into the throat and cause further obstruction.

In addition to a working knowledge of the correct procedures for choking incidents, caregivers should know how to administer mouth-to-mouth ventilation and cardiopulmonary resuscitation. Both initial training and periodic updating should be a requirement for employment.

Suffocation and strangulation

One of the mixed blessings of our civilization is the almost universal use of plastic: plastic bags, plastic mattress covers, plastic baby pants. A plastic bag can be more dangerous than a poisonous snake, and both can kill. No one would place a child and a rattlesnake in the same crib, yet it is not unusual to leave pieces or bags of plastic film within the young child's reach. The resulting deaths are needless and tragic. An infant can suffocate in his crib with or without plastic. He cannot remove a pillow from his face, he cannot move his head from between the mattress and the side of the crib or carriage. The distance between the mattress and the crib or

carriage side should be no more than the width of two adult fingers. An infant may also manage to wedge her head between the slats of a crib or playpen. Slat-to-slat distance should be no greater than 2⅜ inches, or about the width of three adult fingers.

The U.S. Consumer Product Safety Commission (CPSC) periodically releases warnings against products on the market that have a potential to cause death. A recent warning described stuffed animal mobiles designed to be suspended from the ceiling by means of three elastic cords and a cradle gym with an elastic cord strung with wooden beads and rings. The same release repeated a warning about two types of baby cribs that were designed so that an infant could trap her head between the corner post and the head or footboard and strangle. "If it's in the marketplace, it must be safe," is literally a death-defying assumption. The prevention of serious injury or loss of life caused by hazardous furniture and equipment is the direct responsibility of adults: those who manufacture them, and those who buy and use them.

One more avoidable accident: a baby old enough to hold a bottle can literally drown when put to bed with a bottle.

INGESTION OF TOXIC SUBSTANCES
Incidence

In the year 1450, the Court Apothecary in Scotland declared that "all persons are forbidden under the pain of treason to bring home poisons for any use by which Christian man or woman can take harm." Today public service messages and container labels offer repeated warnings to keep all potentially poisonous substances out of the reach of children. However, the problem of poisoning has persisted. More than 500,000 cases of accidental poisoning—at least one every minute of the day—occur in the United States each year. Over 50% of the victims of accidental poisonings in the area served by the poison control center at the University of Iowa are 1- and 2-year-olds.

Development from infancy to toddlerhood is accompanied by an increased accident potential. When infants have learned to coordinate eyes and hands, they reach, and they will reach for anything. Once they start to creep or crawl, they soon will be climbing. Everything is fair game for them to touch, mouth, and swallow, if small enough. They investigate under the sink, under the stairway, and behind and in the toilet. They go into closets and cupboards. The combination of the child's desire and ability to investigate and an unfriendly environment that contains substances that should not be investigated is explosive. Alarmingly, the majority of poisonings occur while the children are under the supervision of their parents or other responsible adults.

Common poisons

Poisons commonly found around the home, and frequently around a child care center, include:

Ammonia	Insecticides	Rodent poison
Aspirin	Iodine	Room deodorizers
Bleach	Kerosene	Rug cleaner
Deodorants	Lighter	Shampoo
Depilatories	fluid	Shoe polish
Detergents	Metal polish	Tranquilizers
Drain Cleaner	Paint/paint	Turpentine
Drugs and	thinner	Varnish
medicines	Perfume	Varnish
Floor wax	Permanent-	Vitamins
Glue	wave solu-	Washing soda
Hairspray	tions	

Plants that poison. Many houseplants are poisonous to human beings. A partial list of common plants is included here to alert us that many of these aesthetically pleasing items are not harmless.

Plant	Toxic parts
Dieffenbachia (dumb cane, elephant ear)	All parts
Caladium	All parts
Philodendron	All parts
Castor bean (*Ricinus communis*)	Seeds

Plant	Toxic parts
Hyacinth, narcissus, daffodil	Bulbs
Oleander	Leaves, stems, flowers
Autumn crocus	Bulbs
Lily-of-the-valley	All parts
Iris	Underground stems (rhizomes)
Foxglove	Leaves, seeds, flowers
Rhubarb	Leaf blade
Yew	Seeds (red berries), leaves
Rhododendron, azalea	All parts
Wild and cultivated cherries	Leaves, stems, bark
English ivy	All parts
Holly	Red berries
Oaks	Foliage, acorns
Plum, apricot, peach, apple	Leaves, stems, bark, pits
Poinsettia	Leaves, stems
Privet (*Ligustrum*)	Leaves, berries
Tobacco	Leaves, cigarettes
Tomato, potato	Foliage

These are just a few of the over 700 species of plants that are poisonous. Effects vary from mild to potentially fatal. If a child has tasted or eaten a plant you think might be poisonous, call the nearest Poison Control Center for advice. Most of the poisonous plants listed are innocuous in small quantities. However, they should be out of reach not so much for their ability to kill, but because a reaction, usually severe gastrointestinal irritation with vomiting and diarrhea, may require hospitalization.

Lists of poisonous plants are constantly changing as we gain new information. Therefore, day care centers would do well to have no plants within the reach of young children. This rule essentially bans all plants, if we realistically assess the extent of a child's reach, which can be lengthened by climbing up on various objects or pieces of furniture and equipment. Of course, children should be taught not to put plants in their mouths, but infants and toddlers are too young to heed this rule with any degree of consistency. We do not stop our teaching efforts, but we do recognize that the extent or permanence of learning is unpredictable and unreliable.

Role of caregivers

It is the adult who mismanages the environment, and it is the adult who frequently mismanages treatment. Many traditional treatments for the ingestion of poisons are useless and, even worse, they can compound and intensify the original damage. The time-honored procedure of using salt water to induce vomiting is both ineffective and potentially dangerous, as is giving doses of vinegar, citrus juices, oil, or milk of magnesia. Too few persons know that inducing vomiting might be the worst possible thing to do! Some substances can add to the irritation or burning of weakened digestive tract tissue as they are regurgitated.

Unfortunately, the antidote charts found in various locations (on drug store counters or in the popular magazines) are almost always out of date or inaccurate. Do not rely on them or on the "childproof" caps on bottles; they may be child-resistant, but are not necessarily childproof.

There is no reason or excuse for ignorance or misinformation about toxic substances; information and advice are readily available and free for the asking. Approximately 500 Poison Control Centers form a nationwide network designed to disseminate information to health professionals and lay persons, to treat poisoned victims, and to engage in continuing laboratory research. The local centers receive almost immediate current information by way of computer from the National Clearinghouse for Poison Control Centers, which analyzes all manufactured products and advises appropriate measures for their mismanagement. The Clearinghouse distributes materials to professional as well as lay persons.

Representative of their printed materials for lay persons are the suggestions for poison-proofing homes and centers, distributed by the University of Iowa Hospitals and Clinics Poison Control Center.

- All cleaners and household products in original safety-top containers out of reach in locked cabinets
- All household cleaning products stored in locked cabinets out of reach
- All cleaners and household products in original safety-top containers
- All bleaches, soaps, and detergents out of reach and in original containers
- All insect sprays, weed killers, gasoline and car products, turpentine, paints, and paint products in locked areas
- All plants out of reach
- All perfumes, cosmetics, mouthwashes, and powders out of reach
- All medications out of reach in locked cabinets

Caregivers and other staff members may be conscientious and follow all of the above precautions, yet leave their purses or knapsacks containing medications, cosmetics, or pointed instruments (e.g., nail files) within easy reach of the children. The prevention of poisoning depends not so much on memorizing lists of rules, but on total awareness of possible risks and removing these risks from the child's environment.

If, in spite of precautions, a child does ingest a harmful substance—and many harmful substances are not labeled as poisonous—follow the directions below, *in the order given*, and *remain calm*.

1. *Do these things before you call someone:*
   a. Remove poisons from contact with eyes, skin, or mouth.
      (1) Eyes
         (a) Gently wash eyes with plenty of tap water for at least 5 minutes with the eyelids held open.
         (b) Do not allow the patient to rub the affected eye.

(2) Skin
  (a) Wash the poison off the skin with large volumes of water.
  (b) Remove contaminated clothing.
(3) Mouth: Remove all tablets, powder, plants, etc., from patient's mouth. Examine for any burns, cuts, irritation, or unusual coloring.
b. If exposed to gases or fumes:
  (1) Get the patient to fresh air.
  (2) Loosen clothing.
  (3) If not breathing, clear the airway and start mouth-to-mouth respiration. Continue until help arrives.
2. *Call for information about what to do next.* Call your doctor or the Poison Control Center. Don't hesitate to call even if you are unsure a poison was ingested. Provide your doctor or the Poison Control Center with the following information:
  a. Identify yourself and the patient. Give the patient's age and weight.
  b. Give your phone number so that you can be reached if your call is accidentally disconnected.
  c. Have the poison container available and read the label. Estimate the amount taken.
  d. *Remain calm.* There is always time to act. Your doctor or the Poison Center will give you instructions on what to do next.
3. *If instructed to induce vomiting:* Have syrup of ipecac available to induce vomiting.
  a. Syrup of ipecac can be purchased from a pharmacy without a prescription. It can be stored at room temperature for years. Keep 1 or 2 ounces available at all times.
  b. Recommended dosage for ipecac syrup:
    (1) Children 1 year old or less: 2 teaspoonfuls (10 ml)
    (2) Children over 1 year old: 1 tablespoonful (15 ml)

(3) Adults: 2 tablespoonfuls (30 ml)
  c. Give the appropriate dose of ipecac with a few ounces of water or a favorite drink.
  d. If the patient has not vomited in 15 minutes, give another dose of syrup of ipecac and more liquids.
  e. *Do not waste time trying other ways to induce vomiting.*
4. *Never induce vomiting if:*
  a. Patient is unconscious.
  b. Patient is having a convulsion.
  c. A caustic (strong acid or alkali) was swallowed.
  d. A petroleum product was swallowed (gasoline, lighter fluids, cleaning products, furniture polish, etc.).
5. *If instructed to go to the hospital:*
  a. Take the poison and its container, plant, etc., to the hospital.
  b. Do not attempt any additional first aid unless your doctor or the Poison Control Center has instructed you to do so.
Remember:
• Keep calm if a poisoning has occurred.
• Do not delay in seeking advice.
To Avoid Poisoning:
• Keep all drugs and dangerous household chemicals locked up.
• Never place a dangerous chemical in a beverage container.
• Do not rely on childproof caps. They can frequently be opened by children.
• Do not store drugs in purses or drawers or in the medicine cabinet.
• Never call medicine candy.

Other toxic substances

Lead poisoning. Insidious because they are not immediately observable, the results of lead poisoning include convulsive disorders, mental retardation, cerebral palsy, blindness, behavioral disorders, and death. When titanium oxide replaced lead in paint in the 1940s, many thought that lead poisoning would soon be an "accident" of the past, but since the mass screening of children started in 1971, 3,000 to 4,000 children have been treated for lead poisoning each year, with thousands more receiving no treatment at all. According to Lin-Fu (1979) "lead poisoning in children is a uniquely neglected public health problem of the 20th century" (p. 1). Data collected during the 1950s and 1960s has clearly indicated that "high risk areas for lead poisoning were almost synonymous with slums, where old deteriorating houses with flaking lead paint and broken plaster prevailed. Children between the ages of one and six were the main victims. Those between one and three years of age comprised approximately 85 per cent of the cases, with the highest incidence occurring at age two" (Lin-Fu, 1979, p. 2).

Unfortunately, the lack of the finances necessary to build centers designed specifically for early child care has necessitated the use of older homes and buildings as the physical facilties for such programs. The combination of older buildings (those built or painted before 1955) and young children's propensity for mouthing and ingesting anything, edible or not, necessitates vigilance. If there is any doubt at all, collect samples of paint peelings and have them analyzed by the local health department.

Poison prevention and control are an excellent focus for parent and staff workshops. Many excellent printed and audiovisual materials are available either at minimal or no cost for such use and distribution, from the National Clearinghouse and other sources. (Appendix A lists selected sources for free materials and sources for films, slide talks, public addresses, and miscellaneous materials.)

Allergens. There are some substances that are poisons for some but not all children. These substances are known as allergens and account for an estimated one-third of all chronic conditions in childhood. Noxious substances may be inhaled (dust, pollen, nasal sprays); contact the skin (cosmetics, fabrics, metals); or be injected through the skin (insect bites, some drugs). A few young children may be allergic to the very objects found in a well-equipped child care environment: paint, glue, dress-up clothes, books, paper, stuffed or live animals, chalk, and plants.

A child who has puffy eyes, a runny nose, skin rash, or repeated sneezing/coughing episodes with no diagnosed cause may be suffering from an allergy that has not been identified. In such an instance we remove the plants and animals; we frequently launder any objects of fabric (including painting smocks, stuffed toys, dress-up clothes); we install a humidifier or air cleaner; we scrub floors and furniture and vacuum carpets frequently; and we use oil-based products, such as clay and marking pens, when available.

At the same time, caregivers convey their suspicions of allergy to the child's parents and suggest they pursue the issue with their family doctor. The sooner an allergy is identified and remedial steps are taken, the better, since allergy is one causal factor of learning disabilities.

Insect bites can be soothed with cold applications and Calamine or similar lotion to relieve the itching. Shortness of breath and/or the eruption of rashlike hives may indicate an allergy to bee stings. These symptoms require the attention of a medical professional.

BURNS AND FIRES

It is hoped that in any day care setting matches and cigarette lighters as well as the pots and pans on the stove are totally inaccessible to young children. Even though children are protected from these obvious dangers, somehow we become emotional and allow lighted candles on a birthday cake or in a Halloween jack-o-lantern.

Infants and toddlers are at high risk from death or injury by fire because of their immobility and their dependence upon adults. Roughly 10% of our population from birth to 5 years of age are injured or killed in fires each year, more than five times the percentage of children from 5 to 14 years of age.

Not all burns are fatal, but all burns are painful, and some cause permanent injury and scarring. Heat registers, radiators, hot water pipes, and floor furnaces should be guarded or insulated so that children cannot come in direct contact with them. Hot liquids or foods and hot appliances and their electric cords must be out of reach and carefully supervised. Hot water temperatures should not exceed 110° at any outlet accessible to children; temperature control mechanisms are readily available.

One of the most tragic—and avoidable—accidents occurs when a child mouths the end of an extension cord that is still plugged into the outlet. This can result in severe burning of the mouth and mucous membranes of the lips and tongue. The damage may not be recognized immediately, but it is serious and irreparable. *Always* unplug a cord when it is not in use or, better yet, never use an extension cord wherever there are children below the age of 5.

Always use safety outlet protectors on wall plugs. Spring-closed outlet covers with a circular or sliding motion and snugly fitting nonconducting plastic cap inserts are available. The inside of electrical outlets must be inaccessible to small fingers and to small pieces of metal such as keys, bobby pins, safety pins. If outlets are not in use, cover them with plastic electrical tape, so that nothing can be inserted. For maximum protection, do not use extension cords. Next best is to tape the plug of the lamp or appliance

into the extension cord outlet. Ideally, any center for young children will have all wall outlets on a strip encircling the room at a height of 5 or 6 feet.

A genuine electrical accident requires fast clear thinking. For accidents involving household electricity:

- Remove source of electricity by cutting off electricity supply. Best to quickly pull master switches.
- If cutting electricity off is not practical, move person from electrical source by pushing with a wooden chair or stick or pulling away with dry cloth.
- Obviously you don't grab the person with your hands because you, too, could get knocked senseless.
- Commence first aid for shocks. (Harmon, 1976, p. 74)

All persons involved in child care should complete at least a basic first aid course. Information about locally available courses can be secured from the Red Cross chapter or from scouting groups. A first aid chart with up-to-date instructions for dealing with accidents should be readily available, and may be obtained from the Council on Family Health, Department FAS, 633 Third Avenue, New York, N.Y. 10017. A list of emergency numbers—doctor, ambulance, hospital, fire department, local Poison Control Center—should be placed by the phone.

PART II: Child abuse and neglect

The safety and well-being of the very young child is endangered not only by motor vehicle accidents, falls, choking and related events, ingestion of toxic substances, and fires and burns; it is also seriously and tragically endangered by the acts or omissions of abusing or neglecting adults. The issue of child abuse and neglect has

the top priority at the U.S. Department of Health and Human Resources.

A prominent pediatrician recently stated, "I was in practice for seven years, and I never saw a case of child abuse." Then he added, "That's because I didn't know what to look for." If pediatricians have been unaware of the everyday reality of child abuse and neglect, how much more unaware are lay persons? The issue is not only lack of awareness. Parents may still be operating under the assumption that what happens in their families is no one else's business, while caregivers in day care centers may be operating under the same assumption about what happens in their centers and in the homes of their children. Neither assumption is valid.

It has been estimated that one in every 30 to 35 preschool-age children is a victim of child abuse and neglect. It has also been estimated that for every known victim, there may be as many as ten unreported, and therefore unknown, victims. But numbers tell only a small part of the story. Effects are far-reaching and serious and may include permanent injury and death. More often than not, the child's personality is seriously damaged. The results of child abuse and neglect can destroy a family, and they extend beyond the family into the community and society, because the emotional harm done to a child can lead to later acts of violence and crime.

The problem of child abuse and neglect should not be ignored by any citizen, but there is no conceivable excuse for any provider of care and education for young children to be uninformed and therefore unprepared to take preventive measures as well as appropriate action when abuse or neglect is suspected. Professional responsibility mandates the day care providers' involvement in the prevention and treatment of abused and neglected children and their families, as a part of their responsibility for the optimal growth and development of children. Their involvement is also mandated by many state laws, required by Public Law 93-247 (Child Abuse Prevention and Treatment Act). State laws differ in definitions of child abuse and neglect, and they differ in reporting requirements, specifying either mandatory or permissive reporting. But regardless of your state's law, any person connected with the regular or intermittent care of young children has a personal and

professional commitment to children. Therefore that person must know what to look for and the appropriate actions to take, both before and after an incident of suspected child abuse and neglect.

BACKGROUND INFORMATION

Some background information is necessary in order to meet this commitment adequately and effectively.

Child abuse and neglect usually occur in the privacy of the child's home, and therefore no one knows exactly how many children or families are affected. The National Center on Child Abuse and Neglect estimates that approximately 1 million children are maltreated by their parents each year. Of these children, perhaps 300,000 are physically or sexually abused, and the remainder are neglected. Each year more than 2,000 children die in circumstances suggestive of abuse and neglect. A rough estimate shows that one-third of the reported cases of abused children are *under the age of 1 year*, and two thirds of the reported cases involve children under the age of 5 years.

Abuse is usually directed toward only one child in the family, although we have yet to determine the specific reasons for this. Neglect usually involves all children in a family and extends across every age group. As in abuse cases, the number of confirmed cases of neglect are probably gross underestimates of the actual neglect taking place. Professional estimates of the ratio of neglect to abuse are sometimes as high as 1 to 10. Some unproved estimates of the incidence of child maltreatment are as high as 4.5 million. Child abuse and neglect are everyday realities.

There are differing definitions of child abuse and neglect within any given state or community. The dividing line between abuse and neglect is often fuzzy, and neglect per se is not mentioned in some state laws. Generally speaking, abuse is the result of a nonaccidental action; neglect is the result of no action when action would be appropriate. The Child Abuse Prevention and Treatment Act defines child abuse and neglect as follows: "The physical or mental injury, sexual abuse or exploitation, negligent treatment, or maltreatment of a child under the age of eighteen, or the age specified by the child protection law of the state in question, by a person who is responsible for the child's welfare under circumstances which indicate that the child's health or welfare is harmed or threatened thereby." More detailed definitions may include injuries sustained as a result of excessive corporal punishment; failure to supply the child with adequate food, clothing, shelter, or health care; abandonment; and failure to provide adequate supervision or guardianship. Within any given community or state there are many different definitions; some are found in laws, some in procedures, and some in the informal practices of related agencies. Day care providers must become familiar with the various formal definitions used in their community.

Although more cases of child abuse and neglect are reported in the lower socioeconomic level, cases occur at all levels of society. There are even some indications that a high level of education and deep religious beliefs are positively correlated with numbers of cases. These parents may have unrealistic or age-inappropriate expectations for children's behavior or attitudes and become frustrated with the apparent failure of their childrearing efforts.

Children themselves may "ask for" abuse, either consciously or unconsciously, as a way of getting attention if all other ways have failed. In addition, not all little children are angelic, and not all little children want to play or do "cute" things on demand. Some children are special; they are born prematurely, or handicapped, hyperactive, or emotionally disturbed. Other children have been adopted. All these "special" children have a higher incidence of abuse than other children.

Child abuse and neglect is a family problem; it is a community problem; it is a societal prob-

lem. It also is a problem within the very day care center or home. Keyserling reports on the findings of the National Council of Jewish Women, whose members surveyed day care needs and services in 77 localities throughout the United States. Two descriptions from this report, one of a licensed center and the other of a licensed day care home, give some indication of what actually does go on behind some center doors.

This center should be closed! Absolutely filthy. Toilets not flushed, and smelly. Broken equipment and doors. Broken windows on lower level near back stairs and doors. Broken chairs and tables. No indoor play equipment. One paper towel used to wipe the faces and hands of all children. Kitchen very, very dirty (1972, p. 48).

This center had an enrollment of 35 children, from 2 to 5 years old. At the time of the visit, the only people in charge were 2 children, aged 10 and 12.

Some family day care is no better. The following description of a licensed family day care home needs no comment.

When Mrs. _____ opened the door for us, we felt there were probably very few, if any, children in the house, because of the quiet. It was quite a shock, therefore, to discover about seven or eight children, one year old or under, in the kitchen. A few of them were in high-chairs, but most were strapped to kitchen chairs, all seemingly in a stupor.

It wasn't until we were in the kitchen that we heard the noise coming from the basement. There we found over twenty children huddled in a too small, poorly ventilated, cement floor area. A TV with an apparently bad picture tube was their only source of entertainment or stimulation.

When we went to look at the back yard, we passed through a porch, where we discovered, again, children, children and more children. The children were literally under our feet. Pathetically enough, it was necessary for Mrs. _____ to reprimand one child for stepping on another.

Mrs. _____ takes care of two families—six children—which the Bureau of Children's Services subsidizes. The other children (41, for a total of 47 children) she takes care of independently, receiving two dollars per day per child. She told us that she has been doing this for twenty years and seemed quite proud to be able to manage as well alone, with no help." (pp. 135-136).

Child abuse? Child neglect? No matter the definition; the urgent problem is to prevent such situations and to protect children both before and after incidents of abuse and neglect.

Child abuse and neglect can result in permanent and serious damage to the physical, emotional, and mental development of the child. Physical injuries include damage to the brain, vital organs, eyes, ears, and extremities. These injuries may result in mental retardation, blindness, deafness, loss of a limb, or death. Abused and neglected children are damaged emotionally. They may be impaired in self-concept, reality testing, defensive functioning, and overall thought processes. The foundations of self-concept, motivation for learning, anxiety, defense mechanisms, and general expectations about the world and the people in it—all of these foundations are laid in the beginning years of life. Persons involved in the care and education of infants and toddlers cannot dismiss the importance of what happens during these years, for the results may be life-long. Maltreated children may develop patterns of antisocial behavior or restricted cognitive behavior that will influence and direct all future growth and development. A fractured arm or a blackened eye may heal; the resulting emotional and cognitive damage compounds itself.

CAREGIVER'S ROLE
Prevention

Day care staff members are in a unique position to provide preventive services to the families they serve. In fact, it is possible that the caregivers are in a better position than anyone else to recognize possible indicators of family stress before a crisis situation occurs. Every incident of child abuse and neglect has three components: the child, the abusing adult, and a

crisis, whether actual or only perceived as such. The "crisis" is sometimes an insignificant, but last, straw.

Abusive parents are often isolated from caring persons or agencies, they move frequently from home to home, are usually young, and often unmarried. If they are married, they seem to have chosen a spouse who is not actively supportive in times when problems become overwhelming. Because of their lack of maturity and stability—and frequently because of their own history of being abused—their immediate response to stress is to strike out. Thus they strike out at someone who cannot strike back—a young child. Most child abusers are just plain people, not emotionally or mentally disturbed people, just plain people who momentarily succumb to the complexities of living. Most infants and toddlers in our day care centers and homes are children of just plain people but people who are subject to more than their share of frustrations and stress.

Fortunately, our current laws no longer prescribe punitive measures for child abusers but take a more compassionate and humanistic approach. Criminal penalties have been replaced by support services, and a vital support service, both before and after child abuse or neglect is discovered, can be offered by day care homes and centers. A quality center or home recognizes the critical role of the parents in the child's development and creates opportunities for enhancing the amount and quality of family interaction with children both in the day care setting and at the child's home. These opportunities include parent involvement in decision-making, policy-setting, and daily operations. They also include both formal and informal individual parent-caregiver conferences and group parent-center meetings, both educational and recreational.

Although the primary intent of such activities is not the prevention of child abuse and neglect, all of these activities can be considered prevention techniques. Day care personnel are frequently the first professional persons to have close daily contact with children and their families, and they are looked upon as "experts" by young parents. Informal conversations between caregiver and parent at pick-up and delivery time can be therapeutic for a parent under stress. The caregiver's sympathetic response to the trials and tribulations of childrearing, as well as other stressful happenings or circumstances, can frequently ease the sense of isolation felt by the parent, as well as promote the parent's self-confidence. All parents need reassurance about their methods of childrearing. There is no more conclusive proof of that statement than the number of advice books sold yearly and the number of related articles appearing monthly in the nonprofessional magazines.

Group meetings for parents can also be therapeutic. Just knowing that other parents face the same or similar (and sometimes worse) problems eases the anxiety, and no one is listened to more carefully than another parent who has faced the same problem and perhaps even solved it. However, there is little gained from a parent-caregiver contact, and much lost, if the caregiver assumes the role of all-knowing expert, shows horror at a parent's abusive feelings, or dictates rules and instructions for appropriate feelings and actions. Warm, open relationships between caregivers and parents are just as essential as are warm relationships between caregivers and children. There is no way to document the number of child abuse and neglect incidents that have been averted by sensitive caregivers, but it seems logical to assume that sensitivity and understanding can help avert many.

Center-parent partnership is an essential component in the delivery of early care and education. Detailed rationale, methods, and techniques are included in Chapter 11.

The root causes of negligence in the care of children are even more difficult to pinpoint than are the causes of abuse. Even the term "neglect" cannot be defined with any degree of specificity.

When is minimal care no longer even minimal? Neglect is the result of the absence of appropriate action. It implies not meeting the psychological or physical needs of children. Again, a sensitive caregiver is alert to suspect conditions in the home through informal opportunities for parents and staff to learn and to share information, both in the center and through visits to the home.

Caregivers must also be alert to the possible characteristics of neglectful or abusive parents or guardians. Possible characteristics include:

1. Isolation of the family from any support system; discouragement by the family of others' attempts at social contacts
2. Reluctance to explain the child's injuries or condition (hunger, apathy, lack of appropriate clothing) or irrational or irrelevant explanations
3. Failure to obtain needed medical care for the child or constant changing of doctors or hospitals
4. Reliance on harsh punishment as the "only way" to make the child mind
5. Continuing criticism of the child; impatience toward the child's crying or other attention-seeking behaviors
6. Misuse of alcohol or drugs
7. Frequent disappearance (failure to pick up a child at the end of the day; failure to keep appointments)
8. Irrational, cruel, or sadistic behavior

Over a period of time, these characteristics will become apparent to caregivers who are committed to the quality care and education of young children. Suspicions of child abuse and neglect need not depend upon visible signs of injury; the visible evidence means that our prevention techniques have not been successful in averting an incident.

Identification of suspected child abuse and/or neglect

Do you remember the pediatrician who said he did not know what to look for? Characteristics of possible child abusers are more difficult to ascertain when contact is infrequent, as is the case with pediatricians and other medical professionals. But both the medical person and the day care staff member should have no problem in suspecting child abuse or neglect when there are visible signs of injury on the child's body. The most usual indications are bruises, welts, scars, fractured bones (sometimes not visible to the naked eye), burns, lacerations, and abrasions. Bruises are by far the most common, and a few bruises on the knees, shins, or even the forehead might be considered normal for a toddler. However, bruises on the back, thighs, buttocks, face, backs of the legs, or in the genital area should create suspicion of abuse.

If any injury is accidental, there should be some reasonable relationship between how the injury happened and the severity, type, and location of the injury. Could a fall from a highchair produce bruises in the genital area? Could a child who pushed a hot tea kettle off the stove have burns on the soles of her feet? Abusing parents are already on the defensive, and when asked for explanations of injuries, they may respond irrationally and illogically—or may claim ignorance of the whole thing.

Even when no physical injury is visible, a child's behavior may be the alerting cue to abuse. The abused child may shrink from adult contact, may become unduly apprehensive when other children cry or when the parent arrives at the end of the day, may demonstrate unusual extremes in behavior (withdrawal or aggression) that are outside the normal range of age-expected behaviors. Unusual behavior in an infant or toddler is a red flag—it means something is wrong. Because one of the several components of caregiving is observation of children, any change in behavior should be readily noticed by an alert staff member.

Very young children (children under the age of 3 years) are also victims of sexual abuse. It is doubly hard to be objective about this type of abuse, but it cannot be ignored. Physical signs of sexual abuse include (1) difficulty in walking or sitting, (2) stained or bloody diapers or undergarments, (3) bruises, bleeding, or scabs in the genital area, and (4) the child's continued rubbing of the genital area. Not all states mention sexual abuse in their definitions of child abuse, but this is no excuse for permitting any suspected case to go unreported.

Physically abused or neglected children almost always are emotionally abused as well. The "failure-to-thrive" syndrome is one possible indicator, especially when the children begin to thrive when taken out of the home and into a treatment center. Other possible indicators include extremes in behavior: passivity, aggressiveness, perseverative rocking, thumb-sucking, or head-banging. The behavioral indicators exhibited by children who are emotionally abused and disturbed are quite similar, and it is the parent's attitude that offers clues to possible abuse. Parents of an emotionally abused child may either blame the child for the problem and related behaviors, or may completely ignore the problem and therefore see no need for help. The parents of an emotionally disturbed child are concerned and actively seek help.

Not all states include emotional abuse in their laws either; emotional abuse is the most difficult type to define and identify. Nonetheless, it is perhaps the type of abuse for which day care personnel can be most helpful. Parents who consistently downgrade their children, consistently ignore them, or who fail to encourage their normal development are guilty of emotional abuse, whether so stated in the law or not. Many young parents do not know the psychological implications of such attitudes and treatment; many young or inexperienced parents do not know constructive approaches to childrearing. There are diplomatic and nonthreatening ways of offering suggestions and ideas to parents, and modeling appropriate caregiving behavior is a good beginning. Parent involvement in the day-to-day program can easily lead to the discussion of alternative attitudes and approaches to children, after the parent has observed the caregiver in action. Fundamentally, abusive and nonabusive parents have at least one thing in common: they all want to be good parents. Some of them just do not know how.

Child neglect can be defined as a parent's or caregiver's failure to act, with such failure impeding the growth and development of the child. Physical neglect tends to be chronic, and all children in the family probably suffer from it. Emotional neglect and emotional abuse are closely related, and are so similar in their causes and manifestations that the terms are frequently used interchangeably. We can suspect neglect of an infant or toddler when the child is constantly hungry or even "steals" food from another; when she is consistently dirty and smelly; when he is listless and apathetic; when medical or physical problems are not attended to; and, of course, when the child is abandoned.

Center policy statements must include explicit procedures for taking care of and reporting the young child who is not called for within a reasonable time after the center has been closed for the day. Parents should be informed of these procedures. More than one youngster has been literally given to a day care center without any announcement that this was going to happen. An example of a policy for late pick-up, and possible abandonment, follows. It is included in the parent manual of the Early Childhood Education Center (ECEC) at the University of Iowa, so that families cannot claim ignorance of the procedure.

Late pick-up

The hours of the Center opening and closing must be respected. A late fee of $5.00 will be charged each time a child is picked up after closing time. Repeated late pick-ups will result in disenrollment of a child.

In the case of a regular scheduling conflict, the parent must make alternate arrangements for another adult to call for the child. However, children can be released *only* to parents or to individuals designated by parents *in writing* on the form "Release of Child to Adult Other Than Parent." Please update this form each semester.

In the rare instances when a parent or another designated individual is more than a few minutes late at the end of the session, staff members will initiate the following procedure:
1. Call the child's home and the parent's place of work;
2. If there is no parental response, call the adult(s) designated on the "Release of Child to Adult Other Than Parent" form(s) to see if someone would come to get the child;
3. If no arrangement has yet been made for the child, call The University of Iowa Campus Police to request that they send a patrol car to the child's home to ascertain if a parent is at home but not answering the telephone;
4. If no arrangement has been made for the child by one hour after closing time, call the Iowa City Police (354-1800) to ask who from the Probation Office is on call;
5. Call the Probation Officer on call and notify him/her that it is possible that a child has been abandoned at the ECEC. (The chief probation officer has indicated that his office has legal authority to take custody of a child who is in emotional or physical danger or who is abandoned.)
6. An ECEC member must be with the child at *all times* until the probation officer or a designated adult arrives. If it is not possible for the ECEC staff member to wait with the child, another ECEC staff member should be contacted and asked to come to the ECEC. Under no circumstances should the child be taken from the ECEC, except by adults designated in writing by the parents or by the Probation Officer. The University of Iowa or Iowa City Police would also be able to take custody of the child in an emergency, but waiting in their facilities might cause the experience to be needlessly traumatic for the child.
7. The ECEC staff member should keep records of which of the above procedures were followed and at what time.

Procedures in cases of suspected child abuse and neglect

If the child appears to need immediate attention, that is the first priority, but as soon as arrangements have been made for medical care, the suspicions must be reported. *Even when in doubt,* a report should be made, because although up to 50% of the families investigated as the result of a suspected child abuse report are not guilty of abuse as legally defined, they are in need of help and support and are relieved to find a source of help. In actual practice, the legal requirement for reporting effectively addresses prevention as well as treatment.

Many states *require* preschool and day care staff to report suspected child abuse and neglect; other states *permit* preschool and day care staff to report suspected cases. Responsible caregivers and teachers will report suspected incidents, whether doing so is mandatory or permissive, if the law provides immunity for the reporter. At the present time all states have an immunity clause in their laws.

Center policy should include statements about the procedures to follow when child abuse or neglect is suspected, and staff members and parents alike should know the policy before an incident occurs. Regardless of the number of children served and the number of caregiving adults involved, one person should coordinate the child abuse and neglect activities. That person should establish and maintain relationships with the community agencies involved in the prevention and treatment of child abuse and neglect, such as state or local department of social services, county attorney, police or sheriff, and medical resources for treatment. The coordinator should

1. Inform the other staff members regarding procedures for identifying and reporting suspected child abuse and neglect
2. Do the actual reporting of suspected cases to the appropriate agency
3. Discuss the reporting with the family when deemed necessary or desirable

Reporting to the family is always advisable (reporting cannot be kept a secret for long), but the timing of notification requires a thoughtful deci-

sion based on previous knowledge and experience with the specific child and family. Abusive parents can become so enraged at the intrusion of the day care center that the life and welfare of the child may be further endangered. The reporting of suspected child abuse is an emotional trigger for all parties concerned.

The procedure varies from state to state, but more often than not, the departments of social services and law enforcement agencies are designated by law to receive the reports. State laws also differ in the information required, but the following items are generally included when possible:

1. Identity of the child; name, home address, age
2. Identity of the child's parents or other persons believed to be responsible for the child's care
3. Nature and extent of the child's injuries
4. Evidence of previous suspicious injuries
5. Name, age, and condition of other children in the home
6. Present location of the child
7. Name and address of the reporter

The report is first made orally, but a written report must be made as soon as possible. As soon as the oral report is made, the appropriate agency assumes the responsibility for the child and the child's family. This agency will advise the day care coordinator as to further action, if any, on the part of the center. Legally, the center's responsibility has been met by making the report, but if the center has continued contact with the child and family, its support can be vital in the rehabilitation.

Child abuse and neglect are no longer viewed as crimes for which adults must be punished; they are viewed as signals that the adults need help. Within that frame of reference, all the laws and all the agencies have as their primary goal the greatest possible protection of the child. In most cases, an intact family is considered the most protective situation. Termination of parental rights is a very last resort, considered only after every other measure has failed.

The following episode gives an indication of a coordinated response to one case of child abuse that was constructively resolved.

This situation occurred in a small community of approximately six hundred people. The abuser was an eighteen year old mother with a small infant, the father was unemployed and the family was new in the community and knew no one. The child had been admitted to the hospital because of severe injuries. It was obvious that the mother had no idea of how to take care of her baby, even diapering or bathing it. After discharge from the hospital the child was placed in a foster home in the same community with a very accepting foster mother. The real mother went every day to the foster home and took care of the baby under the foster mother's guidance. The mother accompanied the local health nurse on home visits and helped with the care given to other individuals. A job was obtained for the father. Both parents attended counseling at a mental health center nearby and the local church brought the parents into the church and town activities. Their loneliness was resolved. The child was returned to the home approximately eight months later. (Solomons, cited in Lakin et al, 1977, p. 103).

This is a beautiful example of coordinated community effort toward the realized goal of a well-functioning intact family.

■ CHAPTER SUMMARY ■

Not only are accidents the number one killer of young children, but also they kill three times the number of children as the total of the three leading childhood diseases. Most accidents are preventable and would not occur if the caregiving adults put into practice their knowledge of the present and emerging behavioral characteristics of children. Infants wiggle and wriggle off of elevated surfaces; they suck on all sorts of things. Toddlers investigate, climb, open doors and drawers. Once toddlers are mobile they are constantly on the move and are amazingly fast. They are driven to prove their auton-

omy and their independence, and constantly imitate others, especially adults.

Thoughtful planning and constant vigilance can result in an environment, both indoors and out, in which caregivers are freed from worries about the safety of the children. They can then devote their time and energies to a developmental program.

State and national laws support and frequently require the involvement of day care personnel in detecting and reporting cases of suspected child abuse and neglect, but quality programs for young children should go far beyond these minimum requirements. Caregivers are in a unique position to help prevent child abuse and neglect and to help with the treatment of abusive families even though they are not the deliverers of primary treatment in such cases.

Persons involved in the care and education of infants and toddlers must acknowledge the existence of child abuse and neglect and must be committed to its prevention and appropriate resolution. In other words, caregivers not only encourage the growth and development of the total child, but also work to ensure the proper conditions for that growth and development to take place. Additional sources of information about child abuse and neglect are listed in Appendix A.

SUGGESTED ACTIVITIES/POINTS TO PONDER

1. Send for the Child Safety Catalog (Safety Now Co., Inc., P.O. Drawer 567, Jenkintown, Pa. 19046). Not only does the catalog describe many innovative products, but it presents at least some safety hazards that have usually been ignored.
2. While at home or in a child care center, get down on your hands and knees and investigate your environment. What safety hazards are accessible? Make a list of the hazards with suggestions for making them inaccessible to infants and toddlers.
3. Interview a social worker, asking questions about local and state laws, practice regarding the reporting of suspected child abuse and neglect, and the procedures followed after a report has been made.

REFERENCES AND SUGGESTED READINGS

Accident Facts, Chicago, 1979, National Safety Council.
Arena, J.M.: The care and safety of young children, New York, 1979, Council on Family Health.
Baker, S.P.: Motor vehicle occupant deaths in young children, Pediatrics 64(6):860-861, 1979.

Broadhurst, D., Edmunds, M., and MacDicker, R.: Early childhood programs and prevention and treatment of child abuse and neglect, DHEW Publication No. (OHDS) 79-30198, Washington, D.C., 1979, U.S. Government Printing Office.

Child Abuse Prevention and Treatment Act: Public Law 93-247 as amended by PL 95-266, April 24, 1978, HEW Publication No. (OHDS) 70-30233, Washington, D.C., 1980, U.S. Government Printing Office.

Curtis, J.C.: "I love my child but I need help . . .", Athens, Ga., 1977, RISWR, Inc.

Department of Transportation: Child restraint systems for your automobile, Washington, D.C., 1980, National Highway Traffic Safety Administration.

Early Childhood Education Center: Parent manual, Iowa City, Ia., 1979, University of Iowa.

Education Commission of the States: Education policies and practices regarding child abuse and neglect and recommendations for policy development, Child Abuse and Neglect Project Report, No. 85, Denver, 1976, The Commission.

Ellis, M.D., editor: Dangerous plants, snakes, arthropods and marine life, Washington, D.C., 1978, Drug Intelligence Publications.

The American National Red Cross: Questions and answers on the updated CPR standards, Washington, D.C., October, 1980.

Fontana, V.J.: Practical management of the allergic child, New York, 1969, Appleton-Century-Crofts.

Fontana, V.J.: A parent's guide to child safety, New York, 1973, Thomas Y. Crowell Co.

Gardner, D.B.: Preventing childhood accidents, Fort Collins, Co., 1979, Commercial Printing.

Gelles, R.J.: Child abuse as psychopathology: a sociological critique and reformulation, American Journal of Orthopsychiatry **43:**611, 1973.

Gil, D.: Violence against children: physical abuse in the United States, Cambridge, Mass., 1973, Harvard University Press.

Gil, D.: A holistic perspective on child abuse and its prevention. In Harris, S.B., editor: Child abuse: present and future, Chicago, 1975, National Committee for Prevention of Child Abuse.

Goldstein, J., Freud, A., and Solnit, A.J.: Beyond the best interests of the child, New York, 1973, Free Press.

Green, M.I.: A sigh of relief: the first-aid handbook for childhood emergencies, New York, 1977, Bantam Books, Inc.

Haddon, W., Jr.: The public's responsibility in protecting children. Paper presented at National Highway Traffic Safety Administration's National Conference on Child Passenger Protection, Washington, D.C., 1979, Insurance Institute for Highway Safety. (Mimeographed.)

Handbook of common poisonings in children, DHEW Publication No. (FDS) 76-7004, Washington, D.C., 1976, U.S. Government Printing Office.

Harmon, M.: A new vaccine for child safety, Jenkintown, Pa., 1976, Safety Now Co., Inc.

Helfer, R.E., and Kempe, C.H.: The battered child, ed 2, Chicago, 1974, University of Chicago Press.

Identification and reporting of child abuse and neglect, policy instruction, Federal Register, Jan. 26, 1977, pp. 1970-1971.

Insurance Institute for Highway Safety: Children in crashes, Washington, D.C., 1980, the Institute.

Johnston, C.A.: Families in stress, DHEW Publication No. (OHDS) 80-30162, Washington, D.C., 1979, U.S. Government Printing Office.

Kempe, C., and Helfer, R., editors: Helping the battered child and his family, Philadelphia, 1972, J.B. Lippincott Co.

Kempe, R.S., and Kempe, C.H.: Child abuse, Cambridge, Mass., 1978, Harvard University Press.

Keyserling, M.D.: Windows on day care, New York, 1972, National Council of Jewish Women.

Lakin, J., Solomons, G., and Abel, C.: Child abuse and neglect: a self-instructional text for Head Start personnel, DHEW Publication No. (OHDS) 78-31102, Washington, D.C., 1977, U.S. Government Printing Office.

Leavitt, J.E., editor: The battered child: selected readings, Morristown, N.J., 1974, General Learning Corp.

Lin-Fu, U.S.: What price shall we pay for lead poisoning in children? DHEW Publication No. (HSA) 79-5144, Washington, D.C., 1979, U.S. Government Printing Office.

Martin, H.P., editor: The abused child: a multidisciplinary approach to developmental issues and treatment, Cambridge, Mass., 1976, Ballinger Publishing Co.

Melvin, J.W., Stalnaker, R.L., and Mohan, D.: Protection of child occupants in automobile crashes. Paper presented at the 22nd Stapp Car Crash Conference, 1978, Ann Arbor, Michigan, Washington, D.C., 1978, Insurance Institute for Highway Safety.

Mohan, D., and Schneider, L.W.: An evaluation of adult strength for restraining lap-help infants, Human Factors **21**(6):635-645, 1979.

North, A.F.: Day care, 6, health services, DHEW Publication No. (OCD) 73-12, Washington, D.C., 1973, U.S. Government Printing Office.

Physicians for Automotive Safety: Don't risk your child's life! Irvington, N.J., Sept., 1980, Physicians for Automotive Safety.

Pizzo, P., and Aronson, S.: Health and safety issues in day care. Paper prepared for the Office of Assistant Secretary for Planning and Evaluation, DHEW, 1976. (Mimeographed.)

Polansky, N.S., De Saix, C., and Shlomo, S.: Child neglect: understanding and reaching the parent, a guide for child welfare workers, New York, 1976, Child Welfare League of America, Inc.

Shelness, A., and Charles, S.: Children as passengers in automobiles: the neglected minority on the nation's highways, Pediatrics 56:271-284, 1975.

Scherz, R.: Restraint systems for the prevention of injury to children in automobile accidents, American Journal of Pediatric Health 66:451, 1976.

Sobel, R.: Vexing problem of poisonings. In You and your health, New York, 1974, Council on Family Health.

Solomons, G.: A basic view, Iowa City, IA, 1976, Child Abuse and Neglect Resource Center, Institute of Child Behavior and Development, University of Iowa.

Williams, A.F.: Restraint use legislation: its prospects for increasing the protection of children in cars, Accident Analysis and Preventions 2:255-260.

Williams, A.F.: Observed child restraint use in automobiles, American Journal of Diseases of Children 130:1311-1317, 1976.

Williams, A.F.: Warning: in cars, parents may be hazardous to their child's health, Washington, D.C., 1978, Insurance Institute for Highway Safety. (Mimeographed.)

Williams, A.F., and Zador, P.: Injuries to children in automobiles in relation to seating location and restraint use, Accident Analysis and Prevention 9:69-76, 1977.

Young children and accidents in the home, DHEW Publication No. (OHD) 76-30034, Washington, D.C., 1974, U.S. Government Printing Office.

CHAPTER 4

THE NUTRITIONAL COMPONENT OF THE CARE AND PROTECTION CURRICULUM

What are little boys made of?
Snips and snails and puppy dog tails.
What are little girls made of?
Sugar and spice and everything nice.
Traditional rhyme

Most adults do not let children play with dangerous toys or equipment. Most adults keep poisons out of the reach of young children. Most adults protect children from obvious harm—*except* when it comes to feeding them. The nutritional component of a child care program is of primary importance. Feeding children is not sufficient.

Our knowledge of the roles of various foods has been greatly enlarged since the period when it was believed that the sex of the unborn child was determined by the mother's diet. A lean diet (snips and snails and puppy dog tails) produced a son; a rich diet (sugar and spice and everything nice) produced a daughter. The mother's diet does have considerable effects on her expected child, but, so far as we know, sex determination is not one of them.

The total nutritional needs of children must be met each day. Therefore, the child care program must provide the foods needed to supplement the food served at home. But the nutritional component includes much more than food service. The socialization and developmental needs of infants and very young children, as well as nutrition education for the children and their parents, also must be considered.

Therefore, even in centers large enough to hire a staff member whose sole responsibility is to purchase, prepare, and store food, each caregiver/teacher is also a vital link in the delivery of the nutrition component of the care and protec-

tion curriculum. Regardless of center size, one person should have the prime responsibility for food service and its related factors, even if combining this with other caregiving activities. In any case, the director is directly involved in the supervision of food service, frequently to the extent of meal planning and food shopping. Consequently, each staff member should know the nutritional needs of children, the nutritional and psychological value of properly prepared and served foods, and safe food practices. Ideally, training in nutrition and its many aspects should be a prerequisite for employment in a day care delivery system. Realistically, this is seldom a requirement, except perhaps for the cook, but important information can be transmitted during in-service workshops or on-the-job training. Expert advice is readily available from the local representative of the Cooperative Extension Service programs. Frequently, faculty members from nearby colleges or universities will volunteer their services or will serve as consultants on a regular basis.

MALNUTRITION AND SUBNUTRITION

This country tends to react to the word malnutrition in terms of crisis: mass starvation, marasmus, and kwashiorkor make headlines and always seem to happen in someplace far away. A more correct concept of malnutrition includes any functional impairment or physical condition that can be prevented or cured by improved nutrition. When so defined, instances of malnutrition exist in every society, whether it is technically advanced or newly developing. There are some 50 identified nutrients, and therefore there are a similar number of types of malnutrition, any of which might cause some measure of stunted physical growth, reduced resistance to disease, or general behavioral unresponsiveness.

There is an increasing amount of evidence from many parts of the world conclusively showing both a direct and indirect relationship of nutritional factors to intelligence and learning. There is even evidence that poor or "picky" eating during the first year of life is related to a depressed IQ score later on. There are many questions still unanswered about the relationship between malnutrition and mental development, but the available knowledge is strong enough for us to insist that children receive adequate nutrition both in day care centers and in their own homes.

The period of rapid brain growth when brain cells rapidly multiply and grow takes place from about the second trimester of pregnancy to 24 months of age. The "brain growth spurt" in humans occurs in two general stages, the first during the second trimester, and the second from the third trimester of pregnancy through the normal period of breast feeding.

The two stages overlap considerably, and many neurons are still multiplying even after birth. . . .Superimposed on the two stages of growth spurt are regional variations in brain development. Some sections of the brain develop earlier than others, and some develop quickly while others evolve more slowly. Throughout its growth spurt, the brain needs adequate nutrients in order to grow. Research findings in animals now indicate that severe malnutrition during this period can produce brain deficits which cannot be rectified nutritionally (Read, 1976, p. 12).

Although the unique human brain may not be this vulnerable throughout the growth spurt, evidence shows that it, like the brain of other animals, is probably more vulnerable to malnutrition throughout the growth spurt than at other times.

The relationship of nutrition to physical growth seems to be universally accepted. Even preschoolers have been told to eat their vegetables and drink their milk so that they can grow up big and strong. The relationship of nutrition to intellectual growth is more complex because of the multitude of interrelated environmental and genetic factors, and it is only in the last three decades that systematic investigations have been made. The War on Poverty and the resulting Head Start programs produced some direct clinical studies that supported the previous survey reports of the high incidence of unsatisfactory diets of young children from the economically disadvantaged segments of the population.

A detailed review of research evidence on the effects of malnutrition on learning and intelligence is included in the Congressional Record of the Senate as a supporting document for the Child Nutrition Act of 1972. A major portion of the summary statement follows:

The evidence we have surveyed indicates strongly that nutritional factors at a number of different levels contribute significantly to depressed intellectual level and learning failure. These effects may be produced directly as the consequences of irreparable alterations of the nervous system or indirectly as a result of ways in which the learning experiences of the developing organism may be significantly interferred with at critical points in the development course.

If one were to argue that a primary requirement for normal intellectual development and for formal learning is the ability to process sensory information and to integrate such information across sense systems, the evidence indicates that both severe acute malnutrition in infancy as well as chronic subnutrition from birth to the school years result in defective information processing. Thus by inhibiting the development of a primary process essential for certain aspects of cognitive growth malnutrition may interfere with the orderly development of experience and contribute to a suboptimal level of intellectual functioning.

Moreover, an adequate state of nutrition is essential for good attention and for appropriate and sensitive responsiveness to the environment. One of the most obvious clinical manifestations of serious malnutrition in infancy is a dramatic combination of apathy and irritability. The infant is grossly unresponsive to his surroundings and obviously unable to profit from the objective opportunities for experience present in his surroundings. This unresponsiveness characterizes his relation to people, as well as to objects. Behavioral regression is profound; and the organization of his functions are markedly infantalized. . . .

In children who are subnourished one also notes a reduction in responsiveness and attentiveness. In addition the subnourished child is easily fatigued and unable to sustain either prolonged physical or mental effort. Improvement in nutritional status is accompanied by improvements in these behaviors as well as in physical state.

It should not be forgotten that nutritional inadequacy may influence the child's learning opportunities by yet another route, namely, illness. Nutritional inadequacy increases the risk of infection, interferes with immune mechanisms, and results in illness which is both more generalized and more severe. The combination of sub-nutrition and illness reduces time available for instruction and so by interfering with the opportunities for gaining experience disrupts the orderly acquisition of knowledge and the course of intellectual growth.

We have also pointed to intergenerational effects of nutrition upon mental development. The association between the mother's growth achievements and the risk to her infant is very strong. Poor nutrition and poor health in the mother when she was a girl result in a woman at maturity who has a significantly elevated level of reproductive risk. Her pregnancy is more frequently disturbed and her child more often of low birth weight. Such a child is at increased risk of neurointegrative abnormality and of deficient IQ and school achievement.

Despite the strength of the argument that we have developed, it would be tragic if one were now to seek to replace all the other variables—social, cultural, educational, and psychological—which exert an influence on intellectual growth with nutrition. Malnutrition never occurs alone, it occurs in conjunction with low income, poor housing, familial disorganization, a climate of apathy, ignorance and despair. The simple act of improving the nutritional status of children and their families will not and cannot of itself fully solve the problem of intellectual deficit and school failure. No single improvement in conditions will have this result. What must be recognized is that within our overall effort to improve the condition of disadvantaged children, nutritional considerations must occupy a prominent place, and together with improvements in all other facets of life including relevant and directed education, contribute to the improved intellectual growth and school achievement of disadvantaged children. (Birch, 1972, p. S13458)

It is very possible that day care homes and centers in our country will never enroll an infant or toddler who is severely malnourished. However, it is necessary to be aware of the major nutrition-related health disorders in order to either prevent or treat them.

NUTRITION-RELATED DISORDERS

In the United States there are four major health problems that are related to nutrition and that may occur or have their origin in childhood: obesity, atherosclerosis, dental caries, and iron-deficiency anemia.

Prevention of obesity

Overnutrition is more prevalent than undernutrition in the United States. Not only is obesity physically unattractive, it is a significant nutritional disease.

It is difficult to be specific about how much is "too much" food, because the amount of food that is barely adequate for one child may actually be excessive for another. There is no medically based definition of obesity, but in general terms, obesity is the excessive ratio of fat to fat-free body mass. Activity patterns, energy expenditures, metabolic rate, and age influence the adequacy of a diet for any one person. Neither parents nor caregivers can be expected to scientifically determine the optimal adequate diet for any one child or group of children. Nutritionists and pediatricians have recommended amounts and types of food as well as meal patterns for children in various age ranges. This information follows the discussion of the nutrition-related disorders.

Although a number of investigators have suggested an association between weight gain in infancy and obesity in childhood, their findings have not yet been verified. However, the cultural belief that a fat baby is a healthy baby is neither correct nor harmless. If a baby puts on too much fat in the early months, this may actually increase the number of fat cells he or she will carry around for the remaining life span. Figs. 4-1 and 4-2 present percentiles of the weight and length of young American children from the National Center for Health statistics based on data from the Fels Research Institute on a cumulative study of children born from 1929 to 1970.

The desire to overeat is tempting in the presence of an abundance of food (as many adults have learned). Many adults have also learned that permanent weight reduction is difficult and elusive. Overeating is a habit and "the earlier in life a habit—good or bad—is established, the more likely it is to persist; hence, the need to begin preventive efforts in infancy" (Fomon, 1977, p. 68).

Babies who are bottle-fed rather than breast-fed tend to gain weight more rapidly, perhaps because nursing mothers are not inclined to urge drinking "the last drop" when baby shows satisfaction and is reluctant to continue sucking. The caregiver who is bottle-feeding the infant seems more inclined to insist on an empty bottle at the end of each feeding, regardless of baby's reluctance or even refusal. The amount of formula or milk in the bottle is somewhat arbitrary and may have little relationship to the amount that baby needs at any particular time. The same psychology applies to the feeding of "biekost" (foods other than milk or formula fed to infants). A clean plate is the goal, and parents and caregivers alike engage in ludicrous antics to convince the child to eat "just one more spoonful." Food also has emotional connotations, and misinformed parents or caregivers use food as a reward, a pacifier, an expression of love, or a bribe, all of which encourage overeating.

It is currently fashionable to introduce biekost in the infant's diet as early as possible, even during the first month (thereby proving the infant is precocious), but there is no medical reason for introducing strained foods before the fourth or fifth or even the sixth month. Commercially prepared foods are expensive and generally unnecessary during the first 5 to 6 months of life. Their use also may encourage overfeeding. Developmental readiness, not adult eagerness, should determine the timing for introducing biekost.

The frequency of eating also appears to have implications in the prevention of obesity. It is far better for the young child to have several small meals than one or two large ones, and until at least 4 months of age, the infant should have no fewer than five feedings every 24 hours.

Diet and atherosclerosis

Atherosclerosis is a thickening of the inner wall of the arteries, which can cause clotting and block the flow of blood to the heart muscle. Atherosclerosis causes angina pectoris, heart attacks, and scarring of the heart muscle. Coronary artery disease has increased greatly because of (1) the universal dependence on the automobile and (2) overnutrition. It seems to run in families with a history of diabetes or high levels of cholesterol.

There is a current controversy about the advisability of modifying the diets of infants and young children for the purposes of decreasing the intake of total fat, saturated fatty acids, and cholesterol. Human milk, of course, is a rich source of these substances. Dr. Paul Dudley White, renowned leader in the fight against

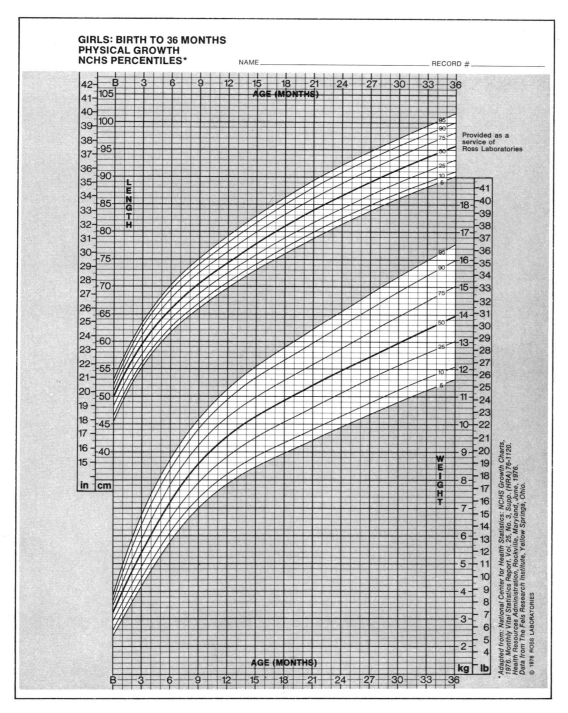

FIG. 4-1   Growth chart for girls.

Courtesy National Center for Health Statistics, 1976.

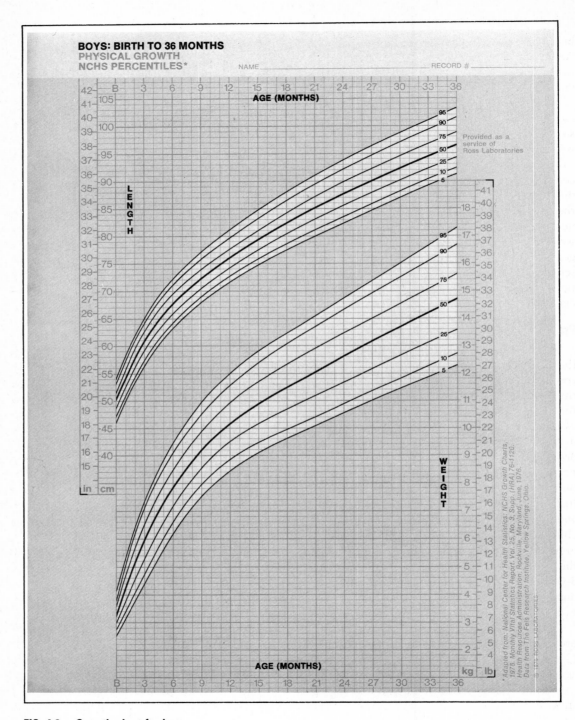

FIG. 4-2 Growth chart for boys.

Courtesy National Center for Health Statistics, 1976.

heart diseases, recommends that each family "control obesity from infancy through retirement years, eat sensible meals in moderation, and take regular exercise" (1974).

A high percentage of normal infants receive commercially prepared formulas for the first and sometimes the second year of life, and these are relatively low in fatty acids and cholesterol. The caregiver should select formulas made with corn, soy, or other vegetable oil. Any other dietary considerations should be prescribed by the family physician and are not considered necessary for normal children at the time of this writing. A small minority of children have genetically based tendencies toward atherosclerosis, and dietary restrictions may be imposed by the family physician or pediatrician.

Prevention of dental caries

Many of the permanent teeth begin to form in the gums during the early months of life, and, of course, one of the developmental highspots is the appearance of the first primary tooth around the sixth or seventh month. Primary teeth are essential for adequate chewing and for the formation of correct speech sounds. Their damage or premature loss can cause malocclusion of the permanent teeth in later years. After a review of nutritional surveys, Fomon (1974) concluded that "at least one-fourth of two-year-old children and approximately two-thirds of three-year-old children have dental caries" (p. 342). In communities without fluoridated drinking water, the prevalence of decayed or missing teeth in 3-year-olds is even higher. However, the primary agent of dental caries is refined carbohydrates, especially sugar.

The American Society of Dentistry for Children has concluded that allowing a young child to nurse for long periods of time on milk, juices, or other sweetened liquids can have a destructive effect on the child's teeth and that this destruction starts as soon as the primary teeth begin to erupt. If long nursing periods continue,

the result is serious. Teeth will need crowns, the nerves or pulps will need treatment, and teeth may even have to be extracted because of extensive breakdown and infection. In addition, teeth affected by prolonged nursing remain highly susceptible to decay long after the nursing stops. This unfortunate condition is called "bottle mouth" or "nursing bottle caries." It is particularly unfortunate because it is easily preventable. The lactose naturally present in cow milk is probably not a major factor, but the sucrose and corn syrup solids in many infant formulas are the true culprits. Most destructive to teeth is the practice of bottle-feeding sweetened drinks or fruit juices. Once the teeth have erupted, bottle-feeding of any sweetened liquid, including formula, should be discontinued, particularly at nap or bedtime. Actually, any liquid other than water will cause dental caries if not swallowed immediately. Nursing bottle caries is most severe when the child is put to bed sucking on a bottle of milk or juice. The maxillary anterior teeth can be destroyed before the child is 1 year old. Therefore, not only should caregivers *not* put a baby to bed with a bottle, but also they should caution parents about the nursing bottle syndrome.

One of the pervasive customs in the United States is eating between meals, and our choice of snacks has a definite relationship to dental caries, obesity, and, possibly, future atherosclerosis. One piece of sticky candy may coat the teeth with sugary substances for up to an hour. Snack choices should be made from fresh fruits and vegetables, nonsweetened enriched crackers, bread or cereals, cheeses, peanutbutter, lean meats, and milk. Cakes, cookies, jams, and jellies are potential troublemakers. Pasteurized honey should *not* be given to children under 1 year of age because they are not able to neutralize the botulism toxins naturally present. Honey is both safe and appropriate in the diet of a child older than 1 year. The suggested snacks in Table 4-1 are low in starch and sugar.

TABLE 4-1   Snack foods low in starch and sugar

Fruits (dried, fresh, or canned in own juice or light syrup)	Fresh vegetables	Protein food	Juices
Peeled apple wedges	Broccoli flowerets	Cheese cubes	Apple
Applesauce	Cabbage wedges	Cottage cheese	Apricot nectar
Apricots	*Carrot sticks or curls	Hard-cooked eggs	Cider
Banana chunks	*Cauliflowerets	Meat slices or cubes	Grapefruit
Berries	*Celery sticks, plain, or stuff-	Peanutbutter	Grape
Cherries (remove pits)	ed with peanut butter, cheese	Sardines	Orange
Dates and figs	spread, or cottage cheese	Liverwurst	Peach nectar
Grapefruit, orange, tangerine	Cucumber slices or sticks	Milk	Pineapple
sections (peel and remove	Green beans	Yogurt	Prune
seeds)	*Green pepper sticks		Tangerine
Grapes (seedless)	Lettuce leaves		Tomato
Melon cubes	Mushrooms		Vegetable or fruit combina-
Peach wedges	Peas		tions
Pear wedges	*Radishes		
Pineapple sticks	Romaine leaves		
Plums (remove pits)	Rutabaga strips		
Prunes (remove pits)	Spinach leaves		
	*Sweet potato strips		
	Tomato wedges or cherry to-		
	matoes		
	*Turnip strips		
	*Zucchini strips		

*Not suitable for infants unless cooked

Most children do not have their first dental checkup until they are 2 or 3 years old at the earliest, and by then nursing bottle caries may have done irreparable damage. It is recommended that the first visit to a dentist, preferably a pedodontist, be made at 9 months of age. This recommendation can be made to the parents of infants in day care, along with the other recommendations about feeding procedures and immunizations.

Every tooth needs cleaning, even that first little tooth that receives so much praise and admiration! There are toothbrush training sets on the market that are designed for use from the time of the appearance of the first tooth. With or without such tools, however, the caregiver can clean a baby's teeth with a damp cloth or gauze pad after each feeding.

Although current evidence shows a relationship between the fluoride content of drinking water and the number of decayed, missing, and filled teeth, there remains considerable uncertainty about the actual intake of fluoride by individual infants. It seems best to delay fluoride supplementation to age 6 months, even for those infants in rural areas or communities with nonfluoridated drinking water. The pediatrician or pedodontist in each locale should be consulted about the need for fluoride both before and after 6 months of age.

Iron-deficiency anemia

Hemoglobin is the part of the red blood cell that carries oxygen to muscles, nerves, and organs. Iron-deficiency anemia occurs when the concentration of hemoglobin is below normal.

TABLE 4-2 Foods containing worthwhile amounts of iron

Vegetables	Fruits	Meat and meat alternate
Asparagus	Apples	Beef
Beans—green, wax,	(canned)	Veal
lima	Berries	Pork
Broccoli	Dried fruits—	Poultry
Brussel sprouts	apricots,	Lamb and mutton
Green leafy vegeta-	dates, figs,	Fish and shellfish
bles—beet	peaches,	Organs (liver, heart)
greens, collards,	prunes,	Eggs
kale, mustard	raisins	Nuts
greens, spinach,	Plums, purple	Peanutbutter
swiss chard, tur-	(canned)	Legumes
nip greens	Rhubarb	
Peas, green		
Squash		
Sweet potatoes		
Tomatoes (canned)		
Tomato juice, paste,		
or puree		

In most countries, including the United States, low concentrations are found most commonly in infants of low birth weight and in full-size infants between 6 and 24 months of age. National nutrition surveys have found that the majority of young children from all income levels receive intakes of iron less than the estimated requirement.

Neither cow's milk nor human milk contains much iron. About 15 quarts of cow's milk would have to be consumed each day to provide enough iron to meet the requirements of normal infants during the first year of life. Babies fed cow's milk should regularly receive an iron-fortified infant cereal or iron supplement. A daily serving of dry, precooked, iron-fortified infant cereals should be fed until 18 months of age. It is very possible that toddlers and preschool children also receive low intakes of iron. Perhaps there should also be moderate restrictions placed on intake of foods low in iron content. These include dairy products, unfortified bak-

ery goods, candy, and soft drinks. Adequate intakes of iron can be provided with supplements, but an overdose can be very dangerous. It is always preferable to offer a more acceptable dietary selection. Meat, poultry, eggs, vegetables, fruits, and cereals are all sources of iron, but the iron from vegetables is generally less well absorbed than that from meats and fish.

A list of foods that contain worthwhile amounts of iron is contained in Table 4-2.

The amounts of iron absorbed by individuals consuming identical diets are influenced by age, sex, iron status, and physiological state. The meal pattern in Table 4-3 contains adequate or better amounts of iron, as well as the other necessary nutrients.

Intestinal parasites: a factor in malnutrition

From a purely nutritional standpoint, anything that feeds upon what the child needs is a cause of serious concern. Intestinal parasites (worms that may grow to over a foot in length, with hundreds of them infesting one child) are native to the Southeastern United States, and may occur in other areas where a warm moist climate is combined with a lack of sanitary toilet facilities, poor personal hygiene factors, overcrowding, and other poverty conditions. Round worms enter the body through the mouth from objects such as toys, food, and hands that come into contact with soil contaminated by fecal waste from infected children. Hookworms enter the body by penetrating the soft skin between toes and fingers, and may live as long as 4 or 5 years in the small intestine. Barefoot infants and young children playing in contaminated soil are prime targets for parasitic invasion.

Caregivers should need no other reason than this for frequent handwashing, both before and after diaper changing, and in connection with food preparation and service, regardless of geographic location. Child advocates in the trouble areas should give high priority to improvement of local sanitary conditions.

TABLE 4-3   Meal patterns for young children in day care programs*

Food components	Infants			Toddlers 12-36 months
	0-4 months	4-8 months	8-12 months	
Breakfast				
Milk (fluid)	4-6 oz. infant formula	6-8 oz. infant formula	6-8 oz. infant formula or whole milk	½ cup
Juice, fruit, or vegetable			0-3 oz. fruit juice	¼ cup
Bread or cereal (enriched or whole grain†)		1-3 Tbsp. infant cereal	2-4 Tbsp. infant cereal	½ slice bread or ¼ cup dry or cooked cereal
Midmorning or midafternoon supplement (snack)§				
Milk (fluid)†	4-6 oz. infant formula	2-4 oz. infant formula or	2-4 oz. infant formula or whole milk or	½ cup
Juice, vegetable, or fruit		2-4 oz. full-strength juice	2-4 oz. full-strength juice	¼ cup
Meat or meat alternate				½ oz.
Bread or cereal (enriched or whole grain)		0-¼ slice crusty bread or 0-2 crackers suitable as finger food	1-¼ slice crusty bread or 0-2 crackers suitable as finger food	½ slice bread or ¼ cup dry or cooked cereal
Lunch or supper				
Milk (fluid)†	4-6 oz. infant formula	6-8 oz. infant formula	6-8 oz. infant formula	½ cup
Vegetable or fruit		1-2 Tbsp. fruit or vegetable (appropriate consistency)	0-3 oz. full-strength fruit juice and/or 3-4 Tbsp. fruit or vegetable (appropriate consistency)	¼ cup (must include at least two kinds)
Bread or cereal (enriched or whole grain)‡		1-2 Tbsp. infant cereal	3-4 Tbsp. infant cereal (or combination of fruit/vegetable and cereal)	½ slice
Lunch meat and meat alternate		0-1 Tbsp. meat, fish, poultry, or egg yolk or 0-½ oz. cheese or 0-1 oz. cottage cheese, cheese food, cheese spread	1-4 Tbsp. meat, fish, poultry, or egg yolk or ½-2 oz. cheese or 1-4 oz. cottage cheese, cheese food, or cheese spread	1½ oz. cooked meat, poultry or 1 oz. cheese or 1 egg or ¼ cup cooked dry beans or peas or 2 Tbsp. peanut-butter

*Adapted from Food and Nutrition Service, 1976 and 1980
†Includes whole milk, lowfat milk, skim milk, cultured buttermilk, or flavored milk made from these types of fluid milk which meet state and local standards.
‡Or an equivalent serving of an acceptable bread product made of enriched or whole grain meal or flour, or enriched or whole grain rice or pasta.
§Select 2 of the 4 components for toddlers 12-36 months.

NUTRIENTS FOR GOOD NUTRITION

The discussion up until now has implied a negative definition of health as the absence of disorder or disease. The positive concept of health, which makes possible optimal development and functioning, is the focus of the remainder of the chapter. There are a few basic facts about food and nutrition that every provider of child care must know and put into practice. These include information about the essential nutrients and recommended meal patterns and practices for very young children.

Nutrients

The total nutrient needs of very young children are relatively low, but for children from 1 to 3 years of age the requirements for protein, calories, a number of minerals, and vitamins A, B, and E are about half those of adults, while calcium and vitamin C needs are about the same. Under the age of 4 years, children often need an iron supplement, because they require 50% more iron than is needed by an adult. Babies gain about 16 pounds during their first year, but only about 3 pounds between 12 and 24 months. Appetite diminishes after the first birthday, and many parents and caregivers become unnecessarily disturbed about decreased food intake and eating "problems."

In general terms, nutrients provide energy (expressed as calories), build and repair body parts, and help control body functions. There are six kinds of nutrients, usually categorized according to their uses in the human body. Each day each person needs a specific amount of each of the six nutrients, which include proteins, minerals, carbohydrates, fats, vitamins, and water.

Proteins are the body's building blocks. They are essential for building and repairing all the body tissues, energy, and resisting diseases. Proteins (or their amino acids) are found in meat, fish, poultry, eggs, milk, cheese, nuts (not recommended before the age of 4), dried peas and beans, breads, and cereals.

Minerals are needed to help build and repair all parts of the body. Four important mineral elements are:

1. *Calcium*, to build bones and teeth, to help make blood clot, and to help muscles and nerves work; milk is the best single source; other sources are milk products and deep green, leafy vegetables.
2. *Phosphorus*, to build and repair all parts of the body, especially bones, teeth, nerves, and glands; found in milk, eggs, bran, and liver.
3. *Iron*, to build red blood cells, which carry oxygen to all parts of the body; found in liver, lean meat, egg yolk, enriched or whole grain bread and cereal, dried fruit, and green, leafy vegetables.
4. *Iodine*, to help control the rate at which the body uses energy, and to prevent goiter; found in seafood and iodized salt.

Carbohydrates are needed to furnish energy for physical and mental activities, as well as the energy needed in body processes such as respiration, circulation, and digestion. Carbohydrates are the sugars and starches, and are contained in breads, cereals, potatoes, corn, dried fruits, and any foods sweetened with sugar, such as syrup, jelly, and jam.

Fats furnish the body with energy and heat, and help keep the skin smooth and healthy. They come from both animal and vegetable sources, such as butter, margarine, cream, nuts, meat, salad oils, and cooking fats.

Vitamins are needed to promote growth and maintain health. They are nutrients, not medicine. A proper diet will provide adequate amounts of all the vitamins needed by any healthy child or adult. The vitamins are:

1. *Vitamin A*, to keep the skin smooth and healthy, to protect the mucous membranes from infection, and to help prevent night-blindness. Important sources of vitamin A are liver, egg yolk, butter, whole milk, cream, yellow fruits, and dark green and yellow vegetables.

2. *Thiamine (vitamin B_1)*, to help keep the nervous system healthy, to help keep the appetite and digestion normal, and to help change food into energy. Important sources are meats (especially pork), eggs, dried beans and peas, enriched and whole grain breads and cereals, and potatoes.

3. *Riboflavin (vitamin B_2)*, to help the cells use oxygen, to help eyes adjust to light, to help keep the skin, tongue, and lips healthy. Important sources are meat, fish, poultry, eggs, ice cream, milk, and cheese.

4. *Ascorbic acid (vitamin C)*, to help make "cementing" materials that hold body cells together, to help keep the blood vessels healthy, and to help heal wounds and broken bones. Because the body does not store vitamin C, it must be supplied *daily* in the diet; important sources are citrus fruits (oranges, lemons, grapefruits, limes), tomatoes, raw cabbage, raw greens, cantaloupes, strawberries, green peppers, and potatoes.

5. *Niacin*, to help keep the skin and nervous system healthy, to help keep the digestive tract healthy, and to promote growth. Important sources are meat, fish, poultry, milk, and enriched or whole grain bread and cereal.

6. *Vitamin D*, (the sunshine vitamin), to help build calcium and phosphorus into the hard material of bones; when the body is exposed to sunlight, vitamin D forms in the skin. Important food sources are fish-liver oils and vitamin D milk.

Water is essential to life, and some nutritionists classify it as a nutrient. Water regulates body temperature, aids in digestion, and helps rid the body of waste products.

MEAL PATTERNS AND FOOD COMPONENTS

The HEW Day Care Regulations, which were completed during the spring of 1980, state:

"A day care center [or home] shall provide adequate and nutritious meals prepared in a safe and sanitary manner. Breakfast shall be provided at parent request. Lunch and mid-morning and mid-afternoon snacks shall be provided. When children are in care during evening and night hours, the center shall provide an evening meal" (Federal Register, March 19, 1980, p. 17882).

Meal patterns

The Child Care Food Program under the National School Lunch Act provided over $3 billion annually (1980) for costs involved in obtaining, preparing, and serving meals that meet U.S. Department of Agriculture requirements to licensed public or private nonprofit institutions providing nonresidential day care services. Although for-profit day care services were not eligible for funds from the Child Care Food Program, the requirements of the program provide excellent guidelines for any infant-toddler day care program. Meal patterns for children from birth to 36 months of age are in Table 4-3.

Description of food components (CCFP, 1980)

Milk. Specified amounts of milk must be served as a beverage at lunch or supper and as a beverage or with cereal at breakfast. Milk may also be served for snack. Fluid, evaporated, or dry milk used in the preparation of foods may *not* be counted as meeting the milk requirement.

Vegetables and fruits. A serving of cooked vegetable is drained vegetable; a serving of cooked (or thawed or frozen) fruit consists of fruit and juice. The following fruit or vegetable foods do not contribute to the requirements: catsup, chili sauce, jams, jellies, preserves, prepared mustard, pickle relish, potato chips and sticks.

Meat and meat alternates. When cooked dry beans, lentils, or peas are counted as part of the meat alternate requirement, they cannot be counted toward meeting the vegetable/fruit requirement as well. A serving of cooked meat is defined as lean meat without bone. A serving of poultry includes meat and skin as normally served.

Breads and cereals. All breads must be enriched or made of whole-grain or enriched flour or meal. Bread must be served at lunch and supper, and may be served at breakfast and for mid-morning and mid-afternoon snacks.

Enriched or whole-grain cereal may be served at breakfast alone or in combination with bread to meet that requirement. Cereal cannot be used in place of bread at lunch or supper. Most ready-to-eat cereals provide an inadequate breakfast; the presweetened cereals cost almost twice as much as the low sugar cereals, and they contribute to tooth decay, heart disease, and other degenerative diseases. The "natural" granolas have an overabundance of fat and sugar for the amount of protein.

Cookies made of enriched or whole-grain meal or flour may be served for snacks, but may not be served in place of bread at breakfast, lunch, or supper. It is recommended that cookies be served as snack no more than twice a week. One-quarter cup of enriched pasta products, enriched or whole-grain rice, corn grits, or bulgur may be counted toward meeting the bread-cereal requirement.

FROM THEORY INTO PRACTICE: INFANT FEEDING
Milk or formula

Breast-feeding is possible for some infants in day care, and occasionally a mother is able to arrange her school or working schedule so that she can feed her child at the appropriate times. Any mother with the least inclination to do so should be encouraged, even though such feedings may "upset" the center routine. Indeed, there should be no routine in infant care that is so rigid that the rights of mother and child do not come first. Babies sometimes get hungry before mother has arrived, and there needs to be an agreement worked out between the mother and center staff as to the appropriate

steps to take when this happens. Once nursing is well established offering an occasional bottle feeding should not cause any problems. There is vigorous controversy about supplementing the diets of breast-fed infants with vitamin D, iron, and fluoride, and of course no one other than the parent and the pediatrician has the right to make this decision.

An iron-fortified, commercially prepared formula is a complete food for infants and requires no supplements of vitamins or minerals. Evaporated milk formulas are acceptable for infants younger than 6 months of age, with supplements of vitamin C and iron. Because of uncertain sterilization, however, preparation of single feedings is preferable to the preparing of all the feedings for a 24-hour period at one time.

"Solid" foods

Today most infants are introduced to foods other than milk or formula by 2 months of age, possibly because of social pressures and the pervasive attitude that earlier is always better. According to Fomon et al. (1979), the starting of solid foods should be delayed until 5 or 6 months of age because of possible interference with established sound eating habits and the probable encouragement of overfeeding. The precautions about overfeeding stated earlier (see pp. 75-76) apply to both bottle-feeding and other foods. Feeding solid foods should be stopped at the earliest indication from the child of willingness to stop. Until the infant is able to sit with support and indicate desire for food by her actions feeding solid foods probably represents a type of forced feeding (Fomon, 1980).

Iron-fortified cereal should be the first food introduced. When it has been accepted, other foods may be introduced, but not more than one or two during the same week. Below are additional tips for adding solid foods to a baby's diet:

1. Using a small spoon, place a little bit of strained food or cereal on the back of baby's tongue (but not so far back as to cause choking).

2. Expect baby to push out the food with her tongue; she needs time to get used to new tastes and textures.

3. Try one new food at a time and use it for several days before adding another. Watch for allergic reactions such as rash, diarrhea, coughing, or vomiting.

4. Try new foods when baby is hungry. A good time is in the middle of the morning.

5. CEREALS: Until baby is at least 6 months old, use only rice, oat, or barley cereal. Measure 1 teaspoon of cereal and mix with 2 or 3 tablespoons of lukewarm formula and feed from a spoon (not in the bottle with the formula).

6. VEGETABLES AND FRUITS: Add vegetables one at a time before adding fruits; start with milder vegetables such as squash, green peas, and green beans. Offer a new vegetable every 4 or 5 days; if baby will not eat it, wait a few days and try again. Introduce vegetables and fruits by serving ½ to 1 teaspoonful, gradually increasing the amount to 2 or 3 tablespoonfuls. When baby has a few teeth, the vegetables prepared for the older children (and adults) may be finely chopped.

7. MEATS AND EGG YOLKS: Commercially available strained foods should be selected with care because there are wide variations in the amounts of total calories and of individual essential nutrients. It is preferable to scrape lean raw meat, form into a pattie, and cook in the top of double boiler until the meat is well done. When baby can handle chopped foods, meats may be baked, boiled, or broiled, and finely chopped.

8. STORAGE: Opened jars of baby food or center-prepared vegetables or fruits should be covered, dated, and refrigerated. The food should be used within 48 hours; raw fruit and meats should not be stored more than 1 day. Many servings of prepared foods may be frozen in ice cube trays and stored in freezer bags for up to 1 month. The need to strain center-prepared foods is temporary; just a few months is both beneficial for the baby, and cost-efficient for the caregiver.

Recommendations for feeding infants in groups

Planners and providers of infant child care should be on the alert about major errors in feeding infants, which include (Fomon, 1977, p. 12):

- Too great dilution or too great caloric concentration of a formula,
- A calorically inadequate diet because skim milk is being fed,
- Hazard from nursing bottle caries, . . .
- An inadequate or excessive quantity of milk or formula consumed (less than 16 oz. or more than 32 oz. of milk or formula),
- Complete avoidance of certain food categories (e.g., an older infant who rarely eats fruits or vegetables),
- Inadequate facilities for food preparation and storage,
- Excessive intake of fat-soluble vitamins,
- Adherence to a special restrictive diet (especially if not under a physician's supervision),
- Pica [craving for unnatural foods].

It sometimes seems that the infant's day revolves around eating, feeding, and related activities—diaper changing, hand and body washing, changing clothes, napping, and then the cycle begins again. These procedures consume much of the caregiver's time, which is one of several reasons behind the adult/child ratio of 1:3 for children from birth-2 years of age, required in the 1980 HEW day care regulations. Although feeding times may be scheduled in the overall daily plan, this is an excellent example of the adage that "rules are made to be broken." Individual schedules should be determined by the individual babies themselves and should be adhered to. Soon each infant will settle into a fairly regular individual feeding schedule, so that caregivers can then plan around it. Adults seem to be less accepting of individual needs and desires in this business of feeding than in any other component of child care (or parenting). Babies should not be forced into predetermined schedules designed for the adults' convenience.

It also might seem more convenient to "bottle-prop" instead of holding the baby while feeding. However, adult convenience and infant group care are not compatible. Both the psychoanalytic theorists and the behavioral theorists would agree on the rule that holding the infant while bottle-feeding is highly desirable and even essential for the development of the sense of basic trust in the world, for laying the foundations of basic social relationships, and for learning about the world from early, repeated experiences. If necessary, adults other than professional caregivers might be utilized during feeding times. Volunteers, senior citizens, the center's nurse, and high school or college students are examples of those who can come in at certain times and be assigned certain babies for feeding and holding. Ideally, however, each caregiver assumes prime responsibility for a small number of babies, and is the deliverer of all the routines as well as many of the social interactions to these same babies.

Until an infant is able to sit up with support at a table or highchair, he should be held when being given foods other than milk or formula. One way of handling this is to sit on the floor with your knees up and cradle the baby on your knees facing you. This frees both of your hands for spoon feeding, and gives excellent face-to-face contact between baby and caregiver.

Between 6 and 7 months of age a baby will delight in finger foods such as hard breads or dry cereals, and should be given the opportunity to drink from a cup. For a while, perhaps, the baby will insist on a bottle for milk but may accept juices or water from the cup.

FROM THEORY INTO PRACTICE: TODDLER FEEDING AND EATING

With a few modifications, toddlers eat just like older people, or at least like older people should! (One modification: if you oil the toddler's face before you spoon pureed vegetables into him, he can be mopped off more easily!) Adults are often conscious of the aesthetics of eating: foods at certain temperatures; interesting combinations of texture and colors; and a variety of sauces and seasonings to tempt the appetite. Toddlers, apparently, could care less about the aesthetics of eating. Foods served at room temperatures are eaten in the same quantities as hot or cold ones. Young children do not

insist upon a crisp salad with a soft entree. With the occasional exception of catsup, they want (or need) no added flavorings or seasonings. Toddlers should be easy to feed, and yet it is during this period, between 12 and 36 months of age, that eating "problems" appear.

Eating "problems"

Some of the problems are in the minds of the adults. Toddlers apparently do not need as much food as infants, and we worry that they are not getting sufficient amounts of nutrients. However, a look at the average growth rates of young children shows that, while 1-year-olds may have gained 14 to 16 pounds during the first year, 2-year-olds will have gained only 3 or 4 pounds during the second year and, of course, their appetites diminish. An adult's insistence on eating more after the toddler indicates "no more" is not only wasteful of time and energy, but also soon changes a pleasant experience into an emotionally charged experience resulting in frustration and even anger. If the child appears alert, happy, and curious, and is gaining some weight, there is no cause for concern. At the same time, the well-developing child is entering the period when a sense of autonomy seems to take priority, even over food, and the child's "No!" to food is an indication of this innate desire for self-assertion.

Very possibly, it is this same drive for autonomy that triggers finicky eating, the seemingly irrational selection of only certain foods or certain types or colors of foods, excluding all others. Usually these are temporary quirks, and they should be accepted and treated casually. However, the persistence of such "quirks" over a period of time suggests that a visit to the pediatrician might be in order. It is possible that some genetic influence has led to poor appetite or strong food preferences or aversions.

Unfortunately, even very young children soon learn that their eating behavior (or misbehavior) can be used to manipulate and control adults. It is very exciting to provoke anger and

TABLE 4-4   Meal plan for one week (12-36 months)

Monday	Tuesday	Wednesday	Thursday	Friday
AM snack				
Orange juice	Apricot nectar	Pineapple juice	Apple juice	Cranberry juice
Dry cereal	Oatmeal cookie	Peanut butter sandwich	Whole wheat crackers	Date bread/margarine
Noon meal				
Meat loaf	Scrambled eggs	Hamburger patty	Vegetable soup with	Tuna casserole
Mashed potatoes	Stewed tomatoes	Scalloped potatoes	noodles	Green beans
Carrots	Grits	Peas	Cheese sandwich	Cornmeal muffin/margarine
Bread/margarine	Bread/margarine	Bread/margarine	Cherry tomatoes	Milk
Apple sauce	Diced pears	Orange slices	Bread/margarine	
Milk	Milk	Milk	Milk	
PM snack				
Wheat crackers and	Apple slices with cheese	Dry cereal mix	Cottage cheese with	Banana chunks
cheese chunks	spread	Milk	pineapple chunks	Milk
Milk	Milk		Milk	

violent reactions in adults, and some young ones seem to thrive on such activities. Mealtime should be one of the most enjoyable times of the day, but it can be the most upsetting. The choice is the caregiver's. Young children are entitled to a pleasant mealtime the same as adults, and threats, rewards, and punishments should not be a part of the experience.

Meal planning for toddlers (12 to 36 months)

The meal patterns for children from 12 to 36 months of age were presented in Table 4-3. An example of their translation to actual menus is given in Table 4-4, which contains a meal plan for morning and afternoon supplements (snacks) as well as a main meal.

Evaluation of menus

The Food and Nutrition Service of the U.S. Department of Agriculture (1976) suggests the following questions for the evaluation of menus:

1. Are all components of the meal included?
2. Are serving sizes sufficient to provide young children the required quantity of: Meat or alternate or an equivalent? Two or more vegetables and/or fruits? Enriched or whole-grain bread or an equivalent? Fluid milk?
3. Are serving sizes planned?
4. Are other foods included to help meet the nutritional needs of young children and to satisfy appetites?
5. Are the combinations of food pleasing and acceptable to children?
6. Do meals include a good balance of: Color—in the foods themselves or as a garnish? Texture—soft, crisp, firm-textured; starchy, and other type foods? Shape—different sized pieces and shapes of foods? Flavor—bland and tart or mild and strong flavored foods? Temperature—hot and cold foods?
7. Are most of the foods and food combinations ones children have learned to eat?

8. Have children's cultural and ethnic food practices been considered?
9. Are foods varied from day to day, week to week?
10. Are different kinds or forms of foods (fresh, canned, dried) included?
11. Are seasonal foods included?

Although young children do not appear to be at all impressed with variety in menus (for instance, banana chunks and milk are favorites day in and day out), menu planners rightfully seek diversity. One of the nutrition-related objectives for any group of children is the introduction of a variety of foods, not only to establish good eating habits, but also to ensure the supply of the essential nutrients. Sources of menu ideas may be found in the senior citizen and public school menus published in local newspapers, although the school menus are inclined to be overloaded with starches and carbohydrates. Excellent snack ideas can be found in the appetizer or hors d'oeuvres section of any cook book (the little hors d'oeuvres knives are ideal for children to spread their own bread or crackers; they are not sharp and just the right size for toddlers).

Little bits of wisdom can be easily learned from any cook in an infant-toddler center. The following suggestions were offered by Marie Jones, cook at the Early Childhood Education Center, University of Iowa:

Cheesespreads work on anything, from crackers to raw apple, potato, and turnip slices. Add oatmeal to all kinds of muffins and to meat loaf. Chinese celery is less stringy and more tasty than Pascal celery. Use flattened (rolled with a rolling pin) hamburger bun halves or refrigerator biscuits instead of English muffins for pizza. Peanut butter is easier to eat if it has been whipped with butter or margarine: use two parts of peanut butter to one part of margarine. Use Grape-nuts or wheat germ in or on top of "everything" instead of nutmeats. Dentists frown on graham crackers.

As is true in all endeavors, experience is the best teacher, and many more practical sugges-

tions may be obtained from interviews with persons involved in the daily preparation and meal
service for very young children. There are also
many printed materials available; a list of addresses from which free materials may be obtained is found in Appendix A.

Involving children in food preparation and service

Even though more food preparation activities
are being included in preschools for 3- and 4-
year old children, adults are inclined to think
that children under the age of 3 would just make
a mess. Many cooks in centers do not want to be
bothered and, of course, young children underfoot in a kitchen increases the risk of accidents
and injuries. An alternative is to bring the foods
and the appropriate utensils for cooking activities to the children's room. The term "cooking
activities" in this instance includes all the steps
necessary in the preparation and serving of
foods, with or without the use of heat. The cooking-related activities that follow are listed in
progressive order. Most 3-year-olds are capable
of mastering all of them.

1. Exploring cooking utensils (banging, nesting, putting away)
2. Exploring cooking utensils with water (cups, bowls, beaters, spoons, funnels)
3. Pouring dry ingredients (corn, rice)
4. Pouring wet ingredients (water)
5. Tasting fresh fruit and vegeables
6. Comparing tastes, textures, colors of fresh fruits and vegetables
7. Comparing tastes, textures, colors of fresh and canned fruits and vegetables
8. Dipping raw fruits and vegetables in dip or sauce
9. Scrubbing vegetables with brushes
10. Breaking or tearing lettuce; breaking or snapping beans; shelling peas
11. Stirring and mixing wet and dry ingredients
12. Measuring wet and dry ingredients (use rubber band to mark desired amount on container or measuring cup)
13. Placing toppings on pizza or snacks; deco-rating cookies or crackers that have been spread
14. Spreading bread or crackers
15. Pouring milk or juices to drink
16. Shaking (making butter from cream or coloring sugar or coconut)
17. Rolling with both hands (peanut butter balls, pieces of dough for cookies)
18. Juicing with a hand juicer
19. Peeling hard-cooked eggs, fruits
20. Cutting with dull knife (fruits, vegeta-bles, cheese)
21. Beating with fork or eggbeater
22. Grinding with hand grinder (apples, cranberries)
23. Kneading bread dough
24. Cleaning up

Participation in cooking-related activities
helps to whet the appetite of even the most
finicky eater. It is hard to imagine the number
of children who have eaten something they
helped to make, even though it was burned to a
crisp! But other areas of development are also
involved: concept development, basic motor
skills, and even social-emotional development.

Involving young children in serving their
main meal at the child care center also has benefits. A suggested procedure for 2- and 3-year-
olds to help with a family-style noon meal is
described below.

Equipment needed

1. Multishelved wheeled cart that holds (a) unbreak-able bowls of food and large pitchers of milk, (b) serving utensils and individual spoons (and forks for the older children), (c) empty dishpan, (d) con-tainer for scraps and plate scraper
2. In classroom supply cupboard: (a) paper napkins, (b) paper towels or sponges, (c) paper plates, (d) plastic cups or glasses, (e) terrycloth bibs with Velcro fastening strips, and small pitchers.
3. Trash container

4. Clean water supply
5. Child-sized tables and chairs (one for each group of 5 children and 1 adult)

Procedure

1. Children are engaged in group activity with adult(s) while another adult brings prepared cart from kitchen to classroom.
2. Adult adds plates, cups, and bibs to cart.
3. Adult places one napkin for each person on tables at appropriate places.
4. Child helpers volunteer or are chosen and come to the cart for suppplies. Helper tasks include: (a) place plate by each napkin, (b) place cup or glass by each plate, (c) place spoon (and perhaps fork) by each plate, (d) put bib on each child's chair, (e) carry bowls of food to tables, (f) carry small pitchers of milk to tables.
5. When tables are ready, adults fasten bibs on children, and all are seated.
6. At each table adult passes or serves food, and all eat. Adult offers seconds or thirds.
7. At each table, adult initiates conversation about the attributes of the food, the morning's activities, plans for the afternoon, or whatever. Adult encourages language interaction among children (but it will mostly be adult-child or child-adult).
8. When the meal is finished, one adult goes to cart, a second adult stands by the supply of water. Children (a) bring plates and cups to be emptied by adult into plastic container, (b) put silverware and cups in dishpan for washing, (c) throw plates and napkins into trash container, (d) are de-bibbed by second adult, who rinses bib, uses it to wipe hands (and face when needed), and puts wet bib into laundry basket, (e) use paper towels for drying themselves, (f) run off to play!
9. Adult wheels cart back to kitchen.

In addition to the many learning possibilities, this procedure is smooth and efficient. No wonder the parents who join their children for lunch are amazed at the capabilities and good manners of their children. "But he would never eat that at home!" is a frequent comment.

An excellent source of information about the food preferences of very young children is, of couse, the caregivers and teachers in a child care program. The list of favorite foods in Table 4-5 was supplied by J. Rosenthal and K. Scheerer (1980), head teachers in the infant and toddler groups at the Early Childhood Education Center. Note the absence of cookies and cupcakes. Indeed, the teacher of the toddlers commented that the children frequently refused a cookie when one was offered!

Many adults have preconceptions about meal service, which may have no relationship whatsoever to what comes naturally to the young child. Adults prefer a variety of color and texture. Children may be perfectly happy with orange carrots, yellow-orange scrambled eggs, and orange gelatin. Adults also automatically assume that dessert follows the main course and

TABLE 4-5   Favorite foods of infants and toddlers

Main dishes	Side dishes	Snacks
Macaroni with cheese	Green beans	Banana bread or muffins
Tacos and sloppy Joe's	Mashed potatoes	Yogurt
Meat loaf	Applesauce	Fresh fruit (except cantaloupe)
Hot dogs (without roll)	Jell-o	Hard boiled eggs with crackers
Bologna (without bread)	Tater Tots	Crackers and cheese
Soup (with lots of "stuff" in it)	Salad with Thousand Island or French dressing	Egg salad with crackers
Liver (with ketchup)	Sweet pickles	Peanut butter with crackers
Ham loaf	Spiced apple rings	White or brown bread and butter
Pizza	Lettuce	Graham crackers
Beef stew (lots of meat)		
Salisbury steak		
Tuna fish		
Egg salad		

that dessert depends on "cleaning one's plate." One infant-toddler teacher serves dessert (fruit, pudding, cookie, even ice cream) with the rest of the meal. In this instance, there is neither a temptation to bribe the child nor the likelihood that the child will accord undue importance to dessert.

Skills and concepts developed during cooking-related activities

The list of beginning skills and concepts inherent in cooking-related activities is extensive. Some are readily apparent. All are essential skills and concepts for later learning and behaviors. For example, typical lists of academic readiness skills include: visual and auditory perception and discrimination, eye-hand coordination, oral language, and the association of print to meaning. What better vehicle for "readiness?" A few examples: peaches and oranges are similar in color and shape, but definitely different in taste and texture. Dishes may all be round, but differ in size and depth. Liquids

bubble when they boil, and frozen liquids crackle when they start to melt. The child without eye-hand coordination will get meaningful practice when measuring and pouring liquids and brush-cleaning or cutting vegetables. Kneading and rolling dough uses the large muscles and coordination of both hands and arms. Using a knife to cut or spread requires a great deal of coordination. Mathematical concepts of sets and numbers, sequence and order, measurement, and time intervals are all parts of many food experiences. Oral language is also a part of the give-and-take of a food preparation experience. And even if the children are far too young to be expected to read, the visual display of a recipe or set of directions to which the teacher refers helps introduce the idea that print does have meaning and is useful. In no way am I suggesting an "academic" infant-toddler program. I am suggesting that beginning learning, understandings, and attitudes should be encouraged at the very earliest ages. They can be encouraged naturally in the course of daily activities.

Academic readiness is an important aspect of any early childhood program. In addition to readiness per se, there are basic nutritional concepts that adults can consciously teach and young children will unconsciously begin to learn. How do we consciously teach basic nutritional concepts to an infant or toddler? By modeling eating behavior (we *like and eat* everything that is served), by talking about our need for good food so that we can run and play and feel good, and by establishing a happy eating environment so that food becomes associated with pleasure as well as physical satisfaction.

Other teaching efforts will be directed to the parents of the children. As is true in most parent-center interactions, center personnel must tread softly. Parents think they know how to raise their children, and this is one of their rights. If we tell them they are not feeding their child correctly, we have probably lost the battle even before starting. If we include in our regular newsletter lists of suggested snacks, the center's menus, and sample recipes for food the children enjoy at the center, most parents will start to compare their food habits with the center's. Possibly they will serve some of the suggested foods. Hopefully, this kind of indirect instruction will initiate a dialogue and perhaps a parent-center meeting or workshop. Parents want the best for their children.

The nutrition concepts that we are striving to teach both children and parents are those developed by the Interagency Committee of Nutrition Education for Project Head Start (1967, p. 24):

1. Nutrition is the food you eat and how the body uses it.
    - We eat food to live, to grow, to keep healthy and well, and to get energy for work and play.
2. Food is made up of different nutrients needed for growth and health.
    - All nutrients needed by the body are available through food.
    - Many kinds and combinations of food can lead to a well-balanced diet.
    - No food, by itself, has all the nutrients needed for full growth and health.
    - Each nutrient has specific uses in the body.
    - Most nutrients do their best work in the body when teamed with other nutrients.
3. All persons, throughout life, have need for the same nutrients, but in varying amounts.
    - The amounts of nutrients needed are influenced by age, sex, size, activity, and state of health.
    - Suggestions for the kinds and amounts of food needed are made by trained scientists.
4. The way food is handled influences the amount of nutrients in food, its safety, appearance, and taste.
    - Handling means everything that happens to food while it is being grown, processed, stored, and prepared for eating.

■ CHAPTER SUMMARY ■

Information about nutrition-related disorders, nutrients, meal patterns, and good and bad snacks has been offered in a nontechnical manner. Suggestions for translating theory into the actual feeding of infants and toddlers in group situations have been offered. Neither the theory nor the suggested practices will have a lasting effect unless the caregiver is personally committed to good nutrition and its importance in the optimal growth and development of young children.

The chapter has not provided recipes for large group cooking or for adult-child food preparation. A multitude of recipes and suggestions can be found in numerous printed materials that are readily available. A sample listing of materials containing recipes for adult-child food experiences is in Appendix A.

SUGGESTED ACTIVITIES/POINTS TO PONDER

1. Using the meal pattern in Table 4-3, design a week's menus for a group of toddlers. Specifiy the time of year and make use of foods that are in season. Include morning and afternoon supplements as well as the main meal.
2. Make up the food shopping list for the menus from activity #1. Include amounts of food to be purchased and current costs. You may assume that staples such as flour, sugar, seasonings, etc., are already available.
3. Prepare a newsletter for parents containing ideas for good nutrition at home for the infant and toddler.

REFERENCES AND SUGGESTED READINGS

Birch, H.G.: Malnutrition, learning and intelligence, Congressional Record-Senate, Aug. 14, 1972, S13455.

Child Care Food Program (Final Rule), Federal Register, Jan. 22, 1980.

Committee on Nutrition: American Academy of Pediatrics commentary on breast feeding and infant formulas, Pediatrics, **57:**278-285, 1976.

Crawford, P.B., Hankin, J.H., and Huenemann, R.L.: Environmental factors associated with preschool obesity, Journal of the American Dietetic Association **72:**589-596, 1978.

Davis, C.M.: Results of the self-selection of diets by young children, Canadian Medical Association Journal **41:**257-261, 1939.

Dell, F., and Jordan-Smith, P., editors: The anatomy of melancholy, New York, 1927, Tudor Publishing Co.

Endres, J.B., and Rockwell, R.E.: Food, nutrition, and the young child, St. Louis, 1980, The C.V. Mosby Co.

Ferreira, N.: Teacher's guide to educational cooking in the nursery school—an everyday affair, Young Children **29:** 23-32, Nov., 1973.

Fomon, S.J.: Infant nutrition, ed 2, Philadelphia, 1974, W.B. Saunders Co.

Fomon, S.J.: What are infants fed in the United States? Pediatrics **56**:350-354, 1975.

Fomon, S.J.: Nutritional disorders of children: prevention, screening, and followup, DHEW Publication No. (HSA) 77-5104, Washington, D.C., 1977, U.S. Government Printing Office.

Fomon, S.J. and others: Skim milk in infant feeding, Acta Paediatr. Scan. **66**:17-30, 1977.

Fomon, S.J., and others: Recommendations for feeding normal infants, DHEW Publication No. (HSA) 79-5108, Washington, D.C., 1979, U.S. Government Printing Office.

Food and Nutrition Service, U.S. Department of Agriculture: Child Care Food Program Final Rule, 7 CFR Part 226, Federal Register, Jan 22, 1980.

Food and Nutrition Service, U.S. Department of Agriculture: A planning guide for food service in child care centers, FNS-64, Washington, D.C., 1976, U.S. Government Printing Office.

Food and Nutrition Service, U.S. Department of Agriculture: Food buying guide for child care centers, FNS-108, Washington, D.C., 1980, U.S. Government Printing Office.

Food and nutrition services in day care centers, Journal of the American Dietetic Association **59**:47, 1971.

Foster, F.: Nutrition and educational experience: interrelated variables in children's learning, Young Children **27**:284-288, June 1972.

Graham, L., and Runyan, T.: Nutrition handbook for staff in child care centers, Ames, Ia., 1980, Iowa State University Research Foundation.

Granger, R.H.: Your child from one to six, DHEW Publication No. (OHDS) 77-30026, Washington, D.C., 1977, U.S. Government Printing Office.

Head Start Bureau: Nutrition: better eating for a head start, DHEW Publication No. (OHDS) 76-31009, Washington, D.C., 1976, U.S. Government Printing Office.

Hines, E.R.: Intestinal parasites: a factor in malnutrition, Head Start Newsletter **6**(3):8-9, Dec. 1971/Jan. 1972.

Howard, R.B., and Herbold, N.H.: Nutrition in clinical practice, New York, 1978, McGovern Hill.

James, J.R.: When kids take over the kitchen, Dimensions **2**:74-79, March 1974.

Johnson, B.: Cup cooking offers highly individualized learning experiences for young children, Dimensions **5**:105-109, June 1977.

Jones, M.: Personal communication, May 27, 1980.

Lloyd-Still, J.D.: Malnutrition and intellectual development, Littleton, Mass., 1976, Publishing Sciences Group.

Mairs, P.: Making baby food, Ames, Ia., 1978, Cooperative Extension Service, Iowa State University.

Mairs, P., and Carlson, C.: Feeding your baby, Ames, Ia., 1978, Cooperative Extension Service, Iowa State University.

Maternal and Child Health Service: Nutrition and feeding of infants and children under three in group day care, Washington, D.C., 1971, U.S. Government Printing Office.

McWilliams, M.: Nutrition for the growing years, ed 2, New York, 1975, John Wiley & Sons, Inc.

National Center for Health Statistics: NCHS Growth Charts, 1976, Monthly vital statistics report, Vol. 25, No. 3, Supp. (HRA) 76-1120, June, 1976, Rockville, Md., Health Resources Administration.

North, A.F.: Infant care, DHEW Publication No. (OCD) 73-15, Washington, D.C., 1973, U.S. Government Printing Office.

Nutrition and young children, Children in Contemporary Society **12**(1): (Special issue), 1978.

O'Brien, M., Herbert-Jackson, E., and Risley, T.R.: Menus for toddlers in day care: Parts 1-4, Day Care and Early Education, Vol 6, Nos. 1-4, 1978–1979.

Preschool Nutrition Education Monograph, Berkeley, Calif., 1978, Society for Nutrition Education.

Read, M.S.: Malnutrition, learning, and behavior, DHEW Pub. No. (N1H) 76-1036, Bethesda, Md., 1976, U.S. Government Printing Office.

Recommendations for day care centers for infants and children, Evanston, Ill., 1980, American Academy of Pediatrics.

Rosenthal, J., and Scheerer, K.: Personal communication, July, 1980.

Sunderlin, S., editor: Nutrition and intellectual growth in children, Washington, D.C., 1969, Association for Childhood Education International.

Thomas, S.B.: Nutrition and learning in preschool children, Urbana, Ill., 1972, ERIC Clearinghouse on Early Childhood Education.

Thomas, S.B., compiler: Malnutrition, cognitive development, and learning, Urbana, Ill., 1972, ERIC Clearinghouse on Early Childhood Education.

Turner, M.D., and Turner, J.S.: Making your own baby food, New York, 1976, Workman Publishing Co.

White, P.D.: Caring for the heart. In You and your health, New York, 1974, Council on Family Health.

CHAPTER 5

THE HEALTH COMPONENT OF INFANT-TODDLER CARE

The health of the people is really the foundation upon which all their happiness and their powers as a state depend.

Benjamin Disraeli (1877)

The health of the American people has never been better.

Surgeon General's Report on Health Promotion and Disease Prevention (1979)

HEALTH GOALS
National Child Health Goals*

- All children should be wanted and born to healthy mothers.
- All children should be born well.
- All children should be immunized against the preventable infectious diseases for which there are recommended immunization procedures.
- All children should have good nutrition.
- All children should be educated about health and health care systems.
- All children should live in a safe environment.
- All children with chronic handicaps should be able to function at their optimal level.
- All children should live in a family setting with an adequate income to provide basic needs to insure physical, mental and intellectual health.
- All children should live in an environment that is as free as possible from contaminants.
- All adolescents and young people should live in a societal setting that recognizes their special health, personal and social needs.

According to the Report to the President of the United States National Commission on the International Year of the Child (1980), the United States is the only industrialized nation that has not adopted in principle and in practice the right to health care for all children. The report points out that:

---

*An Agenda for America's Children
Copyright American Academy of Pediatrics 1980

Eleven other countries do a better job than the United States in keeping babies alive in the first year of life. In the U.S. the death rate for black infants is 92 percent higher than that of white infants. Death rates for other minorities are also high, but accurate data [are] not available. Nearly 10 million American children have no known regular source of primary care. Many children who are handicapped receive no services. One-half of the children who require vision care do not receive it. Of the children under age twelve, 47 percent have never been to a dentist for treatment (p. 91).

According to the American Nurses' Association, "the overriding concern . . . is that the delivery of care to children in this country is in wide disarray, is ineffective, fragmented, uneven, and in many instances non-existent" (Nichols, 1979). Unfortunately, the dominant health approach in our country is crisis care, not prevention. Particularly during periods of inflation and unemployment, families cut back on health-related items. The 1979 General Mills American Family Report states that "among all families, almost half are cutting back on health-related items to cope with inflation; among minority families, six out of ten are forced to make these kinds of cutbacks; among single parents, more than seven out of ten are making health-related cutbacks in order to cope with inflation" (p. 50).

A large percentage of parents (and professional caregivers) think that the health of children suffers when mothers have jobs outside the home and child care is provided by someone other than the mother. But "it ain't necessarily so." We now have the know-how, and in most cases the essential support systems, to provide preventive and corrective health care to every young child in an effective and systematic way. Such provision should be a component of every child care center or day care home.

It is only in the last half of the twentieth century that group care and education of very young children could be recommended. The discovery of vaccines and antibiotics has virtually wiped out the dangers of serious illness and epidemics. Sad to say, not all parents believe immunizations are their responsibility or that they are even necessary. If the day care provider can persuade (or insist) upon appropriate immunizations, it is conceivable that children enrolled in group care centers will be considerably more healthy than those same children if they had stayed at home. This state of affairs comes about only when day care centers or homes follow the guidelines offered in the following pages.

Health goals and policies for infants and young children in day care

What do we want in terms of health for our very young children? We want to improve every child's present functioning and we want to help ensure every child's future health. Day care providers cannot meet these goals in isolation from the parents, from professional health persons and resources, from the community at large. The most often quoted statement of health goals for children in day care was first published in the series of day care handbooks sponsored by the former Office of Child Development and written by Dr. Frederick North in 1973. It reads as follows:

I. To improve a child's present function by:
  A. Finding all existing health problems through:
    (i) Accumulating records of past health and immunization status.
    (ii) Considering the observations of classroom teachers and other staff.
    (iii) Performing screening tests; including tuberculin, hematocrit or hemoglobin, vision testing, hearing testing.
    (iv) Interviewing the child and his parents about his current and past health and function.
    (v) Performing a physical examination as part of a complete health evaluation.
  B. Remedying any existing problems through:
    (i) Applying whatever medical or dental treatments are necessary.
    (ii) Arranging for rehabilitative services, special education, and other forms of continuing care.
    (iii) Applying mental health principles in the classroom or group.
II. To ensure a child's future health by:
  A. Providing preventive services including:
    (i) Immunization against infectious diseases.
    (ii) Fluoride treatment to prevent tooth decay.
    (iii) Health education for children and parents.
    (iv) Introducing the child to a physician and dentist who will be responsible for his continuing health care.
    (v) Assuring that the day care setting and the home provide a safe and stimulating environment.
  B. Improving the health of all members of the child's family through:
    (i) Calling attention to family health needs.
    (ii) Introducing the family to health care services, and to sources of funds for these services.
  C. Improving the health of the community in which the child lives through:
    (i) Increasing the awareness and concern of professionals and the general population with the health problems of children.
    (ii) Stimulating and providing new resources for health care.
    (iii) Making existing health resources more responsive to the special needs of children and parents (p. 8).

I would like to add another health goal for an infant-toddler center. This goal rarely appears in a formal statement. It is to prevent, or at least minimize, the child's resistance to medical procedures or medical persons. Causes of such resistance may be "natural" ones, such as the stranger anxiety syndrome so often evidenced in the months after the first half-year of life. No doubt the white lab coat or uniform emphasizes the strangeness of this new person. Perhaps this is the reason why doctors, nurses, and others who work with young children have discarded their usual attire and dress in street clothes. It would seem that this defeats the purpose. Our efforts to teach a child that the nurse or doctor is a friend will be effective only if the nurse or doctor is dressed in some distinguishing manner and acts like a friend!

Other causes of violent resistance include letting the child "get away" with such behavior, lack of trust in the world and the people in it, and lies or threats. Such statements as "We are just going shopping" (but ending up at the doctor's office), and "It won't hurt" (when it will) naturally build resistance to health care. It is a recognized fact that children, even under the age of 3, understand both the words and actions of other persons and behave accordingly. Their inability to verbally express emotion does not preclude their ability to express emotion in other ways. When the circumstances warrant it, the approach to health care or health personnel might be an appropriate topic for discussion with parents.

Which of these three goals can be met by an individual day care center? All of them, if the following recommendations are put into practice.

Each center or group of centers should involve persons and organizations in planning their health component to ensure that *their* health program is tailored to meet the needs of *their* children, and that it uses the available community resources and does not duplicate already existing services. In order to achieve the comprehensive goals as set forth, the health program must be planned by professionally competent persons who are dedicated to bringing high quality health services to all children. This planning must take place well before the day care program begins and children are enrolled.

A single individual should bear the responsibility for planning and carrying out the health program. This person might be a pediatrician, a public health physician, or a general practitioner with particular interest in and concern for the health of very young children. This person may volunteer services or be paid as a part- or full-time employee or consultant of one large center or several smaller ones. It is wise strategy to include as many relevant organizations and individuals as possible during the planning stages. Those who are involved early in the planning are more likely to cooperate in the implementation of the program. In addition to pediatricians or interested physicians, consider child psychiatrists and psychologists and their organizations; dentists and dental associations, speech and hearing personnel and their associations; hospital administrators; county and state medical societies; and local, regional, and state health officers. Although not usually included in a day care health planning committee, the local fire marshal is not only an expert on fire prevention, but also on all procedures related to any disaster such as tornado, flood, and hurricane. Nonphysician health personnel, such as the pediatric nurse practitioner and the medical assistant in pediatrics are increasing in numbers and are valuable allies for day care centers. And let us not ignore the essential role of the parents of the children to be enrolled. They often know a great deal about what community resources are available and which meet expected standards. Parents can give valuable input as to the feasibility of any plan proposed by "experts."

Keeping in mind the health goals of all children in day care and the various kinds of expertise held by any or all of the above resources, it is possible to formulate a health policy statement for an individual infant-toddler day care center (and, of course, for a center serving older children as well). The example presented on pp. 99-101 is the result of a group endeavor by health professionals, a multidisciplinary advisory council including selected staff members, selected parents, and references to current editions of relevant publications of the American Academy of Pediatrics (AAP). These include: *Standards for Child Health Care,* 1977, *The Report of the Committee on Infectious Diseases,* 1977, and *Standards for Day Care Centers for Infants and Children,* 1980. The AAP standards are nationally recognized as appropriate to follow in providing health care for children. They are updated periodically. Reference was also made to the HEW Day Care Regulations filed on March 18, 1980. The future of these regulations, now known as the Health and Human Services Day Care Regulations, is tenable, if there is a future at all. The same is true of the EPSDT (Early and Periodic Screening, Diagnosis and Treatment) program, referred to in Section 22.c of the sample health policy. Even if these documents are discarded or replaced, their contents are valid and therefore useful in formulating any health policy for an infant-toddler or preschool child care center.

SAMPLE HEALTH POLICY FOR AN INFANT-TODDLER CHILD CARE CENTER

Health policies are based primarily on the following sources of information:
1. *Standards for Child Health Care,* American Academy of Pediatrics, 1977.
2. *Report of the Committee on Infectious Diseases,* American Academy of Pediatrics, 1977.
3. *Standards for Day Care Centers for Infants and Children,* American Academy of Pediatrics, 1980.
4. HEW Day Care Regulations issued March 19, 1980.

10. Administration

The health program will be the joint responsibility of the Center staff and professional health consultants. Periodic reviews of the health program will be undertaken to ensure its implementation and to assess the need for modification or revision. The health policies relate to both children and adults involved in the Center.

20. Admission policies

Parents are required to provide the following information for each child enrolled:

21. Information about the child's previous and current developmental history.

22. A statement from a licensed health practitioner that:

    a. Describes any special precautions for diet, medication, or activity

    b. States that the child has received immunizations in accordance with recommendations of the U.S. Public Health Service or the American Academy of Pediatrics. (These immunization requirements may be waived or modified according to the code of an individual state.)

    c. States that the child has received a health assessment in accordance with the standards of the American Academy of Pediatrics, or the EPSDT National Recommended Health Assessment Plan.

22.1 The above statement for each child must be on record within 60 days of admission, and must be updated according to the American Academy of Pediatrics, or the EPSDT National Recommended Health Assessment Plan.

22.2 Smallpox vaccinations are no longer routine in the United States. However, any infant receiving smallpox vaccine will be excluded from attendance at the Center until the scab has fallen off.

23. Verification that the child has received a tuberculin skin test at the time of, or preceding, the measles immunization, with adequate follow-up for positive reactors.

Continued.

20. Admission policies—cont'd

   24. Source of the child's regular health care (pediatrician, physician, or health resource responsible for on-going health care), including name, address, and phone number. Also an authorization signed by the parent(s) or guardian for emergency treatment of the child.

   25. Name, address, and telephone number of persons in addition to parent(s) or guardian who have agreed to accept responsibility for the child if the child becomes ill and the primary caregivers cannot be contacted.

30. Health supervision

   31. *Center staff responsibility*

     31.1 A staff member shall regularly seek to meet with the parent(s) or guardian to share a summary of the information on the child's growth, development, behavior, nutritional habits, and any special problems. The parents will provide reports of interval immunization and health care and evaluation the child has received. The list of names of professional health persons or resources, as well as the parent(s) or guardian, will be brought up to date. Recommendations should be developed by the parent(s) or guardian and the staff for the child so that there will be a coordinated program of care in the Center and home.

     31.2 There shall be daily communication on problems of diet, illness, and behavior between parent(s) or guardian and staff.

     31.3 Staff shall provide information to parents as needed concerning child health services available in the community, and shall assist parents in obtaining the health services.

     31.4 Children will be assisted in acquiring knowledge and health practices appropriate to their age and development. Consultation with parents will allow reasonable consistency in handling the child between the home and the Center. This includes information about promoting good dental health (daily care, early dental inspection, adequate nutrition, fluoridation, and salvage of injured teeth).

     31.5 It shall be the responsibility of the director (or designated staff) to supervise the administration of medication. Nonprescription medications will be given with signed authorization of the parent. Prescription medication must:

      a. Be prescribed by a physician.

      b. Contain the following information on the container:

        Child's name

        Physician's name

        Name of medication

        Directions for administering

        Duration it is to be given

      c. Be accompanied by a written request and authorization by parent or guardian.

      Records of these prescriptions and authorization will be maintained on file. The Center will maintain a record of the dates and hours the medications are given, as well as the staff member who administered the medication. All medications are to be kept in locked cabinets out of children's reach and in a separate location from where food is stored or prepared.

     31.6 A screening program will be implemented for each child for the purpose of recognizing health hazards or defects. The program includes a minimum of (a) periodic vision screening, (b) periodic hearing testing, (c) periodic weight and growth measurements.

   32. *Sanitary procedures*

     32.1 The Center will provide facilities and promote the practice of washing hands and face before and after meals, and hands after using toilet facilities and after outdoor activities.

     32.2 Wet or soiled clothing shall be changed promptly. An adequate emergency supply will be available at the Center.

   33. *Staff in-service training health goals*

     33.1 To develop increasing ability to appraise the health status of children.

     33.2 To develop increasing ability to recognize deviations (either behavioral or physical) from group and individual health status.

     33.3 To be knowledgeable about appropriate community health resources.

     33.4 To promote the use of preventive and corrective measures in interactions with parents.

     33.5 To teach positive health and safety behavior by example and instruction of children and their parent(s) or guardian.

40. Management of child who appears ill

41. A child who appears tired, ill, or upset will be given the opportunity to rest in a quiet area under frequent observation. Center staff will give the child an appropriate health appraisal, involving, for instance, measurement of temperature, assessment through observation and responses from the child regarding symptoms, general appearance, appetite, and activity level. Parents will be notified either during the day or at the end of the day, at the discretion of Center staff.

42. If a child appears acutely ill and uncomfortable, parents will be informed and asked to seek medical care as soon as possible. If parents cannot be contacted, Center staff will contact the individuals designated as per #24.

43. A child may be cared for at the Center during minor illness at the discretion of the parent and the staff.

44. Any child who frequently requires seclusion and health observation for fatigue, illness, or emotional upset will be discussed with the parents and a complete medical evaluation will be suggested. The Center staff will provide the family with a complete report of the observations of the child. If the special needs of the child cannot be met at the Center, the Center retains the right to disenroll the child.

45. Parents will be notified if their child has been exposed to a communicable disease. When isolated cases occur, children may be asked to remain at home during the time when they are most likely to develop the disease. This may help to prevent rapid spread of the disease. Parents will be told what symptoms to expect.

46. Readmission to the Center following illness is dependent on the individual child's diagnosis and should be a mutual responsibility of parents and Center staff. When the protection of the other children is involved, the director may have the prerogative of requiring a physician's certification of health before the child reenters the Center.

47. Medical consultation will be available to the director to aid in establishing policies for management of current illness or threat of illness.

50. Management of accidents

51. The center nurse or other appropriate persons (local or state social service or health department personnel) shall evaluate the physical facility at least semiannually to determine that it is reasonably free from common hazards, including lead. Daily vigilance will be maintained to "police" the environment.

52. All staff members working with children will be given instruction in first aid principles, including control of bleeding, management of seizures, administration of artificial respiration, cardiopulmonary resuscitation, and splinting of fractures.

53. The Center nurse will assist the staff in developing routine procedures for the treatment of minor injuries. These procedures shall be written and posted with the first aid materials. The current First Aid Chart from the American Academy of Pediatrics will be used as the basic first aid reference.

54. There shall also be written, posted procedures for disaster (including fire), ingestion of poison, and the management of more serious injuries. First aid measures and the procedures to be followed in bringing children to emergency medical care shall also be posted. (First aid measures for more serious accidents will be primarily based on the current edition of *School Health: A Guide for Physicians,* American Academy of Pediatrics.)

55. The Center will negotiate arrangements with the local hospital emergency facilities to provide emergency medical care.

56. First aid supplies will be maintained in the Center.

57. If a child has an accident during the day, the parent or designated responsible person shall be notified. A record of accident or injury shall be kept in the child's permanent health form. Records of accidents shall be reviewed by the medical consultant and staff, semiannually.

60. Employee health

61. An employee with a disease that can be transmitted represents a threat to the health of the children and the other adults. The most important considerations are tuberculosis and hepatitis. All employees, volunteers, and others, including food handlers, housekeepers, and van drivers, should be screened for tuberculosis and hepatitis. The form of screening is dependent upon conditions in the community.

62. Employees will be told that they may not be in contact with children or food service at times when they have respiratory infections, skin infections, or other types of communicable disease.

63. A health examination by a physician will be required before the first day of activities at the Center and should be anually updated. The signed examination form will become part of the employee's file.

As new information is released, the health policy statement of any child care center must be updated.

ADMINISTRATION AND HEALTH POLICY

As stated previously, a single individual should have the responsibility for planning and carrying out the health program. However, unless this person is one of the paid employees of the center, he or she should not be expected to continue with the time-consuming administration of the health program on a routine basis. The outsider who has agreed to assist in the formulation of a health policy and perhaps in setting up the implementation of the policy should then be relieved of the on-going implementation. The role of the health professional becomes that of consultant in case of emergencies or when revisions are needed in policy or practice. Many centers employ a registered nurse or pediatric nurse practitioner (PNP) on a part- or full-time basis for the regular delivery of the health component. Others have been able to employ a person who qualifies as both a registered nurse or PNP and a caregiver/teacher. This arrangement would appear to be both practical and ideal, depending upon the number of children enrolled. However, specific guidelines and time allotments must be agreed upon in writing as to the health component and the caregiving component. It is a common occurrence to use such a person as almost a "permanent substitute" in the classroom, thereby allowing too little time for the health component of the program. Sometimes the services of a visiting nurse may be obtained once or twice a week. If this is the case, there needs to be someone in the center who holds current certifications in first aid and CPR and who will assume the major responsibility for the daily delivery of health services. This person would have responsibility for contacting community resources and the medical consultant and for parent-center relationships with regard to health issues. This person may also be designated to give any medications. Three im-

portant and sometimes difficult tasks to be performed are: (1) being sure every child receives the routine tests, health evaluations, and immunizations; (2) being sure that every child who is found to have a health problem receives the necessary evaluation and treatment; and (3) being sure that every child (and family) is introduced to a physician who can be responsible for the child's future care. In very small centers, the director, owner, or head teacher might assume these tasks, or there might be a division of labor; however, one person should be the coordinator and carry the responsibilities. This person probably will also fill the role of the coordinator of procedures in suspected child abuse and neglect cases, as described in Chapter 3.

ADMISSION POLICIES AND FORMS

Admission policies and their related forms will vary from center to center and from one day care home to another. Regardless of location, number of children served, or sponsorship, each center or home should have an initial information-sharing meeting.

The informational meeting

The initial meeting provides the opportunity for the center representative to explain the program, hours, meal service, facilities, and other information. Ideally, each parent visited the center and had such a discussion before deciding on enrolling the child. Even if this has been the case, many items bear repeating. In addition, each family will have questions of their own. It is a big and important decision to assign the care and education of a very young child to someone other than a family member in a location other than the home. Even when outside care for the child is essential, for whatever reason, many parents are plagued with guilt feelings.

A staff member's willingness to spend an unhurried time period and to answer or discuss any and all relevant items is the first important part of the mental health component of the center's program. The bond between the parents and their infant or toddler is very close. Even before young children can understand the meaning of words, they can sense their parents' fears or doubts, and are adversely affected by them. Therefore we do whatever possible to allay these fears or doubts in the minds of the parents. This is one reason why the initial interview is so important. Another purpose of the interview is to obtain background information about the child that will make the transition from home to center as smooth as possible.

When possible, the caregiver/teacher who will assume major responsibility for the child is the best person to talk with the parent(s). It seems to be the custom in the larger centers to assign admission procedures to the director or

nurse as an efficient use of time. If this is the system in a particular center, it is absolutely essential that the parent(s) and the responsible caregiver also have an unhurried period when they can discuss mutual concerns to minimize any doubts the parents may have.

The admission interview

Shortly before the child begins regular attendance, the parent(s) and caregiver/teacher should meet again, this time for the purpose of obtaining developmental information about the child. Responses should be recorded in an organized way. The kinds of information desired are suggested in the Background Information form (Appendix B). Even though many parents are capable of reading the questions and writing the answers, the center-parent relationship is enhanced when the questions and answers are discussed face-to-face. Parents like to talk about their children! They should be given the opportunity to do so.

At the time of the admission interview or within 60 days of admission, parents are required to provide a statement from a licensed health practitioner describing any special precautions for diet, activity, or medication. An additional statement is also required certifying that the child has received a health assessment in accordance with the standards of the American Academy of Pediatrics or the EPSDT National Recommended Health Assessment Plan. Copies of the EPSDT Health Assessment Plans for infants aged 3 days to 7 months and for children aged 7 months to 30 months are contained in Appendixes C and D. These forms are to be used by health professionals, preferably the family pediatrician or health resource. They are included so that day care personnel will know what kind of information is required.

Immunization requirements. One of the admission requirements listed in the health policy statement (see pp. 99-101) is a statement that the child has received immunizations in accordance with the recommendations of the U.S. Public

TABLE 5-1   Recommended schedule for active immunization of normal infants and children

Age	Immunization
2 mo.	(DTP) Diphtheria and tetanus toxoids combined with pertussis vaccine
2 mo.	Trivalent oral poliovirus vaccine (TOPV)
4 mo.	DTP#2 and TOPV#2
6 mo.	DTP#3; third dose of TOPV is optional
15 mo.	Measles, rubella (and usually mumps)
18 mo.	DTP booster and TOPV booster
4-6 yr.	DTP booster and TOPV booster

Health Service or the American Academy of Pediatrics. The AAP recommends active immunization of normal infants and young children according to the schedule in Table 5-1. Similar schedules are suggested by the American Medical Association, the U.S. Public Health Service, and the American Academy of Family Physicians. Individual circumstances may require modification of the schedule. A pediatrician, family physician, or the public health department will provide current recommendations or requirements for each area.

At the present time, all states require certificates of immunization at the time of enrollment in both public and nonpublic schools, kindergarten through 12. Enforcement of the requirement varies, however, and beginning school age is very late for "baby" shots. Fewer states require certificates of immunization at the time of enrollment in a day care center. If your state does not, it may be difficult to convince the parents of the necessity for immunizations. In order to be convincing, caregivers should know about immunizations and the "big seven" childhood diseases. Although the nurse or health coordinator of a center will be knowledgeable about these diseases, most personal contacts between the center and parents will be with the caregiver directly responsible for the child. It is for this reason that the following information is included.

THE "BIG SEVEN" CHILDHOOD DISEASES
Immunizations

Within a recent 2-year period, almost 100,000 measles cases were identified in this country. Perhaps the sharing of this information will cause parents to pause before rejecting the whole idea of immunizations for their children. The following information was supplied by the Office of Human Development Services, Administration for Children, Youth, and Families.

When full-term babies are born, they have a natural protection from many diseases. But this protection does not last. It wears off anywhere during the first 6 to 12 months of life. When that happens, there is only one thing to do: get special "shots and drops" to take the place of the natural protection which has worn off. These shots and drops are called vaccinations, inoculations, or immunizations. Immunizations are made from very small amounts of the material that causes a specific disease. Immunizations are injected into the body (shots) or taken by mouth (drops). The body reacts to the vaccine by producing antibodies, which build up in the body and guard it for a long time. It takes different kinds of disease-fighters to keep away different kinds of disease. Information about these disease-fighters (immunizations) and the seven childhood diseases which can be controlled by them is presented in the following.

The childhood diseases that can do serious harm to young children are: diphtheria, whooping cough, tetanus, polio, measles, mumps, and rubella.

1. Diphtheria. Diphtheria is an infection that usually develops in the throat, with early symptoms of sore throat, chills, slight fever, and headache. It is most likely to strike children under 15 years of age, and is most harmful to the very young, but adults may also catch it. It is spread by breathing in germs that the sick person throws out while coughing or sneezing. The illness can also be spread by a carrier—a person who carries the germ in his or her body for a long time without getting sick, but meanwhile spreads germs to other people.

Diphtheria germs produce a strong poison that may spread through the body and affect nerves and heart muscles. This can lead to heart failure and pneumonia (lung infection). A thick, grayish coating forms in the throat and may block the windpipe, causing breathing problems and even death.

2. Whooping cough (pertussis). Whooping cough, also called pertussis, is most likely to strike children under the age of 7. Babies have no natural protection against this disease when they are born.

Whooping cough is spread through the air when the sick person coughs and sneezes. It begins like a common cold, but develops into violent coughing fits within one or two weeks. Each coughing spell is followed by a high "whooping" sound, as the children fight to catch their breath.

Whooping cough can lead to pneumonia (lung infection) and convulsions. These conditions are most likely to occur in the very young. This disease can cause death in babies under 6 months of age.

3. Tetanus. Tetanus, also called "lockjaw," can strike people of any age who have not been immunized whenever they have a dirty wound. Babies are born with little or no natural protection against tetanus.

You cannot catch tetanus from another person. Tetanus germs are just about everywhere, mostly in soil, dust, dog saliva, and animal manure. Tetanus is spread by germs coming into the body through a cut or other open wound—sometimes as small as a pinprick, but more commonly in deep cuts such as those made by nails and knives.

The germs grow fast in closed or dirty wounds, and make a strong poison that attacks the body's nervous system. At first, a child with tetanus may be fussy or cross and have a headache with muscle stiffness in the jaw and neck. Later, the sick person will have a hard time swallowing and will have painful muscle spasms in the back, neck, face, and stomach. These muscle spasms (convulsions) may lead to breathing and heart problems. A person who gets tetanus has about a 50-50 chance of living through it.

4. Poliomyelitis. Polio is a very serious disease that can cause permanent loss of use of the muscles (paralysis). It is spread by contact with people who have the disease. It starts with fever, headache, vomiting, sore throat, and sometimes severe muscle pain and stiffness in the neck, back, and legs. In the years before the discovery and widespread use of polio vaccine, the disease often led to paralysis in the arms, legs, throat, and chest, and even to death. There is no cure for polio.

5. Measles. Measles is also called red measles, hard measles, or rubeola. It is different from rubella (German or 3-day measles), which is most dangerous to unborn babies during early pregnancy. Measles is one of the most serious of the childhood diseases.

Measles is caught very easily from persons with the disease by breathing in bits of the measles virus that the sick person throws out while coughing, sneezing, or even talking. Measles usually strikes young children above the age of 6 months, and doctors now report that they are seeing measles in older children.

Measles lasts about two weeks. It begins with symptoms like those of a bad cold—severe cough, chills, watery, light-sensitive eyes, and a temperature that may rise as high as 105 degrees. A few days later a red rash appears on the body. The rash fades away in 7 to 10 days.

These symptoms may not sound very serious. In fact, catching measles used to be thought of as almost a normal part of childhood, like skinned knees. But measles causes children to feel very sick for as long as a week, and other problems, such as ear infection, diarrhea, pneumonia, and infections of the brain, may follow. Some of these illnesses can lead to the loss of sight or hearing, mental retardation, or even death.

6. Mumps. Mumps is a common, usually mild childhood illness that is most likely to affect 5 to 10 year olds. It tends to be more serious and painful in teenagers and adults. Mumps is spread by contact with persons who may have mumps and by eating or drinking from articles they have used (cups, silverware, soda bottles).

Mumps lasts about a week, and may include fever, headache, painful swelling of glands (usually on one side of the jaw or cheeks), and earache. Sometimes, the glands swell so much that air passages are blocked, making it hard to breathe. Mumps may lead to infection of some internal organs and of the brain. On rare occasions, this brain infection may result in deafness. In teenage and adult males, mumps may cause infection of the testicles, which could result in sterility. In adult females, the ovaries and breasts may become swollen and painful.

7. Rubella (German measles). Rubella is also called German measles and 3-day measles. It is different from measles (rubeola), which is most dangerous to young children.

People catch rubella by breathing in rubella virus thrown out by sick persons while coughing, talking, etc. It is almost always a mild disease, with a day of low fever and runny nose, sometimes a day or two of rash and swollen glands in the neck and/or behind the ears. Sometimes it is hard to tell a case of rubella from a bad cold. However, if a pregnant woman catches rubella during the first 3 months of her pregnancy, the baby stands a great chance of being born with heart problems, deafness, blindness, or mental retardation. The woman has an even greater chance of losing the baby.

Possible reactions to immunizations. As the result of an immunization, children may have a low fever, a mild rash, or soreness where the shot was given. Children are frequently tired, cross or fussy, and may not feel like eating. These are common reactions, and should not last for more than a few days. If a child runs a high fever or has a more serious reaction, the doctor or clinic should be contacted.

Miscellaneous forms and information

Information about the health professional or resource responsible for the ongoing health care of the child may be easily recorded on an index card, and is another essential part of the child's folder. At the same time, parents should fill in a "Release of child to adult other than parent" form. Although the parents may have every intention of *always* picking up their child at the end of each daily session, unforeseen happenings may prevent this upon occasion. No child care center should release a child to *anyone* other than the primary caregiver, usually the parent(s) or guardian, unless such written permission is given. At all times we must ensure the child's safety. This policy is particularly important during this period of time when child custody cases and "kidnappings" by one parent occasionally occur. This same precaution is one of the reasons for requesting a "consent for photographs," which may or may not be given. The child's enrollment is not affected by this, however. Such a form might be worded as in Fig. 5-1.

A "consent for travel" form, when secured at the time of enrollment, will save future last minute arrangements. An example is found in Fig. 5-2.

The above forms are indirectly related to the health and safety components of a day care center or home. Of direct relationship to the health and safety component is an authorization for emergency treatment of the child. This authorization is a must. Ideally, it will never have to be used. Because of its seriousness and the possible liabilities that may be involved, it is not phrased in casual terms, but in a formal style, such as that shown in Fig. 5-3.

These admission forms have been adapted

```
                    ABC Day Care Center
                  CONSENT for PHOTOGRAPHS

I/we consent_____do not consent_____to photographs being taken of my/our

child,_____ ,

at the ABC Day Care Center to be used for informational, scientific, or pub-

licity purposes.


This authorization shall remain effective from the time of enrollment until

the next August, and will be updated each August thereafter that my/our child

is enrolled in the ABC Day Care Center.



                              _____
                              Father

                              _____
                              Mother

                              _____
                              Date
```

FIG. 5-1 Consent for photographs.

ABC Day Care Center

CONSENT FOR TRAVEL

I/we consent _____ do not consent _____ that my/our child, _____

_____ , be taken by the ABC Day Care Center on its various field

trips away from the school premises.

This authorization shall remain effective from the time of enrollment until

the next August, and will be updated each August thereafter that my/our

child is enrolled in the ABC Day Care Center.

_____
Father

_____
Mother

_____
Date

FIG. 5-2   Consent for travel.

ABC Day Care Center

AUTHORIZATION TO CONSENT TO EMERGENCY TREATMENT OF MINOR

I/we, the undersigned, parent(s) of _____,
a minor, do hereby authorize the Director of the ABC Day Care Center, or the
Director's authorized representative, as agent for the undersigned, in case of
emergency, to consent to any x-ray examination, anesthetic, medical or surgical
diagnosis or treatment and hospital care which is deemed advisable by, and is
to be rendered under the general or special supervision of any physician and
surgeon on the Medical Staff of _____ Hospital, whether such diagnosis
or treatment is rendered at the office of said physician or at said hospital.
We further authorize the aforesaid agent to consent to any emergency dental
services which may be deemed advisable by and are rendered under the supervision
of dentists on the staff of the _____ Hospital.

It is understood that this authorization is given in advance of any specific
diagnosis, treatment, hospital care, or dental services being required but is
given to provide authority and power on the part of our aforesaid agent to
give specific consent to any and all such diagnosis, treatment, hospital care,
or dental services which the aforementioned physician, surgeon, or dentist in
the exercise of his/her best judgment may deem advisable.

In the event any medical services are rendered to my/our child pursuant to
this authorization to consent, I/we request that the Director of the ABC Day
Care Center notify my/our family physician.

        Physician _____

        Address _____

        Telephone Number _____

This authorization shall remain effective during the entire period that the
aforesaid minor is enrolled in the ABC Day Care Center, _____ .
                                               address

                 _____
                 Father

                 _____
                 Mother

                 _____
                 Legal Guardian

                 _____
                 Date

FIG. 5-3 Authorization to consent to emergency treatment.

from those used by the Early Childhood Education Center, University of Iowa. They have proved themselves over a period of 8 years in serving both infants and toddlers and older preschool children.

Executed forms and information that should be part of every child's folder in any day care center or home include the following:

1. Statement from a licensed health practitioner or health resource that:
   a. Describes special health precautions for the child
   b. States that the child has received appropriate immunizations
   c. States that the child has received a health assessment
   d. Verifies that the child has received a tuberculin skin test
2. Statement of the source of the child's regular health care
3. Statement of authorization of emergency treatment

Optional but highly recommended forms or information include the following:

1. Release of child to adult other than parent
2. Consent for photographs
3. Consent for travel
4. Background information about child

HEALTH SUPERVISION
Information exchange

The responsibilities of the center staff include periodic information exchanges with each child's primary caregiver(s) about that child's growth, development, behavior, nutritional habits, and any special problems. In turn, the parents or guardian will provide reports of interval immunization and health care and evaluation that the child has received. Forms signed at the time of enrollment should be updated. Any changes that have immediate application should be made immediately rather than waiting to set up an appointment. Frequently, parents will wish to add to the list of persons who may pick up the child, for instance, as car pools are formed or as conditions at home change.

In addition to these exchanges on either an immediate or scheduled basis, there should be daily communication between the parent or guardian and the caregiver at the center. This may be no more than a greeting and "How are things going?" However, building into the program the requirement of daily person-to-person contact ensures the opportunity for the exchange of more vital information when necessary. A good rule to enforce is that the parent or other authorized adult personally deliver the child to the center caregiver. Fig. 5-4 clearly shows that this mother is well satisfied with her arrangements for day care, as she delivers her baby to the head teacher. Note that the baby's attention has already been drawn to the ongoing activities of the earlier arrivals. The rule of personal pick-up at the end of the day is equally valid. Fig. 5-5 illustrates the happy reunion of baby and parents. There are definite positive gains derived from this individualized pick-up and delivery system, in addition to providing an opportunity for exchange of information.

Further suggestions and comments about parent-center sharing of information, health and otherwise, will be presented in a later chapter.

Community health resources

Almost every community will have available many health resources. The day care health coordinator and the policy planning committee should investigate each source of funds and services. These sources include:

- Private practitioners of medicine, dentistry, psychology
- Health departments—city, county, regional, state
- Clinics run by hospitals, medical schools, or other agencies·
- Prepaid medical groups
- Neighborhood health centers

FIG. 5-4   Delivery of child to day care center.

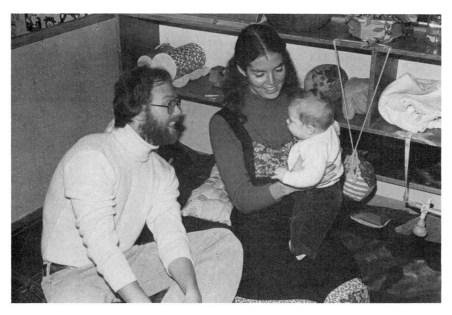

FIG. 5-5   Personal pickup of child from day care center.

- Comprehensive child health centers
- Dental service corporations
- Special voluntary or public agencies, usually concerned with a single category of disease or handicap
- State crippled children's programs, limited to certain categories of illness
- Medical assistance under Medicaid (funds for diagnostic and treatment services for a wide range of health problems for poor children)
- Community mental health programs
- County department of social services
- Community colleges or universities for screening, staff development
- State day care training offices
- State sanitation office
- Preventive dentistry programs
- Area health education centers
- Area education associations
- Red Cross, especially for caregiver instruction in first aid and related fields
- County extension agents, especially for nutrition education
- Hospital emergency rooms

The day care program may contract with existing agencies to provide some or all of the health services, but responsibility for the quality and coordination of these services remains with the day care center staff.

Giving such a list as the above to parents who inquire about (or need) funds or services is worthless. Only the day center or its health coordinator can make this list meaningful by personal contact and investigation of each health resource with regard to the needs of the children enrolled. Some of the resources listed above are nonexistent in a specific community, and some of the resources provide services only for certain categories of children or for certain problems. It is very possible that some of the resources are not available to children below the age of 3 years. Keeping these limitations in mind, the list is a good starting point for on-the-scene investigation.

Knowing the location of support systems and telling parents what they might find and where is merely the first step. For a wide range of reasons, it may be necessary for the center's health coordinator, director or the child's caregiver to encourage the parents to make the initial contact; or the center personnel themselves may need to make contact for the parent and child, setting up an appointment, actually providing transportation, and perhaps providing care for siblings. It is said that love is a many-splendored thing. A quality infant-toddler care center is a many-splendored thing also. Its inherent responsibilities go far beyond the on-site delivery of care and education to young children.

Health education for children and parents

Health education is best taught to both the children and their parents by the example set by the day care center or home. The parents learn from the emphasis placed on the prerequisite doctor's examination, intake interviews, required immunizations, dental care, and other health measures that such activities are important for their children. They also learn that each child is accorded individual concern and care. Parents and children can learn that health care should be a pleasant, continuous experience, and not just a formal physical examination.

Health-related routines and activities within the program can begin to teach children the importance and the routines of personal health care. Infants and toddlers should have their teeth and gums cleaned every day. Toothbrushes can be introduced at about 18 months. Infants and toddlers learn about nutrition as they eat foods containing a variety of nutrients. They learn about personal hygiene by the caregiver's insistence on hand washing at appropriate times (and the caregivers washing their hands at these times, also). They learn about indoor and outdoor safety as they are encouraged to use toys and equipment in appropriate ways. They begin to learn about pedestrian safety during their walking tours of the neighborhood. They learn about automobile safety when they are always fastened into safety restraints and the vehicle's doors are locked before the engine is started. They learn about environmental sanitation and safety when they use wastebaskets or trashcans, and when they observe the housekeeper or caregiver vacuum the carpet after mealtime and spray the tables with a disinfectant. They learn about disease control by using disposable tissues for blowing or wiping noses, and by observing the tissue being thrown into an appropriate receptacle immediately after use. They develop matter-of-fact attitudes about minor accidents and injuries when these are handled matter-of-factly and pleasantly by a caregiver. They begin to learn that sleeping (or resting), eating, and elimination are somehow important as they observe the caregiver noting the occurrence of such activities.

These day-by-day happenings are the means by which our youngest citizens are taught the importance of health and good health care. These activities can also diminish any fears of health-related activities that children may have learned somewhere else. This learning can be "caught" by the parents also as they observe or participate in the center activities.

By providing health education in day care, even in infant-toddler day care, we will decrease the numbers of preschool and school-age children who develop preventable physical and mental health problems. There is no alternative to the conscious and continuous provision of health education in a child care center.

Medications

The policy statement on medications is complete, but needs emphasis. No medications can be given without the parents' consent or authorization. No medications means *no* medications—not aspirin, not cough syrup, not anything. Over-the-counter medications may be given by a designated staff member but *only* with the parents' permission. Prescription medications must be prescribed by a physician for a particular child at a particular time. They also must be accompanied by a written request and authorization by parent or guardian. All prescribed medications are either returned to the parents or destroyed (poured down the drain) at the end of the calendar week. New authorization from both the physician and the parents is required for the following week if the center staff are to resume giving the child medication.

Of course, all medications are to be kept locked up, out of children's reach, and away from food preparation or storage centers. Some medications require refrigeration and none are damaged by it. The staff nurse at the Early Childhood Education Center puts *all* medications in the refrigerator in her office and padlocks the door.

Continued screening and assessment

Any child may develop new health problems at any age. The American Academy of Pediatrics recommends that every child have a health evaluation through interview and examination at least at the following ages (Frankenburg and North, 1974, pp. 63-64):

3-7 days (usually at the time of hospital discharge)
2-6 weeks
2-4 months
5-7 months
8-10 months
11-14 months
17-19 months
21-25 months
3-4 years
5-6 years (usually at the time of school entry)
8-9 years
11-12 years
13-15 years
17-19 years (usually at the time of leaving high school)

If the above schedule is followed, a child would receive 10 health evaluations during the period from birth to 3 years of age. I suspect that few parents, especially those who do not have a pediatrician, arrange for these evaluations on their own initiative. The center's health coordinator can suggest and recommend but has neither the right nor the ability to force parents to follow the schedule. The center can only require the initial health evaluation and immunizations at the time of the child's admission and a statement from a physician for readmittance to the center after absence caused by some diseases.

The center's role in continuous screening goes beyond making suggestions and recommendations to parents. Of course, the health coordinator can weigh and measure, but it is the caregiver in daily contact with the children who can screen by observation during the normal activities. Most centers serving children below the age of 3 may not have access to the services of organizations or persons who periodically screen children for vision or hearing.

Vision. The prevalence of eye problems in infants and very young children is not known. Observable conditions such as unusual sensitivity to light, excessive tearing, inflammation, difficulty with focusing, or persistent deviation of one eye are causes for concern. A visit to an ophthalmologist should be recommended. Sometimes the caregiver is in a better position than the parents to question the child's ability to see because the caregiver spends many hours with the child and with other children of the same age. The child's failure to notice and pick up small objects at the age when he or she should be practicing newly achieved prehension skills is also cause for concern.

Hearing, language, speech. Even at 6 weeks of age, an infant will alert to a spoken word and will respond to vocalizations. If the baby is appropriately assessed, deafness can be picked up in the first few months by a pediatrician. By 6 to 9 months a baby with normal hearing will turn her head toward a soft, familiar sound. At 12 months she should understand simple direc-

tions (for instance to point to a familiar object), use jargon, and perhaps say one or two true words. If an infant's ability to perform any of the above is questionable, a recommendation for referral should be made. As in the case of possible vision problems, purposeful observation by the caregiver may uncover suspicions of possible hearing impairment that have not been noted by the parents. Sometimes deafness in children is not detected until after 2 years of age, which is extremely unfortunate. The optimal time for learning language is from birth to 3 years. The same age period is optimal for teaching children to communicate with alternative methods.

According to the Committee on Standards of Child Health Care (1977), the child with normal language-speech development should:

. . . babble by age 6 months; try to imitate simple words (echolalia); and say two to three meaningful, but distorted words by 12 months. At 24 months this child should: follow at least a one-stage verbal command without gesture cues (e.g., "pick up the block"); spontaneously name familiar objects or body parts; and say meaningful sentences of two or more words. By 3 or 4 years of age a child should be speaking in complete sentences of 4 to 5 words for social purposes (p. 12).

There may be some misarticulation of speech sounds and some sound or word repetition. Both of these occurrences frequently correct themselves—unless undue attention is paid them by well-meaning adults. The Communication Chart (newborn to 3 years) found in Appendix E gives more detailed information about the normal development of speech, language, and hearing.

Other developmental signposts. If the child does not play such games as peek-a-boo, patty-cake, or wave bye-bye by the age of 1; if the child does not imitate adults doing routine housekeeping chores by age 2 or 3; if the child does not enjoy playing alone with toys, pots and pans, sand, etc., by age 3—recommendation for referral is in order. If a child does not react to his own name when called by age 1; is unable to identify hair, eyes, ears, nose, and mouth by pointing to them by age 2; does not understand simple stories told or read by age 3—recommendation for referral is in order.

A trained, experienced caregiver can intuitively sense that something is amiss in the life of an infant or toddler, just as an experienced kindergarten teacher can correctly assess a 5-year-old's readiness to read without a standardized instrument. The educational and medical professions, however, rely on standardized assessment tools to validate their intuitions. This is as it should be. There is a need for a recognized technique for screening and assessment and for any subsequent diagnosis, remediation, and treatment procedures. A widely used screening procedure is the Denver Developmental Screening Test, which is valid as a screening tool up to age 6 if it is used as designed. It seems to be a better instrument for children under age 3 years. It does not yield a definitive evaluation, but it was not designed to do so.

If time and staff are available, it is desirable to screen all the children; if time and staff are at a premium, which is all too often the case, the children whose behavior or progress is questionable or abnormal should be evaluated with an instrument such as the Denver Developmental Screening Test. If the child is under 18 months, the Developmental Screening Inventory (Knobloch and Pasamanick, 1974) is recommended. If the caregiver's suspicions are substantiated, the child should be referred to the appropriate education agency (state, area, or local). The education agencies in many states have both personnel and funds, by virtue of PL 94-142, to evaluate the progress and development of children *below* the age of 3. They will plan and arrange the delivery of an appropriate program, if necessary, either in the child's home or in a group setting. Each community has an established process or local custom; it is the day care provider's responsibility to learn about the local referral system. If the area or local education agency deems it necessary, or if it is not authorized to work with children under the age of 3, the logical referral for suspected developmental disabilities is to a pediatrician in the community (Healy, 1980).

Comments. Caregivers must never forget that they are not trained to accurately screen, assess, or diagnose any developmental problem. These persons may also mistakenly suspect as a developmental problem traits in a child that are purely racial or cultural in nature. Children have been mistakenly labeled as developmentally disabled, and their future development and education have been negatively influenced by such a label. The role of the caregiver in any center or family day care is to *refer* a child about whom there may be questions. It is not to diagnose or label. However, the entire series of processes (screening, assessment, diagnosis, and treatment) must take place if the health program is to be effective. The suspicions of a caregiver may be the first step in this vital course of events.

MANAGEMENT OF CHILD WHO APPEARS ILL: INFECTIOUS DISEASES
Basic facts about infectious diseases

The common agents (causes) of infections in children and adults are bacteria, viruses, fungi, and parasites.

Common diseases caused by bacteria are strep throat, boils, urinary tract infections, conjunctivitis (pink eye), and certain pneumonias. Antibiotics are usually prescribed for bacteria-caused infections. Immunity to the serious diseases of whooping cough, diphtheria, and tetanus can be achieved by a series of triple shots beginning in early infancy.

Viruses, on the other hand, cause colds, "flu," and most of the common childhood infections such as chickenpox, measles (rubeola), german measles (rubella), mumps, and polio. Viruses are not inhibited by antibiotics. The most effective preventive measure is a vaccination that causes the body to build antibodies, which in turn fight off the virus. At the present time there are vaccines against measles, mumps, german measles, and poliomyelitis. This availability, however, does not ensure the immunization of many young children. The General Mills Family Report (1979) includes the following alarming information:

Almost one out of four adult members of minority families (compared to only 12% of all parents) believes that most childhood diseases have been conquered and that there's no need to immunize children against them. More than one out of four of all parents and 44% of minority group family members believe that it is the government's or the school's responsibility—rather than the parents'—to see that children are immunized (p. 51).

When young children are not immunized, tragedies result. When illnesses are contracted during the early years, they may be devastating. Measles may cause brain damage; mumps may lead to deafness. Diphtheria may cause heart and kidney damage. Polio may produce permanent paralysis or death. Pertussis-stimulated convulsions (whooping cough) may bring on brain damage. These tragedies can be prevented by appropriate immunization.

Ringworm of the scalp or body and athlete's foot (not usually found in very young children) are examples of common diseases caused by fungi. There are effective medications for them.

Parasites live on or in animals and humans. Pinworms and roundworms are common parasites in children living in warm or tropical climates. The problem of parasites as one of the causes of mal- or subnutrition was mentioned in Chapter 4.

Young children are especially vulnerable to certain infections because of their small size and anatomic relationships. There is only a short distance between locations in the body where infectious agents are normally found and are harmless, and the locations where these same agents cause disease. Young children are also especially vulnerable to certain infections because of their normal developmental behaviors. Children enjoy playing in the dirt, sand, or mud. They also frequently have a scrape or cut on their skin which allows easy entry of foreign substances. Young children mouth anything and everything and are seemingly oblivious to distinctions between edible and nonedible substances. Close contact with other children or adults in a group setting also increases the likelihood of infection, either internal or external.

Common infections in infant-toddler groups

Upper respiratory infections. Anyone in regular contact with very young children knows that upper respiratory tract infections are by far the most common illness. Complications include middle ear infections. Over 50% of all children experience infections of the middle ear. The most common disease in younger children is otitis media (inflammation of the middle ear). The inflammation may persist for several weeks to months, with fluid remaining in the middle ear space. If it is not treated, it can cause a loss of hearing. Because it is nearly impossible to tell if the infection is caused by a bacteria or a virus, all middle ear infections are treated by antibiotics.

Children under the age of 6 years have small, short, almost horizontal eustachian tubes, which are easily blocked by the swelling and secretions that accompany minor infections. Pizzo and Aronson (1976) suggest that feeding position may be a factor in middle ear disease:

Breast fed infants are normally held in an inclined position in which the child's ear and eustachian tube opening are slightly elevated above the mouth and throat. With bottle feeding in the hands of a person unaware of the problem, and almost inevitably with bottle propping and self-bottle feeding in bed, the child is placed on his back, which favors the entry of liquid and/or the secretions from the nasopharynx through the eustachian tube into the middle ear. Since the secretions of the nasopharynx normally contain some bacteria and viruses which are not welcome visitors to the middle ear, the potential for middle ear problems is greatly increased. (p. 62)

Because of the possible serious results of an upper respiratory or middle ear infection, parents should be advised to seek their pediatrician's (not their pharmacist's) advice for treatment.

Gastrointestinal infections. Also quite frequent in an infant-toddler group setting are gastrointestinal infections, accompanied by diarrhea and/or vomiting. This disease is no doubt the most distasteful illness to be encountered in a child care center. There is no specific treatment other than increasing the intake of clear liquids and decreasing or eliminating the intake of milk and solid foods (biekost). The infection is transmitted by personal contact. Thorough hand-washing and careful disposal of infected materials are essential. If the condition persists for more than 2 days, if there is a high fever (+102°), or extreme loss of fluids, a physician should be called. It can be an emergency situation.

Common rashes. According to the staff nurse at the Early Childhood Education Center, rashes of various kinds are the third most frequent health problem in the infant-toddler group. Rashes have a variety of causes, ranging from chemicals used at home or in the center, to wearing apparel, to medicines, plants, and some foods. Heat and fungi are also agents. A rash may also indicate any of a long list of illnesses such as measles, chicken pox, and scarlet fever. If a rash covers most of the body, the cause is probably internal, either an infectious disease or an allergy.

If the rash is localized, the cause is usually direct contact with an irritating substance. Rashes appear frequently on the infant and toddler, whose skin is more tender and sensitive than an adult's. They are usually transitory when caused by an external agent and if treated appropriately. Most localized rashes are accompanied by discomfort and itching but leave no permanent scars. Of course, scratching increases the likelihood of infection, which in turn may cause scarring.

Heat rash and *diaper rash* are most usually found in very young children. Although they are not communicable, they increase the chance for skin infections and should be treated promptly. Because diaper rash seems to be always a problem, the following care procedure is included.

1. Change the diapers as soon as baby wets or soils. If a baby's bottom is extremely sore, he will cry or fuss when he needs changing, because the urine and stool will sting and hurt. (Ideally, a baby is always changed when needed. If caregivers are conscientious about checking at regular intervals, this ideal can almost be met.)
2. Clean genital area and buttocks twice daily with a hexachlorophene soap (Zest or Dial) and dry thoroughly before rediapering.
3. If ointment or cream has been ordered by the nurse or doctor, apply after the buttocks have been washed and thoroughly dried. Powder is never recommended because of the possibility of inhalation.
4. Expose the buttocks to the air two or three times during the day by removing the diaper completely for 20 to 30 minutes. On warm sunny days the baby can be taken outside undiapered.
5. In case of a severe rash, remove plastic pants during the daytime (two or three diapers folded together will help prevent too much "leak").
6. If nondisposable diapers are used (a real nuisance in a child care center), presoak them for at least 30 minutes before washing in 1 gallon of water and ½ cup of vinegar. Wash them only with soap, not a detergent.

7. A pediatrician should be contacted if the urine has a foul odor, is dark colored or bloody, or if the amount is small when fluid intake is good.

Impetigo is highly communicable, either by direct contact or when skin abrasions or insect bites are present. Hot, humid weather encourages outbreaks of impetigo. Children with impetigo need not be isolated or kept from the center, but there should be an increased emphasis on personal cleanliness and hygiene. The infected children should be referred to a health professional.

Parasites. Infections caused by parasites are wicked! Not only do they cause extreme discomfort for the infected child, but their appearance seems to create a sense of revulsion that is psychologically damaging to the child. Also, parasites are not particular. They appear in elite private centers as well as in publicly supported centers.

Severe itching of the scalp frequently indicates head lice (pediculosis). Small white particles (the eggs) are attached to the hair shaft, usually close to the scalp and behind the ears. The particles may look like dandruff; the lice themselves are dark brown. Personal hygiene, including the thorough cleaning of combs, brushes, clothing, and bedding, is a must, but is not sufficient. Reinfestation or transmittal to anyone who comes into close physical contact with the affected child may occur easily. Head lice are not as dangerous as strep throat, but they are just as contagious. They reached epidemic status in the 1980s. Infected children may be readmitted to the center after application of an insecticide prescribed by a physician.

The most common skin disease is probably scabies caused by small mites that burrow underneath the skin. This results in red bumps and severe itching. Again, personal hygiene, as well as thorough washing or even boiling of clothing, bedding, and towels is essential. The child with suspected scabies or head lice should be referred for treatment.

Ringworm of the scalp or body is a fungal infection and results in a raised reddened circle on the skin. It is transmitted through personal contact, and is communicable as long as the fungi are present. Ringworm on the scalp results in small circular patches, sometimes associated with an area of baldness. The hair becomes dull, brittle, and breaks near the root. Wearing a protective cap and taking a prescribed oral medicine usually result in healing, and the child so treated need not be isolated. Again, it is essential to practice personal hygiene to avoid infecting others. Ringworm in places other than the scalp shows up as flat, circular lesions with raised edges. It necessitates thorough bathing with soap and water with removal of the scabs and crusts. A physician should prescribe ointment or oral medication. Children infected with ringworm may attend the center if they are under a physician's care.

Comments. In no way should the above list of infections be considered all inclusive. Geographic location, living conditions, community sanitation, and home and center practices all influence both the incidence and the spread of infectious diseases. Selection of the problems described was based on personal experience and on recommendations of nurses and others involved in infant-toddler day care. It is hoped that none of the readers of this text will repeat my embarrassing mistake when I saw my first case of ringworm on the neck of a young boy. I assumed that the red oval was the result of a human bite!

Much of the information about infectious diseases was adapted from the Report of the Committee on Infectious Diseases (Steigman, 1977), a copy of which should be in every child care center or home. It presents the current position of the American Academy of Pediatrics.

Expert opinion and research findings

Reliable data about the incidence of infections in day care centers and homes are minimal. The best known research studies have been at the

Frank Porter Graham Center in Chapel Hill, North Carolina, under the leadership of Drs. Loda, Glezen, Clyde, and Collier. Essentially, they found no difference in the incidence of respiratory illness among day care children aged 1 month to 5 years compared to a similar population of children who did not attend day care. There was one exception to this conclusion: Day care infants up to 12 months of age averaged one more respiratory illness per year compared to infants who did not attend a day care. In their summary statement about the Frank Porter Graham research studies, Pizzo and Aronson (1976) state:

> They further demonstrated that with adequate staffing and staff education about care of children, ill children could be cared for in a day care setting without increasing the risk of serious infections. Their center routinely permitted ill children to attend but the children received total health care from the center staff. These results must be interpreted in light of the large amount of health professional consultation available at the center. . . . A review of the health policies used by the Frank Porter Graham staff reveals a high level of consciousness about control of cross-infection, use of sanitation measures and the importance of adequate indoor and outdoor space for each child. The latter is presumed to be related to the concentration of contaminants in the environment (p. 67).

The above findings have been too hastily generalized to all day care centers. The only correct conclusion is that it is possible to maintain a "normal" incidence of infectious diseases under *optimal* conditions. We have many unpublished reports of outbreaks of serious infections in other day care centers.

Children in the under-3 age group are particularly vulnerable, and should not be in a group care situation unless its staff is committed to the practice of the best of the current knowledge about health and safety. Dr. Ann DeHuff Peters, a day care medical consultant, suggests the following important elements in any program of infectious disease control:

1. Personal hygiene of the adults, such as careful handwashing;
2. Environmental control, including proper sewage disposal, care in handling diapers and other contaminated clothing or bedding, proper cleansing of eating utensils, etc.; and
3. Above all, the elements of sound health education for parents, staff and children (cited in Pizzo and Aronso, 1976, p. 69).

She also states, "We need to have an informed staff in each day care program, a source of sound medical consultation, and liberal employment policies to allow adult staff with the 'trots' to be off duty" (p. 69).

MANAGEMENT OF A CHILD WHO APPEARS ILL: RECOMMENDED PRACTICES
Clues to the possibility of illness

The lack of expressive verbal language does not limit the infant's ability to tell us she is sick. Changes in usual behavior, loss of appetite, fever, vomiting or diarrhea, all indicate that something is wrong. If a nonverbal child hurts, his behavior will tell us so. If he has a sore throat, he may drool more than usual and may breathe through his mouth. If a child has an earache, she may pull on the ear or hold her head to one side. A child with his legs pulled up toward the chest and clenched fists may have a tummyache. If an arm or leg hurts, the child may hold the arm or may limp. Remember however, that behaviors that may be symptoms of illness in one child may be normal in another. Donna Schmidt, staff nurse in the infant-toddler center at the University of Iowa, describes illness symptoms as follows:

> One or more of the following findings in a particular child might make a caregiver suspect an illness is present or impending. Some of these findings are very serious and need to be reported to parents at once. Other findings need to be reported, but whether or not they are reported before the parents come to pick up the child depends upon the severity of the findings and how they affect the child's total day.

General appearance

1. Eyes dull and lack-luster
2. Eyes watery or swollen
3. The eyes or lids pink or red
4. Discharge from eyes
5. Breathing heavy, labored, or wheezing
6. Offensive breath odor
7. Skin color pale or bluish
8. Skin red or flushed
9. Lips and nailbeds bluish color
10. Rash or sunburn present
11. Skin hot to the touch
12. Profuse perspiration when others find the room temperature comfortable
13. Limping
14. Refusal to use some part of the body
15. Swollen areas, bumps, lumps, or red spots on head, body, or extremities

Behavior

1. Unusual irritability; has trouble getting along with others
2. Increased activity or unusual lethargy
3. Sleep disturbance; interrupted or restless sleep; inability to sleep
4. Extreme fatigue with or without excessive amount of sleeping
5. Unusual amount of crying, fussing, or whining
6. Seems to get hurt more often than usual; falls easily; bumps into things
7. Clings to parent or caregiver
8. Drinks an unusual amount of liquids

Gastrointestinal

1. Vomiting/diarrhea
2. Poor or picky appetite or refusal to take food or bottle
3. Complaints of pain in abdomen
4. Intermittent loud crying with knees drawn up to abdomen (infants)
5. Blood in stool
6. Dark black tarry stools

Upper respiratory

1. Fever
2. Persistent sneezing
3. Runny nose, crusting discharge or bleeding from nose
4. Coughing
5. Drainage from ears
6. Difficult or labored breathing
7. Difficulty in staying asleep because of obstructed breathing or cough
8. Rubbing or pulling ears
9. Turning head from side to side when lying down
10. Crying while trying to suck bottle
11. Difficulty in swallowing
12. Refusal of juice when child usually would like it

Genitourinary

1. Increased frequency of urination, sometimes with little urine volume
2. Complaint of pain with urination
3. Blood in urine
4. Vaginal discharge
5. Redness, irritation, or discharge in the area of the foreskin of the penis

Central nervous system

1. Convulsions or seizures
2. Blackouts or loss of consciousness
3. Unequal strength on the two sides of the body
4. Projectile vomiting

Dental

1. Teeth emerging in other than usual area
2. Teeth turning dark
3. Refusal to nurse by infant, even though the child acts hungry until he/she starts sucking

It is important to report these findings to parents so that they can relate the symptoms to their pediatrician, thereby helping in making a quick and accurate diagnosis.

Management of ill children

If an adult does not feel well, what does he want? Peace and quiet, and perhaps a caring person to hold his hand, place a damp cloth on his fevered brow, and offer him a cool drink of water. Infants and toddlers have the same desires when they do not feel well. They want peace and quiet, so we provide them with such a spot, away from the stimulation of their peers. They may want to sleep, so we provide a crib in a quiet spot. They may be alert enough to want to play, so we give them a toy or two or a favorite stuffed animal. They may want to be left alone, although I suspect the quiet presence of a caring person provides security and comfort.

All cases of suspected illness should be reported to the parents. Examples of signs and symptoms necessitating a recommendation for referral to a pediatrician include: fever or chills, stuffy or running nose in combination with other symptoms, inflamed or itching eyes, enlarged cervical nodes or neck glands, frequent and persistent cough, difficulty in swallowing, chest pain, abdominal pain, change in rate and character of respiration, blood in stool or urine, or if the child just seems very sick.

Even when some of these signs are present, many caregivers feel themselves competent to care for the child at the center until the end of the day, and do not wish to "bother" the parent at work. But it is considerably more bother if the parent has to contact the pediatrician after office hours. It also is more expensive. If the child's symptoms or behaviors warrant a pediatrician's advice, by all means notify the parent as soon as possible, so that arrangements can be made. This practice seems to be a comparatively minor consideration, but it is an example of a true partnership between center and home.

Meanwhile, the child should be made as comfortable as possible, and no doubt should have his temperature taken. An infant's temperature is easily taken rectally without much fuss. It is difficult (impossible!) to get an accurate reading from a toddler with an oral thermometer, and the well-advertised fever strips have proved unreliable. One suggestion is to hold the child on your lap and look at a book together. With an arm around the child in a friendly hug, the thermometer can be held under the child's arm with no problem.

If for some reason (such as an infected hangnail) the child needs to soak her hand in a water based solution, turn the treatment into an episode of water play by supplying a few pouring utensils.

If a bottle-fed infant needs a liquid medication, give the baby an empty nipple to suck on, then pour the medicine through the nipple. The medication is swallowed almost before it can be tasted.

By using such approaches to health care, the child's experience is nonthreatening and even pleasant at times. Such procedures will help dissipate any anxiety about doctors and nurses.

Guidelines for calling the physician about a child's health and procedures for selected emergencies are presented on p. 122.

It is difficult to set strict criteria regarding when a child is too ill to be in the center. Both Keister (1970) and Collier (1976) maintain that the child may be kept at the center all day if no emergency exists and if appropriate accommodations and surveillance are available. It is the accepted opinion, however, that children as well as adults are more comfortable at home when they are not feeling well. Most day care children do not have this option.

It is advisable for each center to have a specific policy about restrictions of attendance in case of illness. In general, a contagious disease (not a common cold), a fever of 102° F rectally or 101° orally, or vomiting and diarrhea due to illness are sufficient causes for a child to be restricted from coming to the center.

ACCIDENTS AND EMERGENCIES

Accidents will happen in the best of day care centers, day care homes, or family homes. Therefore, even though all reasonable measures are taken to prevent accidents, it is important that each staff member be proficient in at least two basic first aid practices: how to control bleeding, and how to use artificial respiration. Each staff member should also know sources of emergency help and how to use the items in the first aid kit.

First aid should be administered by the staff

SUGGESTED GUIDELINES FOR TELEPHONE USAGE AND HANDLING EMERGENCIES*

Nonemergency calls are handled most easily during the regular workday hours. Emergency care is available around the clock. If the receptionist promises a return call at a certain time and you are not called, do not hesitate to call again.

WHEN DO YOU PHONE?

1. When the child is acting sick—even though the signs and symptoms are vague.
2. If you are concerned by the way the child is acting, even if you can't explain why.

WHEN YOU TELEPHONE

When you telephone the doctor, usually a receptionist-secretary will receive your call. Be prepared to give:
1. Your name
2. Your telephone number
3. The patient's name and age
4. Your main concerns
5. If you believe the problem is an emergency, *say so!!*
   A pediatric nurse practitioner, a doctor or a nurse may return your call. In any case, have a pencil and paper ready and write down the instructions you receive.
When you telephone about an illness, be prepared to tell:
1. The patient's temperature
2. When did the patient become ill?
3. Symptoms such as:
   a. Vomiting and/or diarrhea—frequency of each in a given time period
   b. Urination—the last time
   c. Other—such as headache, sore throat, nasal congestion, cough, difficulty breathing, irritability
   d. General appearances of the patient
   e. Any change from usual feeding pattern, particularly in infants
4. What treatment has been given?
5. Telephone number of your pharmacist
When you telephone about matters other than an illness, it will save time if you tell the receptionist the reason for your call so that the physician may have available when he calls back your account, laboratory results, names of physicians in other cities, etc.

IMMEDIATE CARE OF EMERGENCIES
Poisonings

In case of poisoning
1. Identify the product, if you can

2. Estimate the maximum amount you think might have been ingested
3. Estimate the time of ingestion
4. Give any symptoms or unusual behavior
5. If you are unable to reach [the physician's] office promptly, phone without delay the Poison Information Center _____
6. Have *syrup of ipecac* available
   a. A small sealed bottle should be in every home where there are children in the one- to five-year-old age group. It may be obtained at any pharmacy without prescription.

Accidents
Laceration or "cut"

1. Apply direct pressure, then phone and report the problem
   a. Does it continue to bleed without pressure application?
   b. Does it gape open?

Burns

1. Immerse the part or apply cold water to area
2. Do not apply any salves, creams, butter, cooking oils to burn area
3. Report the extent of the injury
4. Wrap burn area in any clean sheeting or cloth, before transporting the patient to medical facility

Head injury

Many children fall and strike their heads. The injured, but not unconscious, patient cries out immediately following the injury and may vomit a few times. In such instances it is important to:
1. Permit the child to rest or even sleep
2. Observe the child closely, especially the color and breathing
3. *Do not* insist the patient remain awake

Two important do not's

1. *Do not* insist the patient remain awake
2. *Do not* move the patient to a medical facility prior to obtaining medical advice

Phone immediately for advice about the unconscious patient who neither cries out nor stirs following the injury.

*From American Academy of Pediatrics: Standards of child health care, ed. 3, Evanston, Ill., 1977. Copyright American Academy of Pediatrics, 1977.

whenever necessary, and a written report of the accident and the treatment should be shown to the parents when they pick up their child. For serious accidents that may need suturing, parents should be called at once. The responsibility of getting further treatment for their child is the parents'. A few emergency rules are included in outline on p. 122.

If the center is large, a staff member should assume the role of safety coordinator. In smaller centers, the health coordinator may assume this additional responsibility. The safety coordinator should periodically inspect the premises, both indoors and out, develop and maintain posted procedures for emergency situations, and maintain a high quality first aid kit.

According to the staff nurse at the infant-toddler center at the University of Iowa, the essentials for first aid or health maintenance for children under 3 years of age are:

1. First aid manual
2. American Academy of Pediatrics First Aid Chart and First Aid Treatment for Poisoning Chart
3. Towels and soap
4. Liquid soap
5. Covered waste receptacle
6. Isopropyl alcohol
7. Flashlight
8. Bandage scissors
9. Splinter forceps or tweezers
10. Nail clippers
11. Thermometers and storage containers
12. Sterile dressings, 2 × 2 and 3 × 3
13. Band-Aids
14. Roller bandages
15. Adhesive tape
16. Cotton balls
17. Cotton-tip applicators
18. A place where medications can be kept under lock and key. If medicine needs to be refrigerated and must be stored where food is kept, it should be in a locked storage box in the refrigerator.
19. Some kind of accurate measuring device for medications, such as a syringe, a calibrated measuring tube, or commercial medication spoon
20. Ipecac syrup

Some explanations and instructions will be needed before the items are used by a non-health caregiver.

A well-supplied first aid kit is used by center personnel for minor injuries, cuts, bruises, and easily accessible foreign bodies in the eyes. In the case of a serious medical emergency, no time should be wasted in trying to locate the parents. The first action is to request emergency transportation. The second action is to call the hospital or other treatment facility to alert it to the nature of the emergency and to ask for advice. Only then, or after the child is receiving treatment, should the parents be notified. The plan indicating the emergency procedures should be explained to the center staff and parents and should be posted in a prominent location.

Certain severe emergencies (including internal poisoning, skin or eye contact with corrosives, or neck or back injuries) require the immediate intervention of someone trained in first aid or emergency medical care. Necessary lifesaving measures should be applied, and then the child should be transported promptly as described above.

Fortunately, most accidents do not require such prompt action to save life or limb. Emergencies such as dislocation and fractures, large lacerations, animal bites, burns, seizures, eye injuries, and acute high fevers can usually be handled temporarily by any responsible person who can make the child comfortable. The pediatrician or clinic should be called for advice. If contacts with health personnel or parents are delayed, the child should be transported directly to a source of medical care. In any one of the following situations a child may be given medical care without prior parental approval: (1)

when the child needs immediate treatment and the parents or guardian cannot be contacted with reasonable diligence; (2) when any effort to secure approval would delay the treatment long enough to endanger the child's life or seriously worsen the condition, and (3) when the parents have refused permission, but the delay in securing a court order would have serious consequences for the child. A second physician's opinion is usually necessary in this last circumstance. This is the so-called emergency treatment rule. It is nationally recognized, and it applies to all minors, not just those in day care. Ideally, there will be a parent consent form on file for every child in the day care center. An additional consent form for transport of the child for emergency medical treatment would be helpful.

EMPLOYEE HEALTH

Health standards for day care center personnel are established and maintained by the responsible state agency, usually the department of social services. This same state agency or its local office can provide information to each day care center about the availability of child health services in the community and about how the services may be obtained.

The recommendation for staff health standards in the documents submitted during the Federal Interagency Day Care Requirements appropriateness hearings reads as follows.

- All members of the staff of the day care facility shall have a health examination within three months prior to employment and annually thereafter. The report, dated and signed by a licensed physician, shall be on file in the facility.
  a. Within three months prior to employment each staff member shall have a tuberculin test or chest x-ray. Such test shall be repeated bi-annually.
  b. There shall be an annual review and report of the health status of each staff member certified by a licensed physician to include presence or

absence of chronic disease, respiratory or skin infections of childhood.
- Staff members shall be excluded from the day care facility when ill. Persons with contagious diseases such as mononucleosis, [hepatitis], and streptococcal and staphylococcal infections shall have a physician's release before returning to work.
  a. No person with a health history of typhoid, paratyphoid, dysentary or other serious diarrheal diseases shall reside or work in a day care facility until it is definitely determined by appropriate tests that such a person is not a carrier of these diseases.
- Volunteers, persons who agree to give regular or occasional time to work with children in a day care facility, shall be subject to the same health regulations as are applicable to paid staff members. (Pizzo and Aronson, 1976, p. 1974).

I suspect that many day care centers and homes have less stringent health requirements for their staff members. Compliance with the standards as listed is a small price to pay for the maintenance of a young child's well-being. It is recognized that the child's health is the parents' responsibility. When a center or home cares for a child for a significant amount of time each day, it must assume part of this responsibility. The center's health policy involves the center in the maintenance of good health and extends its concerns to the care of children during illness and convalescence.

■ CHAPTER SUMMARY ■

The care and protection curriculum of a group care center or home for children under 3 years of age is as important as the developmental or educational curriculum. Indeed, if young children are not well cared for or protected from the consequences of their natural developmental behaviors and external conditions, there would be few children for whom to plan a developmental program.

Health goals for day care children are directed toward the present and future functioning of young children. They are realized by identifying all existing health problems and assisting in the correction of these problems. They are also realized by providing preventive services, improving the health of all members of the child's family, and by improving the health of the community in which the child lives. Although the family bears the primary responsibility for the health of their children, the day care center or home plays an important helping role in meeting this responsibility.

In order to achieve this helping role, a health policy must be designed by professional health persons, day care staff representatives, and parent representatives. The day care center itself implements the policy. Implementation is initiated by enforcing enrollment/admission requirements, and continued compliance with immunizations at the recommended ages after admission. The on-going provision of a safe and health-promoting environment is a must. A staff knowledgeable about health and safety precautions and about appropriate actions in case of illness or emergency is also a must. Basic facts about infectious diseases, immunizations, symptoms indicating a health disorder, and guidelines for handling illness and emergencies were presented in some detail. Unfortunately, much of the existing knowledge is not put into practice in many day care centers. All too frequently the following conditions are found:

1. Poisons and medicines stored in places accessible to children
2. Broken glass; rusted, broken, and insecure playground equipment
3. Traffic hazards in the play area
4. Nonworking fire extinguishers
5. No planned source of emergency medical care
6. No "panic" hardware on outside doors
7. Hot water temperature over 120° F (scalding)
8. Walls with lead-based paint
9. No fire-resistive drapes or blankets
10. No insurance on center transportation
11. Unsuitable (or no) restraints or seat belts in transporting vehicles

There is a widespread noncompliance with current health and safety standards. All of us, caregivers, teachers, parents, and other adults, should begin to realize the importance of health and safety standards. We need a consciousness-awareness experience. Perhaps the following position statement will increase our recognition of the important stakes.

If the wiping of runny noses is seen as a menial activity which nearly any person can perform, that activity can be delegated to the least-educated member of a care-giving staff. Very little attention will be paid to how nose wiping activity is carried out. It's quite likely that the nose will be wiped with a handkerchief, which is then put back in the caregiver's pocket (with no caregiver handwashing) and/or immediately used to wipe the next child's runny nose, thereby transmitting high doses of infectious agents from one child to the other. The wiping of runny noses doesn't have to be viewed as a "custodial" act. Instead it can be seen as an important public health measure, one which when done with an awareness of causes and control of infectious disease, can make a contribution to the reduction of disease in a community and to the prevention of the spread of viral and bacterial disease among the day care program's children. This preventive measure has implications for promoting the child's total development, since symptomatic viral and bacterial diseases may have negative implications for the total child. (Pizzo and Aronson, 1976, pp. 16-17)

All parents want the best for their children. Every parent experiences heartbreak when her baby is not doing well. But too many parents will not take the initiative to go to a pediatrician, a developmental clinic, or a mental health clinic.

Parents of very young children in day care trust the caregivers and confide in them because both caregivers and parents care about the child. Persons in child care have a unique opportunity in helping parents fulfill their hopes for their children. Caregivers are not alone in this endeavor. There is a large interdisciplinary group of well-educated persons who are continually working to improve the quality of life for children and their families. We in child care can form the bridge between these experts and the parents of "our" children.

SUGGESTED ACTIVITIES/POINTS TO PONDER

1. Which of the national goals for child health could be (or are) included in the goals for infant-toddler day care? Select one and describe appropriate steps that a day care staff can put into practice in order to help meet this goal.
2. Compile a comprehensive list of caregiver behaviors that positively influence the health of infants and toddlers in a child care center.
3. List the information you would use in responding to a parent who thinks immunizations are a waste of time and money.

REFERENCES AND SUGGESTED READINGS

Administration for Children, Youth, and Families: A tale of shots and drops, Washington, D.C., 1979, U.S. Government Printing Office.

American Academy of Pediatrics: An agenda for America's children, Evanston, Ill., 1980, the Academy.

American Academy of Pediatrics: Government activities report, July 1981, pp. 1-4.

Aronson, S.S., and Aiken, L.S.: Compliance of child care programs with health and safety standards: impact of program evaluation and advocate training, Pediatrics 65(2):318-325, 1980.

Cardio-pulmonary resuscitation, Washington, D.C., 1981, American Red Cross.

Clinical infant intervention research programs: selected overview and discussion, DHEW Pub. No. (ADM) 79-748, Washington, D.C., 1979, U.S. Government Printing Office.

Collier, A.: Infections in day care. Supporting document for Pizzo, P. and Aronson, S.S.: Health and safety issues in day care. Paper prepared for HEW as a portion of the study of the appropriateness of the Federal Interagency Day Care Requirement, Sept. 1976. (Mimeographed.)

Collier, A., and Ramey, C.T.: The health of infants in day care, Voice 9(1):7-11, Jan./Feb. 1976.

Committee on Infant and Preschool Child: Recommendations for day care centers for infants and children, Evanston, Ill., 1980, American Academy of Pediatrics.

Committee on Standards of Child Health Care: Standards of child health care, ed 3, Evanston, Ill., 1977, American Academy of Pediatrics.

DHEW, Office of the Secretary: HEW Day Care Regulations, Federal Register, March 19, 1980.

DHHS, Office of the Secretary: Day care regulations, Federal Register, July 17, 1981.

Frankenburg, W.K., and North, A.F.: A guide to screening for the Early and Periodic Screening, Diagnosis and Treatment Program (EPSDT) under Medicaid, Washington, D.C., 1974, U.S. Government Printing Office.

General Mills American family report 1978–79, Family health in an era of stress, Mineapolis, Minn., 1979, General Mills, Inc.

Granger, R.H.: Your child from one to six, DHEW Pub. No. (OHDS) 77-30026, Washington, D.C., 1977, U.S. Government Printing Office.

Healthy people: Surgeon General's report on health promotion and disease prevention, DHEW Pub. No. (PHS) 79-55071, Washington, D.C., 1979, U.S. Government Printing Office.

Healy, A.: Personal Communications, 1980.

Kagan, J.: The growth of the child, New York, 1979, W.W. Norton & Co.

Kagan, J., Kearsley, R.B., and Zelazo, P.R.: Infancy: its place in human development, Cambridge, Mass., 1978, Harvard University Press.

Keister, M.E.: "The good life" for infants and toddlers, Washington, D.C., 1970, National Association for the Education of Young Children.

Knobloch, H., and Pasamanick, B.: Gesell and Amatruda's developmental diagnosis, ed 3, Hagerstown, Md., 1974, Harper & Row, Publishers.

Loda, F.: The health of children in group day care. In Elardo, R., and Pagan, B., editor: Perspectives on infant day care, ed 2, Little Rock, Ark., 1976, Southern Association on Children Under Six.

Loda, F.: Sound health practices for day care infants. In Elardo, R., and Pagan, B., editors: Perspectives on infant day care, ed. 2, Little Rock, Ark., 1976, South Association on Children Under Six.

McCall, R.: Infants, Cambridge, Mass., 1979, Harvard University Press.

Nichols, B.: Remarks to the National Commission of the International Year of the Child, Feb. 8, 1979. (Transcript.)

North, A.F., Jr.: Day care 6 Health services, Washington, D.C., 1973, U.S. Government Printing Office.

Osofsky, J., editor: Handbook of infant development, New York, 1979, John Wiley & Sons.

Pizzo, P., and Aronson, S: Health and safety issues in day care. Paper prepared for HEW as a portion of the study of the appropriateness of the Federal Interagency Day Care Requirements, Sept. 1976. (Mimeograph.)

Report to the President, U.S. National Commission of the International Year of the Child, Washington, D.C., 1980, U.S. Government Printing Office.

Richmond, J.B., and Janis, J.: A perspective on primary prevention in the earliest years, Children Today 9(3):2-6, 1980.

Schmidt, D., Personal communication, 1980.

Standard first aid and personnel safety manual ed 2, Washington, D.C., 1979, American Red Cross.

Steigman, A.J.: Report of the Committee on Infectious Diseases, ed 18, Evanston, Ill., 1977, American Academy of Pediatrics.

Thomas, A., and Chess, S.: Temperament and development, New York, 1977, Brunner/Mazel.

Willis, A., and Ricciuti, H.: A good beginning for babies, Washington, D.C., 1975, National Association for the Education of Young Children.

SECTION THREE

The developmental-educational curriculum

The preceding chapters focused on the care and protection of very young children. It should be evident that it is impossible to completely isolate care and protection from growth, development, and learning. Even the use of safety devices in an automobile has an inherent learning: someone cares about me. It is also impossible to separate growth, development, and learning from the physical and social environment, particularly from the caring and teaching activities of the significant persons in the child's environment. At no other age will the incidental and planned curriculum be so all-inclusive. The care and education of very young children is based on the concept of the total child. The delivery of such a program cannot be achieved by spending a few minutes to provide health care without also using that time for language development and perceptual discrimination. The times allotted to feeding an infant are ideal for establishing social interactions and enhancing visual and auditory discrimination, as well as teaching trust and warmth in the physical and human environment. This totality will become even more apparent in the following chapters. Components of the developmental-educational curriculum have been presented as areas of emphasis only as a way of organizing the text. They should never be considered or put into practice as entities in themselves. The cognitive, physical, social, and emotional components of early child care and education are interdependent.

Learning starts at birth and continues over the life span. Some psychologists claim that the first 2 or 3 years of life are the most important years for learning. The validity of this statement is difficult, perhaps even impossible, to prove. The more accepted opinion is that each period of life is very important and that appropriate experiences in each period of life result in a great amount of learning. The learning accomplished at each stage is very dependent upon the learnings of the preceding stage. The goal of very early education is to maximize the learnings appropriate for the developmental age, thus laying the groundwork for future learnings.

You perhaps remember Topsy in *Uncle Tom's Cabin.* Topsy "just growed," and did a remarkable job of it. However, "just growing" is not enough. There may be moments in a "quality" infant-toddler center when it appears that the children are just growing. Perhaps this is the case during naptime. During the awake times, the influence, guidance, and teaching of the adults and the environment should be readily apparent to even the casual observer. The parents, caregivers, and teachers who are responsible for very new human beings do not start from point zero.

The normal newborn is equipped with three essential tools for learning: (1) the five historic senses, (2) movement as a perceptual activity and an aid to sensory perception, and (3) innate curiosity. A fourth essential tool is the presence of at least one responsible and responsive adult. Chapter 6 deals with these essential learning tools and includes implications for selected learning and teaching activities as well as methods.

Chapter 7 includes issues in goal-setting and a suggested list of goals for the developmental-educational curriculum; issues related to motivation and stimulation; and learning and teaching activities in the perceptuomotor and representational domains. The learning modes highlighted are: exploration with objects, action and interaction, and imitation and participation.

Chapter 8 focuses on the learnings and teachings in the personal, social, and communication components of the curriculum. Incorporated in the presentation of the personal-social components are recommendations for group management and discipline.

Chapter 9 contains the learnings and teachings designed to maximize the motor development expected during the first 3 years. Exercises and activities are suggested for development and coordination of gross and fine motor skills. Play is presented as the teaching technique for the infant-toddler years. Attention is given to the learning and teaching of self-help skills: independent dressing, grooming, eating, and toileting.

The information presented in Section Three is interdependent in spite of its arbitrary separation into chapters.

CHAPTER 6

THE TOOLS FOR LEARNING

I heard is good; I saw is better.

Chinese proverb

Current research findings are beginning to suggest that the newborn is programmed to learn from the very moment of birth, although existing assessment techniques are too insensitive to lead to a definitive statement to this effect. Part of the problem, of course, is the presence of individual differences in effort, activity, and alertness, which are observable very shortly after birth. These differences are indications of the infant's uniqueness. In addition, these differences are also related to the responses the baby receives from persons in the environment.

In spite of these individual differences, every full-term, normal infant is equipped with three essential tools for learning. These are the five historic senses, the ability to move, and an innate curiosity.

The fourth essential "tool" for a baby's learning is a nurturing caregiver. It is this person's responsibility to serve as mediator between the infant and the world. In other words, the caregiver is also a teacher.

There is an inherent danger in assigning the label "teacher" to an adult who is responsible for a very young child. Traditionally, teaching has been defined as transmitting facts and knowledge. It is this misinterpretation of teaching when applied to very young children that has led to the vast number of stimulation programs and "how-to-teach-baby" books that are readily available in super markets, discount stores, and bookstores. In many cases these are "cookbooks" containing an assortment of "recipes" for

things to do to (and with) baby. The activities are presented as single activities. Their objectives are to develop the child's skill or pleasure in that particular activity. The knowledgeable caregiver/teacher selects specific activities for the purpose of enhancing basic fundamental skills and uses them in a sequence. In other words, the activities are not chosen for themselves, but for what baby can learn from them. The sequence should be determined by the baby's activities, apparent interests, and developmental level.

There is little that is new or different in the learning activities and experiences that are incorporated in the following suggestions. When we see a baby, we naturally think of pat-a-cake and peek-a-boo. These games are important in the educational curriculum. These and other activities are designed to follow one another with increasing complexity. Each one is dependent upon the learning derived from the previous one. Both the curriculum and the child's learning can be visualized as an inverted pyramid, expanding up and out.

SENSATION, PERCEPTION, AND THOUGHT

All learning has its groundwork laid in early sensory development and perception. The child is born with receptor organs, which initially introduce information about the sights, sounds, and tastes of the immediate world. The child is also born with motor equipment that soon enables him to focus visually and to turn his head toward the location of an unseen source of sound. Gradually hands follow the eyes, and the impressions from the visual and auditory modalities are enlarged with tactual information. These impressions are mentally organized and stored. Piaget called them sensorimotor schemata. As the child encounters new impressions, the schemata are revised and enlarged to incorporate the new information.

Sensory reception is the term used to describe the mechanical intake of a stimulus. It depends on the completeness of the structures of the sensory organs—eyes, ears, nose, mouth, and skin. These organs are activated by external objects or events. This activation is called sensation, and it requires present stimulation. It does not require previous learning or experience. The newborn receives sensations, or sensory stimulation, from the moment of birth. There are even indications of sensations being received in utero.

Perception is a meaningful experience initiated by sensory stimulation. What one perceives is determined not only by the impression, but also by one's background experience, which provides possible meanings. Very young children have a need to find out, explore, and investigate. At first they "reason" only by doing things and discovering what happens. In this way they build their own background of experience. As a result of these encounters, and guided by a knowledgeable teacher, children internalize the stability and invariance of many aspects of the immediate environment.

An example will illustrate the difference between sensation (reception) and perception. When the very young child looks at a house, the visible parts are seen. Sensation has taken place. When older children look at the same house, they also just see the visible parts, for instance the house front. But older children mentally fill in the parts they do not see by drawing on their past experiences with houses. They therefore perceive a whole house, with a back, roof, sides, and even rooms and furniture inside. Perception is midway between sensation and thought. Sensation requires present stimulation, but does not require previous experience. Perception requires previous sensations and experiences in addition to present stimulation. It involves such mental activities as recognition, interpretation, and association. Perception also involves an understanding of the relationships of one object to another.

Thought grows out of many perceptions. It does not require present stimulation, but does require past sensations and perceptions. Mental classification gives order and structure to our perceptions. When language begins, the first classifications are expressed with nouns. Babies will call all men "Da-da." They soon separate (or classify) unfamiliar men and familiar men, and then assign the term "Da-da" appropriately, based on their perceptions of visual and auditory characteristics and their memories of former experiences. Later, the distinction will be made between foods and nonfoods, and still later, between fruits and fruits and vegetables. Each classification is built upon the memory of many previous perceptions.

In the beginning

The body of the newborn is equipped with the organs to receive inputs from the environment. The typical infant stimulation programs are designed to elicit action of these sensory organs. Artificial episodes of sensory stimulation are not required for the infant whose receptive organs are intact. Indeed, when these episodes are insensitive to a baby's temperament and developmental age, they may even work against optimal development.

From the moment of birth, the baby is in touch with the world and is learning about the immediate. The earliest impressions about the world in general are received from the primary caregiver's actions and responses. Baby and caregiver touch, look, and learn from one another by stimulating each other's senses. There are no recipes for determining the right kinds and amounts of stimulation. These are learned through close contact, observation, and trial and error. When baby cries, she is announcing a need—for food, a diaper change, a bubble, or even for acknowledgement of her existence. By trial and error, by offering various comforts and by observing her response, the caregiver soon learns to interpret the various cries. In other words, the baby's cries, facial expressions, and movements stimulate the adult's ears and eyes. It is by way of the adult's sensory stimulation that baby's needs and desires are interpreted. When the caregiver responds to baby, by picking him up, talking to him, and feeding him, the caregiver stimulates the development and refinement of baby's sensory organs and brain structures. Equally important, baby is learning that someone cares, that his world is a satisfying place, and that he has some control of that world. Caregiver and child learn from one another in the daily nurturance of the child. They are developing a satisfying relationship. Together they are building the child's solid base of trust and confidence.

Different strokes for different folks

Each child (and adult) has differing needs for contact with people, the sound of a voice or music, or things to see and touch. In other words, each person needs differing amounts of sensory stimulation. Some babies are extremely sensitive and cannot take too much stimulation; others seem to need and enjoy more. Also, the amount of stimulation that can be tolerated at any one time varies in each individual. For example, there may be times when an adult who usually enjoys company does not want to be with other people. This is true of babies also. Baby will let us know if she needs or wants company. If she's happy with the attention she is getting, she will respond with coos, gurgles,

and will wave her arms and legs. When she is older she will smile and laugh.

If the baby does not want to be handled or talked to, he may turn his head or body away, or he may become fussy, or just fall asleep as a way of escape. This is his way of letting us know that he has his own individual needs and moods. Particularly in a group care situation, a primary caregiver is needed to protect and shield baby from too much stimulation and attention. When baby is giving escape signals, he should be moved to a less stimulating setting. On the other hand, baby may want more stimulation and attention then the primary caregiver can provide at a particular time. Other children and other adults, of course, can attend to these needs, with mutual satisfaction and enjoyment. If nothing else, baby learns that not all persons look the same, sound the same, or even smell and taste the same. New caregivers are frequently surprised when the baby they are holding actually licks their arm! Just another example of baby's need to find out and her natural ways of learning.

It is only in the extreme cases that lack of stimulation causes problems. If baby does not get at least minimal attention, she shows signs of discouragement and apathy and may even give up trying to get a response. She may stop smiling, cooing, and waving her arms and legs. Development is delayed when a baby is rarely handled, looked at, or talked to. But that is only in extreme cases. It is now conjectured that in the institutions where babies failed to thrive the cause was not necessarily lack of contact between caregiver and infant; it was lack of caregiving behavior *contingent upon* the baby's signals. In other words, for whatever reason, there was little or no mutual stimulation. Only the responses and interactions of a caring human being can provide the stimulating sensory and affective behaviors essential for human growth and development.

SENSORY DEVELOPMENT AND LEARNING
Early visual learning

Normal newborns arrive with the ability to see. Indeed, there is evidence that the human fetus reacts to changes of light even when it is directed toward the mother's abdomen during the last trimester.

Although all the eye parts are present at birth, they are not yet fully functioning. The newborn's eyes and visual abilities are quite different from those of a 4-month or a 4-year-old child. The newborn's eyes are very small and round, the fovea is about 15 degrees off from its eventual permanent site, and the lens is inflexible. For these reasons, the infant cannot accommodate (or focus) longer than momentarily until he is 1 to 4 months of age.

However, almost from the beginning, infants appear to prefer to look at human faces instead of plain circles or other unpatterned stimuli. This preference suggests the first guidelines for caregivers/teachers. Not only should toys and other objects be provided at close range (7 to 15 inches) but also human beings should come within that range also. The distance between baby and caregiver when baby is being held to nurse is best.

Newborns have other visual preferences. They prefer patterned stimuli to plain stimuli, just as they prefer human faces to plain circles. They cannot distinguish spatial relationships, and there is no sustained fixation.

From the first days of life, children have several defensive and orienting visual reactions. These include the pupillary reflex, partial eye closing in bright lights, and eye turning toward a softer light or a gently moving object at the edge of the visual field.

The uncoordinated movements normally disappear in 2 or 3 weeks with the resulting convergence. In the third or fourth week visual fixation (sustained attention) appears. During the second month, it may even last for several minutes. This is critically important for analyzing the environment and for the intentional behaviors that soon follow. Visual perception begins to play a leading role in the child's learning and development in the second or third month. Fixation time constantly lengthens and is the predominant component of the child's behavior. The object that receives the most sustained first visual attention apart from the primary caregiver is the baby's own fist!

At the same time, visual searching is evoked by sound. Baby can turn both head and eyes toward the source of the sound. During the third month, the infant begins to anticipate and intentionally look for an adult when approaching sounds are heard. Soon the infant looks at a moving toy in the hands of the adult, and then at a nonmoving toy or object to which the adult is attracting attention. During this time, the infant primarily interacts with other persons through visual perception. When not gazing at the caregiver, the baby is constantly visually exploring the environment. Baby still prefers faces to inanimate objects, however. At 4 or 5 months of age babies are even more selective. They prefer to look at eyes rather than noses or mouths. So babies should be looked at and given ample opportunity to gaze back. Sometime around the fifth or sixth month, baby begins to recognize his primary caregiver. The closeness of a strange face will often evoke a negative emotional reaction, sometimes labeled "stranger anxiety."

During the first 6 months (and later), visual perception is developed by looking! One responsibility of the teacher is to position baby in different ways. We change baby's position in the crib from front to back, we ourselves come close to baby and talk or sing at times other than during routine care. We hold baby on our shoulder and thereby open up a whole new perspective. We place baby on a blanket on the floor where he can watch us or other children move about. We prop baby on her tummy with her upper body on a pillow in front of a low mounted mirror. We prop baby in an infant seat (for no longer than 10 to 15 minutes at a time) to provide another perspective. In other words, we arrange the baby in the environment as well as arranging the environment itself.

The first "environment" is the cradle or crib, and within the first week or two we fasten a colorful object (toy, plastic spoon) to a stabile, and hang it within baby's visual field. In a few days we add another object and in another few days we add another, this time removing the first one. At 2 or 3 months we replace the stabile with a mobile hanging from the crib or carriage or even the ceiling, but all within the visual field of the infant. A dowel rod with one or two brightly colored ribbons to flutter in the air is a satisfying beginning mobile. By 3 months, the ability to reach and grasp is developing. It is therefore important to securely fasten the objects on the cradle gym, ideally in such a way that they will react with sounds or movement when touched, kicked, or swatted. Even if securely fastened, it is vital to have the objects and their removable parts large enough so that baby cannot choke or swallow them. Any part of an object must be considered removable! A baby's abilities to take or tear apart are incredible. Any caregiver who wears glasses, dangling earrings, a loose scarf, or necktie will have living proof of the baby's attraction to movement and ability to reach and pull. Never underestimate a baby's abilities to do either.

Any object with a diameter between ¾ and 1¼ inch is dangerous. Anything smaller could be swallowed and would pass through the gastrointestinal tract; anything larger could not lodge in the throat and therefore would not cut off the air supply.

Intentional reaching is a milestone. It proves that baby is processing the sensations received visually and has achieved the motor control necessary to direct arms and hands toward the perceived object. The next step is eye-hand co-ordination, then the ability to grasp. By age 6 months, the abilities of visual focusing and perception, reaching, and grasping are usually coordinated. Normal babies do not need specially designed learning cards, materials, or activities to develop their visual and reaching-grasping skills. Normal babies develop these skills through daily contact with objects and nurturing persons. The teacher ensures the availability of a variety of objects and encourages baby's spontaneous play and exploration. The teacher calls verbal attention to objects ("See what I have—a little red block."), and perhaps demonstrates looking at, touching, and moving the block. Teachers sometimes encourage reaching and eye-hand coordination by holding the object slightly beyond baby's grasp. The teacher's major responsibilities are to introduce familiar and new objects to baby's visual and reaching range, to verbally describe the objects and to call them by name, and to talk about what baby is doing, what the object is doing, and perhaps what the teacher is doing.

For the first 6 months (more or less) "out of sight, out of mind" holds true. After that period a baby's ability to receive visual sensations is almost mature, and he is beginning to process, or operate on, what he sees. We capitalize on this new development with many activities, including two traditional ones. Both peek-a-boo and hide-and-seek involve the beginning understanding that out of sight does not mean out of mind, that objects exist whether they are seen or not seen. Baby is beginning to establish mental images (or memories) of things seen and heard. As is appropriate for all learning, the progression is from simple to complex. Peek-a-boo can start with the teacher covering his own eyes with his hands, and saying "Where's baby? I can't see baby." The next step comes several times later after baby shows interest and delight instead of just puzzlement. The teacher covers baby's eyes, and asks "Where's baby? Baby can't see teacher." (The names of the persons involved should of course be used, not the labels "baby" and "teacher.") After a few more games of this type, baby is ready to look for and find the teacher whose face might be covered. Later, teacher can be found when only an arm or leg show from behind a door or chair. Many games of the teacher disappearing momentarily by the side of the crib or of covering baby's head or body end in squeals and laughter from both. They also lead to the tacit knowledge of object permanence.

Hide-and-seek is a version of peek-a-boo, using objects instead of people. A small toy is partially hidden under the blanket, while baby watches. The question "where's the ball?" is accompanied by some assistance in finding the ball, until baby catches on. After two or three episodes, the ball and blanket should be left with baby. If she is developmentally ready for this important step, she will engage in the game by herself. Trial-and-error attempts will eventually lead to success. This self-initiated activity is one basis of learning and should continue as a major learning mechanism throughout life. Particularly during these very early years, children need to explore, manipulate, and find out by themselves. They refine their sensory skills and coordinate their body movements in this manner. True intellectual development is rooted in exploration. As increased mobility enlarges the range of exploration, baby has more encounters with the environment. The wider the experiences, the more is learned. (Additional comments about exploration and sensorimotor learning are contained in a later section of this chapter.)

In the game of hide-and-seek the resulting lump when the ball was hidden under the blanket gave a clue to its whereabouts. The next step is to hide the toy behind a piece of cardboard, again while baby watches. If baby seems puzzled, teacher demonstrates reaching around (or over) the cardboard, with baby watching. At later times, the toy may be placed in an open container; still later, in a small, lidded box; and then in a small lidded box within a bigger box.

Each game should follow the same plan: the object is hidden while baby watches, teacher demonstrates how to find the object if baby has difficulty, and baby is allowed time to manipulate, explore, and master the task. Variations of peek-a-book and hide-and-seek continue through the early school years. They give a feeling of controllable suspense and much pleasure. A more advanced version is part of every county or state fair—the shell game. It, too, can be played with a toddler if cans or cups of different sizes or colors or with different labels are used. The toy is always placed under the same container, the positions of the containers are shifted, and baby uses mental imagery to choose the correct container.

It is impossible to isolate visual perception and learning from the other sensory modalities or from movement. The baby who is creeping or crawling is also the baby who has achieved reaching and grasping. Learning proceeds from a combination of visual-motor-tactual encounters and experiences. The emphasis is on the visual, as baby and toddler become competent in perceiving likenesses and differences and in matching objects. Both of these skills are foundation skills for later classification and conceptualization.

In addition to the visual experiencing of actual objects, baby is ready to enjoy and learn from pictures and picture books by her first birthday or before. Fig. 6-1 shows the progression of interest in books during the infant-toddler years. There is nothing more exciting than a homemade picture book containing photographs of the persons and objects baby is familiar with, including pictures of all the children in the group. Even simple lotto games are age-appropriate; they can involve matching pictures, shapes, or colors. One-piece puzzles help baby perceive shapes and objects, as well as practice eye-hand coordination. Picture books,

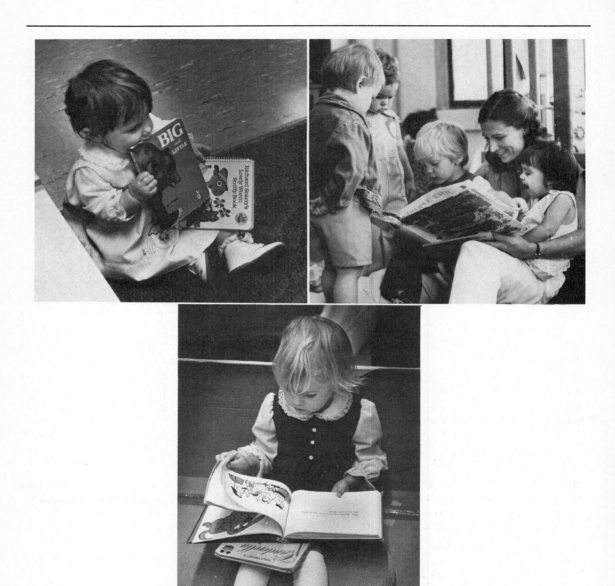

FIG. 6-1 Progression of interest in books during infant-toddler years.

lotto games, and puzzles need not be purchased. They can be easily made by adults or school-age children.

Some young children have difficulty in recognizing that the picture of an object stands for that object. This ability is just one of many that most adults take for granted. Experience with Head Start and Title I children has shown that this understanding is not innate. It must be learned—and it can be taught. After the children are able to match small cubes of the same color or size and to match more diverse objects such as clothespins, spoons, or bottle caps, they are ready to match objects and pictures or sketches of these objects. While the child watches, the teacher might trace the outline of a familiar object: a mitten, a block, or the child's hand on a piece of paper. During the tracing, teacher "talks through" the drawing. "First, I'll draw your thumb, then your finger, and then another finger, and another finger, and then your little finger." Similarities between the child's hand and the drawing should be discussed. This tracing activity can be repeated with objects chosen by the child, with the teacher "talking through" the drawing and pointing out similarities and the differences between two-dimensional and three-dimensional objects. Continuing exposure to real objects and their drawings or pictures (a real cup of milk, and a picture of a cup of milk) will ease the transition from object to a pictorial representation of the object.

Long before baby can assign a label to an attribute (red, big), she will be able to visually match objects on the basis of shape and color. Again, the teacher reinforces a correct match by verbalizing "yes, they are both red" and by acting pleased. A more difficult match is between an object and its cut-out shape in a shape sorting box or form board. Many trials and errors will gradually result in matching correctly. Matching activities afford practice in visual perception, tactual perception, and eye-hand coordination.

The ability to discriminate shapes is a prerequisite to symbol recognition, including the letters of the alphabet.

Perceiving visual patterns is a prerequisite to mathematical understandings. The newborn prefers patterned to plain stimuli and human faces to plain circles. Teachers capitalize on these preferences by frequently being within baby's visual field and establishing eye contact. They also introduce patterns into baby's activities. As soon as eye-hand coordination has somewhat developed, teacher introduces "necklace-making" with large wooden beads. Teacher demonstrates stringing beads while baby watches. Baby is rewarded by having a necklace that is long enough for him to wear, and to put on and take off. The putting-on and taking-off are developmental tasks in themselves. Soon the teacher refines the stringing action by selecting beads of alternating colors and stringing two or three pairs, and then asking baby to pick out the next one from an assortment of beads of the two colors (same shape and size). After going through progresssively more difficult steps over a period of time, the toddler will be able to repeat patterns of four colors, and perhaps different shapes also.

In all these teacher-led activities, the adult verbally describes what is happening, shows pleasure (gives social reinforcement) when the child is successful, and gently corrects when the child does not imitate the pattern correctly. There are 4-year-olds who cannot replicate patterns because they have not had previous experiences such as this one. The understanding of patterns leads to the understanding of sequence: what comes first? what comes next? what comes next? Some 3-year-olds can even tell stories based on events in a logical order. Some can "read" a story from strips showing sequenced pictures of getting dressed, or of building a block tower, or of a flower growing from a seed to full bloom.

By the age of 2 years, after many develop-

FIG. 6-2   Sorting by colors and shapes.

mentally appropriate activities, the child can accurately sort all kinds of objects—buttons and spools, blocks and marbles, circles and squares. Items that require finer visual discrimination should be introduced gradually, such as buttons of different shapes and colors, or paper circles of different colors and sizes. Any new material should lead to a small leap forward. In other words, circles of two colors are introduced first. When the child masters their differentiation, a third color is added. Step by step the number of choices is increased. Time for manipulation and mastery should be allowed before the next step is introduced (Fig. 6-2).

If these and other visual-perceptual activities have been included in the daily routine of caregiving and teaching, the 3-year-old should be able to point to six or seven pictures when named, name four or five pictures of familiar objects, understand such position words as in, under, and behind, and perhaps copy circles and horizontal and vertical lines. In three short years, baby has progressed from receiving virtually meaningless visual sensations to a child who perceives visually, who acts upon the visual perceptions, and has a somewhat organized view of the world.

Early auditory learning

Although hearing ability is not fully developed at birth, newborns can hear moderately loud sounds and can distinguish different pitches. In fact, a fetus in the last trimester will respond to a loud sound. It has long been recognized that babies startle at loud and sudden noises. We now know that babies also react to softer sounds. In the first days of life infants not only react differently to sounds of a tonal and nontonal nature, but are also able to differentiate them according to pitch and timbre. They can distinguish sounds separated by one octave (McDonald, 1979). There is little information about the development of the more complex auditory skills. We do know that low-frequency, rhythmic sounds are soothing and loud or sudden sounds are distressing.

The usual indoor environment, whether in a home or a center, is full of the activity sounds of people. People talking and walking, snapping lights on and off, opening and closing doors and drawers, splashing water, using kitchen appliances, as well as radios and television sets—all these immerse the child in a sea of sound. Fortunately, infants seem to prefer sounds made by humans, just as they prefer to look at human faces instead of blank shapes or inanimate objects. The most meaningful human sounds are verbalizations. Gordon (1970) advised us to surround baby with a "language envelop."

In the second or third week a new reaction to a relatively strong auditory stimulus appears, in terms of inhibition of general motor activity. Some researchers call this *auditory fixation.* Shortly thereafter auditory fixation can be obtained in response to verbal expressions by an adult. As is true of visual fixation, auditory fixation is critically important. Fixation is the forerunner of attention. There can be little learning without attention. Adult verbalizations can be nonsensical, rhythmic, or include comments about the weather or what's cooking for lunch. Almost from the beginning, the adult should talk about what baby is doing or looking at in addition to explaining what the adult is doing or looking at. As soon as baby responds by cooing or gurgling, good teachers imitate these sounds and initiate a "conversation."

There seems to be an interaction between baby's body movements and the sounds of an adult's voice. It is conjectured that baby's rhythmic responses to changes in the adult's verbalizations may be a part of early speech development. Baby needs to be talked to and sung

to in order to develop the human quality of language. Talking or singing to baby while holding or rocking her will incorporate several sense modalities and movements. This is the true "stimulation" program. Children use all their mental images when learning a new skill or understanding. These images are the result of a variety of experiences with sounds, sights, smells, touches, and motions.

Not only is the environment sound-laden, but baby delights in adding to the sounds. Clapping hands, banging blocks or spoons, jingling bells on an elastic bracelet, rattling rattles and keys— these all give pleasure, and of course add to general confusion.

In addition, the teacher encourages baby to discriminate sounds. Discriminations and the resulting classifications follow the same developmental sequence as those of visual perceptions. Without a teacher's language, body movements, and demonstrations, progress in auditory perception is less than optimal. Statements such as "I hear something. It sounds like a bell," or questions such as "What is it?" "What do you hear?" "Is it loud or soft?" accompanied by directing visual and auditory attention to "it" gradually refine the discrimination ability. The effectiveness of the direction to "turn on your ears" is uncertain, to say the least. In the case of auditory learning, as with all other learning during this developmental period, it is necessary to associate the sensation with an actual concrete object or experience. "Turn on your ears" does little to focus the child's attention. Table 6-1 follows the development of auditory perception during baby's first year.

It is rare to find music included as part of the educational curriculum for infants and toddlers, yet what more natural means to encourage auditory perception and pleasure? McDonald (1979) states that "attention to musical sound, and interest in producing musical sounds, begins in infancy. Several studies have noted the focused attention given to music by infants in their first six months, their attempts to carry on 'musical

TABLE 6-1 Auditory perception during the first twelve months

Age	Perceptions
By 3 months	Differentiates tonal and nontonal sounds
	Differentiates pitch and timbre
	Auditory fixation to adult's verbalizations
	Looks for source of sound
	Soothed by soft, rhythmical sounds
By 6 months	Differentiates tones of voice
	Differentiates speech sounds
	Likes to "talk" to self
	Coos and gurgles
By 9 months	Associates sound with its source (toy or person)
	Enjoys listening to musical sounds
	Attempts "conversation"
	Babbles
By 12 months	Imitates adult vocalizations
	Responds rhythmically to music
	Knows own name
	Knows names of other persons
	Understands more than verbalizes
	Tries to comply with verbal requests

conversations' with others before the age of one year, and their rhythmic and dancelike movements when music is present. . . . In view of these findings, the starting time for learning about music is the same as the starting time for any learning" (pp. 3-4). Musical sounds *are* special for our very youngest babies. Although recorded music and sounds may soothe, they do little to nourish the developing brain or to strengthen the relationship between caregiver and infant. Constant stimulation by impersonal sounds may even teach the baby to tune out, thereby dulling the ability to listen, to discriminate, and to perceive auditorially.

Even in the first few weeks of life, babies can discriminate sounds, and they attend to changes of the characteristic sounds (timbre) of various instruments. Baby's first "instruments" include many rattles with different sounds, musical mobiles, ticking clocks, music boxes, and record-

ings. Recordings for the very young child contain excellent enrichment possibilities if used as a supplement to adult-to-child music and movement. Some recordings are really imitations of environmental sounds—thunder, ocean waves, bird calls, etc. Others contain songs and rhythms. The selection of tapes or records should not be limited to childish music. This is the time for the introduction of selected classical music as well.

Music education should start at birth or as soon thereafter as baby can attend to a sound or differences in sound. The first objective is to match the sound with its source. We sing, croon, and talk to babies as they watch us. We dance with baby in our arms to the music from recordings or make our own music. We rock baby rhythmically as we croon and sing. We give baby his own sound makers. If rhythmic activities are included during the first few weeks, by 6 to 8 months of age, baby may initiate her own rhythmical movements to music. When we feed baby, we can make up little songs: "Up comes the spoon, down goes the food" with appropriate changes of pitch.

Adults should imitate the baby's coos and engage in "singing conversations" long before actual words can be understood or used. Babies also enjoy and profit from listening to actual songs. Lullabies have probably been sung or hummed since the first baby fretted about going to sleep. They are now viewed as an important means of developing a close relationship between baby and caregiver. If singing is part of the usual daily activities, children will start to sing snatches of songs by 18 to 24 months, and by the time they are 36 months old, many of them will sing whole songs. Such songs as Twinkle Twinkle Little Star, Hot Cross Buns, Jingle Bells, This Old Man, and My Bonnie Lies Over the Ocean, are appropriate because of their range in pitch.

For a toddler, singing is playing with sounds. Once a toddler discovers a pattern she likes, she works at it, refines it, and changes it, until it becomes part of her repertoire. Adults can imitate the child's songs, thus reinforcing them. Adults can also make up little songs to fit activities or happenings, and these soon become part of the child's repertoire. Spontaneous singing by 2-year-olds involves a surprisingly wide range in pitch. When learning a song taught by a teacher, the most comfortable range seems to be from D to A (above middle C), and with intervals no larger than a fifth (McDonald, 1979).

If adults "think music," music will become a natural part of living with infants and toddlers. We provide the foundation for future enjoyment from music, but we are also providing an excellent foundation for auditory perception and therefore for speech and language development.

Early tactual learning

Touch is necessary for human development, and touch sensitivity is highly developed in the newborn. Indeed, an infant seems to be "programmed" for early tactual stimulation. Touch sensitivity emerges during the prenatal period in the area of the mouth and nose, and spreads throughout the entire surface of the body in the early postnatal period. In the first days of life, a touch on the infant's cheek evokes exploratory responses, including mouth opening, lip wrinkling, and sucking movements. Localized reactions, such as moving the hand toward the body part being touched, have been observed as early as the end of the first month. Actual hand rubbing of the stimulated part appears during the second or third month. During the third to sixth month period, a "tactual fixation" emerges. The baby freezes in response to stimulation on some portion of his skin instead of reaching his hand toward that portion. All movements stop, and the baby seems to be attending only to the ongoing stimulation. Tactual fixation is another component of learning to attend.

A baby's mouth is even more sensitive to touch than the skin and hands. No doubt this is why the infants and toddlers put everything in their mouths. They are feeling the object with their most sensitive receptor.

As is true with all sensations and perceptions, teachers should capitalize on the innate abilities. In the case of touch and feel, the following sequence might be followed during the first year. Even during the first month, baby's position in the crib can be shifted from back to front. Baby's arms and legs, shoulders, back, and tummy can be gently massaged during diaper changes and before and after feeding. Baby should be cuddled during feeding, and perhaps gently rocked back to sleep. Cuddling and rocking should be part of every baby's experience almost from the beginning, and should be continued as long as the baby or toddler finds them satisfying and comforting. During the second and third months, we gently move baby's arms up over the head and back again. When she is on her tummy, we push on the soles of her feet. Do not neglect the making up of song snatches to accompany the movements—"Your arms go up, up, up; your arms come down, down, down"—with appropriate rhythm and pitch. "This little piggy" includes good touch sensations as baby's toes or fingers are grasped and wiggled in turn. It will not be too long before baby will respond by pointing when asked "Where are baby's toes?" and "Where is baby's nose?"

The body massages may be extended by rubbing baby with a soft cloth, a terry cloth towel, or even a feather, during the fourth and fifth months. Give baby soft balls or rag dolls to clutch, textures to feel, and hard spoons or plastic rings to feel and probably to mouth. By age 6 or 7 months, physically and verbally encourage baby to roll back and forth on the floor or in the playpen; place baby in a propped sitting position; give her more objects to feel and grasp (and release); put her hand on the radio to feel

FIG. 6-3   A "sniffing" game for toddlers.

the sound vibrations; have fun splashing and feeling water. When baby has learned to creep or crawl, let her experience smooth tile floors and shaggy carpets. As soon as she is mobile, she will feel and touch any and everything!

Baby is also sensitive to temperature. Application of hot or cold to the newborn's skin will cause physical withdrawal. It is not necessary, however, to heat a baby's milk or first foods to make them palatable, nourishing, or digestible. Room temperature formula is just as beneficial and acceptable as warm. It is not the temperature of the food that is important to baby's development, but the emotional warmth given during the feeding time.

The development of tactual reactions is complete by the end of the sixth month. Thereafter, the reactions become more refined in terms of accuracy and differentiation. Contrived feeling activities continue for several years. The "feelie" boxes, clutch balls, texture balls, play dough, whipped soapsuds, and finger paints all provide tactual as well as muscular experiences. Edible materials are recommended until baby stops exploring with his mouth.

Early taste and olfactory learning

Although there are mixed research findings about the newborn's ability to differentiate tastes and smells, it is now generally thought that all of the full-term newborn's senses are fully or nearly fully functioning.

When smells or tastes are purposely introduced to sharpen the ability to discriminate, there are at least two general rules to follow. Stimuli that produce extreme sensations should be offered at first, and then the range is gradually decreased. A pleasurable taste or smell should be the last one in the "lesson." "Smelly" things include perfume or cologne, peanut butter, slices of onion, vanilla, and vinegar. A few drops may be placed on a cotton ball for sniffing, but first let the children sniff the plain cotton ball and conclude that it has a "nothing" smell. Again, this activity should be "talked through" while it is happening. After the toddler has some command of words, he can play the "sniffing" game (Fig. 6-3). First the child labels real objects (food, flowers, scented soaps, onion, perfume) by sight, and then identifies the same objects by their smell, with eyes closed. The same types of procedures may be followed with tasting foods, liquids, and condiments. A next step is the classification of tastes and smells under headings such as sweet and sour, pleasant and unpleasant, sharp and soft.

All objects in our environment can be classified and described in terms of at least one sensory perception—sight, sound, feel, taste, or smell. Opportunities for refining perceptions abound in the natural and manmade world. The senses put us in touch with the world. They are also essential tools for continued learning. However, beyond the first few weeks, utilization of sensory equipment depends to a large extent upon the infant's developing abilities to move.

MOVEMENT AS LEARNING

Movement as a perceptual experience depends upon the internal (proprioceptor) organs located in the skeletal muscle tissue and in the tendons and joints. These organs are referred to as organs of muscle sense, or kinesthesis. They enable us to experience sensations of movement itself, equilibrium, and position in space. According to Sinclair (1973) these receptors are "activated whenever movement occurs, and they are doubtless functioning before birth. They are thought to constitute the earliest input system of the body. This sensory-motor mechanism, ac-

tivated through movement, thus provides the first learning or experience system and is of prime importance in maturation and growth during infancy and early childhood" (p. 3).

There is a predictable pattern of motor development and behavior. There are also variations because of individual differences and interactions with the physical and social environment. Normative studies chart the developmental sequence, but do not include what the child can do given a variety of opportunities. Norms change over time, and also over different populations. The motor skills and behaviors that follow a fixed sequence of development are the phylogenetic skills. They develop in three general directions. First, development proceeds from head to feet. Infants gain control of head movements before they control leg movements. They learn to visually fixate before they attempt to reach the object. Second, development proceeds from the central regions of the body outward. Upper parts of the arms are used for deliberate reaching long before wrists, hands, and fingers are used. The use of the hand for grasping develops from an overall palm grasp to a pincer-like grasp using thumb and finger. Third, development proceeds from gross muscle movements to fine muscle movements. When a newborn cries, he uses his whole body—face, voice, lungs, arms, and legs. Later, crying involves only the breathing and vocal organs and facial muscles.

The ages at which these particular skills emerge may vary, but their sequence is fixed. Variations may result because of different activity levels, sexual and cultural factors, or differences in opportunities for motion and moving. The chance to move during infancy is particularly important for motor skill development. Motor retardation is largely caused when children are restricted in their opportunities to move. Movement-restricted children may be as much as 3 months behind other children by the time they are 4 months old (Slovin-Ela and

Kohen-Raz, 1978). In addition, Zaporozhets and Elkonin (1971) remind us that when young children are excluded from socialization with adults, they do not master upright movement, typical human postures, or other important features of human movement.

The major phylogenetic skills are locomotion and prehension. The usual timetable of their development is found in Table 6-2.

It is impossible to completely separate movement from perception. Some psychologists claim that perception not only initiates movement, but also regulates it. Just as we cannot separate movement from perception, we cannot separate movement from objects in the environment. This interdependence is clearly shown in the following description of the young child's motor development and explorations.

During infancy

By the age of 1 month, many babies can raise their head slightly from a prone position to look at something. When held in the feeding position, they will open their mouth as the nipple comes into view. Early in the third month, baby begins to reach out and bat at dangling objects, although he does not open his fingers and try to grasp. By the time he is 4 months old or can be propped in a sitting position, he reaches out to take hold of things and spreads his fingers to grasp, although his thumb is not yet opposed to his fingers. When he attempts to pick things up, he usually sweeps them toward his body with his forearm. Even when he does manage to pick up an object, he cannot intentionally let it go.

As baby approaches 5 months, he studies and plays with his hands, often using one hand to bring the other into his visual field and into his mouth. From then on, for about a year's time, everything he picks up will go into his mouth. If for some reason he cannot pick up something, he may even pull his mouth to it.

Between 5 and 6 months of age, baby can grasp, hold on, manipulate, and let go of rattles and toys. She uses both hands in a coordinated way. Now she mouths objects not so much to feel them, but for their chewability since baby teeth are beginning to push through. At about 6 months, she discovers her feet, and they are tasted and chewed too! Baby may also hide her face with a blanket corner, and peer out from time to time to see if anything has changed. This action might be interpreted as a beginning awareness in object permanence.

During the seventh month, baby can sit up without support but may need help in getting to

TABLE 6-2   The development of locomotion and prehension skills*

Age	Prehension	Locomotion
Newborn	Reflexive arm movements Uncoordinated eye movements	Reflexive head and body movements
1-4 months	Spontaneous hand-to-mouth movements Objectives placed in hand or grasped	Reflexive head and body reactions disappear
4-7 months	Successful reach for and grasp of objects in the palm of the hand	Voluntary control of head and arms
7-10 months	Grasp with thumb and forefinger	Trunk control Unsupported sitting
10-12 months	Eye-hand coordination (can place pegs in board)	Control of legs Creeping or crawling
2nd year		Walking· Running

*Adapted from Appleton, Clifton, and Goldberg, 1975.

a sitting position. Now he amuses himself by banging objects on the table top or tray or banging them together. Soon he discovers the game of dropping things intentionally. Careful observation will show that he watches and listens for the impact of the object. This is a first step in the exploration of spatial relationships. His delight is enhanced by a caregiver who retrieves the object, and retrieves the object, and retrieves the object again. Several authors of "baby activity books" suggest attaching the object with a string, so that it only falls a few inches and is therefore easier for the caregiver to retrieve. This may save the caregiver's back, but it defeats the learning possibilities of the game. Baby will also be enthusiastic about the game of peek-a-boo, with someone putting a small blanket or cloth over her head. However, visual information has become so important that baby should not be deprived of seeing her world for more than a few seconds at a time.

Between 8 and 9 months of age baby's thumb is fully opposed, and he can grasp objects with accuracy. He practices this new skill tirelessly, picking up real bits of fluff and imaginary specks of sunbeams and shadows.

By 8 months baby will also probably be able to creep or crawl. By 9 months, baby may stand upright, holding on, and by 12 to 18 months will probably walk. Some babies do not crawl or creep; they may scoot or even attempt upright walking without the usual preliminaries.

The beginnings of memory are shown by baby's imitation of other's actions. Imitation is paying attention to what other people do and acting in a like manner. The game of pat-a-cake is a good one late in the first year. First she will clap her fists but soon her palms. We learn much of our fine motor behavior through imitation and we learn most if not all of our social behavior through imitation.

If babies have learned to trust the world and the people in it, if they have been lovingly cared for and appropriately taught, expect the following accomplishments by the first birthday. They can remove a bead from a wide-mouth jar, unscrew caps from bottles and toothpaste tubes, work simple cardboard latches, tug at door and drawer knobs, and switch on a radio or television set. They like to empty cabinets of pots and pans, bang them together, mouth them, and take apart double boilers and coffee percolators. They may be able to put wooden disks on a cone, but not in order of size. In addition, they wave bye-bye, can build a "tower" of one small block on another, can sometimes get a mouthful of food in their mouth, and can drink from a glass. If they have achieved some steadiness in walking, they delight in carrying large or small objects hugged close to the chest.

During toddlerhood

Increased opportunities to learn are the result of the transition from infancy to toddlerhood. Sometime around 15 to 20 months, the child has mastered all types of locomotion except running. The perceptions of the sense organs are now corrected or reinforced by the motor movements of reaching, grasping, and manipulating almost everything within range. These movements are called orienting-exploratory responses.

Initially, infants indiscriminately rotate a small block from hand to hand, perhaps touch the angles, and perhaps let it go in order to grasp another one. Later, the infant may visually fixate or gaze at a block, apparently trying to internalize its properties. Baby needs time for looking at, touching, and manipulating a variety of blocks in order to learn "block." It might facilitate adult understanding of this process to mentally visualize a square block. Looking from above, all that is seen is a flat square and four right angles. A slightly turned block viewed from the side reveals three sides, each of an apparently different shape, four right angles, two larger angles, and two smaller angles. A single view from whatever direction does not suggest "block," until it is picked up, turned over, and perhaps rolled. Baby needs to repeat these actions until absolutely certain that the block looks and feels the same no matter what its position. Given the opportunity, baby will naturally go through this sequence of actions.

It is difficult for adults to fully appreciate the complexities involved in the early learning of a young child. When we analyze a task or concept down to its basic parts, we begin to understand the necessity for repeated and varied manipulations and explorations. Kamii and DeVries (1978) suggest the following steps in learning "ball-ness."

> It is only by dropping the ball on the floor, rolling it, throwing it into the air, throwing it against the floor, throwing it against the grass, throwing it against a wall, varying the force applied, trying to catch it, chasing it down a stairway, kicking it, and so forth, that the child can come to know the ball. (p. 234)

In too many instances, children of all ages are expected to learn by visual stimulation only. The labeling of colors does depend solely on visual perception; labeling and understanding sizes, shapes, weights, and space depend on vision, touch, and movement.

In addition to the child's self-initiated learning, as in the ball episode, children can also be taught how to "learn" an object. Teaching can enhance self-perceptions, and thereby enrich learning. Teaching should never be a substitute for the child's actions and interactions. How does one teach "square"? Teacher can demonstrate tracing or following the outer edges with her finger or hand and guide the child's hand to do the same thing. Verbalizations such as "up this way, across, and down again" will alert the child's attention to changes in direction. After repetitions with the same object (a small block) over a period of days, similar procedures can be applied to a triangle or rectangle. In addition to the directional comments, we call attention to the differences between the two blocks. Some

time later, these and similar teaching episodes will enable the child to visually recognize likenesses and differences in shapes without the motor behavior. The groundwork for form perception and for whole-part distinctions has been laid. Both are forerunners of reading and mathematical readiness.

The process of perception is not developed in isolation but in the course of the child's manipulations and interactions with the perceived object. Motor behaviors correct or reinforce the perceptions triggered by the sensations of the sensory organs. Observant parents and teachers have long recognized the cumulative effects of first-hand experiences involving the sense and motor activities. Piaget also recognized these beginning experiences and called them sensorimotor intelligence. Our debt to him is not that he discovered the importance of sensorimotor learning, but that he popularized the idea. His writings describe, in minute detail, such learnings in the lives of his own children and the children attending the Montessori school next to his Institute in Geneva. Piagetian theory has been interpreted as attributing all the knowledge gained by the very young child to the child's manipulations in the environment. Many Swiss preschools, and particularly those that follow the Montessori method, downplay the instructional or mediating role of the teacher. They also emphasize individual activity over social activities. Perhaps this is the reason that Piaget gives little attention to persons in the child's life-space. Sensorimotor learning is the primary mode of learning, but it is not the only one.

CURIOSITY

The curiosity that may have killed the cat is the motivation for all human learning. (It is probably the motivation behind all cat-learning, also.) There are differing theoretical perspectives about the phenomenon called curiosity. Some hold that curiosity is a personality disposition. Others say that curiosity is developed from perceptions that differ from previous understandings. A third view is that curiosity is a learned attribute designed to satisfy the need for mastery. Bradford and Endsley (1978) define a curious child as "one who reacts positively to new, strange, incongruous, or mysterious elements in the environment by focusing attention on them, moving toward them, manipulating them, and/or seeking information about them" (p. 2). Regardless of the theoretical explanations, it does seem that the curious child is the child who learns.

Children have a natural curiosity about their world. Even before they are physically able to reach out, they are mentally reaching for answers with all their being. Teachers of very young children do not need to awaken or teach curious behaviors. Children come equipped with a need to find out about the world. However, this is not an excuse for letting Topsy "just grow"; Topsy needs a teacher to provide developmentally appropriate experiences and the time and opportunity to learn from them. Every normal environment is rich in objects that elicit curiosity. It is up to the teacher to recognize these objects and to capitalize on them.

Appropriate learning is the result of a properly nurtured curiosity. It does not depend upon external stimulation or incentives. Everything is new to the newborn, and many things are new to the toddler. If the young child's curiosity needs are met and enhanced, that child is on the road to a life-long approach to learning all kinds of things. It is the teacher's responsibility to so arrange the environment that it serves as stimulation. After the environment has been arranged, the teacher's responsibility is twofold: he provides the opportunity for child-initiated exploration, and he directs the child's attention (or curiosity) to pertinent factors in the environment.

It has already been noted that during the first 2 years of life, infants will indiscriminately feel, manipulate, and mouth objects. In addition to this random activity, the young infant will fixate (attend). Teachers use this fixation ability to attract the child's attention to a specific object or action. They use a combination of gestures and words. Toward the end of the toddler period, children may remain attentive to words alone for short periods of time. At 2 or 3 years of age children can listen attentively to short poems or stories and derive meaning from the content.

We can predict and therefore somewhat control the focus and duration of attention if we consider the following guidelines:

1. Children pay attention to what they can see or hear. After the first 5 or 6 months, these sensory abilities are similar to the adult's abilities.
2. There are individual differences in the amount of attentiveness. Also, children attend more at some times than at others. Attentiveness is directly related to physical well-being and psychological security, in addition to unique differences.
3. The degree of attention is directly related to the intensity of the stimulus. Loud noises and bright colors attract more initial attention than do subdued noises and colors. Intense sights and sounds may attract the child's attention but will not necessarily hold it. The physical environment should not be overwhelming with its use of bright colors or bright lights. Understimulation has the same effect. There is no conclusive research evidence as to appropriate intensity. Indeed, it is probably impossible to accurately pinpoint appropriate intensities by age for normal children because of their individuality. The teacher's experience with each child is the best guide.
4. Although the attributes that hold a child's attention have not been identified, it has been shown that a child's sustained atten-

tion is influenced by associations to former perceptions. Even the youngest infant has acquired meanings from previous events. Hungry babies stop crying when they hear the approaching footsteps of the caregiver. A toddler's attention is attracted when she hears her name or the voices of her parents at the end of a day in a center program. She ignores the voices of another child's parents.

5. A young child's attention is influenced by how well the event or object matches previous knowledge. A totally new experience frequently causes a young child to ignore or even withdraw from the encounter. A totally new experience may even frighten.

The young child's attention is attracted and held by happenings that are only moderately discrepant from previous understandings. Therefore, attention patterns shift with each new understanding. Children are most curious about familiar objects or events that have one or two discrepancies from the former perceptions. Teachers should build on (or from) the familiar. Discrepancy (or novelty) may be introduced by changing the pictures hanging on the wall, rearranging the furniture in a familiar environment, or alternating the toys and objects available for investigation. The use of a somewhat flexible schedule based on children's needs and interests also introduces novelty in a familiar situation. The introduction of a totally new object or activity may help relieve "boredom" of a teacher. It may be exciting for the adult, but it may be completely ignored by the young child. In order for the child to be interested, there needs to be some relationship of the new with the already known. A balance between the unfamiliar and the familiar is particularly important for the infant and young toddler. If too much is given too soon, these younger children may withdraw mentally, if not physically.

At the very beginning, baby's attention is attracted by whatever or whoever moves or makes a sound or satisfies biological needs. With an increasing sense of physical and psychological security, a baby then attends to the novelty of a newly provided object or a change in the environment. Somewhat later, the infant's attention is attracted to stimuli that can be associated with previous sensations, and baby begins to refine the sensations into perceptions. The child progresses from "What is it?" to "What can be done with it or to it?" The motor behaviors that are developing concurrently enable the learning to proceed.

It has already been noted that during the first 2 years (more or less), babies will indiscriminately feel, manipulate, and mouth objects. By 2½ a child will attempt to establish relationships or associations between the perceived objects. Of course she has been associating objects and events that have emotional meanings for a long time before this. At 4 or 5 months of age she learned to anticipate a bottle when she heard approaching footsteps. She even determined the appropriate time by vocally demanding it!

Children are curious throughout the infant-toddler period, and throughout life, but it is during the first 2 to 3 years that sense information is all important. Toward the end of that period, another dimension is added. Toddlers become attentive to verbal descriptions of objects and events. The 3-year-old can listen attentively to short poems, nursery rhymes, and simple stories, and can understand what is being said. There is some indication that the 3-year-old can also go beyond the verbalized content and engage in imaginative wonderings. Of course, imagination is a more sophisticated version of curiosity. Instead of asking "What is it?" and "What can it do?" the question becomes "What would happen if . . . ?"

The development of creative and imaginative behavior in the young child has been sequenced in terms of behavioral objectives (Table 6-3). These objectives are part of a larger list, most parts of which are included in following chap-

TABLE 6-3 Developmental objectives for imaginative and creative behavior*

Age	Objectives
By 1 year	Manipulates paintbrush and crayons in free art situation.
By 2 years	Sings songs with group. Dances creatively to music. Memorizes little rhymes and songs with group or teacher (up to 4 lines). Can paste a smaller piece of paper on a larger piece of paper. Can effectively manipulate clay (makes hotdogs, bird's nest, etc.). Enjoys working with paints and color in free art situation. Enjoys games (participates) and imaginative role playing either in home or in block center. Given items, child will engage in spontaneous dramatic play.
By 3 years	Eagerly participates in musical activities. Expresses self through the media of paint, color, clay, pasting, paper cutting, paper tearing.
By 4 years	Will engage in spontaneous dramatic play having complex plots, differentiated roles, etc.

*Adapted from Caldwell, 1980.

ters, where relevant. The objectives indicate dimensions of development in addition to the curious imaginings mentioned above.

THE TEACHER

The extent of the utilization of child-related tools of learning is dependent upon the actions and attitudes of the significant adults in the child's environment. Therefore, the fourth essential tool is the teacher.

When most parents who need or want day care for their little ones are asked what they hope to find, their answers reveal their primary concern is to find someplace where someone will take good care of their child. A small number of parents will mention other children to play with or an enriched environment. When day care staff members are asked what their responsibilities include, there are mixed answers about caregiving and teaching. When both groups are asked what is important for children to learn by age 3 years, responses will cover a wide range of learnings, with only a few agreements (Weiser, n.d.). These responses are presented in more detail in the next chapter. At this time it is sufficient to point out that there is confusion about the teaching activities of day care personnel and the educational goals of infant-toddler day care. The confusion is related to lack of knowledge about young children, as well as differences in adult priorities. The problem is intensified by the various meanings accorded the terms "caregiver" and "teacher." Does a caregiver teach? Does a teacher give care? The confusion increases when the children are very young.

Honig (1976) suggests that quality caregivers:
1. Nourish children
2. Arrange environments so that they "ask for" child actions and interactions
3. Notice and heed child behaviors and interests
4. Encourage competency
5. Encourage thinking
6. Are good match-makers
7. Encourage creativity and individual expression in a variety of ways
8. Provide positive contingent reinforcement
9. Encourage language development
10. Notice and use teachable moments
11. Promote mental health
12. Integrate the experiences of children
13. Form trusting, loving relationships with children
14. Are good models

With the exception of #10, notice and use teachable moments, the idea of teaching per se is not addressed directly. It is, however, implied in each item.

Fowler (1980) states that good teaching of infants and children depends on:

I. Planning a developmental learning sequence, from the simple to complex, and matching children to programs.
II. Monitoring and pacing presentations (stimulation) to match each child's rate of learning.
III. Ensuring children maintain developmental progress instead of learning isolated facts or merely enjoying the play.
IV. Adapting teaching methods to learning and personality styles. (p. 329)

In this list Fowler has been able to separate teaching from caregiving. I was not able to do this even in the presentation of the child's essential tools for learning. The difficulty becomes apparent in the following episode of routine caregiving, taken from a typical day in the life of 3½-month-old Luther (the complete day is included in Chapter 10).

Episode 1. At 10:15 A.M. Luther's eyes open slowly. He holds them open for only a moment. A deep sigh follows. Then he rubs his face on the sheet. He stares a minute, and then begins to focus in. He lifts his head off the crib mattress, looking around. "Hey there, Luther, ready to get going?" asks the caregiver. "Have a good rest?" she continues, as she offers a finger for a palm grasp. "You took such a long nap, I'll bet your diapers are soaked. Let's take care of that right now." She snuggles close to his face and rubs noses. She hums a snatch of a song, then moves back. He makes a gurgling sound that she repeats. They "talk" face to face.

With one hand still gripped by the baby, she taps his nose with her free hand, "boop," and then runs her finger around his ear, down his neck, and under his chin. She gives his tummy a pat and says, "Okay, let's change those diapers. . . . "One snap, boop, boop, boop, there's that tummy," she says as she rubs his bare skin. Luther laughs. "Where are those feet?" she asks, as she pulls one leg out of his sleeper. "There it is," and the other leg is pulled out. Holding both legs at the ankles, she moves his legs in a running motion. "Look at those legs go!" She smiles. Holding both ankles in one hand, she raises his body, loosening and removing the damp diaper. She quickly slips a dry one under him, laying one end loosely over his front. She cleans the diaper area with a towelette, and again loosely replaces the diaper over him, allowing him to airdry before fastening the diaper. "Better, huh? In go those toes, and snap, snap, snap, you're all fixed up and ready to go."

Caregiving? Yes. Teaching? Decidedly yes. A shorter episode about a 16-month-old boy (Eric) also includes the teaching-caregiving dichotomy:

Episode 2. The teacher is sitting on the floor in the middle of the room with Eric on her lap. The teacher is talking to him, and is interrupted when he points to her belt. She immediately responds enthusiastically, "Hey, I have a belt!" She asks if Eric has a belt, too. He looks and then shakes his head. "But you have buttons," continues the teacher, pointing to Eric's shirt buttons. Then she points to her own blouse. "No buttons." Then she points to Eric's shoes and her shoes, Eric's pants and her pants, naming each one in turn. The child responds verbally, and the teacher continues by naming the nearby objects: a ball, the indoor slide, other children and adults. Eric points to each in turn and laughs.

Teaching? Yes. Caregiving? Very definitely, because immediately before this incident, Eric had been frustrated in his attempts to grab a toy truck from another child and was observably angry.

The traditional teacher's role in the elementary school and even in kindergarten and prekindergarten classes has been either that of facilitator (the humanist approach) or of enforcer (the behaviorist approach). Both approaches separate the child from the teacher. Neither role is appropriate in the care and education of very young children. An adult is a necessary part of the infant's and toddler's learning network. It is the adult who serves as the mediator between the individual child and the world. Perhaps at no other time is a "teacher" more important. It is the teacher who screens the experiences and encounters of the child, and who makes available the interactions with the physical and social environments from which the child forms the foundation for all subsequent learning. In Piagetian terms, it would appear that the teacher preassimilates and preaccommodates experiences in the intentional choices of objects, persons, and experiences, as well as attitudes toward these encounters and toward the individual child.

An adult mediates the child's learning, either

consciously or unconsciously. Some special education researchers are even claiming that the children who are labeled as moderately mentally disabled or retarded are perfectly normal children whose past experiences have lacked an adult mediator.

The responsibile adult in a day care center or family day care home is a teacher, regardless of the label. Teaching and learning take place continually. Intentional planning of this teaching and learning is a prerequisite of the group care and education of infants and toddlers.

■ CHAPTER SUMMARY ■

Very young children have all the essential tools for learning at birth or shortly thereafter. The organs for sensation are activated by things to sense. In a very short time random sensations are internalized and become random perceptions. Young children need to build their own warehouses of sensory experiences. These sensory experiences become more meaningful if they are shared and talked about. The processes of perception are not developed in isolation, but in the course of the child's manipulations and interactions with the perceived and in the context of related adult-child interactions. The increasing number of sequenced encounters and experiences with the environment, both physical and social, lead to the formation of mental images. In turn, these mental images (percepts) lead to concept formation. The broader the perceptual base, the greater is the child's potential for learning.

The development of motor behavior, particularly locomotion and prehension, enables the child to greatly extend the field of exploration and the number of perceptions. Appropriate perceptuomotor experiences are difficult to repeat or replenish after the first few years.

The senses and the ability to move are the mechanisms by which the young child meets the need to know (curiosity). Although curiosity is innate and is the intrinsic motivation to learn, adult participation and guidance are needed to convert random learning to an organized body of information.

Planning ways to motivate very young children to learn is a misuse of time and energy. It is inappropriate and unnecessary. Children want to learn and devote every awake minute in trying to learn. Good teaching is the provision of opportunities for learning. It is guiding and extending child-initiated activities and interests. Caregiving and teaching are inseparable, regardless of the title given the adult. Topsy cannot be allowed to "just grow."

SUGGESTED ACTIVITIES/POINTS TO PONDER

1. Visit a toy store or study catalogs containing toys and equipment for very young children. Evaluate three items in terms of their relationships to sensory learning, and in terms of their relationships to sensorimotor learning.
2. What are the possible results of placing a baby in a playpen or infant seat? There are both advantages and disadvantages, but who gets the most benefit?
3. Infant-toddler caregivers/teachers (and parents) usually view baby's curiosity as a mixed blessing. Why? How should it be handled?

REFERENCES AND SUGGESTED READINGS

Note: There are a number of books containing recommended learning activities for infants and toddlers. They are listed in Appendix A. Lists of learning and teaching activities are not included in the suggested readings for this or following chapters, with the exception of a few specific ones as illustrations.

Appleton, T., Clifton, R., and Goldberg, S.: The development of behavioral competence in infancy. In Horowitz, F.D., editor: Review of child development research, vol. 4, Chicago, 1975, Univesity of Chicago Press.

Babska, Z.: The formation of the conception of identity of visual characteristics of objects seen successively. In Cognitive development in children: five monographs of the Society for Research in Child Development, Chicago, 1970, University of Chicago Press.

Bower, T.G.R.: The perceptual world of the child, Cambridge, Mass., 1977, Harvard University Press.

Bradbard, M.R., and Endsley, R.C.: Developing young children's curiosity, Urbana, Ill., 1978, ERIC Clearinghouse on Early Childhood Education.

Bryant, P.: Perception and understanding in young children, New York, 1974, Basic Books, Inc.

Caldwell, B.: AID Chart (working draft), Little Rock, Ark., 1980, Center for Child Development and Education, University of Arkansas.

Carter, A.: The transformation of sensory motor morphemes into words. In Clark, E., editor: Papers and reports of child language development, No. 10, Palo Alto, Calif., 1975, Stanford University.

Cazden, C.: Suggestions from studies of early language acquisition. In DeStefano, J., and Fox, S.E., editors: Language and the language arts, Boston, 1974, Little, Brown & Co.

Clark, J.E.: Movement experiences for the young child, Della Ward Presentation, Iowa City, Ia., 1978, University of Iowa. (Unpublished.)

Fowler, W.: Infant and child care, Boston, 1980, Allyn & Bacon, Inc.

Gewirtz, J.L.: On designing the functional environment of the child to facilitate behavioral development. In Dittmann, L.L., editor: Early child care: the new perspectives, New York, 1968, Atherton.

Gibson, E.J.: Principles of perceptual learning and perceptual development, New York, 1969, Appleton-Century-Croft.

Greenman, G.W.: Visual behavior of newborn infants. In Stone, J.L., Smith, H.T., and Murphy, L.B., editors: The competent infant, New York, 1973, Basic Books, Inc.

Gordon, I.J.: Baby learning through baby play, New York, 1970, St. Martin's Press.

Gordon, I.J.: The infant experience, Columbus, Ohio, 1975, Charles E. Merrill Publishing Co.

Honig, A.S.: The training of infant care providers, Voice for Children 9(1):12-15, Jan./Feb., 1976.

Kamii, C., and DeVries, R.: Physical knowledge in preschool education, Englewood Cliffs, N.J., 1978, Prentice-Hall, Inc.

Lowe, M.: Trends in the development of representational play in infants from one to three years: an observational study, Journal of Child Psychology 16:33-48, 1975.

McDonald, D.T.: Music in our lives: the early years, Washington D.C., 1979, National Association for the Education of Young Children.

Meier, J., and Marlone, P.J.: Facilitating children's development, vol. 1, Baltimore, 1979, University Park Press.

Sameroff, A.J., and Cavanagh, P.J.: Learning in infancy: a developmental perspective. In Osofsky, J.D., editor: Handbook of infant development, New York, 1979, John Wiley & Sons.

Sinclair, C.B.: Movement of the young child, Columbus, Ohio, 1973, Charles E. Merrill Publishing Co.

Slovin-Ela, S., and Kohen-Raz, R.: Developmental differences in primary reaching responses of young infants from varying social backgrounds, Child Development 49:132-140, 1978.

Spitzer, D.R.: Concept formation and learning in early childhood, Columbus, Ohio, 1977, Charles E. Merrill Publishing Co.

Thomas A., and others: Behavioral individuality in early childhood, New York, 1963, New York University Press.

Weiser, M.G.: Continuity between home and child care programs (unpublished ms).

Yardley, A.: Young children thinking, New York, 1973, Citation Press.

Zaporozhets, A.V.: The development of perception in the preschool child. In Cognitive development in children: five monographs of the Society for Research in Child Development, Chicago, 1970, University of Chicago Press.

Zaporozhets, A.V., and Elkonin, D.B., editors: The psychology of preschool children, Cambridge, Mass., 1971, MIT Press.

CHAPTER 7

LEARNING AND TEACHING PERCEPTUOMOTOR AND REPRESENTATIONAL SKILLS AND ABILITIES

I hear and I forget; I see and I remember; I do and I understand.

Chinese proverb

The very young child is born with the essential tools for early learning: the sense organs, the developing motor abilities, and a perpetual and persistent curiosity. The first 3 years are dedicated primarily to sensory development, many motor achievements, and some major steps in satisfying the curiosity drive. If all goes well, by age 3 years the child will have a capacity for reflection, manipulating ideas, and understanding complicated verbal expressions. Individuality and imagination are developing.

Unlike physical, emotional, and personality development, the milestones in cognitive development do not dramatically appear. Normative models should not be applied after the first year of life, because the rate of cognitive development is partly a function of environmental stimulation. As baby grows from infancy to toddlerhood, environmental factors become increasingly important determinants of both development and learning.

Although the proverb cited at the beginning of this chapter applies to persons of all ages, it has the most significance for the early years of human life. Learning-by-doing is the primary mode of learning in the infant and toddler. It is hard to find anyone who disagrees.

Why, then, does this chapter include "teaching" in its title? If very young children learn primarily by doing, perhaps tender loving care is all that is necessary. Perhaps good infant-toddler caregivers and teachers are just good babysitters. Many adults think that "good babysitting" is the beginning and the end of infant-toddler care and education. These are the same adults who are critical of many preschool programs. They ask, "Why preschool, if all they do is play?" Teachers of young children need to be ready to respond to the issues of teaching vs. babysitting, and learning vs. play, as well as other issues involved in good quality caregiving and teaching. Education during the first 3 years is the first link in the educational chain. Experience has shown that any chain is only as strong as its weakest link. Therefore this chapter and the next three are devoted to the issue of teaching and learning in the infant-toddler center.

GOAL-SETTING

The setting of goals is an appropriate first step in considering educational programs for persons of any age. Without goals a program goes willy-nilly like a rudderless boat. It may contain all kinds of wonderful opportunities for learning but without a preconceived direction, the time and energy expended by both adults and children will have less than optimal results. The setting of goals for an infant-toddler educational program is more difficult than the traditional setting of goals for an academic kindergarten or the elementary grades. Many times goals for the public school years are expressed in terms of completed basal texts and levels of reading and mathematics achievement. Teachers of the very youngest children cannot state that the child will learn colors, shapes, letters, and numerals. They cannot offer a program designed to teach reading, writing, and arithmetic. They cannot even state that the child will learn the social skills of sharing and cooperation.

What is left? What are appropriate goals? What should be taught to children under 3 years of age? Who should decide? On what should the decisions be based?

Child development specialists are sometimes inclined to base their programs on developmental norms and to design programs to enhance the achievement of developing abilities. Early education specialists and psychologists are sometimes inclined to base their programs on societal expectations for later academic achievement. Other specialists from these and other disciplines design programs based on both the developmental norms and societal expectations. The model programs for very young children fit into one of the above designs. To date, we do not have conclusive evidence that one is significantly better than another.

White (1980) suggests that the parents of the infants and toddlers are the appropriate source for program goals. However, it might prove difficult to find a group of parents who agree on goals for their children in any particular center or day care home. It is not unusual to find a mother and father in the same family who disagree about goals for their own children! In addition, there seems to be a relationship between goals and socioeconomic status, and between goals and cultural or ethnic status. Some groups are more oriented to academic readiness, obedience, and "good manners." Other groups are more concerned about individuality, creativity, and social relationships.

On the surface, it appears relatively easy to assign the responsibility of goal-setting to the parents. However, a parental consensus is elusive, and even if reached, may be developmentally inappropriate. It also may be difficult

to put into practice in the daily life at the center. As part of a larger study, I recently conducted a survey of the parents of 30 infants and toddlers enrolled in university-related day care programs in four Midwestern states. One of the questions called for an open-ended answer to "What three things do you consider very important to be learned by the time your child is 3 years old?" The same question was asked of the caregivers/ teachers of these children. The responses of both groups are contained in Table 7-1. In some instances, parental answers revealed overly high expectations, caused by a basic lack of child development knowledge. Some parents gave no answers at all! Others apparently considered toilet training the only important thing to be learned during the first 3 years.

The teachers' responses were more closely related to developmental norms. The information suggests a lack of agreement among the parents, a lack of agreement among the teachers, and a lack of agreement between the groups.

There can be a compromise approach to educational goal-setting, which involves both parents and teachers. In this approach, the teachers take the lead instead of parents. All persons involved in the delivery of the educational components (directors, teachers, aides, and perhaps the nurse and social worker) should initially explore the full range of goals suggested by the authorities in the field and their own value systems. They select the most desirable goals. From this list they then select the goals that are achievable in their particular situation. These desirable, achievable goals are then presented to the parents for discussion. The parents are asked to choose from them, or to list them in terms of their priorities. It is possible in this way to arrive at mutually agreeable goals. Parental goals are important and must be included in any goal-setting by the staff of any center.

Still another approach to goal-setting is to ask what should be taught and learned. The list that follows contains the major components of an

TABLE 7-1 Responses to the question: What three things do you consider very important to learn by age 3 years (results given in percentage of total responses)

Responses	By parents (Percent)	By teachers (Percent)
Attitudes toward self		
"I am important"	11	18
"I am loved"	5	13
"I can succeed"	—	2
"I am unique"	1	5
"I am happy"	—	2
Attitudes toward others		
Trust adults	—	2
Respect for adults	9	—
Respect for others	—	7
Playing with others is fun	1	—
I can get help if I ask for it	1	—
Personal-social skills		
Toilet-training	10	11
Feed self	8	7
Dress self	3	9
Large motor skills	—	2
Language and communication	5	11
Acceptable behavior (good manners)	11	—
Share toys	8	—
Cooperate	5	2
Obedience	6	2
Sense of responsibility	4	—
Beginning independence	1	4
Specific knowledge		
Name, address, age	4	—
Body parts	—	1
Sex-role identification	—	1
Safety limits	3	—
"Learning is fun"	3	2

educational program, accompanied by suggested teaching methods. We want to teach very young children:

1. *How to learn the physical environment.* We provide opportunities and encouragement for self-directed perceptuomotor play. We include a variety of experiences and objects with different characteristics: shape, size, color, texture, sound, taste.

2. *How to learn from the physical environment.* We provide opportunities and encouragement for a variety of large and fine motor activities. We provide objects, materials, and experiences that relate to one another and that respond to the child's actions on them. We direct the child's attention to relationships, similarities, and differences among things and persons.

3. *Increasing competence in representational tasks.* We lead the child from object perception to perception of pictures and diagrams representing three-dimensional objects. We provide materials for role play and pretending. Children at the toddler stage re-enact home experiences, meal preparation, doll care. These are the beginning steps in representational thought.

4. *Self-awareness and a positive self-concept.* We attend to the child's actions, communication, and attempts at mastery. We give outward expressions of love, approval, and praise. We treat each child as a unique person who is enjoyable and has value for us. We increase the number of alternatives in the repertoire of child behaviors by suggesting, demonstrating, or facilitating new or different strategies. We encourage and praise any new strategy or behavior of the child. We value the child's attempts to learn, regardless of the success of the endeavor.

5. *How to learn the social environment.* We provide opportunities and encouragement for the development of self-help skills. We provide meaningful child-adult interactions, and opportunities to observe other adults and other children and to engage in small group activities.

6. *How to learn from the social environment.* We provide opportunities and encouragement for self-directed activities in the presence of others. We provide teacher-directed activities with one or two other children. Snack or mealtimes, and music, art, and motor activities may include up to six children. We do not expect any group endeavors, just individuals who happen to be doing similar things at the same time. We demonstrate approved behaviors in our interactions with each child and each adult. We redirect unacceptable behavior by providing an alternative behavior.

7. *The use of verbal language for communication and social exchange.* We talk to the child in all adult-child interactions, focusing on the child's interest or experience at that particular time. We engage the child in "conversations" at the child's level, progressing from sounds to words to phrases and sentences. The child's level is never "baby talk." We play with language, imitating and repeating the child's vocalizations and verbalizations, repeating rhymes, singing songs. We listen attentively and responsively to the child's vocalizations and verbalizations.

8. *How to learn and control the physical body.* The goal is the development of motor skills leading to the desired self-help skills, body control, and the manipulation of developmentally appropriate objects and materials. We provide opportunities and encouragement to roll over, sit up, creep or crawl, stand up, walk, jump, and climb. We provide objects for increasingly finer manipulation.

Our main goal is to teach each child to become a more effective learner. In so doing we will be teaching the child that living and learning are both satisfying and exciting.

Learning will not occur unless there is motivation. Even learning how to learn the environment is ineffective if there is no motivation to learn the environment.

MOTIVATION AND STIMULATION

Motivation is an intrinsic quality; stimulation is an extrinsic quality. Therfore the term *motivation* is misused when teachers are admonished to motivate their children to learn. According to Samples (1975):

> I cannot motivate you (although I can move you to action), and you cannot motivate me (although you can arouse my motivation). . . . What school teachers generally think of as motivation is what psychologists call stimulation. . . . Stimulation is something I can do to you and you can do to me, but in terms of motivation the actual inner drive that is created in each one of us and that provides us with the impetus to do something has to come from within ourselves (p. 136).

Teachers of infants and toddlers are fortunate indeed. Their children are motivated by an innate curiosity, one of the essential tools of learning. We would hope that these children have not yet had their curiosity suppressed for the sake of a smooth routine or an exaggerated view of safety precautions or for the adults' convenience. Teachers do not need to stimulate curiosity. They do need to arrange for its continuation. Studies of human infants who are satisfied with their lives suggest that "they are avid seekers of information who scan their environment, make fine distinctions, and prefer certain types of complex stimuli. Children appear to be biologically programmed to seek, explore, and respond to gain increased information and competence in dealing with their environment" (Coopersmith, 1975, p. 18).

Even with this biological programming, teachers cannot sit back and let baby "just grow." Motivation to learn has a somewhat elusive quality. Although it comes with the baby, it can actually be eliminated, or at least driven underground, unless baby has the security and stability of a positive concept of self.

A positive concept of self

Self-concept is learned. It therefore begins at birth. By the time most children have reached their third birthday they have learned two of the most complex tasks to be confronted during their lifetime: to walk and to talk. The other children (excluding those with developmental delays) very possibly have not learned to walk or to talk because their early environment discouraged their attempts to learn. Lack of psychological support leads to a negative concept of self, which leads to fear, anxiety, and noticeable withdrawal from the normal activities. The time and energies of these children have been focused on developing their defense mechanisms, instead of seeking new challenges. Defense mechanisms of infants and toddlers include regression to earlier behaviors, denial, and withdrawal. Murphy (1962, 1976) reports that young children develop characteristic ways of coping that remain fairly consistent over childhood. The necessity of an early positive concept of self should not be questioned.

It is appropriate here to mention two extensive studies of public school systems, even though the children involved were well beyond the infant-toddler age period. The Coleman study (1966) found that only two factors made a difference in school achievement. These were not the traditional factors of class size, teacher preparation, or per-pupil expenditure. They were the *child's sense of self-worth* and the *child's socioeconomic background*. The second study by Platt (1974), involving school children from 20 countries, resulted in essentially the same findings. Although neither the public schools nor the day care centers can control the socioeconomic factors in a child's life, they can and must help each child develop feelings of self-worth. This development should occur during the first 3 years, long before the children attend elementary school.

This period may even be a critical one. Attitudes toward self determine openness to new experiences. They determine approaches to and relationships with other persons. They influence the intrinsic motivation to learn.

There are few research studies concerning the developing feelings of self-worth in very young children. The research findings and statements of expert opinion are usually directed toward the elementary school years. Coopersmith (1975) has no reservation when he states "children with high self-esteem perform better and will do less poorly in their schoolwork" (p. 96). There are research conclusions that indicate that the kindergarten child's feelings about self are a better indication of reading readiness than are the scores on intelligence tests (Wattenberg and Clifford, 1964). Perhaps no more need be written here about the importance of a positive self-concept, except that most educators and psychologists agree about its influential role.

Our immediate concern is how to teach positive self-concepts. The following episodes, which were observed in an infant-toddler center, highlight a few of the recommended teaching techniques.

Episode 3. Four-month old Margie was sitting contentedly in the infant seat playing intently with some bells that were strung above her just within her reach. She was batting the bells, looking quite pleased with the resulting sounds. Suddenly her mood completely changed. She arched her back, began kicking her feet and waving her arms wildly. She began to whimper and continued whimpering until one of the caregivers came to her and said, "Margie, you must be tired of sitting in your chair." The caregiver unfastened the restraining belt and moved Margie from the chair to the adult-sized rocking chair. The bottle of formula was ready. Margie nestled into the caregiver's arms and greedily sucked the bottle. Her eyes were wide open and were focused on the caregiver's face as she talked softly to Margie during the feeding. Margie's body was very still as she concentrated on sucking and gazing into the caregiver's eyes. After about 5 minutes the caregiver removed the bottle, placed Margie in a sitting position on her lap, and patted her firmly on the back. After a clearly audible bubble, the caregiver resumed Margie's feeding and began to gently rock. Margie finished the bottle, her eyes still glued to her caregiver's face. After a few more pats (and another bubble), Margie was placed on her tummy on a blanket in front of the long low mirror fastened to the baseboard of the wall. She promptly rolled over, smiled at the caregiver, and then began to smile at herself in the mirror.

Episode 4. Eighteen-month-old John has been greeted by a caregiver after waking from his nap. The caregiver tended to his emotional and physical needs by caressing, kissing, holding, changing and dressing, and getting his lunch. After eating eagerly, and just as eagerly washing his hands, John walked to the caregiver and raised his arms saying "up!" The caregiver responded, "Let's go play," and swooped John up in his arms. John smiled and giggled. He was put down on the floor where he began to play with a pull toy near the caregiver. John gradually moved away, after giving the caregiver a smile.

Episode 5. Thirty-month-old Tommy was having a bad time. He and the other children were on the outside playground on a gusty, nippy day. Every time another gust of wind came, he would start to scream, look terrified, and run for the storage shed in the corner of the playground. The teacher would pick him up, and talk and comfort him while standing inside the shed. When the wind died down, Tommy went back out to play. After two such episodes, the teacher suggested that he stay in the shed and play for awhile. She put a sleeping bag on the floor so he could pretend he was camping out. She also opened the window shutters so that he could see out and watch the other children at play. As soon as he heard another gust of wind he would back into the corner of the shed. The teacher stayed with him most of the time. When she did leave to attend to other children, she returned every few minutes to check on Tommy. A trash truck backed into the pick-up area on the other side of the fence. With this new excitement and noise, Tommy ventured outside the shed and seemed to forget the wind, but it was at his back. After the truck left, he started to cry again. The teacher suggested they both back into the wind, and soon they were both playing "backing up into the wind." In a minute it was time to go inside. Tommy ran happily into the center with the rest of the children.

Each episode contains teaching techniques appropriate to both the ages and the personalities of the individual children. Each episode includes teaching and learning a positive self-concept. In each instance, there was a caregiver/teacher who cared enough to respond to signals appropriately and affectionately. As the result of teacher-child interactions, each child in his or her own way felt acceptance and love in the day care setting.

Attitudes toward self are learned in the same way attitudes toward other persons, experiences, things, and places are learned. They are the result of consistent responses from things, experiences, or persons. Attitudes can be strengthened, weakened, or destroyed. The responsibility of the caregiver/teacher is to strengthen each child's concept of self. It is not difficult, if we remember that desirable attitudes result from emotionally satisfying experiences. We also need to remember that even very young children are not fooled by superficial words of praise or demonstrations of physical affection. Teachers must be genuinely interested and concerned; they must involve themselves in the child's activities; they must appreciate what the child is doing and can do. Good teachers offer support in times of stress and encouragement in times of uncertainty.

There is a subtle but important difference between encouragement and praise. Praise is external recognition given to the child for a successful performance. It is intended to motivate and to stimulate further performance. However, praise can have harmful side effects. It might suggest to children that their value or relationship to the praiser is dependent upon success. Encouragement is not dependent upon success or achievement. All of us need encouragement when we have not succeeded. Encouragement may take many forms in an infant-toddler center. "Try again" is appropriate sometimes. At other times the teacher can rearrange the environment or subjects in it to enable the child to succeed. Also, comforting words and temporary redirection (e.g., the sleeping bag for Tommy) are powerful encouragers.

Motivation and basic needs

Maslow (1943) is sometimes called the father of the needs theory of human motivation. He contends that basic needs are arranged in hierarchical order, and that the emphasis on one need grows out of the satisfaction of a previous need. Maslow's list of basic needs can be adapted to very young children in the following manner.

1. Needs relating to physiological survival and well-being: food, water, oxygen, clothing, shelter, hygiene, and health care.

2. Needs relating to physical safety and psychological security in the environment: Young children show strong reactions when they are suddenly disturbed or startled by loud noises, flashing lights, or other intense stimuli. They are upset by rough handling and by loss of physical support. They perceive danger when their world is unorganized and unstructured and therefore unpredictable. Even a physical illness may be threatening to the very young child and apparently leads to a feeling of loss of safety.

3. Needs relating to love and belongingness: All children (even the "unlovable") need to be loved, cared for, attended to, and given emotional support. Human love needs include both receiving and giving love.

4. Needs relating to self-esteem or self-worth: Infants and toddlers need to be accepted, appreciated, and valued as individuals. They also need to achieve and to be independent. Of course, achieving and independence are closely related to, and somewhat determined by, the developmental stages. Nonetheless, very young children have these needs and constantly strive to meet them under normal circumstances. Satisfactions of the self-worth need leads to self-confidence and a positive concept of self.

5. Need to know and to understand: Curiosity is readily observable in any infant or toddler. The need to know (or to learn) is as basic a need as are the needs for physical well-being and emotional satisfaction. The need to know is activated only when these other needs have been met. It will be expressed automatically and naturally if the teacher(s) have adequately met the prerequisite needs. A satisfied need no longer motivates behavior, and the child is freed to attempt to satisfy the next higher need.

Motivation and stimulation

Many theories have been forwarded in an attempt to analyze what motivates children to learn. Some claim that basic drives of hunger, thirst, and sex spur us to action. Others suggest love and a sense of belongingness as learning incentives. Still others rely on a planned system of rewards and punishments. Robert White (1959) emphasizes the need for competence as the basic motivation. He includes three characteristics of the competence need: (1) the need for activity, (2) the need for mastery, and (3) the need for excitement and stimulation.

Behaviors directed by these needs are readily observable. Very young children continually explore their surroundings by moving, touching, grasping, lifting, pulling, pushing, dropping. Young children are active whenever the opportunity is there. They do not need external stimulation to cause or provoke activity. Young children strive for mastery. Picture the baby just learning to grasp and later learning to let go. Watch the toddler work and work and work to master "chair-sitting." She backs up and plops, usually on the floor a foot away from the chair. She starts again, this time facing the chair and putting her hands on the chair, thereby gaining tactual knowledge of its location. She twists and turns her body so that one hand remains on the chair seat while she backs up again, and tentatively sits down on the front edge of the chair. She wriggles back into position and shows pure delight at her mastery of chair-sitting. The moment of delight is short-lived, and she now attempts mastery without hand-help. When finally successful, her beaming face and loud chuckles prove without a doubt that she has satisfied her need for mastery. No one had offered a gold star or a cookie; no one had instructed or consciously demonstrated. Such intrusive actions might even have led to loss of interest in the activity.

The third characteristic, the need for excitement and stimulation, is the characteristic that has resulted in controversy regarding desirable techniques for teaching very young children. According to Bromwich (1977), "the term infant stimulation is misleading and should not be used in identifying educational programs appropriate for young infants" (p. 81). Brazelton (1979) tells parents that so much cognitive development goes on in a young child *who is being nurtured properly* that any artificial or imposed stimulation is superfluous. The National Institute of Mental Health (1970) assures parents that:

> Stimulating your baby is just a natural part of caring for her. It doesn't take great investments of time and effort, and it can be fun for both of you. When you relax and enjoy yourself, your baby will tend to do the same (p. 8).

In an interview on a National Public Radio broadcast, Burton White (1979) said that "almost anything the kid does is enough to move the child forward."

Cognitive development is related to a match between the child's developmental level and the quantity and quality of environmental stimulation (Hunt, 1961). The child shows interest in objects and events that are mildly discrepant from previous experiences. Too much discrepancy will result in noninterest or even avoidance. Too little (or no) discrepancy produces boredom and even apathy when continued over a period of time. Previous experiences, natural abilities, and chronological age all influence the child's developmental level. It is for this reason that norms of cognitive development are questionable when applied to an individual beyond the first birthday.

Environmental stimulation. Infants generally receive large amounts of environmental stimulation from the time of birth. Therefore there is no need for imposing a specially designed infant stimulation program. However, there is a need for observing each baby to discover the optimal environmental match. Stimulation programs that are not related to individual behavior or temperamental patterns, as well as to maturational changes and needs, could interfere with cognitive development. Reciprocity of interaction is the cornerstone for optimal development. If the child is allowed the opportunity to explore and interact with a varied environment, he will encounter novel or discrepant stimuli that introduce new learnings. It is now thought that stimulation that proceeds in a somewhat predictable order will lead to formation of the basic concepts of object permanence and causality. However, given the appropriate environment, the child must be given freedom to pace his own encounters with stimuli.

General guidelines for planning the stimulation in the physical environment follow the stages of perceptuomotor development during the first 2 years. During the first month, baby responds only to stimuli relating to the innate reflexes. These include the sucking and rooting behaviors related to hunger and thirst, and the crying and other vocal behaviors related to discomfort or stress. After the first month, baby's reflexive behaviors begin to be modified by sensory experiences. All stimuli possess novelty when first presented. The environment now should contain a variety of sights, sounds, textures, and shapes. Baby will smile at some and will gaze at others for a long time. Now is the time to use bright patterned sheets, crib mobiles within visual range, decals on the inner sides of the crib, and pictures on the wall. Soft

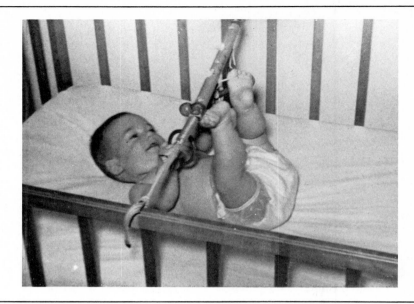

rhythmic music both stimulates and soothes. There is no substitute for a caregiver's song or hum. Now it is time to start placing rattles and different toys and textured objects in baby's hand and to offer help in grasping (wrap baby's fingers around the object). Baby should accomplish a firm grasp by 4 months of age and then will start to adjust the grasp to the specific object. The ability to integrate seeing, reaching, and grasping has not yet developed. Sometime during the fifth or sixth month, baby will be intrigued by an attractive object just beyond reach and will attempt to reach it. Continuing frustration is nonproductive, and the object should be moved close enough for baby to be successful. The mobiles that have been used up until now should either be removed or moved within the baby's physical reach if they are safe for baby to grasp.

When the baby's position in the crib is changed periodically (this should happen well before the sixth month), a whole new perspective is gained. An even larger perspective with many new stimuli is opened up when baby is placed on the floor. Intentional behavior is observable between 6 and 12 months of age when baby becomes mobile and able to reach a desired object. The sequence of behaviors will be continued in a later section, "Exploration and experimentation."

Selected principles about the stimulation qualities of the physical environment include the following:

1. The best environment at one stage of development is not the best at another stage. The rattles and toys that intrigue the 6-month-old have lost their fascination for the 1-year-old, who is beginning to enjoy the banging of real pots and pans. The child who is walking (or toddling) is attracted to objects with removable parts, and to manipulative toys, push-and-pull toys, and small cube blocks, but only when he is not working on the mastering of walking skills. By the time the third birthday occurs, the child is ready to encounter the world!

2. The best physical environment is one that

provides encounters and experiences with a variety of objects that can be investigated and manipulated with a minimal number of restrictions. To assure challenging stimulation for children at different developmental levels, there must be an even wider range of stimuli.

3. Optimal stimulation occurs when events or objects are mildly discrepant from previous experiences. The experiences of any parent or teacher of very young children testify to this principle. The well-known story of a trip to the zoo is a good example. The adults are intrigued by the bizarre make-up of the giraffe, the 3-year-old is intrigued with the different kind of knob on the entrance gate, and the 1-year-old is busy attending to the crinkly candy wrapper on the ground. The giraffe was too discrepant from previous experiences with animals to create any interest at all on the part of the young children. This example, of course, should also be related to the preceding principle.

Human stimulation. The caregiver/teacher of very young children is a multimodal stimulus. No matter how varied the physical environment, the young child will not go beyond a certain developmental stage in learning if only the enriched environment is provided. The physical environment needs a teacher to serve as mediator between the child and the environment. Teachers mediate by structuring the child's interactions, by giving emotional support and encouragement, and by providing stimulation by playing with and talking to the child. Because young children differ in their responsiveness to actual stimuli and to the pace of stimulation, a responsive teacher structures both quantity and characteristics of stimulation. As an example, babies are more visually attracted to bright colors than to differences in form or shape. The responsive teacher also structures the rate of introduction of new stimuli for each child. The environment should be arranged so that the young child learns that specific actions have specific effects. Crying leads to comfort,

pulling a toy produces sounds, playing an instrument produces music or rhythm.

Horowitz (1969) suggests that the retardation in children raised in institutions might result from the poor match between the environment and the children's individual needs. When a few adults are responsible for the care of too many young children, individual differences are more difficult to accommodate. In order to facilitate a good match between the child's abilities and the physical environment, teachers need to be alert, enthusiastic, and genuinely interested in what the child is doing. Such teachers are more likely to interact with the child in a meaningful way. Genuine interest does not involve pressure to achieve. An optimal match implies that the child is not being pushed or overstimulated. An optimal match ensures enjoyable learning.

Teachers in day care centers and homes can profit from a study of Burton White's (1972) findings about parents who produced competent 3-year-olds. Not only were the parents genuinely interested in their children's activities, but also most parent-child interactions occurred at the child's request. In addition, these parents engaged in frequent conversations related to what the child was doing at the time. White (1972) concluded that exposure to live language directed toward the child's understanding level is related to the development of competence. Language from a radio or television set does little to develop a child's competence. White (1980) summarizes his recommendations to parents as follows.

Newly crawling infants should be given maximum access to the house. They should be allowed to practice their climbing and other emerging motor skills. For most of their waking hours, they should have easy access to people who have a very special love for them. These people should talk to them about what they are focusing on at the moment, using ordinary language. They should lavish affection, encouragement, and enthusiasm on the baby, thereby intensifying her interest and excitement in learning. They need not make use of elaborate educational toys or programs. (p. 3)

Bronfenbrenner (1978) reinforces this recommendation when he states "in order to develop, a child needs the enduring, irrational involvement of one or more adults" (p. 773).

Teaching responsibilities include the initiation and mediation of stimulation and response to the child's behaviors. The teacher initiates stimulation by holding, cuddling, playing with, and talking to the child. Physical contact continues to be important until the child's growing sense of independence no longer permits it. The teacher of the very young child also initiates stimulation by:

. . . bringing the child in contact with appropriate materials and objects, manipulating situations in order to elicit appropriate intellectual and personal-social responses, as well as varied forms of indirect and focused teaching—that is, encouraging the child to attempt his own solution of problems as well as demonstrating and guiding him in the solution of problems. (Yarrow, 1968, p. 20)

The teaching event described in Episode 6 illustrates one example of manipulating a situation in order to elicit an appropriate intellectual response.

Episode 6. The teacher was seated at the table with three children, from 2 to 3 years of age. They were placing colored cube-blocks on color-matched squares on a game board. Each card contained squares of only one color; there were blocks of three colors from which to choose. Dottie joined the group, but did not appear to understand the game. She watched the others, and then began to place blocks of any color on the card with yellow squares. The teacher noticed and said, "Can you put a yellow block on top of a yellow place?" Dottie did so immediately. The teacher gave reinforcement by saying "good" and then led her a step further. "Now can you put a yellow block on all the yellow places?" Dottie correctly completed the yellow card, and asked for a card of a different color. She happily completed this one independently.

As mediator, the teacher regulates the amount, intensity, variety, and complexity of stimulation, as well as its timing and back-

ground conditions. As an agent of response, the teacher responds to and interacts with the child's behavior instead of merely doing things to and for her. Caregivers or teachers who pride themselves on having well-behaved but passive babies who grow into toddlers who never get dirty or noisy deny these children their opportunities to become intelligent. Even when infant-toddler centers are somewhat stimulating, if the primary concern is for efficient routine care, the results may include delayed motor skills, delayed social language, and abnormal passivity, all of which are cumulative.

Three more principles of stimulation may be added.

4. Each child should be given the freedom to choose those stimuli that are interesting at any particular moment.

5. Each child should be free to investigate and interact with the stimulus according to the child's timetable of development, not to the teacher's timetable for teaching.

6. In order to reach the developmental potential in learning, each child needs a genuinely interested adult who will initiate and mediate stimulation, and will respond to and interact with the child.

Motivation to learn is an intrinsic quality. It is also an elusive and highly personal quality. It is dependent upon the fulfillment of basic needs, a positive concept of self, and appropriate interactions with both the physical and the human environment. The most powerful force for learning at all ages is the inner sense of excitement that results from having learned something by and for one's self.

PERCEPTUOMOTOR AND REPRESENTATIONAL INTELLIGENCE

The learnings and teachings contained in the following pages focus more directly on the development of perceptuomotor and cognitive-academic skills and abilities. They are examples of activities related to the first three goals: how to learn the physical environment; how to learn from the physical environment; and increasing competence in representational tasks. The goals are met by activities that involve exploration and experimentation, action and interaction, and imitation and participation.

Piaget's name is frequently associated with sensorimotor (perceptuomotor) intelligence and learning. However, the importance of such learning has been recognized for well over 100 years.

The word *perceptuomotor* implies the coordination of sensory and motor functions. It is difficult to totally distinguish between sensory acts and motor acts. Sensory perceptions are instrumental in all motor acts, whether consciously or subconsciously. The infant who is beginning to physically reach has achieved visual perception and is now concentrating on the act of reaching the perceived object. The abilities of looking, grasping, and arm and hand controls are interconnected in the final ability to reach. As soon as reaching is achieved, the infant tackles new challenges and moves toward the skills of using objects together, putting one inside another, stacking one on top of another, and using one as an arm extension in reaching another. As is true for persons of all ages, current learning is based upon the successful completion of prerequisite learning.

Perceptuomotor intelligence is intelligence in action. It might be said that the child "reasons" and "thinks" with actions. There is no reflection and therefore no thought in the traditional sense of the word. The child's perceptuomotor intelligence is dependent upon the availability of objects and of persons who mediate their use.

The ability to represent is a natural result of the child's developing abilities in a facilitative environment. It is essential for mental thought but not for "action thought." Representation describes the ability to function symbolically, to remember past experiences, and to anticipate future ones. The coordination of representa-

tional ability and language leads the child to socialized and conceptual thinking (Sigel and Cocking, 1977). According to Flavell (1963), Piaget likened perceptuomotor (or sensorimotor) intelligence to a:

. . . slow motion film which represents one static frame after another, but can give no simultaneous and all-encompassing purview of all the frames. Representational thought, on the other hand, through symbolic capacity has the potential for simultaneously grasping, in a single internal epitome, a whole sweep of separate events. It is a much faster and mobile device which can recall the past, represent the present, and anticipate the future in one temporarily brief, organized act (pp. 151-152).

A milestone in the progression from action thought to mental thought is that of goal-oriented behavior. The very beginnings can be observed at age 10 to 11 months, when the child is manipulating different objects or toys in different ways. He squeezes a rubber toy, swings or bangs a rattle, and drops or rolls a ball. These manipulations are simple, but they are of great significance in intellectual development. As the result of exploration and experimentation with objects, the child's perceptions and motor activities lead to goal-oriented behavior. During this period, the visual characteristics of objects are of more importance than the tactile or auditory characteristics. Visual perception maintains its prime importance during the second and third years. It is the combination of recognizing that one's own actions have results and discriminating between effective and ineffective actions that determines the level of goal-directed behavior achieved by age 3 years.

The progression of perceptuomotor development, involving motor control, prehension, and manipulation skills is outlined in Table 7-2.

Another milestone is the conceptualization of object permanence. Numerous normative studies reported by Appleton and colleagues (1975) have led to the following description of its development. Abilities during the first 4 months

TABLE 7-2   Progression of perceptuomotor development*

Age	Motor control	Prehension and manipulation
By 4 months	Control of eye muscles and movement	Hand watching Objects brought to mouth Hand-swiping Beginning reaches for seen objects
By 7 months	Control of head and arms	Successful reaching Palmar grasp
By 10 months	Control of trunk and hands	Refined grasp Partial thumb opposition Fingering holes in pegboard
By 12 months	Control of legs	Placing pegs in pegboard Opening and closing boxes
2nd year	Walking and running	Holding crayons; scribbling Building cube towers Using spoon Using trial and error with form board
3rd year	Jumping, climbing, balancing Integration of large and fine motor skills	Making visual comparisons between holes and objects of form boards before intentional insertion

*Adapted from Appleton, Clifton, and Goldberg, 1975, pp. 131-134.

include recognition and anticipation of events and smooth visual tracking of objects. The infant visually follows an object as it is hidden, but shows no surprise when a different object appears in its place. Between 4 and 7 months the baby will show surprise when the reappeared object is not the same one that was hidden, but will not look for a hidden object. From 7 to 10 months, the baby acts puzzled if a different object is pulled from the hiding spot, and will search for a hidden object if the actual hiding has been observed. By the end of the first year, the child will continue looking for the hidden object in the same place it was first found, even if the adult has been observed while moving it to another hiding place. During the second year, the child will extend the search and will achieve success in finding the object in the last place it was hidden, ignoring the temporary hiding spots. Object permanence has now been solidly conceived, and the road to the mental

representation of objects is opened. The child's initial ability to mentally represent an object does not include the ability to classify on the basis of more than one characteristic. Even the 3-year-old child is perception dominated, and will attend to one visual perception only (usually length and not width, or amount of space covered and not the number of objects occupying that space). The child under 3 or 4 years of age will not group objects according to adult logic. Child logic leads to groupings based on the child's former experiences with the objects.

The cognitive landmarks related to child-object relationships and representational competence are summarized in Table 7-3. Implications of goal-oriented behavior are included, with the child moving from random actions to purposeful ones.

As is the case with all statements of age-expected behaviors, environmentally adequate conditions are implied. As is also the case, an

TABLE 7-3   Cognitive landmarks related to object exploration and representational competence

Age (months)	Child-object relationships	Means-end	Representation
0-3	Undifferentiated action	Random	
3-9	Beginning repertoire of action specific to object By 9 months, object permanence	Repeats actions that please	At end of 9 months, will imitate own actions
9-12	Knows functional use of common objects (to play with, to drink from)	Idea that an object can be used to do something else	Imitates adult's action, if the act is already in baby's repertoire
12-18	Knows functional use of more objects; may combine objects	Understands there are tools or intermediaries, including people, to achieve goal	Imitates new behaviors; starts to associate object or event with representation of another object or event (e.g., Adult gets coat, baby says "go bye-bye.")
18-24	Relates to objects; will use one to represent another (block as car, tissue as dolly blanket)	Makes more use of tools and persons	Object or event is represented by a word (true internal representation); demonstrates deferred imitation of action occurring up to 2 weeks ago (usually household activities)

enriched environment that includes competent teachers will enable the child to reach certain stages before the normative age. One example concerns the visual and tactual differentiation of shapes. If toys have been well seqenced, babies under 1 year can successfully work with form boards. The sequence of learning shapes progresses as follows: one circle; two circles; one square; two squares; one triangle, one circle, and one square; one square and one triangle.

Intelligence is but one aspect of adaptation to the environment, but it seems to attract the most interest in discussions of the education of even the youngest infant. It is true that mental functions derive from motor actions on concrete objects. Motor actions derive from sensation and perception.

EXPLORATION AND EXPERIMENTATION WITH OBJECTS

All babies and young children are naturally interested in examining objects, acting on them, and observing the object's reactions. Certainly at the infant-toddler stage, this spontaneous interest should be used in teaching children to gain knowledge in ways that are natural to them.

Actions that can be performed on objects to make them move (or react) include pulling, pushing, rolling, kicking, jumping, blowing, sucking, throwing, swinging, balancing, and dropping. Kamii and Devries (1978) suggest the following criteria for the selection of appropriate objects: "(a) the child must be able to produce the movement by his own action, (b) the child must be able to vary his action, (c) the reaction of the object must be observable, (d) the reaction of the object must be immediate" (pp. 8-9).

Such objects will enable the child to progress from random exploration (sucking, shaking, squeezing) to experimentations in producing desired effects or object reactions. Even after baby has used a spoon for eating, she will use it as a noise-maker by banging it on a table. Indeed, all kinds of things can be done with a spoon, as shown in Episode 7.

Episode 7. Timmy, aged 15 months, was playing near the water table, where four 2- to 3-year-olds were playing. He wandered over, peeked in, and ran his hands through the water. He reached in and grabbed a spoon, which kept his attention for the next 5 minutes. First he splashed it in the water. Then he put a spoonful of water in his mouth. He stuck out his tongue and rubbed the back of the spoon on it. He stooped down and tried to dig the carpet with it. Next, he found a small plastic container in the water table. He banged the spoon against it, put the spoon in it, and used it as a rattle. Then he pointed the spoon at John, who was walking by. Then he used the spoon as a "weapon"—he hit John with it!

Timmy's actions showed a mix of "adult-appropriate" and "toddler-appropriate" uses for a spoon. The episode came to an end before John had a chance to react, when the teacher announced that it was time to go outside.

Exploratory activities and suggested objects for the first 12 to 15 months including the following:

1. Looking and inspecting—mobiles, stabiles, pictures, photographs of known persons and places, magazines, catalogs, cloth books, safety mirrors, living people (considered as objects by the child)
2. Listening—metronome, ticking clock, bells on booties, variety of rattles, musical kicking toys, music boxes, records or tapes of music and familiar sounds, people's activities, verbalizations
3. Touching and fingering—hand-sized objects differing in texture, shape, edges; miniature copies of large objects; piano keys and guitar strings; simple form boards and shape-sorting boxes; people
4. Turning—book and magazine pages
5. Hammering and pounding—drum or other percussion instruments; wooden pegboard with 1-inch thick pegs or dowels; cube blocks; modeling materials such as clay or play dough
6. Emptying and filling—sand, water, buckets, blocks, containers, nesting toys, one- or two-piece puzzles.
7. Threading—wooden beads, empty thread spools, heavy cord or shoelaces
8. Opening and shutting—doors and drawers, boxes; pots and pans with lids
9. Stacking and knocking down—cube blocks, color cones
10. Picking up—counters, bottle caps, checkers, cotton balls, paper scraps
11. Twisting—knobs and switches; lock and lever boards
12. Bouncing—mattresses; "baby bouncers" (preferably people)
13. Rolling and retrieving—balls, beanbags, round bell rattles
14. Dropping—spoons, cereal bowls, anything loose
15. Scribbling—crayons, newspaper, paper bags
16. Creeping or crawling through or under—boxes, barrels, classroom furniture
17. Pulling and perhaps pushing—pull-string wagon, toy animals on wheels, wheelless wooden cars and trains, pop-beads

A similar listing of appropriate objects for 15- to 36-month-old children would be very long indeed. Sources of suggestions include infant-

toddler curriculum and activity books and the many manufacturer's catalogs available for the asking (see Appendix A).

During this age range the recommended activities will grow in number as well as in complexity of small motor abilities. For instance, hammering and pounding have been replaced by the use of carpentry tools on a sturdy small workbench. Walking, running, jumping, and climbing will replace creeping and crawling, requiring climbing equipment both indoors and outside, jumping or tumbling mats, tricycles, and lots of space. The stacking and knocking down of small blocks will progress into building with cartons and boxes, hollow blocks, and full

and half-unit blocks. The pull-string wagon has been relegated to "babies," and replaced with wagons and wheelbarrows to pull and push and to carry things and children. Now there is a fascination in vehicles that work, such as trucks that dump or carry freight.

Crayon scribbling has developed into "writing" on the chalkboard as well as on paper, finger and easel painting, drawing with felt-tip pens, and making collages out of pasted scraps. The infant objects for touching and fingering are replaced with multiobject sets and interlocking toys (log cabins, erector sets, connected trains), wind-up toys, hand or finger puppets, design blocks and mosaics, as well as toys, books, or

clothes designed to teach self-help skills. Magnetic boards with brightly colored shapes, flannel boards with pieces of felt, picture puzzles of four to twelve pieces, and picture lotto games all enhance perceptual, manipulative, and representational skills. The addition of an infant bathtub or small water table (water 2 to 3 inches deep) will extend touching and fingering in another dimension.

Role-playing has been added to the toddler's repertoire of activities. Therefore it is necessary to provide child-sized housekeeping equipment, dress-up clothes of all kinds, and washable baby dolls and doll equipment.

The provision of selected objects in sequence will even enhance the pre-reading skills of toddlers. These are included not as an argument for teaching baby to read but as the appropriate means for preparing the child for much later learning-to-read activities. Reading-related objects for exploration are listed in the order of their presentation.

1. Catalogs and magazines to look at, to touch and finger, to mouth, and otherwise explore
2. More catalogs, magazines, and cloth books
3. "First" books with pictures of everyday objects (sturdy cardboard pages, perhaps protected by transparent stick-on material)
4. Photographs or books containing photographs of persons and objects in baby's life, including baby
5. "Sense" books that call for touching or smelling
6. Picture books, ABC books, illustrated nursery rhyme books, pop-up books
7. Alphabet and number books
8. Books containing simple stories with which the child can identify
9. Books, books, and more books

The exploration and manipulation of objects other than books also have clear-cut implications for later reading (and writing) endeavors, as well as representational competence. The list of developmental objectives for reading and writing contained in Table 7-4 were drawn from the working copy of Caldwell's AID (Advance in Development) Chart (1980). Many reading methods textbooks include at least some of the objectives in lists of prereading and prewriting skills. They are included here as reminders that experiences during the very early years have a direct relationship to future academic learning.

The development of numerical concepts also has its foundation in these early years. These developmental objectives are even more closely related to the exploration and manipulation of objects. Table 7-5 lists these objectives for the first 4 years, again taken from the AID Chart.

Object exploration is an important part (but not the whole) of the infant-toddler curriculum being recommended. Its importance has been noted by designers of many intervention programs for 3- and 4-year-olds who have been considered educationally disadvantaged. Some of these programs have included the same kinds of activities and opportunities for object exploration that have been recommended here for the infants and toddlers in group care and education programs. Moore et al (1975) give a satisfactory concluding statement for this discussion of exploration and experimentation.

A specific, concrete base for learning comes from the freedom to explore and discover a relatively predictable environment and to manipulate actively the materials in it. This active involvement with even relatively simple surroundings is more productive of mental development than continual sensory stimulation which reduces arousal level and produces a long-range dulling effect. Material enrichment and equipment are less necessary than accepting and responsive people for an environment conducive to learning (p. 92).

ACTION AND INTERACTION

There has been a recent shift in the psychological position about how young children learn. The child is no longer viewed as a passive re-

TABLE 7-4   Developmental objectives for reading and writing*

Age	Objectives	Age	Objectives
By 1 year	1. Can mimic animal sounds or calls animal by sound (minimum of 3 animals). 2. On request points to one body part. 3. Points to picture of familiar object when asked (shoe, ball, etc.) 4. Points to 3-5 pictures in a book.		22. Can name eleven body parts. 23. Draws an acceptable circle with a model to copy. 24. Draws an acceptable square with a model to copy. 25. Can follow design when allowed a half inch track, staying within lines most of the way.
By 2 years	5. Knows whether a boy or girl. 6. Knows his/her age. 7. Can identify objects in pictures by their use (ten common objects.) A child can be given a choice of pictures and will respond correctly to the question, "Which one do you wear on your head?" 8. Names six body parts 9. Can match textures without visual clues. 10. Perceives missing parts of objects from the actual objects. 11. Draws circle and vertical/horizontal line free-hand with demonstration. 12. Imitates folding paper in half, like a book.	By 4 years	26. Identifies 8 colors (red, blue, yellow, orange, purple, green, black, brown). 27. Understand "just alike" and "different." (Example: compares picture of house and apartment). 28. Can repeat whole sentences containing six words. 29. Knows day and night. 30. Correctly labels a rectangle when asked, "What shape is this?" 31. Correctly labels a line when asked, "What is this?" 32. Can group an assortment of objects according to function.
By 3 years	13. Uses particular color on request. 14. Knows common shapes (circle, square, triangle). 15. Can classify on basis of simple distinctions (big ones here, little ones there). 16. Perceives missing parts in pictures. 17. Knows labels for common perceptual phenomena (hot, cold, heavy, soft, hard, etc.) 18. Can verbally supply information about function of objects. 19. Identifies primary colors verbally (red, blue, yellow). 20. Can copy rhythm patterns with either hands or feet. 21. Points to an object that should not be grouped with others ("Show me the one that does not have wheels.").		33. Can tell ways in which two objects are alike and different. 34. Remembers missing object when one is removed from a group of five. 35. Holds crayon or pencil between thumb and forefinger, resting pencil on third finger. 36. Traces along both vertical and horizontal lines. 37. Draws an acceptable triangle freehand but with a model to copy. 38. Can follow a straight edge (ruler, template) with a pencil. 39. Can draw recognizable man, woman, or child (drawing will include head, body, arms, and legs). 40. Names twenty body parts.

*Adapted from Caldwell, 1980.

TABLE 7-5 Developmental objectives for object manipulation and numerical concepts*

Ages	Objectives	Ages	Objectives
By 1 year	1. Puts small objects in and out of a container. 2. Pulls string to secure out-of-reach toy. 3. Looks for toy that has disappeared. 4. Finds toy hidden under a pillow or other object. 5. Demonstrates knowledge of function of common objects. 6. If given an array of small objects and a container, will, upon request, put *all* objects into container. 7. Can stack 2 small items (spools, blocks, etc.). 8. Can stack 3 graded boxes in a tower (boxes will measure approximately 8 inches, 6 inches, 4 inches). 9. Can nest 3 loose fitting boxes (boxes will measure approximately 8 inches, 6 inches, 4 inches). 10. Can successfully place at least one piece of single-unit puzzle of no more than 5 pieces.	By 3 years	17. Stacks all disks on color cone correctly. 18. Given the choice of 3 and 2 blocks, will say three means more. 19. Counts correctly to 10. 20. Understands one-to-one correspondence up to 3. 21. Uses lacing toys correctly accomplishing a uniform stitch. 22. Successfully places graded cylinders in Montessori boards. 23. Replaces nesting cups correctly. 24. Works 6 to 8 piece puzzle. 25. Copies pegboard designs involving only one direction depicted in drawing. 26. Takes toys apart that involve manipulation (nuts and bolts, etc.).
By 2 years	11. Manipulates pull apart and put together toy (e.g., pop-beads) 12. Counts to 3. 13. Can successfully work a puzzle of at least 5 whole units (fruits, cars, etc.). 14. Can string large beads getting ten or more past tip in five minutes. 15. Builds with small table blocks, stacking as high as six or seven. 16. Plays with lacing toys appropriately, correctly accomplishing the in and out effect.	By 4 years	27. Assembles toys (nuts and bolts). 28. Works 9 to 12 piece puzzle. 29. Copies pegboard designs involving two directions depicted in drawings. 30. Constructs objects with Tinker Toys or other small building toys. 31. Establishes one-to-one correspondence up to 10. 32. Knows positional terms (second, middle, next to last, etc.). 33. Copies pegboard designs involving two directions given by a concrete example.

*Adapted from Caldwell, 1980.

ceiver of information. In the case of the infant or toddler, learning is not accomplished by exposure to an enriched environment. The current position is that the child acts on the environment, which is designed to react to the child. The environment, of course, includes living persons as well as inanimate objects. Out of the action-reaction sequence comes an expectancy for future interactions. At 4 months of age, for instance, the infant smiles more readily at an "object" that smiles back. If the environment is somewhat systematically ordered and appro-

priately stimulating, the infant learns that the world is predictable.

This newer view of learning emphasizes interaction. It implies that a maturational view of development is not the total answer, because the maturational theory allows no room for reciprocal interactions. Maturation is a necessary condition for development and learning, but it does not provide the motivation for learning. The child's experiences, including interactions, are important and necessary. In addition, it is superficial to attribute individuality to genetic tendencies and environmental influences. From the moment of birth these two are interacting. They modify the adaptational pattern of the baby as well as that of the significant persons in the baby's life space. Different components of the physical environment also direct baby's growth and development. A highly active baby may be limited in space exploration (for the convenience of the caregiver/teacher) but given many toys and play objects within that space. Another equally active baby may be given free rein to explore a wide area, with only a few toys. Would this make a difference? Probably. The space-limited baby will concentrate on the mastery of available objects. The space-free baby will gain exploration-of-space skills, but perhaps will not master specific objects in the same time period.

Interactions between child and object and child and teacher have been stated or implied repeatedly in the preceding discussion. It is the reciprocal interplay that binds the child to the world of things and people. Recognition of this fact leads to the question of teacher/child ratio. Teachers with too many children cannot be effective as teachers, or even as caregivers. Children need many individualized reciprocal exchanges. Teachers must have time and an interest in being with children. They must honestly want children to learn. Lichtenberg and Norton (1971) state that "each child must be dealt with actively and individually, spontaneously and yet in connection with known constitutional and other predispositional factors. In no other way can the reciprocity entailed in binding the organism to the environment be carried to fruition" (pp. 16-17).

There appears to be common agreement that growth, development, health, and high levels of cognitive and affective functioning in children are all associated with continuous ongoing participation in actions and interactions that contain pleasure and playfulness. If caregiver/ teachers and young children "laugh, play at

words, satisfy each other, act in an animated and joyful way, glory in their mutual liveliness, the infants and children will grow into intelligent, happy, searching, curious, creative human beings" (Lichtenberg and Norton, 1971, p. 17).

Developmental sequence of action and interaction

The information that follows is expressed in terms of what the child does and what the teacher does in responding.

From birth to 3 months. The infant makes baby noises and gurgles. The teacher imitates the baby's noises, uses them in conversation with the baby, and makes new vocalized noises with changes in pitch. The infant engages in mouth play. The teacher allows baby to taste a finger or arm, etc. The infant engages in hand play. The teacher chews or kisses baby's hand or lets baby grasp a finger or two. Baby shows surprise at a discrepancy in the usual. The teacher makes faces and different vocal sounds. The baby moves arms and legs; the teacher pushes gently on the soles of baby's feet, and alternately raises and lowers baby's arms. Baby responds to rhythmic movements; teacher dances with baby in her arms, and also gently rocks baby. Baby visually explores the environment; teacher provides things to look at (patterns, colors, movement) and persons to look at, including the teacher.

From 3 to 6 months. The baby plays with food; teacher supplies finger foods. Baby recognizes familiar things; teacher provides stability in objects and persons. Baby shows surprise at a novelty in the context of the familiar; teacher gradually introduces slightly different objects and persons and experiences. The baby engages in object play and power play; the teacher provides toys that do something as a result of the child's actions. Baby is excited by movement and rhythm; the teacher dances, sings, and plays with baby; he bounces baby on his knee, holds baby up in the air; provides mobiles within visual range. Baby enjoys predictable excitement; teacher plays "this little piggy went to market," "pat-a-cake," "rock-a-bye baby," "there was a little mouse," etc. Baby explores the environment visually and tactually; teacher provides objects to look at and touch and positions baby in visual range of on-going activities.

From 6 to 12 months. Baby explores visually, tactually, and motorically; teacher permits as much freedom as is reasonable and safe and introduces new objects (or places baby in different locations of the room). Baby imitates new sounds or sights; teacher converses with vocalizations, verbalizations, and facial expressions, including funny faces and sounds. Baby wants an audience; teacher is a frequent observer and an appreciative responder; teacher makes "mirror" faces. Baby enjoys total body movement; teacher gently rough-houses. Baby enjoys predictable surprises; teacher plays peek-a-boo and hear-a-boo. Baby enjoys fun and games; teacher makes baby laugh, and plays with baby.

From 12 to 24 months. Toddler explores sensually and motorically; teacher adds new objects to investigate, such as pegboards, containers to fill and empty, doors and drawers to open and close, balls, modeling materials, crayons and paper; also occasional "field trips" to other rooms in the center. Toddler likes to put together and take apart, to fill and empty; teacher provides pop-beads, blocks for stacking, train cars that hook together, one- to three-piece puzzles; nesting toys. Toddler likes to hide and look for (self and objects); teacher plays hide-and-seek games, pretends to lose things, including the toddler, supplies corners or big boxes for toddler to hide in. Toddler likes to test her strength; teacher plays tug-of-war. Toddler likes to chase and be chased; teacher chases and "runs" from child. Toddler enjoys people and simple social rituals; teacher engages in verbal and action messages associated with "hello" and "good-bye." Toddler also tests social behaviors and imitates the actions of others; teacher provides opportunities to observe others and grad-

ually introduces interaction episodes with other young children. Teacher includes toddler in small group activities (two or three) and adult activities when possible and feasible. Toddler enjoys pretending; teacher provides realistic toys, gradually moving to less realistic; also dress-up clothes, baby dolls, stuffed animals, blocks and boxes, simple child-sized housekeeping equipment. Toddler tests his motor abilities; teacher provides opportunities to run, throw, climb, hit, jump, march, and balance; also to hide and to search for a hidden object or person.

From 24 to 36 months. The young child likes to explore; the teacher enlarges the environment for exploration and provides "field trips" to other parts of the building and in the neighborhood adjoining the center. The teacher allows unhurried times for exploration and investigation. The young child likes to build; the teacher provides unit blocks, toys (hammers, soft wood, paper, scissors, paste), small interlocking blocks, beads to string, puzzles, pegboards, materials to use as musical instruments. Young children like to test their physical prowess; the teacher increases the complexity and opportunities in the 12-to-24 month list; provides an obstacle course; balance beam, set of two or three steps, appropriate trampoline, balls of all sizes. Young children imitate and represent; teacher provides opportunities for role-playing, including objects and toys that may but do not have to represent their real counterparts. Teacher introduces imitation games such as "Simon says," and uses many finger-plays and action songs. Young children enjoy people; teacher plans for and encourages participation in small group activities of many kinds, some of which are teacher directed.

Comments about the teaching role

The very young child needs two major things from the teacher: (1) attention and interaction and (2) sufficient time to allow the cognitive processes to develop. Teachers of older children sometimes think they should be directly teaching most of the time. The correctness of this approach is not the subject of this text. However, it is within the scope of this text to emphasize the absolutely essential provision of sufficient time for the very young child to mentally organize perceptions, actions, and interactions. White and Watts (1973) found that their most competent infants were directly taught only 1–4% of their waking hours.

Teachers of infants and toddlers are inclined to use one of two approaches to teaching. They either let Topsy "just grow," thereby failing to promote adequate stimulus content for the child to make optimal perceptual and motor use of the environment, or they intrude in the child's "continuity of processing time needed for coping" (Murphy, 1976, p. 145). As with many questions, the answer is not one or the other. The answer is an appropriate compromise of the two positions. In the instance of infant-toddler education, the answer for each child can be arrived at only by close observation of the individual child. The timing, quantity, and quality of teacher input, or lack of input, is unique for a particular child.

Infants and toddlers are action oriented. It is the teacher's responsibility to react and to interact with the child and the child's actions in order to further the child's learning and development.

IMITATION AND PARTICIPATION
"Don't stick out your tongue at a newborn"

Recent studies suggest that newborn infants have sophisticated perceptual and motor abilities. Until quite recently, developmental psychologists assigned the ability of precise sequential imitation to babies between 8 and 12 months of age. Now Meltzoff and Moore (1977) have shown that infants as young as 12 days old can and do imitate "tongue-sticking-out." They even found an infant 1 hour old who imitated adult actions! It is therefore conceivable that the ability to imitate is innate rather than a learning that develops during the first several months after

birth. If imitation is an innate skill, it should be considered as the fourth essential learning tool present at the time of birth (or very shortly thereafter).

Although most day care centers and family day care homes do not serve newborns, the advice "Don't stick out your tongue" applies to older children also. From 6 months of age, imitation appears to be the most powerful motivation for behavior throughout childhood. The imitations of very young children may not be conscious behavior, but children are constantly learning by imitation of the adults with whom they identify. Toward the end of the perceptuomotor stage, imitation is active and intentional (Piaget, 1951). "Awareness of imitation is inseparable from the development of the notion of self in the child. Imitation enables the child to see himself in the person of another" (Guillame, 1926, p. 207).

Imitation and learning

Imitation provides a shortcut to many learnings at all ages. It is the only way to teach some things to children too young to follow verbal directions. Imitation plays a large role from the simplest version of pat-a-cake to the complexities of self-dressing skills.

Because imitation is such a strong motivator in young children, the teacher's repertoire of values and behaviors must be worthy of imitating. Children will imitate those persons with whom they identify. This is clearly shown in Episode 8.

Episode 8. Bobby and Clara, both 2 years, 10 months old, were sitting close on the floor. Their "conversation," which was too quiet to be overheard, came to an abrupt end when Bobby hit Clara. Clara began to cry. She continued crying and loudly announced "I don't like it when Bobby does that!" Her perfect imitation of a teacher's verbal response to aggression rang out loud and clear. There was a dramatic pause in the classroom activities, as teachers and children alike realized that Clara was "teacher" for a moment.

All social learnings during the early years are developed out of the imitation of significant others. Of course, it is possible to teach "please" and "thank-you" by rote, if the adults insist on the words and provide a tangible reinforcer. But "please" and "thank you" are more than meaningless words to be used when needed. They represent an attitude of respect and consideration of others in social relationships. The words and their meanings are best learned by the imitation of consistent adult behaviors, including but not limited to verbalization.

Toward the end of the second year, children will incorporate imitations in their dramatic play. The housekeeping corner in the center is proof of the influence of parents and teachers on a child's behaviors and developing attitudes. It is an interesting side note that children rarely imitate the play of adults. For whatever reason, it is the work of adults that is reflected in their behaviors. (Perhaps adults play only when baby is elsewhere.)

Teachers of very young children recognize that the ability to imitate progresses in stages. Until we learned that newborns will stick out their tongues, the first imitative behavior was noted when an infant assimilated the crying of other infants. It is common knowledge in an infant center or nursery that crying is contagious. Babies cry when others are crying. They also stop crying when others stop.

Next, the infant imitates actions or sounds of a significant adult, but only if the adult has first imitated the child's own actions or sounds. Deliberate imitations of sounds and movements follow, but they are limited to those already in the child's repertoire, and are visually or auditorially perceptible. In the last stage (about 18 months), the child's ability to remember (or represent) enables imitation of actions or sounds not immediately perceptible. The child begins to imitate the actions and sounds of objects as well as those of persons. This ability has been called symbolic functioning. It is the beginning of the make-believe world. Pretending reaches its forte during the preschool years (ages 3 to 5).

The activity of stringing beads is a usual activity in the toddler curriculum. It involves imitation in almost every step. A description of a suggested learning sequence follows.

1. From a group of wooden beads, similar in color and shape, the teacher demonstrates stringing the beads onto a shoelace with a firm tip.
2. Baby imitates the action, using a pincer grasp to pick out beads from the same group.
3. Teacher gives the baby opportunity to explore and manipulate spontaneously.
4. When baby has conquered the act of bead-stringing, the teacher adds beads of a second color (but same shape) and demonstrates stringing beads of alternate colors.
5. Baby imitates.
6. Teacher again gives the baby the opportunity to explore and manipulate spontaneously.
7. Teacher adds beads of a third color, and so on.

After beads of more than one color (or shape, which should be added later) are being used in a pattern set by the teacher, it is worthwhile to let the toddler make up patterns for the teacher to imitate.

Participation

Taking part in group endeavors is closely related to imitation. Younger children learn participation skills by first observing others who are interacting or engaging in a common endeavor. Even after several observations, they may need encouragement to join in.

Few 2 or 3-year-olds will actively attempt to include others in their play. They are still somewhat nonsocial, and their own needs and interests predominate. The teacher gains little by directing children to play together. The teacher gains much by joining in the fun and gradually pulling in another child or two. If the activity calls for specific actions (clapping or moving on cue), taking the child's hand and guiding him through the appropriate actions will help ease the transition from observer to participant.

Social relationships and interactions are learned in the same way that the physical environment is learned. Social learnings result from exploration, investigation, and manipulation. Many incidents of "aggression" are really incidents of exploring people as objects. The teacher should treat these incidents accordingly.

All very young children, not just the extremely shy ones, need to be taught how to participate. Any shared experience, such as action songs, finger-plays, and rhythmic movements, is an appropriate vehicle for teaching participation. Even the simple social rituals of greeting children when they are delivered to the center and saying "good-bye" when they are picked up are an important part of teaching social behaviors. In too many instances the teachers and parents greet one another and talk on an adult level, virtually ignoring the child. This is an easy routine to establish and must be consciously avoided. It tells the child that only grown-ups are important.

Social learnings and teachings are presented in greater detail in the next chapter. It is sufficient to call attention to the importance of early experiences for social learnings. White and Watts (1973) have pinpointed the period from 10 to 18 months as the most crucial in determining the child's later competency in social skills and attitudes. Social competency is learned through imitation and participation.

■ CHAPTER SUMMARY ■

The meanings underlying the proverb quoted at the beginning of the chapter ("I hear and I forget; I see and I remember; I do and I understand") have been expanded and deepened. The main message of this chapter is that young children learn by doing. They learn better when their "doing" is guided and encouraged by a responsive teacher.

The following goals for a developmental-educational curriculum for infants and toddlers are suggested. We want to teach very young children: (1) how to learn the physical environment and how to learn from it; (2) competence in representational tasks; (3) self-awareness and a positive self-concept; (4) how to learn the social environment and how to learn from it; (5) the use of verbal language for communication and social exchange; and (6) how to learn and control the physical body. The overall goal is to teach the young child that both living and learning are satisfying and exciting.

The learning necessary to meet these goals is dependent upon motivation and stimulation, a positive concept of self, and the satisfaction of physiological, safety, love, and self-worth needs. The need to know, present in the newborn, is never completely satisfied. Motivation is an intrinsic quality that expands with appropriate teacher behaviors and teacher-child interactions. Artificial or imposed external stimulation to learn is unnecessary and superfluous for intact children who are nurtured properly.

The infant-toddler teacher's role is three-fold: (1) to initiate appropriate stimulation; (2) to mediate the stimulation by structuring the child's interactions (by giving emotional support and encouragement, and by playing with and talking to the child); and (3) to act as an agent of response.

During the first 18 months, the child reasons and thinks with actions (perceptuomotor intelligence). Then the child begins to function symbolically, to remember past experiences, and to anticipate future ones. The coordination of those abilities (representation) and language lead the child to socialized and conceptual thinking.

Young children learn through exploration and experimentation with objects and persons, action and interaction with objects and persons, imitation of significant persons' behaviors and attitudes, and through participation in activities involving other persons.

The most learning and the best teaching are based upon the teacher's close observation of each child and individual curriculum planning based on these on-going observations.

SUGGESTED ACTIVITIES/POINTS TO PONDER

1. Identify specific teacher behaviors or attitudes in Episodes 3, 4, and 5 that should encourage the development of a child's positive concept of self.
2. Based on your own evaluation, prepare a list of children's books suitable for children below the age of 3 years. Include the reason(s) why each book was chosen for your list.
3. Make a beanbag, texture toy, or clutch ball.

REFERENCES AND SUGGESTED READINGS

Appleton, T., Clifton, R., and Goldberg, S.: The development of behavioral competence in infancy. In Horowitz, F.D., editor: Review of child development research, Vol. 4, Chicago, 1975, University of Chicago Press.

Brazelton, T.B.: Infant learning. Options in Education Program No. 202, Part I, Washington, D.C., 1979, National Public Radio and the Institute for Educational Leadership.

Bromwich, R.M.: Stimulation in the first year of life? A perspective on infant development, Young Children 32(2): 71-82, 1977.

Bronfenbrenner, U.: Who needs parent education? Teachers College Record 70(4):767-787, 1978.

Caldwell, B.: AID Chart (working draft), Little Rock, Ark., 1980, Center for Child Development and Education, University of Arkansas.

Chance, P.: Learning through play, Pediatric Round Table 3, New York, 1979, Johnson & Johnson Baby Products Co.

Coleman, J.S., and others: Equality of educational opportunity, Washington, D.C., 1966, U.S. Government Printing Office.

Coopersmith, S., editor: Developing motivation in young children, San Francisco, 1975, Albion Publishing Co.

Coopersmith, S.: The role of emotions in education. In Coopersmith, S., editor: Developing motivation in young children, San Francisco, 1975, Albion Publishing Co.

Dodson, F.: How to parent, New York, 1970, The New American Library, Inc.

Fein, G.G.: Play and the acquisition of symbols. In Katz, L.G., editor: Current topics in early childhood education, II, Norwood, N.J., 1979, Ablex Publication Corp.

Flavell, J.: The developmental psychology of Jean Piaget, Princeton, N.J., 1963, D. Van Nostrand Co., Inc.

Fowler, W.: Infant and child care, Boston, 1980, Allyn & Bacon, Inc.

Garvey, C.: Play, Cambridge, Mass., 1977, Harvard University Press.

Garden, I.J.: The infant experience, Columbus, Ohio, 1975, Charles E. Merrill Publishing Co.

Gordon, I.J.: Baby to parent, parent to baby, New York, 1977, St. Martin's Press.

Gratch, G.: The development of thought and language in infancy. In Osofsky, J.D., editor: Handbook of infant development, New York, 1979, John Wiley & Sons, Inc.

Guillaume, P.: Imitation in children, Chicago; 1971, University of Chicago Press. (Translated by E.P. Halperin; originally published in 1926.)

Horowitz, F.D.: Learning, developmental research and individual differences. In Lipsitt, L.P., and Reese, H.W., editors: Advances in child development and behavior, Vol. 4, New York, 1969, Academic Press.

Hunt, J.M.: Intelligence and experience, New York, 1961, The Ronald Press Co.

Kamii, C., and DeVries, R.: Physical knowledge in preschool education, Englewood Cliffs, N.J., 1978, Prentice-Hall, Inc.

Languis, M., Sanders, T., and Tipps, S.: Brain and learning: directions in early childhood education, Washington, D.C., 1980, National Association for the Education of Young Children.

Lichtenberg, P., and Norton, D.: Cognitive and mental development in the first five years of life, Washington, D.C., 1971, U.S. Government Printing Office.

Maslow, A.H.: A theory of human motivation, Psychological Review 50:370-396, July 1943.

McCall, R.B.: Infants, Cambridge, Mass., 1979, Harvard University Press.

McCarthy, M.A., and Houston, J.P.: Fundamentals of early childhood education, Cambridge, Mass., 1980, Winthrop Publishers, Inc.

Meltzoff, A.N., and Moore, M.K.: Imitation of facial and manual gestures by human neonates, Science 198:75-78, 1977.

Moore, R.S., and others: Influences on learning in early childhood: a literature review. Berrien Springs, Mich.: Hewitt Research Center, 1975, (ERIC Document Reproduction Service No. Ed. 144 711).

Murphy, L.B.: The widening world of childhood, New York, 1962, Basic Books Inc.

Murphy, L.B., and Moriarty, A.E.: Vulnerability, coping, and growth, New Haven, Conn., 1976, Yale University Press.

National Institute of Mental Health: Stimulating baby senses, Washington, D.C., 1978, U.S. Government Printing Office.

Osofsky, J.D., editor: Handbook of infant development, New York, 1979, John Wiley & Sons, Inc.

Piaget, J.: The origins of intelligence in children, New York, 1952, International Universities Press. (Originally published, 1936).

Piaget, J.: Play, dreams and imitation in childhood, New York, 1962, W.W. Norton & Co.

Platt, W.: Policy making and international studies in educational evaluations, Phi Delta Kappan 55:7, March 1974.

Sameroff, A.J., and Cavanagh, P.J.: Learning in infancy: a developmental perspective. In Osofsky, J.D., editor: Handbook of infant development, New York, 1979, John Wiley & Sons, Inc.

Samples, R.E.: Serving intrinsic motivation in early education. In Coopersmith, A., editor: Developing motivation in young children, San Francisco, 1975, Albion Publishing Co.

Sigel, I.E.: Psycho-educational intervention beginning at age two—reflections and outcomes. Paper presented at Second Annual Blumberg Symposium, Baltimore, Md., 1972.

Sigel, I.E., and Cocking, R.R.: Cognitive development from childhood to adolescence, New York, 1977, Holt, Rinehart & Winston.

Singer, D.G., and Revenson, T.A.: How a child thinks: a Piaget primer, New York, 1978, New American Library.

Sutton-Smith, B., and Sutton-Smith, S.: How to play with your children, New York, 1974, Hawthorn Books, Inc.

Wattenberg, W.W., and Clifford, C.: Relation of self concepts to beginning achievement in reading, Child Development 35(35):461-67, 1964.

Weiser, M.G.: Continuity between home and child care programs (unpublished ms).

White, B.L.: Fundamental early environmental influences on the development of competencies. In Meyer, M.E., editor: Third symposium on learning: cognitive learning, Bellingham, Wash., 1972, Western Washington State College Press.

White, B.L.: Infant learning. Options in Education Program No. 202, Part II Washington, D.C., 1979, National Public Radio and the Institute for Educational Leadership.

White, B.L. The knowledge base, the development of intelligence, Part II, Newsletter of the Center for Parent Education 1980, 11(4), 1980.

White, B.L., and Watts, J.C.: Experience and environment: major influences on the development of the young child, Englewood Cliffs, N.J., 1973, Prentice-Hall, Inc.

White, R.W.: Motivation reconsidered: the concept of competence. In Almy, M., editor: Early childhood play: selected readings related to cognition and motivation, New York, 1968, Simon & Schuster, Inc.

Yarrow, L.J: Conceptualizing the early environment. In Dittmann, L.L., editor: Early child care: the new perspectives, New York, 1968, Altherton Press.

CHAPTER 8

LEARNING AND TEACHING PERSONAL, SOCIAL, AND COMMUNICATION SKILLS

The difference between a lady and a flower girl is not how she behaves, but how she is treated.

Eliza Doolittle in *My Fair Lady*

"Positive self-concept," "socialization skills," and "learning to get along with others" are usually included in lists of goals for young children attending organized care and education programs. The goals suggested in Chapter 7 include: (1) self-awareness and a positive self-concept; (2) how to learn the social environment; (3) how to learn from the social environment; and (4) the use of verbal language for communication and social exchange. The satisfactory achievement of these four goals at the appropriate level will result in a young child who is socially competent.

SOCIAL COMPETENCY

A definition of social competency is elusive. In 1973 the now-defunct Office of Child Development requested that a panel of experts define social competency in young children. Their final report (Anderson and Messick, 1974) included the following essential components of "young" social competency:

1. Differentiated self-concept and consolidation of identity
2. Concept of self as an initiating and controlling agent
3. Habits of personal maintenance and care
4. Realistic appraisal of self, accompanied by feelings of personal worth
5. Differentiation of feelings
6. Sensitivity and understanding in social relationships
7. Positive and affectionate personal relationships
8. Role perception and appreciation
9. Appropriate regulation of antisocial behavior
10. Morality and prosocial tendencies
11. Curiosity and exploratory behavior
12. Control of attention
13. Perceptual and perceptuomotor skills
14. Gross motor skills and fine motor dexterity
15. Language skills

The list also contains cognitive and intellectual skills, such as critical and creative thinking and problem-solving skills, which are probably not appropriate for very young children, although foundations for these higher level skills are laid in the beginning years.

There are three distinct processes in the development of social competency, all of which extend beyond the very early years. The first process is social cognition. Lewis and Brooks-Gunn (1979) define social cognition during the first years of life as "the relationship between three aspects of knowledge: (1) knowledge of the self; (2) knowledge of others; and (3) knowledge of one's relations to others" (p. 2).

The second process is the acquisition of skills and techniques for initiating and responding to persons and social events. The third relates to the development of appropriate reactions that undergird and motivate social behavior.

The second and third processes are traditionally included in definitions of socialization. For instance, Zigler and Child (1973) define socialization as a "broad term for the whole process by which an individual develops, through transactions with other people, his specific patterns of socially relevant behavior and experience" (p. 36). A more limited view of socialization concerns "the various ways people learn about what is approved and disapproved by their culture" (Margolin, 1974, p. 55). The more limited definition might be easily misinterpreted as saying that socialization consists of learning rules. A follow-up statement might be: All a teacher does to socialize a child is to teach rules and perhaps punish when the child does not follow the rules. Here, as in all other areas of the curriculum, the definition of teaching as telling is very inadequate. True, social skills and behaviors must be learned, but they are learned from relationships with others.

The parent-child relationship is the first major teacher. For the infant or toddler in a group setting for a significant number of hours on a regular basis, the teacher-child relationship is also a major teacher. There is a third teacher: relationships with peers and the related social accommodations necessitated by group living.

Selected landmarks of the personal and social development of a very young child have been summarized, based on the assumption that all goes well in the child's relationships with others.

0-1 mo.	Primary identification with mother or mother-substitute; interested in faces
1 mo.	Is quieted by touch; responds to speech
2 mo.	Turns head toward speaking voices; spontaneously produces responsive smiles
3 mo.	Is quieted by a voice; cries when adult leaves; shows anticipation
4 mo.	Adjusts position in anticipation of being lifted; nonselective smiling; aware of strange situations
5 mo.	Is quieted by voice or caress; disturbed by strangers; smiles at other children; dislikes being left alone
6 mo.	Can distinguish between friendly and angry talking; holds arms up to be picked up; recognizes familiar people; smiles only at recognized persons.
7 mo.	Reacts to image in mirror; differentiates known and unknown people.
8 mo.	Pats and smiles at own mirror image; interested in other children's play; begins to imitate movements and sounds.
9 mo.	Is developing preferences for people and objects; knows mother; possible separation anxiety.
10 mo.	Imitates movements of other children; responds to pat-a-cake and peek-a-boo
11 mo.	Strives for attention; will repeat a behavior for an appreciative audience
12 mo.	Enjoys watching other children, but the ability to play considerably with anyone else is still far in the future. The playmate may be pushed or bitten or sat on! The playmate has not been mentally separated from objects-to-be-explored.
12-18 mo.	Learns that some actions please adults and that others do not; tests limits of caregivers; pursues new relationships and is less shy toward strangers.
18-24 mo.	Begins to understand "mine"; other children are still explored. Murphy and Leeper (1976) suggest that 1- to 2-year-olds will benefit by occasionally playing with other children (4- or 5-year-olds) instead of always with other toddlers. Not only do the older children model more mature interaction skills, but also the toddler will not have to fend off the aggressive attacks that are likely to come from peers. Of course the older children

may be dictatorial, and supervision is advisable. Toward the end of the second year, the toddler may offer a toy to another child. At this point, the realization that a child is not an object has been achieved.

24-30 mo. Engages in solitary play and spends a lot of time watching other children. May engage in occasional parallel play as well as some physical/aggressive acts.

30-36 mo. The number of social intractions increases, although they may be negative or destructive. Usually unwilling to share toys, but during the next months, a preschooler will begin to play cooperatively. The importance of having a friend soon follows.

It is readily apparent that the development of social skills is closely tied to the child's other developing motor and vocal skills. If a peer is available, the infant will direct a particular skill to that peer as soon as it is mastered. Peer-directed smiles appear at about 6 months. As infants become mobile, they approach, follow, and reach for their peers. Between 9 and 12 months of age, infants have been observed playing games with each other (run-and-chase, peek-a-boo, and ball games); at 13 to 14 months they imitate one another and begin to make noises back and forth (Mueller and Vandell, 1979). It appears that after the first 15 months, the repertoire of social encounters is fairly complete. The child spends the next 2 years (and many more) in increasing the frequency and complexity of social behaviors.

The summary lends credence to the suggestion that social responsiveness is an innate human capacity, and that from the moment of birth the infant is ready to communicate with others (Bower, 1978). Babies usually learn to communicate most frequently and effectively with their mothers (or mother substitutes). When baby is left with someone who does not "speak" the same language, the baby is left without a communication partner. This is the case when babies under 6 months are placed in out-of-home care. All efforts must be made to enable the new caregiver to get to know the baby as well as possible within the shortest possible period of time. The frequent smiles of a baby at this age will elicit warm responses (physical and verbal) from the responsible caregiver, and —voila!—a new communication partnership is on its way.

If babies are first taken to a day care center or home during the second half of their first year, these same efforts are needed. But this time, it is the mother who should arrange her other commitments so that she and the new caregiver mutually care for the baby in the new surroundings for a time. If mother can stay long enough for the caregiver to become a familiar person to the baby, many emotional upsets will be avoided. The ideal situation, of course, would be having the caregiver spend time at baby's home, interacting with baby and mother, before baby starts to attend the center. Unfortunately, the ideal is rarely obtainable. It is included here to emphasize the importance of a gradual transition for baby from one primary caregiver to another, and from one setting to another. The emotional upsets referred to above may not be exclusively the baby's. Most mothers of very young children are also emotionally involved and concerned when they relinquish caregiving responsibilities to a nonfamily person.

Perhaps the issue of stranger anxiety should be mentioned. First, it must be recognized that not all babies are afraid of strangers. If baby has had experiences with many people (family members, neighbors, even "strangers") there will be little or no stranger anxiety. Much depends on the way the new person approaches the baby. If the mother is present and the approach is gradual, the anxiety level is markedly decreased. The recommended approach is one in which the newcomer pays no attention to baby, but engages in friendly conversation with mother. Shortly, baby's curiosity will overcome any uncertainty, and baby will approach and "explore" the stranger. The adult's warm response will initiate a social interaction, and the person is no longer a stranger. The following incident illustrates such a resolution of the stranger anxiety of a 2½ year old girl, who solved the problem for herself, with the assistance of a knowledgeable mother.

Episode 9. Carol could talk of nothing else but her desire to see Santa Claus. Mother and Carol made a special trip downtown to one of Santa's headquarters, and joined the line of other adults and children. But when Carol's turn came, she burst into tears and clung to her mother. They both moved away, and when Carol calmed down, she said, "Just watch." They watched for awhile at a safe distance.

During the next week, mother and Carol saw several Santas as they went in and out of stores Christmas shopping, and one night Carol saw Santa on a television program.

Eight days after her first encounter with him, Carol announced, "I want to go see Santa Claus." She and her mother again went to Santa's headquarters and joined the line. When Carol's turn came, she jumped up on his lap and happily responded to his questions, "What is your name? . . . What do you want for Christmas?" Her answer to both questions was "Two in August!" He laughed and gave her a hug and a candy cane. Carol hurried back to her mother, obviously very pleased with the whole affair.

So many good things happened in this story, and all of them happened because the mother did not pressure, scold, or ridicule her daughter's anxiety and fear. Mother gave Carol the time and opportunity to solve the problem for herself, and the little girl made a giant step forward in her development.

Most persons anticipate that all children will go through the stranger anxiety crises and dismiss the episodes with little thought. Although the amount of recent research knowledge about the early years is considerable, there is much still to be learned. Brazelton (1978) suggested a new view of the so-called stranger anxiety at a national pediatric round table discussion. He suggested that it is possible that the strong reactions to strangers in infancy are really "peaks of intense curiosity, and that they accompany

spurts of learning about new areas of his world" (p. xv). Certainly we know that baby's reaction to a new person is very much a function of that person's method of approach to the baby. The fear implied by the term "stranger anxiety" is not universal.

The preceding sequence in the development of social competency has been fairly well established by observation and empirical research. Let's turn our attention to the processes involved in the sequence, which have been labeled social cognition and socialization.

SOCIAL COGNITION

In 1934 George Mead wrote that the main outcome of socialization is the development of self. In 1968 Abraham Maslow included the need for self-actualization in his list of universal human needs. In 1978 Louise Kaplan, director of the Child Clinical Services at the City University of New York, described the child's efforts to establish its own identity as a second or psychological birth that occurs around the age of 18 months. According to Kaplan, the child's resolution of the oneness-separateness conflict between the ages of 18 and 36 months will shape the adult he or she will become.

Who am I?

Self-knowledge is learned through interactions and relationships with others in the social world, just as object knowledge is learned through interactions and relationships with objects in the physical world. Freedom to explore and manipulate objects not only gives information about these objects, but also much information about oneself. "I can move my arms and hands . . . I can reach . . . I can grasp . . . I can make something happen . . . I can control what happens . . ." More important in the development of self-knowledge, however, are the social relationships and interactions. Objects may or may not react in a predictable manner; many objects are not readily available to the infant who is not yet mobile. On the other hand, caregivers are more consistent in their responses and reactions, and are usually available when needed (and at other times also). According to Erikson (1964), the first awareness of self as a separate entity develops out of the quality of care and personal trustworthiness experienced by the infant through the caregivers.

The sense of self is prerequisite knowledge for the formation of self-concept. The importance of a positive self-concept was stressed in the preceding chapter. It is difficult to distinguish between self and self-concept. In real life they are tightly interwoven. Both are learned from the same social activities and interactions; both are closely related to body image. The child's body image is influenced by the caregiver's attitudes and reactions to such things as exploration of one's body and the bodies of others, thumbsucking, and masturbation. The achievement of object permanence enhances self-awareness and also allows the infant to relate to other individuals in a more effective way.

The basic sense of trust in persons and in the physical environment is a prerequisite for a positive self-concept, as well as for the later achievements of autonomy and initiative. The sense of autonomy further differentiates the child's view of self as distinct from other persons and objects. It frees the child to relate to the ever-expanding world of the 3-year-old.

Lessons from Head Start. One of the several surprises that came out of the first few years of the Head Start and other poverty programs was that severely deprived 4- and 5-year-olds did not realize that they were individual persons or that they had names distinguishing them from anyone else. The director of the local Head Start Center tells of taking a group of 4- and 5-year-olds to the grocery store to buy fruit for the afternoon snack. On the way back, some of the children were reluctant to leave the front of the store. Investigation showed that these children were seeing the reflection of their full-length

bodies for the very first time in the store window. They were actually discovering their "selves," and they were both curious and excited. As the result of many, many similar episodes, an overriding goal of all Head Start programs became the child's development of self-awareness as a precurser to the development of self-esteem and self-confidence. The teachers were given many suggestions and techniques to reach this goal. They provided full-length mirrors so that children could see all of themselves (a triple mirror that will give front, side, and back views is ideal for this purpose). They took pictures of the children and attached them to each child's locker or cubby. They drew pictures or silhouettes of the children; they drew outlines of the child's whole body on butcher paper or newsprint. They made up songs and games that included the children's names. They always used a child's name in direct conversation to that child. They consciously worked at establishing a warm friendship with each child and his or her family. Their guideline was that each day, each child would go home with his head just a little bit higher.

These economically deprived youngsters had missed a necessary step in their earlier years. Today's infants and toddlers should be given these experiences in our group settings.

Teaching "who am I?" Action games, songs, and finger-plays all help young children become aware of parts of themselves and of themselves as persons who can do things. For the younger toddlers, activities involving the larger body parts are more suitable than finger-plays. Beginning favorites include the following:

JACK-IN-THE-BOX

Jack-in-the-box
Sit so still
   (Children squat or stoop down, placing hands overhead as cover.)
Won't you come out?
Yes I will!
   (Children open their hands and jump up.)

HERE IS A BALL

Here is a ball,
  (Fingers of both hands touch to form first ball.)
Here is a bigger ball,
  (Bowed arms with fingers touching, form the second ball.)
And here is the biggest ball of all
  (Arms form biggest ball, no fingers touching.)
Now let us count the balls we made:
One,
Two,
Three.
  (Repeat making balls, showing increasing size.)

RAIN

Rain in the green grass,
  (Bend hands at wrists, wiggle fingers for rain.)
And rain in the tree,
  (Raise both hands for tree.)
Rain on the roof top,
  (Make roof above head with palms down.)
But not on me.
  (Point to self.)

After the toddlers have some idea of the names and motions of the various body parts, as well as a beginning ability to follow directions, they are introduced to the various action songs and games. Following directions at this point is mostly imitating the teacher's actions. Traditional favorites include the following:

TEDDY BEAR

Teddy Bear, Teddy Bear, turn around.
Teddy Bear, Teddy Bear, touch the ground.
Teddy Bear, Teddy Bear, climb the stair.
Teddy Bear, Teddy Bear, hop into bed.
Teddy Bear, Teddy Bear, turn out the light.
Teddy Bear, Teddy Bear, blow a kiss "Goodnight!"

RING AROUND A ROSY

Ring around a rosy,
A pocket full of posies.
Ashes, ashes,
All fall down!
(The children form a circle, holding hands, and skip around until the word "down", when they squeal and fall down on the rug.)

THE MULBERRY BUSH

Here we go round the mulberry bush,
The mulberry bush, the mulberry bush,
Here we go round the mulberry bush,
So early in the morning.
2. This is the way we wash our clothes,
  So early Monday morning.
3. This is the way we iron our clothes,
  So early Tuesday morning.
4. This is the way we scrub the floor,
  So early Wednesday morning.
5. This is the way we mend our clothes,
  So early Thursday morning.
6. This is the way we sweep the house,
  So early Friday morning,
*7. This is the way we bake our bread,
  So early Saturday morning.
*8. This is the way we go to church,
  So early Sunday morning.
(The children join hands and skip around in a circle. Beginning with the second verse, they act out the words of the song.)

Action songs and games might be called body-plays. Finger-plays come into their own as toddlers begin to gain control over their finer muscle movements. Such all-time favorites include Open, shut them, Eentsy weentsy spider, Here is a beehive, Five little squirrels, and Two little blackbirds. Good collections of finger-plays and action songs and games are available at any bookstore. The children's departments of many public libraries distribute their own collections at little or no cost.

Most important, however, in teaching "Who am I?" is the use of the child's name whenever talking to or about the child. Adults must consciously refrain from using "honey" or "sweetie" when talking to individual children. In addition, self-awareness is enhanced when teacher mentions such things as "John is wearing red socks

---

*Some children and their families go to church on Saturday, and some do not go at all. Also, some families wish complete separation of religion and the center program. Adjustments might be made in the last two verses to meet the needs and wishes of the families in a particular center.

today" or "Mary washed her hands all by herself."

The use of children's names when talking to or about them is an important part of teaching "who am I?" First names or nicknames, however, are only half a name! A 2-year-old may know his name is Sam, but that will be of little help if he is ever separated from the group or family members. When Sam knows that his name is Sam Jones, he can be of some assistance when he is found. Soon after learning his full name, he can learn his street address or at least the name of the town or section of town where he lives. By 3½ or 4 years of age children should also know their phone numbers. Our hesitance toward having children learn by rote memory should not apply with this kind of information. Carol's answer "two in August" (Episode 9) to Santa's question "What's your name?" was cute and funny to adults. But this same response to that question if she had become separated from her mother in the crowd would have been more frustrating than cute or funny.

Birthday parties and "king" or "queen" for the day celebrate the specialness of a child. Conversations about each child's favorite color or food, or about pets, a new baby, or family outings all help children get to know themselves. Pictures of children by themselves, in the day care group, with the teacher, and with their families posted on bulletin boards or included in teacher-made picture books further increase the understanding of "Who am I?"

It is possible, and it happens all too frequently, to completely negate the "I am somebody" learnings at the times of arrival and departure from the center. Visualize the following and its unspoken message to Jonathan:

> **Episode 10.** Mrs. Andrews and 1-year-old Jonathan arrive at the center breathlessly at 7:45 AM. Mrs. Andrews must punch in on the time clock by 8:00 at her job across town or have her pay docked. Mrs. Andrews: "Hi, Ruth, here's the baby. I've got to run. Oh—I'll be a little late tonight. I have a doctor's appointment after work." Ruth (as she takes Jonathan from Mrs. Andrews): "I hope nothing is wrong. Don't forget we close at 6." Mrs. Andrews: "O.K.," and she rushes off.

Poor Jonathan! He had no more status than a sack of potatoes! Unfortunately, the end of the day is typically just as rushed as the beginning—working mothers or fathers have to grocery shop, get dinner, do the laundry, and tend to other childrden. It is conceivable that Jonathan both starts and ends his day like a bag of potatoes! Treating people like objects is not limited to toddlers. An example of a more humanistic beginning of a day is described in "a day in the life of Travis" in Chapter 10.

It is difficult to pinpoint a specific time frame for the child's development of the concept of self. One of the first attempts is described in the many reports from the Gesell Institute of Child Development. Ames (1952) traced verbalized concepts of self, starting at age 2 years. Typical remarks of the 2-year-olds are "Me . . . Mine . . . I need . . . Do it all myself" (p. 299). More recently, Smart and Smart (1978) and others have suggested that the average age for recognition of self in a mirror is 15 months. Most 3-year-olds talk in terms of "we," but still demand "me too!" Children who have attended day care over a period of time may reach the consciousness of others before the traditional age expectancies.

Recognition of self vs. others leads into self-regulation, which is also a product of both maturation and appropriate environmental influences and experiences. The developmental sequence of self-regulation skills in Table 8-1 was taken from Caldwell's AID Chart (1980).

TABLE 8-1   Developmental objectives for self-regulation*

Age	Objectives	Age	Objectives
By 1 year	1. Tolerates solitude 10 to 20 minutes without crying. 2. Takes daily naps on fairly regular schedule. 3. Is undisturbed during sleep by ordinary household or center noise. 4. Can be distracted during crying episode. 5. Recovers fairly quickly (3 to 5 minutes) from painful experiences. 6. Can carry out certain types of play activities by self for 5 minutes (e.g., looking at book). 7. Interprets clues indicating time for regularly scheduled change in activity (e.g., bringing in lunch tray, bringing forth outdoor toys, etc.). 8. Changes from one activity to another—if given appropriate notice—without getting upset.		9. Can delay gratification of impulses for 5 minutes or so. 10. Does not bite people. 11. Can carry out certain types of play activities by self for 10 minutes (e.g., looking at a book). 12. Occupies self unattended while adult is otherwise engaged—as getting lunch, talking, etc. 13. Occasionally will look at book by self, turning pages and pointing to recognized pages. 14. Does not have temper tantrums more than about once a week. 15. Waits without constant surveillance while adults get ready to move—as to go outside, to go home, to go on a trip.

*Adapted from Caldwell, 1980.

TABLE 8-1   Developmental objectives for self-regulation—cont'd

Age	Objectives	Age	Objectives
	16. Is beginning to comply with adult's request without stormy protest or ignoring the request. 17. Can carry out certain types of play activities by self for 15 minutes (e.g., working puzzles, playing with doll). 18. Does not exhibit hostile behavior without discernible reason (e.g., toy taken away, hit first). 19. Cries or fusses only when hurt or angry. 20. Happy, smiles, enjoys life. 21. Occasionally will look at book by self, labeling recognized pictures.		36. Gets book and signals (verbally or otherwise) a desire to be read to. 37. Knows to stay near adults when outside or on field trips (e.g., does not try to run off, run in street, etc.)
By 2 years	22. Is not easily distracted by the activities of others around him. 23. Generally expresses needs or desires without whining or screaming. 24. Complies with adult's request without stormy protest at least one fourth of the time. 25. Delays gratification of impulses for 10 minutes. 26. Will persist at a task requiring 10 minutes to complete. 27. Responds with joy to praise and compliments. 28. Anticipates schedule (e.g., time to get ready to go outside) and carries out necessary preparatory routine (goes for coat, etc.). 29. In free periods child finds things to do to occupy time constructively. 30. Can wait as long as 15 minutes for something he/she has expressed a desire for. 31. Does not have temper tantrums more often than once a month. 32. Can shift activities if given a reasonable warning. 33. Expresses pleasure at the completion of an activity. 34. Seldom initiates hitting, biting, scratching, etc. 35. Occasionally reacts to provocation with some response other than retaliation (e.g., hitting).	By 3 years	38. Is not foolhardy on equipment for large muscle activity. 39. Acts disturbed (concerned) if he/she breaks a piece of equipment. 40. By an occasional statement, demonstrates budding self-confidence (e.g., "Look at what I can do!"). 41. Does not have temper tantrums more often than once every 2-3 months. 42. Works and plays with minimal supervision for up to a half hour. 43. Will work for future reward (up to 15 minutes). 44. Demonstrates remorse (patting victim, saying "sorry") after show of aggression. 45. Enjoys "reading" book to self or peers. 46. Is eager and curious to explore his/her environment and ask questions. 47. Can be trusted not to bolt and run when group is moving from one locale to another. 48. At least half of the time will comply with adult's request without being cajoled or persuaded. 49. Can be trusted on field trips. 50. Enters classroom without dawdlng, wandering about, running off, etc.
		By 4 years	51. Is willing to try new tasks and to share achievements (e.g., volunteer to show something). 52. Does not have temper tantrums more than twice a year. 53. Will generally comply with adult's request without stormy protest. 54. Will work for future reward (up to 30 minutes). 55. Rarely attacks another child, and generally finds nonaggressive ways to solve problems.

The establishment of self vs. others is the fore-runner of all social relationships and interactions. It is the necessary first step for learnings and accomplishments in every area of human endeavor. The mastery of the self-regulation skills in Table 8-1 further enhances the child's development as a social person. In this area of development and learning, it is important to remember that it is the uniqueness of the child that adds spice to caregiving and teaching.

There are four major sources of the child's sense of "Who am I?" These have been listed in a publication of the Cooperative Extension Service, Iowa State University, as follows:

- A child listens and watches for cues from other people to see what they think about him or her. This is where all the smiles, comments, pats and hugs become important.
- A child watches his or her own progress in learning basic skills. Whether a tower of blocks will stand up or whether he or she can ride that tricycle or tie his or her own shoes are all important clues.
- A child checks to see how well he or she lives up to your expectations. Your comments about goodness or badness, right or wrong, success or failure all begin to add up.
- A child begins to set his or her own standards. "I can do it!" becomes a personal battle cry and an important step toward deciding "who I am" (Bakawa-Evenson, 1979, p. 1).

Children are constantly tuned in to what their significant adults are saying, doing, and even thinking. It is the adults who set the standards, both directly and indirectly, for the child and for the child's sense of self.

Who are you?

Mother-child relations. Any account of social development must begin with the responsive behaviors between infant and mother. Mother is the primary target for the infant's looking, smiling, crying, and reaching. This is not because the baby "knows" mother. It is because mother is usually available and is usually responsive to baby's communication behaviors. Out of this initial partnership between mother and child has come the psychological concept of attachment. There are many theories of the development of attachment in human infants, some growing out of studies of human mother-child dyads, others out of studies in which monkeys were induced to become attached to terrycloth cylinders (Harlow and Zimmerman, 1959), dogs to people (Scott, 1967), and even sheep to television (Cairns, 1966).

Theoretical speculation about human attachment is far ahead of empirical knowledge. Further discussion is beyond the scope of this text, but two excellent sources of information are by Ainsworth (1971) and Schaffer and Emerson (1964), both listed in the suggested readings at the end of the chapter.

There is evidence that suggests "the social stimulation provided by the mother is the critical variable in the formation of the infant-mother tie" (Corter, 1974, p. 179). The development of a mother-child bond has been recognized as essential for normal development. It has been seriously disrupted too many times. The most frequently cited "experiment" involving very young children (under 1 year of age) without a consistent parent or caregiver has been reported by Freud and Dann (1951). They were involved in the care of a group of six German-Jewish orphans, victims of the Hitler regime, who were sent to England in order to protect them from the Nazi bombings. In writing about the experience, Freud and Dann state that the children were:

. . . without doubt, "rejected" infants. . . . They were deprived of mother love, oral satisfactions, stability and relationships in their surroundings. They were passed from one hand to another during their first year, lived in an age group instead of a family during their second and third years, and were uprooted again three times during their fourth year. . . . But they were neither deficient, delinquent nor psychotic (p. 168). It was evident that they cared greatly for each other and not at all for anybody or anything else (p. 13).

There are research indications now that relationships between a child and significant others are also essential for optimal social development (Greiff, 1977). It might be said that detachment is as significant as attachment.

Knowledge about mother-child relations and attachment may be limited, but it is much greater than current knowledge about child-child relations.

Child-child relations. The young child's developing sense of other children is a recent research interest. In a review of the research on children's social cognition (1978), Forbes proposes four stages in the development of a cognitive sense of other:

1. Early fusion between self and other
2. Initial recognition of other's continued existence at about 10-12 months of age
3. Development later in infancy of a rudimentary sense that the other has independent inner states
4. Awareness by middle or late childhood that

others have personal histories and general life circumstances that contribute to their inner states of the moment (p. 129)

Detailed observations of infants during their first year have shown that their initial question is not "Who are you?" but "What is it and what can I do with it or to it?" When babies become mobile, they approach one another because of their attraction to a new and different object. Sometimes two babies will collide because of a mutual attraction to the same toy or other object. Infants may play side by side, may tug each other's hair and clothes, and may handle the same objects, but there seems to be little recognition of the alive-ness of one another. Episode 8 shows this clearly, as does the following:

Episode II. Mary (10 months) is sitting on the floor, playing with pop-beads, close to Shelley (9 months) who is lying on the rug. Neither child seems aware of the other. Mary starts to swing her arms, and drops her "necklace," which lands on Shelley's arm. At this moment, both babies stop short and fix their attention on one another. Mary reaches over to retrieve the

beads, drops them again, starts to wave her arms, and accidentally hits Shelley. There is no observable reaction from Shelley, who has been watching Mary attentively. Mary suddenly stops her arm waving and gazes at Shelley. She leans over and puts her face directly in front of Shelley's. She puts out her hand and touches Shelley's hair, eye, nose, and mouth, gurgling and cooing the whole time. Shelley returns a small "coo," and they both touch noses several times. Shelley starts to kick her legs, and moves back. Mary sits up and resumes playing with the beads. Both babies ignore each other once again.

These initial getting-to-know-you behaviors will gradually lead to the realization that one does not act the same toward a peer as toward a new toy. Mary and Shelley had already spent several months at the day care center and were probably more at ease with their investigations than babies who had not yet been in a group setting. Lois Murphy's observation of Colin's first days in a nursery school (1956) offers the same getting-to-know-you behaviors at an older age. Colin was 2 years, 9 months old when he was taken to the nursery school.

Colin progressed quickly from a quiet, friendly, watching relationship on the first few days to actively hugging the other children. The hugging seemed to be in an excess of friendliness and was only mildly aggressive. Having started hugging he didn't know how to stop, and usually just held on until he pulled the child down to the floor. This was followed very closely by hair pulling. He didn't pull viciously, but still held on long enough to get a good resistance from the child. (p. 12).

When babies have been in a happy group setting from their earliest months, there are indications of beginning social interactions with peers toward the end of the first year. The 1-year-old is aware that a peer is someone who both initiates and responds to social behaviors. Once discovered, this awareness develops at a rapid pace, although all does not go smoothly.

Episode 12. Two-year-old Jimmy was contentedly playing with a toy telehone in the middle of the playroom floor. Mark, also 2 years old, decided he had to have that particular phone. (There were two more on the toy shelf.) Mark grabbed the phone and pushed Jimmy down. Jimmy screamed. Mark ran to the playhouse with Jimmy in hot pursuit. The teacher arrived on the scene, and held Jimmy's arm to get his attention. He tried to calm Jimmy by talking to him slowly and directly and holding him close. "Jimmy, you took a little fall. Are you alright?" Jimmy continued to sob. His attention was on Mark. The teacher took Jimmy over to Mark and said, "Jimmy, Mark, let's play a game with the phone together. I'll start first." He pretended the phone rang, answered it, and said, "Yes, Mark is right here." He handed the phone to Mark who started an imaginary phone conversation. The teacher withdrew, and both boys happily took turns with the phone.

This incident and the teacher's response give a clue to appropriate methods of discipline for toddlers, and will be referred to later in that context. At this time, it serves to point up the negative or destructive interactions that are to be expected sometimes in children who are learning the complexities of social behavior. Aggressive encounters between young children rarely last more than a minute. Often they are completed and apparently forgotten within 30 seconds. Common and normal behaviors during these episodes are pushing, pulling, pinching, and throwing relatively harmless objects. Two- and 3-year-old children have little understanding of the rights or desires of other children. They also have little capacity to express their feelings verbally (Feldman, 1975).

Teachers of toddlers have observed enough instances of cooperative play among 2-year-olds to question the usual description of their social interactions as egocentric and noncooperative. Laboratory stories by Rheingold and others (1976) demonstrated that sharing is a characteristic of children 18 months of age and younger. The child's sharing was defined as: (1) showing—directing a person's attention to a toy by pointing; (2) giving—releasing a toy in a person's hand or lap; and (3) partner play—manipulating a toy given to someone else and still in the possession of the other. Incidental observations of younger children revealed that sharing by pointing, showing, and giving occurred in babies as young as 10.1 months. The incidents reported involved sharing with mother, father, and experimenter (all adults). The study shows that very young children exhibit social behaviors much sooner than has been traditionally expected. These children had been reared at home. It is reasonable to expect that these "early" ages for sharing behaviors would exist in a group center also.

Developmental objectives for the child's involvement with people (Caldwell, 1980) are presented in Table 8-2.

If they have been taught and have had the opportunity to learn, children 2½ or 3 years old are capable of the sustained attention, turn-taking, and mutual responsiveness usually observed and expected in the social interactions of older children and adults.

SOCIALIZATION OF THE INFANT AND TODDLER
Where have we been?

The definitions of socialization presented in the introductory comments of this chapter refer to learning socially relevant behavior and the ways people learn about what is approved and disapproved. Socialization, therefore, includes the learning of the rules for group living. This

TABLE 8-2   Developmental objectives for involvement with people*

Age	Objectives	Age	Objectives
By 1 year	1. Recognizes familiar faces. 2. Follows people with eyes as they move about the room. 3. Indicates some negative reaction when a stranger approaches. 4. Shows displeasure at the departure of a favorite person. 5. Develops favorites among the people he/she knows. 6. Enjoys the company of others. 7. Accepts presence of strange adults or children in home territory. 8. Imitates pat-a-cake. 9. Follows people physically for short distances. 10. Smiles and talks to image in mirror. 11. Accepts, enjoys, "loves" teacher. 12. Responds positively to affection offered by another person. 13. Expects attention on demand—looks at teacher when he/she cries. 14. Plays with one other child while each child is doing separate activity. 15. Seems to try to elicit affectionate interchange with other children.		20. Gives indications that he/she recognizes the needs of others. 21. Will permit other children to have a turn at the teacher's suggestion. 22. Seeks outside help in frustrating situations (not whining). 23. Responds with pleasure to compliment or praise.
		By 3 years	24. Is accepted (chosen) as a playmate by other children. 25. Generally complies with adult's request without stormy protest. 26. Demonstrates internalization of social graces (says "please," "thank you," "excuse me," etc.). 27. Engages in cooperative play with other children. 28. Can play simple group games (e.g., follow-the-leader). 29. Permits other children to have a turn at teacher's suggestion. 30. In general gets along well with peers. 31. Can accept constructive criticism when he/she makes a mistake and can modify behavior accordingly.
By 2 years	16. In general gets along well with peers. 17. Is friendly (greets visitors, initiates contacts with visitors). 18. Displays sympathy for children or adults. 19. Accepts rules of social graces (when reminded says "please," "thank you," "excuse me," etc.).	By 4 years	32. Verbally requests aid when needed. 33. Under the direction of adult can participate in organized group games (e.g., follow rules).

*Adapted from Caldwell, 1980.

learning starts at birth and continues far past the infant-toddler years. Indeed, many elementary schools claim that the socialization of children is their major responsibility. Some parents think their teen-agers are not socialized. How has the learning of rules evolved to its current theory and practice?

In the beginning of civilization, children who did not learn the rules of living by imitation were severely punished and frequently ostracized. Accurate imitation meant survival in those days. The pedagogical rule in early Egypt was that since a boy's ears where on his back, he heard better when he was beaten. A fourteenth century theological dictionary approved of both child beating and wife beating. In the eighteenth century, teachers were "often very ignorant and not infrequently graceless scamps, drunkards, or ruined people who handed out barbarous punishments" (Gillett, 1966, p. 158). In 1844, Horace Mann reported an average of 66 separate floggings per day in one school for 250 pupils (in the United States). Instead of corporal punishment, which had fallen into disfavor, the following substitutes were used: imprisoning in dark and solitary places, bracing open the jaws with a piece of wood, torturing the muscles and bones by fastening in unnatural positions, and encouraging the class to ridicule and shame the hapless culprit. Mann commented, "these, and such as these, are the gentle appliances by which some teachers, who profess to disregard corporal punishment, maintain the empire of the school room" (cited in Harris, 1928, p. 55).

In 1973, the Group for the Advancement of Psychiatry described a poster that was displayed in a Washington toy shop. It read:

1910	Spank them
1920	Deprive them
1930	Ignore them
1940	Reason with them
1950	Love them
1960	Spank them lovingly
1970	THE HELL WITH THEM!

Our "advanced" society has not yet reached consensus on what to do with "them." How would you complete the line for 1980? for 1990?

Where are we now?

We are in a state of confusion! Recently, the father of a 1½-year-old bragged that he had found the answer to temper tantrums. "All you do is throw a bucket of cold water on him—it sure works fast!" True, it probably did work fast. We might wonder, however, about the child's learnings as a result of the unexpected bath. (The child's tantrums continued for several months.)

One of the current theories about teaching and learning social rules is exemplified in Episode 9. The teacher ignored Mark (the aggressive child), attended to Jimmy (the victim), and initiated an associative play interaction. Piagetian theory suggests that children under the age of 4 or 5 years are unable to reason. Even if Mark had been able to think logically, the situation was too emotional at that point for him to do so. However, the key time for learning how to handle aggressive drives and feelings is between 2 and 3 years of age (Lourie, 1973). How can it be taught if reasoning ability has not yet developed?

Aggression

There are at least two kinds of aggression. One is hostile and involves an intent to hurt another person or an object. Should it be assumed that Mark pushed Jimmy down because he wanted to hurt him? Was the act premeditated? The other kind of aggression, according to Feshback (1970), is instrumental aggression. The child wants to get or retrieve something and there is a block in the attempt (of course, the "block" in the episode was Jimmy). Instrumental aggression can be viewed as an assertion of self-interest. It is quite possible that Mark's primary concern over possession of the telephone completely eclipsed his developing cognizance that Jimmy was another human, and that pushing him down was a normal reaction to an object in the way of a goal. The intent to hurt should never be assumed in the infant-toddler group.

Behavioral management. The teacher applied principles of behavioral psychology in his approach (or nonapproach) to Mark. He completely ignored Mark immediately after the incident. He devoted all his attention to Jimmy. In a few moments, when both he and Jimmy returned to the scene and the teacher engaged both boys in play, he was subtly reinforcing Mark for his (Mark's) nonaggression after the pushing down. The three principles of teaching that are useful in helping children stop unacceptable behaviors are:

1. Remove all positive reinforcement for the behavior.
2. Ignore a child who is not behaving acceptably. This ignoring is especially effective if the teacher immediately attends to (reinforces) the child when the unacceptable behavior stops.
3. Structure unpleasant consequences for a particularly unacceptable behavior. In this instance, the teacher assumed lack of intent to hurt and also knew the usual developmental sequence of social behaviors. He did not consider Mark's behavior "particularly unacceptable" for his age.

   The incident finished happily, but the learning had just begun. In order to increase the frequency of an acceptable behavior, the following guidelines for teaching behavior have been derived from the principles of learning. The sequential steps are:

4. Careful observation to determine what toys, activities, or forms of attention are reinforcing for the child.
5. Arranging the environment so that the child can observe significant persons performing the desired behavior. (One teacher is looking at a book; a second teacher approaches and says, "May I look at the book, please?" First teacher responds, "I'm not finished reading it. Would you like to read it with me?" or even "I'm not finished with it, but I'll give it to you when I am finished.") Note: It would be next to impossible to structure such a situation with the other toddlers, although such interactions do sometimes occur. The best way for a child to learn a new behavior response is to observe it in another child. Our teaching should not wait for happenstance, however. Children do imitate behaviors that receive observable reinforcement, and we therefore do not limit our positive reinforcement only to those who specifically need it.

6. Immediate reinforcement for increasingly successful steps in the right direction (usually called "shaping"). (In Mark's case, a successful step in the right direction might be to come close to a child playing with a truck and to stand close by to watch. An observant teacher might say, "I like the way you are waiting for your turn.")
7. Immediate reinforcement (within 3 seconds) for each successful performance of the desired behavior. ("You asked for the truck nicely, Mark. Good asking!").
8. Giving verbal cues or suggestions to help the child identify situations where the new behavior is appropriate and to serve as a reminder. ("Maybe if you asked Terry for the trike, he would let you have a turn.")
9. Gradual decrease in reinforcement when the child has mastered the behavior and is performing it at appropriate times.

One or two final comments should be made before we leave Jimmy and Mark. If an uninformed observer had watched (1) Mark grabbing the phone and pushing Jimmy down and (2) the teacher's complete ignoring of Mark immediately afterwards, the observer would feel justified in saying, "that teacher lets kids get away with murder!" At the very least the observer would classify the teacher as very permissive. The teacher was neither permissive nor did he use any form of punishment. He taught in the way that was appropriate for the situation.

Temper tantrums. Although not considered an act of aggression, temper tantrums are the ultimate in negativism. They can be eliminated using these same principles of teaching. The child is removed from the group if necessary, so that she receives no attention from the other children or adults (Principle No. 1); the teacher, after moving the child, ignores her completely (Principle No. 2); the teacher immediately pays attention to, and invites the child back to the group, as soon as the child is under control (Principle No 3). If the tantrum continues, a natural consequence very probably would be missing snack or outdoor play or music or whatever was next on the schedule. If the timing of the schedule does not coincide with the need, the teacher might rearrange the schedule on the spur of the moment. However, a time-out of even a minute is a very long time for a child under 3 years of age. Probably the child will be ready to rejoin the group before even a spur-of-the-moment change can be put into action. Pediatrician Brazelton (1974) maintains that tantrums are necessary and appropriate around 12 to 15 months of age. He defines a tantrum "as a reflection of the inner turmoil of decision-making that one is faced with when decisions become one's own" (p. 21). Neither a bucket of cold water nor any other punishment will solve this inner turmoil.

A tantrum can be a frightening experience for a very young child. The child is temporarily out of control and loses all sense of reality. What is needed is a close-by compassionate adult who offers psychological security, as well as physical affection and verbal soothing as soon as possible. There is nothing to be gained by reasoning with the child. The most quieting and reassuring environment is away from the group, where the child can gradually regain control with the support of a responsive adult.

As the children get older, there is a subtle change in the stimulus for tantrum behavior. The tantrum becomes a somewhat intentional method of obtaining one's way that conflicts with expectations or requests. If adults allow themselves to be manipulated by these tantrums, the frequency and duration of the tantrums will increase because they have been reinforced. Caregivers who know their children should be able to differentiate between the inner-turmoil and the manipulative tantrum, and therefore can respond appropriately. An appropriate response to the intentional tantrum is removal from the group with as little fuss as possible. In this case, the adult's role is to teach acceptable behavior, not to support inacceptable behavior. It is taught by the complete absence of all reinforcement from both children and adults. Close adult supervision is necessary, however, to prevent any self-inflicted injury.

Selected conclusions from research. One of the many valuable conclusions of the Sears, Macoby, and Levin, (1957) longitudinal study of child-rearing patterns is as follows:

> The way for parents to produce a non-aggressive child is to make abundantly clear that aggression is frowned upon, and to stop aggression when it occurs, but to avoid punishing the child for his aggression. Punishment seems to have complex effects. While undoubtedly it often stops a particular form of aggression, at least momentarily, it appears to generate more hostility in the child and lead to further aggression outbursts at some other time or place. . . . The most peaceful home is one in which the mother believes aggression is undesirable . . . and who relies mainly on non-punitive forms of control. (p. 266)

Caldwell (1977) suggests that if we substituted the word "teacher" for "parents" and "mother," and "classroom" for home, the statement would be just as true.

One last word about aggression. It has now been learned that providing clay to pound on, a doll or pillow to pummel, or a tree to kick is not the way to reduce the frequency of aggressive behaviors toward persons. "Contrary to popular beliefs, children encouraged to behave aggressively toward inanimate objects are likely to try out their aggressive skills learned in these situations on their peers" (Roedell and others, 1976, p. 11). This finding has been well documented by several research psychologists (Borke, 1972; Chandler and Greenspan, 1972; Grusec, 1974; and Hoffman, 1972).

Punishment and discipline

Punishment per se need not be addressed when the topic is the socialization of the child under the age of 3. Punishment has no place in a group or home setting for infants and toddlers. These children do not "misbehave"; they behave in ways that lead to their learning. Misbehavior, like beauty, lies in the eyes of the beholder. Somehow, even the teachers who encourage the children to explore and experiment with physical objects in the environment do not extend their encouragement or even their permission to explore personal and social behaviors.

It is easy to get tangled in a jumble of words when we think about punishment and discipline. There are almost as many definitions of the words as there are teachers of young children. I am defining punishment as an act by an adult that is intended to physically or psychologically hurt the child (a slap, a spank, abusive language). These acts are mistakenly viewed as teaching acts. They do teach, but they do not teach the hoped-for learnings. They do not even teach the child "to mind."

The young child who has been removed from positive reinforcement probably views the removal as punishment. The adult should view the removal as a teaching act. It helps the child learn which behaviors are acceptable and which are not. Even so, removal from reinforcement should be a last resort that is used infrequently in the infant-toddler age group.

The process of socialization (rule-learning) does not proceed in a straight line. A zigzag line is the usual sequence. The child tests limits,

adults, and the other children. When the initial testing is frustrated, the testing behaviors may intensify. But if the frustration is consistently enforced, the testing behaviors will soon decrease in number and intensity. If the adult gives in, the testing is reinforced and will continue.

The popularization of the phrase "terrible two's" has sometimes led teachers to overlook the positive growth of this stage. In the first place, any coined phrase or label tends to blur the individuality of the child. Any label, therefore, is deceiving and dangerous. Second, every 2-year-old—it might be said that every person regardless of age—wants and needs to be self-assertive. During the early years, self-assertion is a part of the establishment of self-identity and autonomy. This drive is most easily observable in the child's use of the word "no". Brazelton defines the child's "no" as "a fragile barrier behind which a child this age can hide. If he is taken too literally, he will be surprised and disappointed" (1974, p. 101). When a child says "no" out loud she has asserted her ability to make a decision. Most frequently the child's decision will coincide with the adult's, as shown in Episode 13.

Episode 13. Two-year-old Karen was busily engaged in caring for her doll baby right before lunch time. The teacher approached, saying "Let's go to the sink, Karen, and I'll help you wash your face and hands." Karen: "No!" The teacher smiled, took Karen by the hand, and said "Come on Karen, it will only take a minute, and then it's time to eat. Let's go." Karen smiled, and teasingly pretended a reluctant walk over to the sink. Her reaction to the cool water on her face and hands was one of delight. Karen even had to be reminded that the other children needed a turn, also.

If a teacher had reacted in a completely opposite way ("Don't you say 'no' to me, young lady!") a serious confrontation of wills would have followed. Teachers rarely win a serious clash with young children. They wear out and give in. In so doing, they make certain that future confrontations will occur.

When adults follow the suggested principles

of teaching they are in control of the situation, and the child is subconsciously assured of a sense of security. The overall sense of trust is reinforced, because the adult's behavior is predictable and consistent. However, the teacher sequence presented so far is not complete. If an alternative to crying or breath-holding or tantrums is not offered the child, we have not taught an acceptable way to obtaining one's wants. We leave an empty spot in the child's repertoire of behaviors. Specific alternatives cannot be suggested for each incidence each time and for each child. The following statements have proved useful and indicate the general philosophy:

Blocks are to build with.
Hammers are to pound nails with.
Dolls are to be played with.
You may color on the paper, or you may find something else to do.
You may leave the playground walking or I'll carry you.

How much better than "Don't throw the blocks" or hammers or dolls, etc. How much better than nagging a child to come in from the playground. Our job is to teach, and we teach by providing an alternative.

Adults are prone to dismiss a child's clinging behaviors (to skirt or pants or legs) as a bid for attention, and they react in one of two ways. They give the attention, thus reinforcing the child's techniques of getting attention, or they say "Stop it" or "Get away," giving the child neither the needed attention nor an acceptable alternative. A positive way to respond to the attention-seeking child is to say "I know you want me to hold you, but I won't hold you until you stop hanging on (or crying, or whining) and ask me to hold you." If the child is too young to ask verbally, suggest she raise her arms up, or even lead her through the action. Immediately reinforce, and pick up the child. According to Brazelton (1974) almost 75% of the infants are able to make word demands by 1 year of age:

The first words are the simple vowels attached to an explosive consonant. As the exploration of such speech sounds proceeds, the baby senses that certain ones . . . produce a more rewarding response from the environment. He quickly learns their value and by nine months of age has fixed them as producible responses (p. 3).

There are many nonverbal ways of showing attention to a child. These include smiling, nodding, establishing eye contact, watching a child's activities with interest, really listening to a child's language, helping the child when appropriate, and making a physical contact. It is frequently the case in a group setting that a teacher may be involved with one or more children, and yet want to attend to another one. This is why the above suggestions should be part of a teacher's repertoire of attending behaviors. Whenever possible, a direct interaction involving language is preferable. Note the teacher's verbal interaction with Melissa while she was busily engaged with Luther in "a day in the life of Luther" in Chapter 10.

Limits in an infant-toddler group should be confined to the three major ones: (1) you may not hurt yourself; (2) you may not hurt someone else; and (3) you may not hurt the materials or equipment. These limits must be consistently enforced in order for learning to take place.

Pertinent to all teacher behaviors in teaching (disciplining) a young child is the statement that a child who is never shouted at never learns to shout at others. It can be applied to hitting or biting or kicking equally as well. We can learn from the experiences at the Enep'ut Day-Care Center in Fairbanks, Alaska, where "at all times, the children . . . are held, picked up, carried around, tickled, fondled, and most of all, listened to" (Butler, 1973, p. 18). Eskimo adults are models of gentleness; their children grow up as gentle to others as their parents and teachers were to them. In an atmosphere of acceptance, encouragement, trust, respect, joy and fellowship, children can function as friends and playmates. Such an atmosphere is well described in the three "days" in Chapter 10.

The teacher's goal for discipline in the center where these children spent many hours each day was to provide an environment that was rich in positive self-concept, concern for one another, and the security of equitable treatment. To meet this objective, the focus is on desired behaviors by teacher attention, facial expression, tone of voice, and verbal interaction. Teachers point out to children what it is about their behavior that is likeable: "I like the way you hold your glass with both hands. It really helps you drink without spilling." "That's a careful way to go down the slide. You waited for David to be out of the way. Thanks, Jean." A good teacher also supports social compatibility. "I can tell that Julie likes you, John. You make her laugh when you talk to her." "Tammy is feeding the doll right now. Let's look on the shelf and see if you can find one too." "I like the way you are building together. It's fun to build with a friend." Teacher requests include reasons, and are carefully worded to avoid confrontations. "Books are to read. When you tear out the pages, we can't read the whole story. The pages need to stay in the book." "It is time to go to the bathroom. Would you rather walk or be carried?"

I suspect that when adults observe a basketball or football game, they "behave" basketball or football. These same adults would not yell or stamp their feet in a post office or library. Little children can be taught to act in accordance with whatever behaviors are deemed acceptable and desirable in a group setting. Barker (1968) concludes that the principal determinant of behavior is the nature of the situation that the child or adult perceives himself or herself to be in. The nature of the situation is in the hands of the caregivers and teachers. The situation contains reasonable and definite limits, clear-cut guidelines, and a few necessary taboos.

Appropriate techniques for discipline with in-

fants and toddlers involve distraction, substitution of alternative activity, and a change of subject. In all instances we must enable the child to "save face."

The Group for the Advancement of Psychiatry (1973) summarizes the position expressed here: "Good discipline is a positive force directed toward what the child is allowed to do rather than what he is forbidden to do. It is based mainly on mutual love and respect. In childhood it has to be reinforced with teaching, firmness, and reminder" (p. 74).

SOCIALIZATION AND COMMUNICATION

Teach your child to hold his tongue; he'll learn fast enough to speak.

Ben Franklin

In spite of Ben Franklin's usually timeless wisdom, his approach to language learning leaves much to be desired in the 1980s. Perhaps in former days when children were to be seen and not heard, his advice was appropriate. Today our responsibility is to both see and hear children, and to take an active role in encouraging and enlarging upon their abilities to communicate and converse.

During the first few months, the caregiver's role is that of a conversational partner even though baby is prelinguistic. In the later months the teacher and other adults continue as speaking partners, and by the time a child is in the last half of the second year, age-mates also become speaking partners to a limited degree. Without such partners, the development of language is impossible.

Language development

The main focus on the following pages is on communication and conversation as a necessary part of the child's socialization. It is not on language and speech development per se. Nevertheless, an overview of this development can serve as an introduction to the major focus. It is

TABLE 8-3   Developmental objectives for language*

Age	Objectives	Age	Objectives
By 1 year	1. Turns toward sound. 2. Interprets mealtime clues. 3. Responds (looks, glances, or smiles) when talked to by teacher or other adult. 4. Gurgles and coos. 5. Looks in direction indicated by pointed finger. 6. Responds nonverbally to vocalizations (e.g., when Mother says, "Let's go," child raises arms). 7. Responds vocally to vocalizations. 8. Reacts to name being called by looking or reaching to be picked up. 9. Waves bye-bye. 10. Imitates adult in touching (e.g., eye, chin, nose, etc.). 11. Can use some appropriate, easily interpreted gestures to indicate positive or negative reaction (e.g., shakes head yes or no). 12. Imitates adult in making sounds (e.g., ba-ba, ma-ma, la-la, da-da). 13. Mimics words. 14. Uses one-word labels. 15. Can generally signal needs and wants using gestures or gestures and words. 16. Can say 6 or more words (e.g., mommy, baby, no, go, up, down, all gone, cookies, juice, hi, milk, see). 17. Can follow instructions including, "Bring me," "Give me," "Come here," "Take it." 18. Knows the names of all regular caregivers in his/her group (looks at person when name is said, goes to person on request). 19. Interprets clues indicating time for regularly scheduled change in activity. 20. Knows the names of all other children in his/her group. 21. Will listen to a short story read on a one-to-one basis. 22. Combines two words. 23. Responds to question "Want to play pat-a-cake?" given without gestures. 24. While playing with several common objects will respond appropriately to at least 2 requests. (e.g., Child is given a doll, tissue, spoon, bowl and he/she will feed baby and wipe nose). 25. Will listen to short book if read to in groups of 2 or 3. 26. Uses three-word sentences.		30. Says first names of all other children in own group. 31. Looks at a speaker who is talking to him/her. 32. Demonstrates by action knowledge of common prepositions (e.g., on, in). 33. Can answer questions (knows that a question means an answer is expected). 34. Can give simple descriptions or explanations. 35. Can verbalize the action depicted in pictures (e.g., "What is the baby doing?"). 36. Labels pictures of known common objects (e.g., ball, car). 37. Can correctly respond to instructions involving broad categories of location (inside, outside, in the kitchen etc.) without help from gestures. 38. Speech is clear, distinct, and audible. Child can be understood by a stranger.
By 2 years	27. Can say first name when asked. 28. Listens when spoken to. 29. Responds to "What is this?" when asked casually about common objects.	By 3 years	39. Delivers simple messages (e.g., "Mary's hurt."). 40. Can say first and last name when asked in conversation. 41. Spontaneously relates experiences (tells something that happened on playground, etc.). 42. Understands prepositions (e.g., under, beside, in front of). 43. Can listen to a story or record for at least 10 minutes. 44. Can respond appropriately to "where" and "when" questions. 45. Uses positional terms (e.g., first, last). 46. Gives full name distinctly when asked by a stranger in the classroom.
		By 4 years	47. Can give name of city in which he/she resides. 48. Uses compound sentences (e.g., "We went to the zoo and we saw a lion."). 49. Answers roll call with both names in a complete sentence (e.g., "My name is Reggie Berry."). 50. Responds to informal questions based on symbolic representation (e.g., "Tell me about this picture."). 51. Uses four- to five-word sentences. 52. Can retell main facts from a story. 53. Can describe pictures in sentences. 54. Enjoys "reading" book to small group or class.

*Adapted from Caldwell, 1980.

presented in the form of the language objectives adapted from the AID Chart (Caldwell, 1980). The Speech, Language, and Hearing Communication Chart in Appendix E contains the information in another form.

It is obvious that a partner of some kind is a necessary prerequisite in each step of language development.

Communication and conversation

Infants start to communicate from the time of birth. By one signal or another, babies let the world know they are hungry or uncomfortable or fatigued. Although babies can neither walk or talk, they communicate in a forceful manner. The frantic pulling-up and stretching out of legs is readily understood as meaning "I have a pain in my tummy." For the first 3 months, baby's responses to the self-state and the other-than-self state are reflexive: smiling, grasping, gazing, and orienting to sound. These all give messages to the caregiver. The child, therefore, learns that these reflex actions are signals, because the adult attaches meaning to them. The cry is also a reflex response during the first few months, and is neither controlled or designed to exploit the caregiver. Bell and Ainsworth (1972) found that mothers who respond to their babies' cries and other signals have babies who cry less often and for shorter periods of time at 1 year of age. They also noted that the babies who cry least are more mature in ways to get attention and are more independent at 1 year than are the babies who are left to "cry it out." Cries soon become cause-specific, and can be differentiated by a caregiver as hunger or pain or fatigue cries.

Between the third and ninth month, baby becomes more active in using signals to communicate. Baby will look and smile, will usually follow the caregiver's line of regard, will respond to adult vocalizations, and begins to anticipate events, as in peek-a-boo. Also during this period, baby coos, gurgles, and laughs, and makes many vocal sounds. Osgood (1957) claims a baby can make all possible sounds; McNeill (1970) and Ingram (1976) say nearly all. All babbling starts around 6 months and reaches its peak between 9 and 12 months. Baby has developed conversational skills even before 9 months. Baby learns to engage the attention of the caregiver by vocalizing or crying. The adult responds with attention, and the baby responds by smiling, quieting, grasping, etc. Before reaching the first birthday, baby has made a remarkable discovery: certain sounds result in certain reactions from caregivers. Sounds such as ma-ma-ma-ma have no meaning for baby, but they certainly create an excitement in the caregiver. Baby repeats the syllables because they evoke pleasure, thereby initiating the first social conversation. It is the caregiver's feedback that leads baby to the attachment of meaning to sound experiments such as ma-ma and da-da. If no one responds to these or other sounds, the baby loses interest in trying new ones and will remain content with babblings and other vocalizations. The child will eventually stop even these, because no one gave any indication that sounds can communicate meaning. The advice of Huntington and colleagues (1972) is that the infant-toddler environment must supply:

- a relatively small number of adults having continuing, focused and affectively meaningful relationships with the child; adults who encourage reciprocal interactions.
- frequent contacts with adults and other children, contacts that are predominantly gratifying, expressive and warm.
- verbal interaction; a "speaking partner." Sound alone does not stimulate speech development; verbal exchanges do. Free and open verbal communication is essential (p. 9).

Toward the end of the first year, babbling contains variation in intonation and perhaps even a word or two. A stream of babbling sounds like talking with meaning. Pflaum-Connor (1978) observed "a puzzled three-and-a-half year old listening intently to a baby with this pseudo-language. Finally the older child said that the baby was funny because she sounded like she was saying something but it did not come out like talk" (p. 25).

Until recently, research on language acquisition has been directed toward the production of sounds, the length of word utterances, and the size of vocabulary at different ages. For instance, at age 1 year, baby uses one or two words meaningfully, and by age 2, the average number of vocabulary words is 272 (Leopold, 1971). An average is often misleading, because of the very large range of vocabulary size, even at age 2. We know that in favorable conditions, a 3-year-old child understands most of the words that are used in everyday adult conversations and is able to produce many of them.

The current emphasis in research on language acquisition is directly applicable to infant-toddler programs. Carter (1974) and Cazden (1972) have concluded that activity, motor involvement, and play are significant in the establishment of a language system. There are numerous studies of early utterances that support the idea that meaning is gained through actions. An early language development program, therefore, should provide opportunities for the action-development of meanings before and during the expectations for verbal expressions. Children always know more than they can verbalize. They need continuing opportunities to engage in both monologues and dialogues with adults who are involved active listeners as well as talkers. Certainly, the labeling of an object that has been learned motorically will greatly enlarge communication. *Ball*, for example, depending on eye focus, intonation, and gestures may mean: "This is my ball. . . . Where is the ball? . . . I want to play ball. . . . Play ball with me. . . . I found the ball." (Languis and others, 1980).

Between 9 and 12 months, there appears a primitive intention to communicate, although baby is still preverbal and prelanguage. Baby will deliberately try to get the caregiver's attention by vocalizing and using eyes and gestures. A concurrent understanding is the differentiation of self from object or other person. At 12 months, babies may not be very articulate, but they understand most of what is said to them and will babble and jabber in response.

Sometime between 9 and 18 months the toddler moves from prelinguistic communication to intentional one-word utterances with a purpose. They are directed to a responder in order to (1) satisfy needs, (2) exert control over the responder's behavior, (3) express self-awareness, (4) ask why, (5) play or pretend, (6) inform, or (7) ask for help (Halliday, 1975). These may be considered social utterances because they are addressed to someone, and they request a response of some kind. These utterances are frequently accompanied by gestures of pointing, showing or giving objects, or an indication of "give it to me." The combination of word, intonation, and gesture is usually correctly interpreted. Therefore the sequence of a conversation is established (baby points to cookie, caregiver gives baby cookie, baby vocalizes, caregiver verbalizes in return). Occasionally two one-word utterances will be offered sequentially with a pause in between ("car . . . bye-bye"). The sequence shows a beginning insight into word and meaning relationships. Not all intentional utterances are addressed to persons. Children will practice the labeling of an object and will repeat words they or others have said. In other words, they practice talking.

From 18 to 24 months, the major gestures are still used, but the toddler makes sequential or adjacent utterances that sometimes deal with past events and objects not immediately perceivable. "Truck go" is not a story yet, but it is important for conversation. During this period the child seems to recognize that listeners may have different conversational needs. For instance, how the child talks to his mother is different from how he talks to a stranger. The child seems aware of previously shared information or experiences and adjusts the choice of words accordingly. It appears that the child is able to relate past experiences, but this is because the familiar adult structures the conversation. According to Halliday (1975), the child engages in a verbal dialogue before the age of 2 years. "Dialogue can be viewed as essentially the adoption and assignment of roles. The roles in question are social roles, but of a special kind: they exist only in and through language, as communication roles—speaker, addressee, respondent, questioner, persuader, and the like" (p. 48). The child knows that when a question is asked, an answer is expected. Also, the child knows that a conversation can be initiated with a question. The roots of these conventions are in the ritualized turn-taking games of caregiver and child.

Young children combine words intentionally sometime between 18 and 24 months of age. They seem to be sensitive to the adult conventions for ordering words in sentences. This is the first grammatical rule they will learn. Children talk about actions, what happened to what, who does what, locations, recurrences, and nonexistence. Sample utterances include: "We go bye-bye. . . . Mommy outside. . . . More milk. . . . Soup all gone" (de Villers, 1979).

The 2-year-old's language is not always used in conversations or interactions with others. The following episode illustrates the fact that Elaine did not wish an interaction, but that she was willing and able to respond to the questions of an adult.

Episode 14. Elaine (2 years old) is playing in the kitchen corner of the toddler playroom. A teacher is tending to the caged rabbit, about 10 feet away. The teacher asks, "What are you cooking Elaine?" She casually answers "ot dog," and continues getting out the utensils and ingredients. The teacher moves close and asks, "Do you need any help?" Elaine shakes her head "no," and works diligently, pouring, measuring, and mixing in the bowl. The teacher asks, "Did you get your hot dogs cooked?" Elaine replies "Almost." Then from a wooden block she pours another imaginary ingredient into the bowl. "Sh sh sht." She carefully measures a spoonful from an empty spice box and adds it to the mixture. "You tell me when the hot dogs

are done, O.K.?" Elaine continues making her hot dogs and then, "Done. Ot." She puts her materials away and joins the teacher for a story.

Elaine apparently felt no desire to share her activity with anyone else—she was alone in the kitchen corner, and matter-of-factly refused the teacher's offer to help.

Although not an example of child-child interaction, the next episode illustrates a growing social awareness of other persons' feelings.

Episode 15. The teacher was sitting on the floor, reading to a group of five children, all around the age of 2 years. Sadie, aged 17 months, began to cry. Teacher: "Sadie, why are you crying? Can you tell me what's wrong?" Sadie didn't answer, and continued her crying. The teacher asked, "Does anyone know why Sadie is crying?" Jeff (28 months) suggests "Maybe she's hungry." Tom (24 months) says "Is she tired?" Jeff adds, "Maybe she wants to be picked up." The teacher picks up Sadie and puts her on her lap. Sadie stops crying, and the story continues.

Although the cause for Sadie's crying was not discovered, it is easy to attribute it to her "youth"—17 months is very young to be expected to listen contentedly to a story when part of a group containing four other children.

From age 2 the child builds on the communication accomplishments of the first 2 years. During the third year, the number of conversations in adult-child interactions multiplies rapidly, with rapid changes in topics. In child-child relationships, the monologue predominates and there are few real dialogues. Children typically use three- and four-word utterances.

The conversation tasks, in addition to grammar and vocabulary, are internalized. Children consider the perspective of the listener and the give-and-take rules of conversation. The child is learning to distinguish a referent from alternatives. An adult should supply a referent such as "I want the truck," not just "I want it." The child must learn when he can presuppose information, because what we choose to say is based on the presupposed information known by the other. "Peter is lost" could refer to another child, a stuffed animal, even to an Uncle Peter. In this case, Peter was a live pet rabbit.

The child presupposes that the listener already has that information. Other rules that make utterances acceptable in conversations include: don't interrupt; don't bore people; answer questions when asked; be truthful; be relevant; and use the common courtesy phrases, such as "please" and "thank you." These rules are not always put into practice in everyday living, by either children or adults.

McAfee (1967) gives some excellent suggestions for the teacher's language when working with Mexican-American children. They apply equally well to the teachers of infants and toddlers. She suggests that teachers speak in complete sentences, and that they be specific in their use of words (not "over there" but "under the chair"). It is also helpful if a word denoting a classification is used whenever possible. For instance, "The *animals* in the cage are bunnies," or "The blocks are all the same *color*—red."

Most of the developmental research has been confined to the child's first 3 years. It has been noted, however, that the conversations of 3- and 4-year-old children resemble adult conversations in that a single topic is continued over several successive utterances. Shatz and Gelman (1973) and Sachs and Devin (1976) found that 4-year-old children modify their speech as a function of the age of the listener. The observed 4-year-olds used simpler and shorter sentences when talking with 2-year-olds than when talking with adults. Other researchers have noted that children around age 4 years include direct or indirect hints in their language: "My mother always lets me have *two* cookies!" I have observed these same behaviors in children who were below the age of 3 in a day care center. These children had been in day care for more than 2 years. It is quite logical to expect a more mature approach to communication by language in children who have been in group situations over a period of time.

Language in an infant-toddler program is developed primarily as a means of communication.

The active participation of the children is vital. The best teachers are the natural language models (teachers, caregivers, parents), who actively participate in the child's language acquisition. Many of the language development or stimulation programs for very young children do not match the young child's development. An interest in colors, numerals, or possessive's is not normal at this age. Teachers need not spend time, money, or effort in directly teaching language. They will do better spending their time in talking about things that are happening, that have happened recently, and that will happen soon. They also should remember that in order to learn to talk, children must talk. Adult-child interactions must include *both* persons talking and responding.

■ CHAPTER SUMMARY ■

There are three distinct processes in the development of social competency, all of which have their foundations in the first days and months of a child's life. These processes include social cognition (knowledge of self, others, and relations with others); the skills for initiating and responding socially; and the development of social behaviors.

The parent-child relationship is the first major teacher of social cognition and socialization. If the infant or toddler spends a significant number of hours in a group setting away from home, the caregiver/teacher-child relationship is also a major teacher. It is the responsibility of the teacher to ensure that: (1) each child recognizes his or her similarity to and distinctness from others; (2) each child is so treated that a sense of trust, autonomy, and mastery is developed; (3) each child is able to take advantage of the sense of initiative when it appears; (4) each child is provided opportunities to learn the skills of interpersonal relations; and (5) each child achieves a measure of success and confidence in these relationships.

Prerequisites for socialization include a basic sense of trust in the social and physical environment, a positive sense of self, continuing interactions with significant adults, and opportunities to observe and then to interact with peers. There should be no punishment for the "misbehavior" of children under the age of 3 years. However, there should be teaching. One effective technique for teaching acceptable behavior is the application of the principles of behavior management. Alternative behaviors must always be made known to the child.

Limits for behavior in an infant-toddler group should be related to three major types of behaviors: hurting themselves, hurting other persons, and hurting or damaging equipment or materials.

Child-child interactions in an infant-toddler group primarily center around objects. During the third year, children begin to gain sufficient skill in language production to use language as a means of communication. From then on, the frequency and complexity of child-child interactions increases rapidly.

The best teachers of language are adults who use natural language.

SUGGESTED ACTIVITIES AND POINTS TO PONDER

1. Start a card file of finger-plays and action songs and games that will encourage the development of personal and social skills.
2. List and discuss methods useful in teaching courteous behavior, in addition to the insistence on "please" and "thank you."
3. How would you react to a parent who claims, "But he *never* throws a tantrum at home?"

REFERENCES AND SUGGESTED READINGS

Ainsworth, M.D.: The development of infant-mother attachment. In Caldwell, B.M., and Ricciuti, H.N., editors: Review of child development research, vol. 3, Chicago, 1971, University of Chicago Press.

Ames, L.B.: The sense of self of nursery school children as manifested by their verbal behavior, Journal of Genetic Psychology, **81**:193-232, 1952.

Anderson, S., and Messick, S.: Social competency in young children, Developmental Psychology **10**(2):282-293, 1974.

Bakawa-Evenson, L.: Helping children learn "who I am," Ames, Ia., 1979, Cooperative Extension Service, Iowa State University.

Barker, R.: Ecological psychology: concepts and methods for studying the environment of human behavior, Stanford, Calif., 1968, Stanford University Press.

Bates, E.: Pragmatics and sociolinguistics in child language. In Morehead, M., and Morehead, A.E., editors: Language deficiency in children: selected readings, Baltimore, 1976, University Park Press.

Bell, S., and Ainsworth, M.: Infant crying and maternal responsiveness, Child Development **43**:1171-1190, 1972.

Berkowitz, L.: Control of aggression. In Caldwell, B., and Ricciuti, H., editors: Review of Child Development Research, III, Chicago, 1973, University of Chicago Press.

Blount, B.: The prelinguistic systems of 100 children, Anthropological Linguistics **12**:326-342, 1970.

Borke, H.: Chandler and Greenspan's "Ersatz Egocentrism": a rejoinder, Developmental Psychology **7**:107-109, 1972.

Bower, T.G.R.: The infant's discovery of objects and mothers. In Thoman, E.B., and Trotter, S., editors: Social responsiveness in infants, Pediatric Round Table 2, New York, 1978, Johnson & Johnson Baby Products Co.

Brazelton, T.B.: Infants and mothers, New York, 1969, Dell Publishing Co., Inc.

Brazelton, T.B.: Toddlers and parents: a declaration of independence, New York, 1974, Dell Publishing Co., Inc.

Brazelton, T.B.: Foreword. In Thoman, E.B., and Trotter, S., editors: Social responsiveness in infants, Pediatric Round Table 2, New York, 1978, Johnson & Johnson Baby Products Co.

Brazelton, T.B., Koslowski, B., and Main, M.: The origins of reciprocity: the early mother-infant interaction. In Lewis, M., and Rosenblum, L., editors: The effect of the infant on its caregiver, New York, 1974, John Wiley & Sons, Inc.

Bronson, W.C.: Developments in behavior with age mates during the second year of life. In Lewis, M., and Rosenblum, L., editors: Friendship and peer relations, New York, 1975, John Wiley & Sons, Inc.

Brown, R.: A first language: the early stages, Cambridge, Mass., 1973, Harvard University Press.

Brown, R., and Bellugi, U.: Three processes in the child's acquisition of syntax, Harvard Educational Review **34**:133-51, 1964.

Bruner, J.: Overview of development and day care. In Grotberg, E.H., editor: Day care: resources for decisions, Washington, 1971, U.S. Government Printing Office, 90-108.

Butler, J.G.: Enep'ut: a hot idea from the Eskimos, Day Care and Early Education **1**(1):15-18, 1973.

Cairns, R.B.: Development, maintenance, and extinction of social attachment behavior in sheep, Journal of Comparative Physiological Psychology **62**:298-306, 1966.

Caldwell, B.M.: Aggression and hostility in young children, Young Children **32**(2):4-13, 1977.

Caldwell, B.M.: AID Chart (working draft), Little Rock, Ark., 1980, Center for Child Development and Education, University of Arkansas.

Cazden, C.B.: Suggestions from studies of early language acquisition. In Cazden, C.B., editor: Language in early childhood education, Washington, D.C., 1972, National Association for the Education of Young Children.

Cazden, C.B., editor: Language in early childhood education, rev. ed., Washington, D.C., 1981, National Association for the Education of Young Children.

Cazden, C.B., and others: Language development in day-care programs. In Cazden, C.B., editor: Language in early childhood education, Washington, D.C., 1972, National Association for the Education of Young Children.

Chandler, M.J., and Greenspan, S.: Ersatz egocentrism: a reply to H. Borke, Developmental Psychology 7:104-106, 1972.

Corter, C.: Infant attachments. In Foss, B., editor: New perspectives in child development, Baltimore, 1974, Penguin Books, Inc.

Dale, P.S.: Language development: structure and function, ed. 2, New York, 1976, Holt, Rinehart & Winston.

Eckerman, C.O., and Whatley, J.L.: Toys and social interaction between infant peers, Child Development 48:1645-1656, 1977.

Eckerman, C.O., Whatley, J.L., and Katz, S.L.: Growth of social play with peers during the second year of life, Developmental Psychology 11:42-49, 1975.

Edge, D., editor: The formative years: how children become members of their society, New York, 1970, Shocken Books, Inc.

Elardo, R., and Caldwell, B.M.: Value imposition in early education: fact or fancy, Child Care Quarterly 2(1):139-157, 1973.

Elkin, F., and Handel, G.: The child and society: the process of socialization, ed. 3, New York, 1978, Random House, Inc.

Elkind, D.: The child and society, New York, 1979, Oxford University Press.

Emde, R.N., and Harmon, R.J.: Endogenous and exogenous smiling systems in early infancy, Journal of the American Academy of Child Psychiatry 11:177-200, 1972.

Erikson, E.: Childhood and society, rev. ed., New York, 1964, W.W. Norton & Co., Inc.

Ervin-Tripp, S.: Some strategies for the first two years. In Moore, T.E., editor: Cognitive development and the acquisition of language, New York, 1973, Academic Press, Inc.

Escalona, S.K.: Basic modes of social interaction: their emergence and patterning during the first two years of life, Merrill-Palmer Quarterly 19:205-32, 1973.

Fafouti-Milenkovic, M., and Uzgiris, I.C.: The mother-infant communication system. In Uzgiris, I.C., editor: Social interaction and communication during infancy, New Directions for Child Development 4:41-50, 1979.

Feldman, R.E.: Teaching self-control and self-expression via play. In Coopersmith, S., editor: Developing motivation in young children, San Francisco, 1975, Albion Publishing Co.

Feshbach, S.: Aggression. In Mussen, P.H., editor: Carmichael's manual of child psychology, New York, 1970, John Wiley & Sons, Inc.

Feshback, N., and Feshbach, S.: Children's aggression, Young Children 26:364-377, 1971.

Forbes, D.: Recent research on children's social cognition: a brief review. New Directions for Child Development (1):123-139, 1978.

Fowler, W.: Infant and child care, Boston, 1980, Allyn & Bacon, Inc.

Fraiberg, S.H.: The magic years, New York, 1959, Charles Scribner's Sons.

Freud, A., and Dann, S.: An experiment in group upbringing. In Eissler, R.S., Freud, A., Hartmann, H., and Kris, E., editors: The psychoanalytic study of the child, Vol. VI, New York, 1951, International Universities Press, Inc.

Gillett, M.: A history of educational thought and practice, New York, 1966, McGraw-Hill Book Co.

Greif, E.B.: Peer interactions in preschool children. In Webb, R.A., editor: Social development in childhood: day care programs and research, Baltimore, 1977, Johns Hopkins University Press.

Group for the Advancement of Psychiatry: The joys and sorrows of parenthood, New York, 1973, Charles Scribner's Sons.

Grusec, J.E.: Power and the internalization of self-denial, Child Development 45:248-251, 1974.

Halliday, M.A.K.: Learning how to mean: exploration in the development of language, London, 1975, Edward Arnold Publishers, Ltd.

Harlow, H.F., and Zimmerman, R.R. Affectional responses in the infant monkey, Science 130:421-432, 1959.

Harlow, H.F., and Harlow, M.K.: The affectional systems. In Schrier, A.M., Harlow, H.F., and Stollnitz, F., editor: Behavior of nonhuman primates, Vol. 2, New York, 1965, Academic Press, Inc.

Harris, P.E.: Changing conceptions of school discipline, New York, 1928, Macmillan, Inc.

Hipple, M.: Classroom discipline problems? fifteen humane solutions, Childhood Education 54(4):183-187, 1978.

Hoffman, M.L.: Symposium on development of altruism. Presented at Annual Conference of the American Psychological Association, Honolulu, August, 1972.

Horowitz, F.D.: Receptive language acquisition in the first year of life, New Directions for Exceptional Children 3:1-20, 1980.

Huntington, D.S., Provence, S., and Parker, R.K.: Day care 2 serving infants, Washington, D.C., 1972, U.S. Government Printing Office.

Ingram, D.: Phonological disability in children, London, 1976, Edward Arnold Publishers, Ltd.

Irwin, O.: Infant speech: consonantal sounds according to place of articulation, Journal of Speech and Hearing Disorders 12:397-401, 1947.

Jenkins, G.G., and Schacter, H.S.: These are your children, ed. 4, Glenview, Ill., 1975, Scott, Foresman & Co.

Kagan, J.: Change and continuity in infancy, New York, 1978, John Wiley & Sons, Inc.

Kaplan, L.: Oneness and separateness, New York, 1978, Simon & Schuster, Inc.

Kearsley, R.B., and Sigel, I.E., editors: Infants at risk, Hillsdale, N.J., 1979, Lawrence Erlbaum Associates, Inc.

Languis, M., Sanders, T., and Tipps, S.: Brain and learning: directions in early childhood education, Washington, D.C., 1980, National Association for the Education of Young Children.

Leopold, W.F.: Semantic learning in infant language. In Bar-Adon, A., and Leopold, W.F., editors: Child language, Englewood Cliffs, N.J., 1971, Prentice-Hall, Inc.

Lewis, M., and Brooks-Gunn, J.: Toward a theory of social cognition: the development of self. In Uzgiris, I.C., editor: Social interaction and communication during infancy, New directions for child development, No. 4, San Francisco, 1979, Jossey-Bass, Inc.

Lewis, M., and Rosenblum, L., editors: Friendship and peer relations, New York, 1975, John Wiley & Sons.

Lewis, M., and Rosenblum, L.A., editors: Interaction, conversation, and the development of language, New York, 1977, John Wiley & Sons, Inc.

Lourie, R.S.: The roots of violence, Early Child Development and Care 2:1-12, 1973.

Mahoney, G., and Weller, E.L.: An ecological approach to language intervention, New Directions for Exceptional Children 2:17-32, 1980.

Margolin, E.: Sociocultural elements in early childhood education, New York, 1974, Macmillan, Inc.

Waslow, A.: Toward a psychology of being, rev. ed., New York, 1968, D. Van Nostrand Co.

Maudry, M., and Nekula, M.: Social relations between children of the same age during the first two years of life, Journal of Genetic Psychology 54:193-215, 1939.

McAfee, O.: The right words, Young Children, 23:74-78, 1967.

McCall, R.B.: Smiling and vocalization in infants as indices of perceptual-cognitive processes, Merrill-Palmer Quarterly 18:341-348, 1972.

McNeill, D.: The acquisition of language, New York, 1970, Harper & Row Publishers, Inc.

Mead, G.H.: Mind, self, and society, Chicago, 1934, University of Chicago Press.

Menyuk, P.: Methods used to measure linguistic competence during the first five years of life. In Kearsley, R.B., and Sigel, I.E., editors: Infants at risk, Hillsdale, N.J., 1979, Lawrence Erlbaum Associates, Inc.

Moore, S.G.: Child-child interactions of infants and toddlers, Young Children 33(2):64-69, 1978.

Moore, S.G.: Social cognition: knowing about others, Young Children 34(3):54-61, 1979.

Montague, A.: The nature of human aggression, New York, 1976, Oxford University Press.

Mueller, E., and Brenner, J.: The growth of social interaction in a toddler play group: the role of peer experience, Child Development 48:854-861, 1977.

Mueller, E., and Lucas, T.: A developmental analysis of peer interaction among toddlers. In Lewis, M., and Rosenblum, L.A., editors: Friendship and peer relations, New York, 1975, John Wiley & Sons, Inc.

Mueller, E., and Vandell, D.: Infant-infant interaction. In Osofsky, J.D., editor: Handbook of infant development, New York, 1979, John Wiley & Sons, Inc.

Murphy, L.B.: Colin—a normal child. Personality in Young Children II, New York, 1956, Basic Books, Inc.

Murphy, L.B., and Leeper, E.M.: Language is for communication. Caring for children, No. 10, Washington, D.C., 1973, U.S. Government Printing Office.

Murphey, L.B., and Leeper, E.M.: From "I" to "we." Caring for children, No. 8, Washington, D.C., 1976, U.S. Government Printing Office.

Osgood, C.E.: Motivational dynamics of language behaviors. In Jones, M.R., editor: Nebraska Symposium on Motivation, Lincoln, 1957, University of Nebraska Press.

Pflaum-Connor, S.: The development of language and reading in young children, ed. 2, Columbus, Ohio, 1978, Charles E. Merrill Publishing Co.

Prutting, C.A.: Process: the action of moving forward progressively from one point to another on the way to completion, Journal of Speech and Hearing Disorders 49:3-30, 1979.

Rheingold, H.L., Hay, D.F., and West, M.J.: Sharing in the second year of life, Child Development 47:1148-1158, 1976.

Risley, T.R., and Baer, D.M.: Operant behavior modification: the deliberate development of behavior. In Caldwell, B.M., and Ricciuti, H.N., editor: Review of Child Development Research 3:283-329, 1973.

Roedell, W.C., Slaby, R.G., and Robinson, H.B.: Social development in young children, Washington, D.C., 1976, U.S. Government Printing Office.

Rubin, Zick: Children's friendships, Cambridge, Mass., 1980, Harvard University Press.

Sachs, J., and Devin, J.: Young children's use of age-appropriate speech styles in social interaction and role playing, Journal of Child Language 3:81-98, 1976.

Schaffer, H.R., and Emerson, P.E.: The development of social attachments in infancy, Monographs of the Society for Research in Child Development 29(3):Serial No. 94, 1964.

Schiefelbusch, R.L.: Synthesis of trends in language intervention, New Directions for Exceptional Children 2:1-15, 1980.

Scott, J.P.: The development of social motivation. In Levine, D., editor: Nebraska Symposium on Motivation, Lincoln, 1967, University of Nebraska Press.

Sears, R.R., Macoby, E.E., and Levin, H.: Patterns of child rearing, Evanston, Ill., 1957, Row, Peterson, and Co.

Shatz, M., and Gelman, R.: The development of communication skills: modification in the speech of young children as a function of the listener, Monograph for the Society for Research in Child Development, vol. 38, 1973.

Smart, M.S., and Smart, R.C.: Infants, ed. 2, New York, 1978, Macmillan Inc.

Stroufe, L.A.: Socioemotional development. In Osofsky, J.D., editor: Handbook of infant development, New York, 1979, John Wiley & Sons, Inc.

Templin, M.: Certain language skills in children: their development and interrelationships, Minneapolis, 1957, University of Minnesota Press.

Thoman, E.B., and Trolter, S., editors: Social responsiveness of infants, Pediatric Round Table 2, New York, 1978, Johnson & Johnson Baby Products Co.

de Villiers, P.A., and de Villiers, J.G.: Early language, Cambridge, Mass., 1979, Harvard University Press.

Vinoze, M.: The social contacts of infants and young children reared together, Early Child Development and Care 1:99-109, 1971.

Webb, R.A., editor: Social development in childhood: daycare programs and research, Baltimore, 1977, The Johns Hopkins University Press.

Yarrow, M.R., and Wayler, C.Z.: The emergence and functions of prosocial behaviors in young children. In Smart, M.S., and Smart, R.C., editors: Infants: development and relationships, ed. 2, New York, 1978, Macmillan Inc.

Zigler, E., and Child, I.L., editors: Socialization and personality development, Reading, Mass., 1973, Addison-Wesley Publishing Co.

CHAPTER 9

LEARNING AND TEACHING MOTOR SKILLS

Motor development is also mental development.

Ira J. Gordon

The last of the goals listed in Chapter 7 reads: "How to learn and control the physical body." The maturational viewpoint of the development of physical (motor) skills is that they unfold naturally in an appropriate environment. Evidence seems to reinforce this concept—apparently all normal children walk, climb, and run without instruction. Research in the 1930s and 1940s by McGraw, Gesell, and others, using the co-twin experimental design in which one twin received enriched motor experiences and the other sat in a crib, provides evidence that motor skills do unfold. McGraw (1954) concluded that Johnny, the "enriched" twin, and Jimmy, who received no exercise or movement experience, did not differ. Both boys learned to walk, run, climb, and so on. Walking, running, and climbing are the phylogenetic motor skills. They are common to the species. It can be reasonably argued that they require very little stimulation for their appearance.

There is a quantum leap, however, in the argument that all motor skills develop naturally. How many of you have an under-par golf score, or can hit a winning tennis serve? Does the ballerina's arabesque just develop? Does the football punter's kick just develop? Of course not. Efficient, skillful movement must be learned and then practiced over and over again.

There should no longer be any questioning of the importance of the early years for all components of development. The importance of the environment, including interacting objects and persons, has been accepted in relation to the learning of cognitive skills. Recent research is leading to the same conclusion about the learning of motor skills. As a result, there is a relatively new component of the curriculum called movement education. It is designed to teach motor skills and to provide specific movement experiences for children of all ages.

A survey of the journal articles and books written by persons involved in physical and recreational education results in the following list of the values of movement.

- Movement is a medium to get in touch with ourselves. Moving provides a concrete, sensorily rich experience with ourselves. It leads to self-awareness. Descartes wrote "I think—therefore I am." A paraphrase might be "I move—therefore I am."

- Movement is a medium for the development of a positive sense of self. The ability to move in various ways is the first major development in the young child's life. A sense of mastery through physical actions is achieved long before mastery in language, social relationships, or cognition. Carefully planned movement experiences present challenges that can be met successfully. Physical development progresses rapidly in the early years. It deserves our attention. Body image is an important factor in feelings about self.

* Movement is a medium for self-expression. Young children do not need to have speaking, writing, or drawing skills to express their feelings of joy, anger, or sadness when they have been taught nonverbal communication skills.
* Movement is a medium for learning about the environment. The exploration, manipulation, and interaction components of learning have already been stressed in all kinds of learning. Piaget, among others, believed that movement is the foundation for cognitive learning. Although infants and toddlers learn much by sensory observation, their ability to move greatly enhances their observational data. Each episode in the preceding chapters has been heavily dependent on the children's ability to move purposely.
* Movement is a medium for interacting with others. The interactions of infants and toddlers are primarily physical. Their social and language skills are just beginning to play a role in their encounters with people.
* Movement is important for its own sake. To learn to move skillfully is to learn to enjoy living. All early play episodes are based on some ability to move and to interact with movement.

Whitehurst (1971) states that movement "means life; self-discovery, both physical and social; freedom, both spatial and self expressive; safety; communication, enjoyment and sensuous pleasure; acceptance" (p. 55). We can therefore conclude that motor, cognitive, language, and social development are interrelated.

SEQUENCE OF MOTOR SKILL DEVELOPMENT

Motor development does progress systematically. However, all children do not progress at the same rate. Nor do all children reach the same level of skills and abilities. Norms are useful, but we need to pay attention to the normal age ranges, instead of specific ages, for the de-

velopmental milestones. There is little information on gross motor movements of young children other than locomotion.

Motor skill development can be divided into six phases. The first year encompasses the first two: reflexive and prelocomotor. From birth through the first month of life, the infant's movement behavior is best characterized as reflexive. Behavior is a stereotypic response to a given stimulus in the environment. The reflexes are designed for survival (sucking and rooting). The "pure" reflexive phase lasts for the first month, but already other movements begin to show increasing adaptability and intention. Before the appearance of upright, bipedal locomotion (walking) the infant gains control of the many segments of the body. Much of the first year is spent in acquiring voluntary control of the trunk, head, arms, and legs. Rolling over, reaching for objects, sitting up, and crawling are major developmental milestones of this period. All reflect the continuous progression toward greater and greater control of the body's movement, eventually terminating in upright walking, usually around the first birthday.

Once the child starts walking (phase 3—locomotor), the whole world is opened up. The second year of life is filled with exploring, discovering, and learning. Unfortunately, but understandably, these activities bring the child into conflict with caregivers and teachers. Mobile children want to practice their skills: creeping, crawling, and walking wherever and whenever they want. They want to grasp, hold, and drop anything they can reach. They glory in exploration, and have no concept of safety or valuable personal property or breakability. During the locomotor phase, walking and dynamic postural control are refined.

The appearance of running (usually around 2 years) begins a long period of motor skill development, frequently referred to as the "fundamental movement" phase. Lasting until the beginning primary grades, this phase marks the child's acquisition of the fundamental or basic motor skills upon which subsequent, sport-type skills are built. By the age of 3 years, most children have acquired some abilities in throwing, catching, and kicking. They need many opportunities for running, hopping, jumping, hitting, kicking, catching, and throwing.

The last two phases encompass the development of specific abilities, as specified by game rules, and of specialized abilities, when motor skills are efficient, flexible, and automatic. Many of us do not reach the "efficient, flexible, and automatic" phase.

A more detailed list of the early developing motor skills is contained in Table 9-1, the developmental objectives for motor development in the AID Chart (Caldwell, 1980).

There are three key principles that should di-

TABLE 9-1 `Developmental objectives for motor development*

Age	Objectives	Age	Objectives
By 1 year	1. Follows objects with eyes both horizontally and vertically. 2. Kicks legs. 3. Reaches for object. 4. Head is held erect and steady when child is held in a sitting position. 5. Sits with support. 6. Bounces up and down while sitting. 7. Picks up object left in reach. 8. Pivots about when placed on floor on stomach. 9. Rolls over front to back and back to front. 10. Clings, or adapts muscles when picked up. 11. Sits erect without assistance. 12. Rocks back and forth while on hands and knees. 13. Crawls on hands and knees. 14. Pulls self to standing position. 15. Cruises. 16. Stands alone. 17. Walks with assistance. 18. Uses finger and thumb to pick up small objects. 19. Reaches for offered object. 20. Bends over or squats to pick up toy and returns to standing position. 21. Walks without assistance. 22. Climbs on and off sofa or large chair. 23. Climbs on and off small chair. 24. Climbs up and down stairs without assistance. 25. Overcomes or removes obstacles to reach a goal. 26. Operates a push or pull toy while walking. 27. Propels a sit and ride toy. 28. Walks up and down stairs with assistance.	By 2 years	29. Walks up and down stairs without assistance. 30. Throws a ball to an adult who is approximately 5 feet away. 31. Can walk a balance beam for 6 feet (6-inch board). 32. Can hop one hop on either foot. 33. Can jump from still position. 34. Can pour from a small vessel into another small vessel (e.g., pour from a cup into a cup.) 35. Can unscrew a lid on a jar. 36. Can cut with scissors. 37. Can ride a tricycle, using pedals and steering mechanism accurately.
		By 3 years	38. Can do forward somersaults with assistance. 39. Walks up and down stairs with alternating feet. 40. Can put puzzle in puzzle rack correctly. 41. Can hop on same foot for 2-3 feet. 42. Can walk balance beam for 6 feet (4-inch beam). 43. Can throw a ball to another child or adult reasonably well. 44. Can catch a bounced ball with hands on chest. 45. Can throw a beanbag so that it lands in a basket from a distance of 6 feet.
		By 4 years	46. Can cut out a simple design involving curves with reasonable accuracy. 47. Extends fingers and touches thumb to each finger. 48. Walks balance beam heel to toe. 49. Catches thrown ball with arms and body. 50. Catches bounced ball with both hands. 51. Skips.

*Adapted from Caldwell, 1980.

rect any instruction or guidance in the development of motor skills. They need to be remembered as you study (and put into practice) the exercises and activities that follow.

1. A wide variety of movement experiences will lead to better learning of more movement responses. Refining of skills comes later. The early years (birth to 6 years) should be filled with variety.
2. Movement tasks should be developmentally appropriate. Infants and toddlers will be in various substages of the prelocomotor and locomotor phases. Tasks and activities should be planned that encourage the continued development of these skills. They should incorporate flexibility of choice. For example, when the children are working on catching, beanbags and balloons as well as balls of various sizes should be provided.
3. Movement tasks should be staged so that children can solve them without adult help (interference). Learning to do somersaults might start with a child being asked to roll over a small rolled-up mat or even a large ice cream carton. Throwing to hit a target might start with "Can you throw the ball to me?"

Children need time and practice to learn the skills of movement. They need time and freedom to explore, manipulate, and interact with their physical bodies. They learn motor skills in the same way they learn cognitive and social skills. It is the teacher's responsibility to provide the environment and the challenge. Teachers of children of all ages often fail to include the nonlocomotor skills of bending, stretching, twisting, turning—all the movements done "in place." They are just as important as the locomotor skills.

The movement learnings of infants and toddlers cover a wide range of activities. At first, the child is moved by a teacher or caregiver. Before the age of 3, the child should be moving independently and efficiently.

PHYSICAL FITNESS AND THE INFANT

Immediately after birth the infant is able to lift her head unsteadily for a second or so, kick her legs, grasp with her fingers when the palm of her hand is touched, and grasp with her toes when her foot is touched. When held in an upright position, the infant can move forward with crossed legs, and will use toes and feet to push against a surface. Baby will even try to climb when held against a caregiver's body. These physical/motor activities are the reflexive behavior repertoire of the normal full-term baby. For the most part they are involuntary. Some of these activities fade out and are replaced later by intentional activities.

As is true with each facet of development and learning, guided stimulation and encouragement are required for optimal progress in motor skill development.

"Moving" the baby

At first baby usually lies on his tummy on a firm mattress, which should absorb movement and support the body. The prone position helps baby learn to help himself. Baby learns to raise his head through the strength of the back muscles; he realizes success as he sees more of the surroundings, and he breathes deeper and more quietly. Even during the first few days, baby's position in the bed should be changed, and baby should be carried and held in different positions. Above all, baby needs freedom to move—no tight diapers or swaddling bands, and a room temperature that requires as little clothing as possible. The debate about swaddling continues. It is possible that swaddling is relaxing and adds to a sense of security for some babies. As is true with almost everything, there is a happy middle-of-the-road position. It is a certainty that infants need unswaddled freedom during their waking times. Because the sense of movement is sensitized by the skin receptors, baby should be held closely, and cradled slowly and quietly, against bare skin if possible. Kinesthesia (perception of one's own movements) is strengthened when baby moves freely during the bath, also. The water temperature should not be more than 88° F. Warmer water will decrease movement impulses. After the second month baby can join an adult in the big bathtub to give needed room for the stretching movements of the legs and feet.

Baby also practices movement and sensory abilities during the caregiving routine—the way she is touched, turned over, dressed, and undressed. A first step in learning to move is the orientation to the movements of the caregiver. Diem (1974) suggests that the caregiver should:

- Carry the child around as much as possible
- Carry the child in different ways and manners (vertically, horizontally, on the hip, on the back, and later on the shoulders)
- When carrying the child, change the rhythm, tempo and direction of the pace. The child should feel the change in movement . . .
- Repeat motions to which the child reacts happily and let him gradually consciously play along
- Avoid hastiness, violence, and all too-sudden changes (p. 4)

Holding a baby over one's shoulder in an upright position increases the amount of quiet alert time of a newborn. Rocking a baby is a time-honored custom. Even the rate of optimal rocking has been investigated. One researcher found that fast rocking (one time per second) is what baby likes best (Smart and Smart, 1978).

A program of planned stimulation (exercises) should be undertaken during the third or fourth month. These exercises are play. They give direction to the motor skills that are available and will be used if baby is given the freedom to use them. Baby's limbs are moved first. Knee-bends, arm cross-overs and stretches, sit-ups, push-ups, and bicycle pedaling, which are traditional exercises in an adult fitness program, are equally beneficial for the infant. The teacher "walks" baby through the exercises, holding baby's lower arms or lower legs.

By 9 weeks of age, baby can be encouraged to stand up, with feet firmly placed on the floor or table, and trunk gently supported during the up and down movements. Babies will also attempt walking movements in this position.

By 3 months of age, baby can be helped in rolling over from back to side in the crib or on a flat surface. The procedure is to:

1. Take the child's upper arm gently and pull to the opposite side.
2. Stand facing the child's back and attract the child's attention by talking, singing, or ringing a bell. The child may roll back without assistance.
3. If assistance is needed at first, give it, but withdraw it as soon as possible.

Rolling can also be encouraged by placing toys or other objects to the side of the child, just out of reach.

The baby should be able to do knee push-ups alone by the age of four months, when placed tummy-down. Prudden and Sussman (1972) offer step-by-step directions.

Turn your baby on his tummy. Grasp him by his hips and lift his body up 3 or 4 inches. Don't be dismayed if he lands on his nose at first. . . . Eventually he will get the idea and push up with his hands and arms. When he does, hold him up for a count of 4, then lower him. Repeat 5 times. As your baby becomes proficient, lift him at the thigh instead of the hip. Work your way down until he can hold his body straight while you hold him at the ankle. (p. 89)

Jumper seats (used during the fourth, fifth, and sixth months) move the baby toward independent orientation of self in addition to strengthening the leg and foot muscles needed for walking. The seats should be hung in such a way that the child can push up off the floor or ground with his feet or the tips of his toes. Jumper seats are *not* babysitters. They should be used for short periods of time, and only as long as baby is actively using them.

Rocking and swinging have commonalities in movement and sensation. Ideally, babies have been rocked from the very first time they were picked up for feeding. Introduction to the swinging motion starts when the baby is held around the torso and swung gently (and carefully) up and down. Babies can also sit on a caregiver's folded hands to be swung between her legs. After the first year, children enjoy hanging onto an adult's hands and being swung back and forth and up and down.

All of these rhythmical movements through space should be accompanied by rhymes or songs.

> Rock-a-bye baby, on the tree top,
> When the wind blows, the cradle will rock,
> When the bough breaks, the cradle will fall,
> And down will come baby, cradle and all.
> (Rock the baby until the word "fall." Then let
> the baby fall slightly backward, and bring
> back to a sitting position on the last line.)

Bouncing the baby is fun, too. Place the baby on your lap (or knee or leg) and bounce up and down so that baby:

> Rides a cock horse to Banbury Cross
> To see a fine lady upon a white horse.
> With rings on her fingers and bells on her toes,
> She shall have music wherever she goes.

Baby moves

By age 6 months or so, babies should be traveling—rolling, creeping, or scooting. Soon after they will be able to crawl. The sheer ability to move is exhilarating in itself. Even so, some babies need encouragement. All babies react to moving objects: they will crawl after a rolling ball, a "crawling" adult, or another child. They may even push a ball away from themselves, for the challenge of going after it. The caregiver builds upon this interest by rolling the ball in different directions, sometimes close and sometimes further away from the child. "The more the child learns to follow a motion in different directions and to recognize different speeds, the more agile he will become" (Diem, 1974, p. 13).

When crawling ability is well established, a new challenge is to crawl over the rungs of a ladder placed down on the floor. Crawling up

and down a sturdy ramp with an incline of about 12 inches is also recommended. A more advanced crawl is required when baby is placed in a cardboard box and encouraged to crawl out. Even 2- and 3-year-olds are tempted to crawl under an obstacle or through a narrow opening. They are attracted to challenge. Teachers create additional challenges by letting children crawl through their straddled legs, through a hoop held vertically, or a tunnel on the floor.

By 8 or 9 months, children may be pulling themselves to a standing position. A caregiver can place a toy or bit of food on a chair or table (of appropriate height) and call the child's attention to it. If the child is having difficulty, the teacher can offer index fingers for him to grasp and pull himself up. If necessary, transfer his hands to the edge of the chair or table and allow him to reach the object. The next step, of course, is to stand unsupported. As the child's leg muscles gain strength, and when she is standing and holding onto a piece of furniture or equipment, she can be offered a toy or two to occupy her hands so that she will release her hold. Another way of encouraging standing alone is to support the child lightly with your hands by his sides and gradually remove your hands. The child should be praised immediately when he stands independently. In this "exercise," the teacher should support the child, rather than have the child hold onto her.

The last milestone of the infant stage is the first step, first with support and then independently. These first hesitant steps may be encouraged by having the child hold onto the lowered handles of a buggy or stroller. The child can hang on, push, and walk, all at the same time. The toddler may not understand what is expected at first. If this is the case, the teacher should stand behind the child, place the child's hands on the handles, and gently push both child and vehicle until the child goes it alone. The buggy or stroller might hold some blocks or toys to give it some weight so that it will not tip over easily.

Physical and recreation educators extend their recommendations for planned movement activities throughout the life span. Caregivers and teachers of infants and toddlers should review their sequenced programs for children up to age 3 years for the specific details and instructions for very young children. Good sources of information and programs will be found in the books by Diem (1974), Sinclair (1978), Levy (1975), Prudden (1964), and Prudden and Sussman (1972). The Uzgiris-Hunt Ordinal Scales of Psychological Development (1975) suggest age-appropriate motor activities, as do other development scales or assessment instruments.

TEACHING AND LEARNING GROSS MOTOR SKILLS

Once a child has learned to walk, many adults seem to take large muscle development for granted. They let Topsy "just grow." They assume that Topsy will learn to run, skip, hop, and climb. These are the caregivers who view outdoor playtime as a time to use excess energy (children) and to catch up on the latest gossip (adults). It is true that most children develop these abilities with little or no instruction *if* they are provided with encouragement, appropriate equipment, space, and time and opportunity to practice their developing skills.

The toddler moves instead of relying on an adult to do the moving. At first the sheer joy of independent moving is almost overwhelming to the child. The child and the adults should be equally excited. Although the first "moving" is not coordinated or efficient, it is an accomplishment that changes an infant into a child.

Walking and running

The prerequisites for walking include an upright posture and a satisfactory progression through the creeping-crawling stage. A few children neither creep nor crawl, but suddenly stand up and attempt to walk.

If the baby has engaged in exercises to strengthen chest and upper back muscles during the first year, good posture will be the natural result. Both a sense of balance and muscle strength are components of good posture. A sense of balance is the sense of stability produced by maintaining an equal distribution of weight on all sides of the vertical body. Arm cross-overs, arm stretches, push-ups, wheelbarrows, headstands, and leg stretches (up over head) can all be done by an adult moving the specified limbs of the baby. After baby is walking, a continuing program of exercises will maintain and strengthen good posture. The walking child can engage in arm swings and handstands and can hold onto a horizontal bar, hanging, swinging, or kicking without adult help.

By the time children are 2 to 2½ years old, they walk with a smooth heel-to-toe gait. They are combining walking with pushing, pulling, dragging, and carrying about everything movable. Running, however, is still stiff and awkward. The child has trouble stopping quickly or turning sharp corners.

When the children are developing a smooth, coordinated walk (and later), the following activities are useful and appropriate.

WALKING THE TRACKS

First crawl over the rungs of a ladder placed on the floor or ground. Then step over ladder rungs. Walk forward and beside the ladder on right and left sides. Walk backward close to the ladder sides. Walk backward in the between-rung spaces. Walk forward on the rungs. Walk backward on the rungs. (Note: not all 3-year-olds can manage rung-walking.) An adult must always be close enough to the child and ladder to give physical support or assistance when needed.

In the above, as well as the following activities, young children may get started in one of several ways. It is preferable to let the children discover instead of having an adult demonstrate the desired activity, or even to make verbal suggestions. The unexpected appearance of a ladder on the floor will lead the more adventurous children to explore its possibilities and even perhaps crawl or walk over the rungs. Others will soon follow, if they are ready developmentally. Imitation of another child's activities motivates to a much greater degree than imitation of an adult's actions. The teacher should wait to see if it will happen before intruding, directing, or even suggesting. In this instance, the teacher is a close-by active observer. Former knowledge and present observation of individual children should enable the teacher to offer suggestions or support only when needed. Whenever a child indicates a psychological or physical need for an adult hand to hold, it should be available and readily offered. But *never* deprive a child of a sense of accomplishment in a job done "all by myself." After a period of experimentation, the teacher may suggest a new or different approach, such as walking close to the outside, or walking backward, etc.

The ladder activities and those that follow should be "taught" in the same way. In the examples that contain different activities around the same theme, the activities have usually been presented in the order of difficulty. The final activity in each category may take weeks (or months) to be achieved. In the "ladder" sequence, crawling over the rungs may be accomplished in the 12 to 15 month period, and walking between the rungs in the 12 to 18 month period. The ability to walk backward and sideways may come around 18 months. The difficulty of walking backward between the rungs may delay this particular pattern for several more months.

FOLLOWING THE PATH

The first path may be a straight line, two or three feet wide, on the floor delineated by large hollow blocks or cardboard boxes. As the toddlers become more mature walkers and less wobbly, the width of the path may be decreased as well as the height of the sides. By 30 months of age, most children can successfully walk on a path 8 inches wide. The path at

this point (or before) may be formed by two parallel lines of masking tape on the floor. Also during the second year, the path may be curved or angled so that children must change their forward motion in order to stay within the parallel lines. The path may also be indicated by lengths of cord or rope stretched knee high, thigh high, or waist high. Three-year-old children can be expected to walk on a 1-inch path. All of these path-walkings are equally appropriate for outdoor play. The children can crawl, walk, tiptoe, roll, and even run on a masking tape or chalk path. They will be challenged, perhaps, to walk backward on a one-inch path but may not succeed.

WALKING THE PLANK

Related to path-walking is walking on a balance beam. The beam or plank is first laid on the floor, and the children first crawl and then walk on it from one end to the other. It can be gradually raised, perhaps an inch at a time, up to 4 to 6 inches. Walking backward on a beam may not be achieved by age 3. Children 20 to 24 months old will probably be able to travel sideways using a closed step pattern. If the beam is wide enough, children can pretend to be four-legged animals and move forward and return backward. When the children have achieved a sense of confidence in walking the beam, they might be asked to walk forward with their arms held straight from the shoulders or with the arms straight up over their heads. In the very beginning, however, children will probably walk the plank with one foot on and one foot off.

CROSSING THE RIVER

Large paper cut-outs of various sizes and shapes may be taped to the floor, serving as flat rocks on which to cross the river without getting wet. Cut-out paper footprints accomplish the same thing when traveling on "dry land." If the room is carpeted, hollow blocks placed close together also serve as stepping stones. On the outside playground, ideally in a nonslippery area, children will sometimes line up their own stepping stones (large blocks) and play follow the leader.

WALKING THE DOTS

The teacher may place large paper dots on the floor in straight rows or curving lines or at sharp right angles. Children follow the path by stepping on the dots.

TIPTOE THROUGH THE TULIPS

This time the paper cut-outs serve as tulips, and in order to walk through the garden, one must avoid stepping on the flowers. Some children will be able to tiptoe by 18 months. Children at this age are not yet able to represent or symbolize. Therefore, it might add to the fun to use paper tulips or other flowers. Vinyl cut-outs will outlast construction paper cut-outs many times over. For those children who have not yet conquered the skill of tiptoeing, a cookie or toy may be placed on a table or window sill just high enough to necessitate rising on tiptoes.

MERRY-GO-ROUND

Tape a large circle on the floor. Play follow-the-leader in walking on the line, beside the line, straddling the line, both frontward and backward. Moving up and down during the walking activities is an additional accomplishment in body coordination and control.

SQUATTER'S RIGHTS

Children stand erect with feet together and hands on hips. They bend their knees to a squatting position, then stand tall again. (The jack-in-the-box action game turns this into fun instead of exercise.) Squatting seems to be a natural position for young children. It is the stretch up that is important.

GIRAFFE WALK

The children stretch their arms overhead, clasping their hands together forming a giraffe's head and neck. They imitate a giraffe's movement by walking with knees stiff. Arms and trunk may sway slightly, but they must point upward. Children may also walk on tiptoes for the giraffe walk.

LEG SWING

Children hold onto back of a chair or railing with one hand and stand on one foot. They swing their free leg forward and backward. An arm swing should accompany the leg swing.

MOVING DAY

A self-initiated activity in which a child may carry, or use a wagon or cart to move, all the blocks (or toys, cars, dolls, etc.) from one place to another, and probably back again!

Rhythmical walking and other movement activities should frequently be directed by musical sounds or rhythms. The use of records or tapes or drum or tambourine beats, as well as piano accompaniment, can direct the speed of the motions, as well as indicating when to start and stop. Taking giant steps and baby steps around the room or outdoor play area will help increase coordination and body control. These children are old enough to play statues (move to music and freeze in position when the music stops). Statues are fun but will not be very stable. These children will not be finished performers.

A mature walking skill usually develops through the following stages: creeping-crawling; walking with support; and stepping independently. Babies do not need walkers in order to learn to walk. Indeed, walkers might even delay the natural progression of prewalking skills. Walkers steal time from the development of the creeping and cruising movements that help establish the rhythmic patterns of leg movements and coordinated arm and leg movements. Babies will walk when their bodies and nervous systems are developmentally ready. Many centers encourage toddlers to go barefoot as a way of encouraging good motor development and healthy feet.

During the second year, walking becomes an insatiable need and is constantly practiced. Walking skills become automatic during the second and third years. Teacher-arranged obstacle courses (pillows, blocks, boxes, narrow pathways, free-standing stairs, ramps) will enhance walking skills and balance, and perhaps encourage some ingenuity in ways to get over or around. Obstacle courses should include low objects to climb over, large crates or tunnels to crawl through, a table or other large object pushed close to the wall or fence so that the child must turn sideways to get through, and any other similar challenge. They are fun both indoors and out.

Running ability develops out of coordinated walking. It requires sufficient leg strength to propel oneself upward and forward with one leg, and enough balance to accommodate the body weight on one foot when landing. At first, children will walk fast with feet spread far apart and hands held at waist level. The fast walking (or beginning running) will be stiff and probably accompanied by many falls. Practice makes perfect, and the children will practice on their own initiative. Soon the child will run with his hands held below the waist and his head leaning forward in front of the rest of the body. A mature run is achieved when the head is held high and the arms swing alternately at the sides. It may not be accomplished by age 3.

At the infant-toddler levels (crawling and toddling), preliminary walking and running skills are encouraged by games of people-chasing and ball-chasing. Marching in place, and then around a space, with arms swinging, will help the arm movements develop. Whenever feasible, walking and running are done best without shoes and on a variety of surfaces. By the time children are 2 or 2½ they will walk with a smooth heel-to-toe gait. They will combine walking with pushing, pulling, dragging, and carrying anything that is movable. Running is still somewhat stiff and awkward.

Climbing and jumping

The ability to climb stairs with alternating feet (with no support) is achieved sometime before the third birthday. Descending stairs independently is more difficult and will be conquered after the fourth birthday.

It is possible in these days of apartment living that some toddlers will not have an opportunity to practice step-climbing skills. Steps in some form should be provided in the day care center or home. A set of sturdy free-standing steps backed up against a corner wall or a combination step-platform-slide is recommended.

The baby who is creeping or crawling is also

interested in climbing and can climb onto a step or platform 6 inches off the floor. Climbing is an all-fours (hands and feet) movement, and therefore is a natural outgrowth of crawling. Children are exhilarated by being up high and looking down for a change. They have not yet learned to be afraid, and therefore need sturdy objects to climb on and nearby supervision. The supervision should not prevent the child from testing, however. Toddlers should be free to attempt "daring" feats. The report of the following observation, written by a nearby adult, illustrates both the challenge of climbing and appropriate supervision.

Episode 16. Kathy (10 months) was quietly sizing up the long stairway leading to the upstairs hallway. She hiked herself up the first step, looked up again, conquered the next one, rested a minute, and then crawled to the very top. She surveyed her world (including the teacher at the bottom of the steps). She turned herself around carefully, and after several complicated body movements, she felt her way backward and arrived at the first step down in 5 minutes. She negotiated the next one in half the time, and continued downward slowly. Her beaming face shown with her sense of accomplishment when she arrived back down.

The "appropriate" supervision was the availability of the adult who wisely refrained from saying "Be careful", or "That's too high." There was no distraction whatsoever, as Kathy devoted her total being to her self-set task.

By the first birthday, most babies will be able to climb on and off chairs and other furniture several feet high. They can manage climbing intervals of about 12 inches and show much ingenuity in reaching higher levels. Low stepladders or combinations of block-chair-table will offer appropriate climbing opportunities, unless one of the rules is "no climbing on the table." Diem (1974) states that 14-month-olds should be able to climb up and down a slightly tilted ladder of 3 to 5 feet in height. In a normally developing child, climbing is even less of a teaching responsibility than walking. The problem is to keep the toddler from climbing! In the early stages of climbing, the action itself is the goal. By age 2 or 2½ climbing becomes purposeful. The child will use an object as a climbing-off space to reach even higher levels. After reaching the heights, there may be cries of frustration over the inability to get down. Young children and kittens have much in common in this respect. Therefore many opportunities for safe climbing should be provided to enable children to learn for themselves what they can and cannot do.

Jumping really begins when a toddler has climbed up and wants to get down. Preparatory exercises include crouching, squatting, using arms for balancing on a balance beam, and using the legs together for hopping. If a climber indicates uncertainty about getting down, the adult can grasp both her hands and lift her off and down quickly, directing her to keep legs somewhat bent. A soft landing spot is best (rug, mattress, grassy spot). The child will rapidly progress from relying on two adult hands, to one adult hand, to the security of an adult close by, to complete independence. The best height for safe jumping is about half the child's height.

Many of the walking activities lend themselves to jumping also. Children may jump over a rope or yardstick on the floor, which is then gradually raised; over cracks in the sidewalk; or in and out of the "pond" (masking tape circle on the floor). Bouncing on a flexible board and then jumping off lends excitement and challenge to other jumping activities.

Throwing and catching

Throwing and catching activities are usually thought of in terms of balls and beanbags. But baby starts to throw soon after he discovers that a dropped spoon or cereal bowl causes a commotion! Prethrowing skills are the grasp-and-release motions, which progress to intentional releasing (or dropping), and then throwing just to see what happens or as a release for frustration. Random throwing is not toward anything. The throwing itself is important. Dropping can be led to a goal-oriented behavior, as baby drops clothespins, blocks, or buttons, into large-mouthed containers. In the first stages, each child should have his or her own objects and a container to drop them in. Gradually child and container can be moved further apart, necessitating the need for aimed throwing with the application of some force.

Sometime around the first birthday, the teacher can sit on the floor behind a seated child and can help the child push a ball away. After the child gets the idea, teacher and child can face each other for a beginning game of ball-rolling. Once a child has internalized the idea of needed force, all kinds of throwing opportunities are available. Balls and beanbags may be

rolled or thrown across taped lines, circles, or squares, into wastebaskets, or to teacher or another child.

Light-weight beach balls are best as begining balls. Gradually the size of the balls may be decreased down to tennis ball size. As the balls become more hand-sized, children should be shown over- and underhand approaches to throwing. As was suggested earlier, teacher and child can throw the ball together, so that the child gets the feel of the motions. Games such as ring toss help refine throwing skills. The upright legs of an overturned chair serve as well as any purchased piece of equipment. At first the child may simply drop the rings in the right place, and then gradually back away. Aiming a ball or beanbag toward a target is a little more ad-

vanced. The target must be such that the child can see the result (a container) rather than a hoop or target board that the ball contacts only momentarily.

Catching is harder than throwing. Balloon-tapping and catching give the child the opportunity to coordinate catching motions with body position. A balloon-pass game will initiate catching movements, with children standing in a circle and passing the balloon from one to another. Using two balloons at the same time will ensure the involvement of each child without much waiting for a turn. Later the same game can be played with balls, first passing them, and then throwing them to children in a spread-out circle.

Balls are favorite playthings during the second year, and teachers and children should have lots of ball games. A 2-year-old will also walk up to a large ball on the floor or ground and kick it.

It takes several years to refine throwing and catching skills. The suggested activities lay the foundation skills.

TEACHING AND LEARNING FINE MOTOR SKILLS

The coordination of gross and fine motor skills proceeds rapidly through the second and third years of life. The beginnings are laid during the first few months of life.

The first year

During the first 7 to 9 months, baby has progressed from grasping with whole hands or palms to grasping and picking up small objects with the thumb and index finger (pincer grasp). Teachers encourage the initial steps by first placing an object (plastic keys, rattle, small squeeze toy) in baby's hand and closing his fingers around it and then removing her hand. Another object can be substituted for the first one. Later, two objects may be offered at the same time. The child should have the opportunity to use both hands, either singly or together. In other words, toys should be offered from each side, instead of always from the right or left side. Baby will probably be able to grasp and release an object before his first birthday. If there is a reluctance to let go, sometimes the request "Please give it to me" will trigger the release. The development of the pincer grasp in a normal child needs no more encouragement than a few bits of dry cereal spread on a tray or table, or a few crumbs on the floor. Dust balls are also intriguing. If baby needs help, a one-time "walking through" with teacher's hand over the baby's should initiate the independent action. As soon as baby is able to grasp (around 7 or 8 months), a crayon may be placed in her hand with her fingers wrapped around it. The teacher and baby together can mark on a piece of paper. It is premature to instruct or show

baby the "right" way to hold the crayon. The grasping and holding on are sufficient at this stage.

Adults sometimes postpone the introduction of finger-plays and action games until baby can imitate or initiate the called-for motions. This postponement overlooks some opportunities for fun, and for a beginning awareness and interest in hands and fingers. In addition to the traditional nursery rhymes and made-up jingles that are used since baby's early weeks, finger-plays and motion games should be included in the daily activities. As was the case in the early activities for gross motor development, the teacher either demonstrates or moves baby in response to rhythms and words. A few examples are sufficient to start thinking about others.

1. Teacher recites:
   Knock on the door (tap baby's forehead)
   Peek in (lift baby's eyelid)
   Lift the latch (tilt baby's nose)
   Walk in (put baby's finger in mouth)
   Go way down cellar and
   Eat apples (tickle baby under the chin).
2. The teacher makes a fist and shows one finger at a time while baby watches:
   Here is a beehive—where are the bees?
   Hidden away where nobody sees!
   Soon they come creeping out of the hive—
   One! Two! Three! Four! Five!
3. The teacher pulls baby's arms back and forth, while singing "Row, row, row your boat."
4. The teacher moves baby's arm with his, while going through these motions:
   Over there the sun gets up (extend arm horizontally),
   And marches all the day (raise arm slowly),
   At noon it stands right overhead (point straight up),
   At night it goes away (lower arm slowly).
5. Again with teacher's help:
   These are grandmother's glasses (make finger circles at each eye)
   This is grandmother's hat (both hands over head)
   This is the way she folds her hands (fold hands)

And puts them in her lap (all four hands in baby's lap).

6. Arms are raised, and then lowered while moving fingers to represent raindrops:
   Pitter-patter, pitter-patter,
   Hear the rain come down,
   Pitter-patter, pitter-patter,
   All around the town.

If such games as these are introduced to baby motorically as well as verbally, baby will soon begin to imitate the motions, and a developmental milestone will have been reached.

As you know by now, the baby's drive to explore seems to be all-encompassing. This drive can be channeled so that baby is introduced to clasification skills, or at least to relationships. Objects provided should have some connection to one another. Self-care items include a comb, brush, washcloth, empty powder can, and a spoon and cup. Food-related items include cooking spoons, measuring spoons and cups, egg beaters, and pots and pans with lids. Even babies under 1 year of age are intrigued by toys that react, or do something, and toys or objects with simple parts that move.

Of course, the most fascinating game of all is grasping and dropping, soon followed by intentional dropping and then throwing. Around the first birthday, baby can drop clothespins into a container with a two-inch opening. Old fashioned wooden clothespins may be slid over the rim of a round container so that baby will learn a pulling-off action in addition to the dropping. Later, a plastic-lidded, large coffee can, with a slit cut in the lid, is a perfect receptable for buttons and the like. Further refinement of finger muscles comes when spring-type clothespins are introduced.

In a group situation there cannot always be a one-to-one interaction between teacher and child. Indeed, baby needs time alone periodically. One self-teaching piece of equipment can be a collection of many small objects (too large to mouth) of a variety of shapes, sizes, and tex-

tures placed in a container with a wide opening. A gallon ice cream can works well. The objects should be changed periodically so that baby's interest will continue. Natural curiosity along with the skills of grasping and manipulating are the only motivation necessary.

By the end of the first year, babies are beginning to recognize at least one shape visually and tactually. The circle is the appropriate first shape, and with a little maneuvering it can be dropped through a matching hole in the top or side of a box. The first form board or box should contain a round hole and a square hole. Squares are much more difficult to drop in because they require some rotation to fit into the hole.

The second and third years

No doubt balloons and large balls and beanbags have been enjoyed for several months. By the time baby is 15 or 16 months old, ping pong balls can be handled with some degree of success. They are light weight and easily thrown. They are not easy to catch, but they are fun to chase.

The toddler has also been manipulating the colored small cube blocks, stacking them and knocking them over with much glee. Some nesting toys are good stackers also if they have lids. The teacher can demonstrate stacking progressively smaller ones. Stacking activities lead to size awareness and discrimination, size comparisons, and eye-hand coordination. They also provide the opportunity for language development if there is a stacking partner. Stacking is a readiness skill for ordering and seriating activities. Almost any set of objects can be used: different sized toothpaste boxes, detergent boxes, candy boxes, paper cups and plates, even shoes (doll, baby, child, adult).

When children can order objects from little to big, labels can be introduced. "This one is little, this one is big, this one is the biggest," etc. The game should be started with two objects, one big and the other little. Gradually in-between-sized objects can be introduced. Matching objects of the same size should also start with just two sizes, with the in-between sizes gradually added. As soon as possible, the child should be moved from manipulative ordering and matching to pointing, and then to verbalizing in response to "Show me the biggest one" and so on. The containers that have been used for ordering should be used in the sandbox or the water table for the experiments that will reinforce the notion that biggest is really biggest because it holds more than any of the others.

Sorting games can use all kinds of homemade materials, starting with large bowls, cans, or milk cartons, and progressing to TV dinner trays and egg cartons. Actual objects can be taped in the corner of each section to give a visual direction to the sorting. Pasted-on paper cut-outs may also indicate the desired color or shape or size. Later, line drawings or pictures can provide the clues.

Beginning teachers face many time-consuming tasks and learnings. If they have a collection of homemade teaching-learning tools in advance, they will be able to devote their time and energies to their children and to the program itself. It is difficult to store large cardboard boxes, or even coffee cans, but it is both practical and advisable to begin collecting pictures. Mounted pictures can be used in a number of ways: for matching, sorting and grouping, lotto games, language development, story telling, and beginning symbolization skills. A good assortment of pictures, line drawings, and silhouettes will supply sets for matching by color, size, and shape, by relationships (e.g., fork and spoon), by function (e.g., things we wear, things we ride on, things we eat), and by location (e.g., indoors or outdoors, kitchen or bedroom, zoo or farm). There is a very important caution about using pictures, however. They are appropriate and useful *only* after the child has had many real experiences with the ideas and concepts in planned and incidental activities.

Suggestions for gross and fine motor activities have been included throughout the chapters devoted to the developmental-educational curriculum and need not be presented at length here. Also, the many toy and equipment catalogs, which are free for the asking (names and addresses are listed in Appendix A), and the many printed materials available (also listed in Appendix A) contain an assortment of activities designed to promote the development of perceptuomotor, gross, and fine motor skills. With these resources readily obtainable, there is no need to present them here.

When a child is able to sit, stand, walk, reach, and retrieve, that child is freed to become an individual and to make use of developing social and intellectual abilities. It is during these first 3 years that motor abilities and patterns of movement should be developed, so that the preschooler is freed from physical limitations on further and expanded activities.

COORDINATION OF MOTOR SKILLS

The older toddler is glorying in his mastery of body movements and control, and should be given ample opportunity (time and space) to put them to use and to enjoy them. The older toddler is also becoming socially aware of other children and is beginning to realize the benefits of cooperation and "togetherness," but on a limited basis. One of the several techniques of building on this social awareness and of extending the already-present motor skills is the introduction of action games and circle activities.

Action games and circle activities

One of the traditions of early childhood education is the use of group activities that require movement, following directions, and paying attention. At first they are led by the teacher, but then an individual child may assume the teacher role. The following games are samples of those which should be a part of every toddler program. In each of them the children stand in a circle, facing inward, and move through the called-for actions.

REACH FOR THE CEILING

Reach for the ceiling
Touch the floor,
Stand up again
Let's do more.
Touch your head,
Then your knee,
Up to your shoulder,
Like this . . . see?
Reach for the ceiling
Touch the floor,
That's all now—
There isn't anymore.

I'M A LITTLE TEAPOT

I'm a little teapot, short and stout.
Here is my handle; here is my spout.
   (place left hand on hip for handle, and raise right
   arm with palm down.)
When I get all steamed up then I shout,
"Tip me over and pour me out!"
   (Bend over toward the right.)

The following games call for a leader and a small group of children. Children should be leaders occasionally for the fun of it. When the teacher is the leader, the suggested actions can challenge the children's motor skills more than the child leader will.

COPY CATS

The leader engages in any physical action—walking frontward, backward, and sideways; marching; crawling; hopping; turning around; stooping—with the children following behind copying the actions. Sometimes two simultaneous actions can be presented to make the copying more challenging. Walking on all fours, flopping as a rag doll, and animal walks are other suggested movements.

THE TALKING DRUM

The teacher will be the first drummer, but all the children should be given the opportunity. The game is to move as the drum directs: fast, slow, loudly, softly, fast and softly, slow and loudly, etc.

MARCHING

Children face teacher, and imitate his marching in place, with arms swinging. Teacher should face the children. It is helpful to tie a colored piece of yarn on the teacher's right shoe, and on each child's left wrist and shoe.

GUESSING GAME

One child (with eyes closed) is in the center of the circle of children. Children repeat the verse, and stand tall or stoop low when appropriate. At the end of the verse, the teacher motions to the children to be tall or small, and the child in the center guesses.
We're very, very tall
We're very, very small
Sometimes tall, sometimes small
Guess what we are now.

A HUNDRED WAYS TO GET THERE

Children watch as one child walks or crawls or runs around the room. Children then imitate. There might be pillows or blocks scattered on the floor to make an indoor obstacle course.

Awareness of body parts and movements is a necessary understanding for the young child. Such awareness helps the child to recognize body limits and its position in space in relation to other objects.

GETTING TO KNOW ME

Children should lie flat on their backs on the floor. The teacher calls out names of body parts, and the children raise the named part. The teacher can also call out the names of paired body parts (arms, hands, legs, feet) and the children raise both together.

ANGELS IN THE SNOW

This activity gets progressively harder, and not all 3-year-olds will be able to do the variations. Children should lie flat on their backs on the floor (or in the snow), with their arms down at the sides. Keeping the arms touching the floor, children slowly move them out and up until they are above the head with backs of hands touching. Then children move their feet apart as far as possible (touching the floor). Bring arms and legs back together. Children repeat, moving arms and legs at the same time.

Variations: move one arm at a time; one leg at a time; move left arm and left leg; move right arm and right leg.

Games like the above contribute to motor coordination and perception, both of which are forerunners of academic readiness. The components of motor perception are:

1. Body image—the complete awareness of its potential for movement and performance
2. Laterality—the awareness of two sides of the body
3. Directionality—the projection of the body into space in all directions
4. Balance—the stability produced by maintaining an equal distribution of weight on all sides of the body
5. Temporal projection—behavior made up of synchrony (the harmonious working together of body parts), rhythm (recurrent actions at ordered intervals), and sequence (arrangement of events in time)

Eye-hand coordination

High on any list of academic readiness skills is the coordination of eyes and hands. The toddler has made giant steps in this connection, even before the first birthday, when directed reaching has been achieved. Teachers can further develop eye-hand coordination by providing activities and play equipment with this goal in mind.

Scribbling with crayon or felt-tip pen on paper or with chalk on the chalkboard leads to a desire (and ability) to make the marker do certain things. Every infant-toddler environment should have a reachable chalkboard. It encourages full-arm movements using elbows and shoulders, as well as movement of fingers, hands, and wrists. The child should use both hands together and each hand individually. Chalk can be fastened to a long string taped to the wall of chalkboard frame. For reasons of their own, some children reject chalk as a drawing instrument. When this happens, the teacher can cover the entire chalkboard with chalk (using its side) and ask the child to erase some of it with arms of palms, using large circular motions.

After the children have engaged in chalkboard drawing, they can be encouraged to draw a line between dots placed progressively farther apart, but never so far that the child cannot reach while standing still. We are working for directional movements of the arms and hands, with the child's body at the center of the task. Children can trace straight lines, curves, or circles with each hand, moving their hands and arms but not the trunk. An adaptation of follow-the-leader can incorporate chalkboard drawing. The teacher draws a line, the child follows, the teacher draws another, and so on. A more advanced dot game can be introduced in this way, with the teacher drawing lines between dots that will form a recognizable shape (circle, square, triangle). The next step, of course, is to draw arrows between the dots, so that the children do not rely on direct imitation.

Pegboards can be used in the same way. The teacher may place two pegs as end points for horizontal, vertical, and diagonal lines. After a child has filled in the missing pegs and formed a continuous line, a line of the same direction can be drawn on paper with crayon or on the chalkboard.

Paper, chalkboards, and even pegboards may be considered two dimensional. Their use should come only after considerable time has been spent in working with three-dimensional objects (blocks, toys). The transfer from three to two dimensions is not automatic and must not be rushed.

Playing catch with balloons or keeping a balloon in the air by gently tapping it with both hands and then either hand requires the coordination of eye-hand muscles, in addition to the larger muscles. Dropping objects into various sized containers, putting disks through slots, matching shape inserts with form boards or shape boxes, joining pop-beads, stacking rings, hammering pegs, throwing beanbags to a target or in a container—these are examples of the activities that help consolidate the desired eye-hand control and coordination.

Concluding statement

A room full of infants and toddlers is a room filled with motion. The actions, both random and intentional, are directed toward practicing developed motor skills and learning new ones. It is the practice that is important, and good teachers capitalize on the child's innate need to move by guiding the movements in increasingly coordinated patterns.

PUTTING IT ALL TOGETHER IN PLAY

Motor development is promoted by action, and young children at play are involved in motor actions. Running, climbing, riding wheeled toys, chasing balls, and playing in the sandbox are all influential in the development of gross motor skills and their coordination. Fine motor skills are exercised and developed through activities that involve cutting and pasting, crayoning, and painting; table games and puzzles; and pouring water, sand, rice, or cornmeal in and out of containers.

Play is the vehicle used in infant-toddler teaching and learning. It is the means by which the young child discovers and learns. Play involves stimulation, exploration, experimentation, manipulation, action, and interaction.

In more recent years there has been an emphasis on the role of play in the development of intellectual abilities. Arnold (1971) tells parents that "your child becomes teachable through play" (p. 29). Fowler (1980) reminds teachers that the "most obvious function of play is the production of learning" (p. 144). Phrases such as these and others ("play is serious business"; "play is children's work") have sometimes been interpreted as references to academic learning. So many issues, including the issue of play, seem to follow a pendulum course, and opinions swing from one extreme to the other. It has always been recognized that playing en-

hances motor skill development. Up until the 1950s play was viewed as essential for both social skill development and emotional stability. I suspect the current emphasis on play as an intellectual exercise is partly a reaction to society's desire for instant observable results. I also suspect that those persons who are stressing the seriousness of play are attempting to counteract this societal concern for intellectual results by stressing the intellectual or academic learnings in any play episode. Their goal may not be to identify play as an academic tool per se, but to ensure the inclusion of play as an essential component in any program for young children. The problem stems from the general misinterpretation of the terms "teaching" and "learning."

Development of play skills

Various schemes have been presented to describe the evolution of play skills. As a social phenomenon, children move through the following stages:

1. Solitary—no ability or desire to play with others. Another child is viewed as a plaything to explore, and maybe to poke or pinch.
2. Parallel—two or more children occupy the same space environment and take pleasure in each other's presence but engage in unrelated play.
3. Associative—two or more children are in the same space environment and are engaged in the same activity (making mud pies, pushing trucks in the sand box, stacking blocks), but with no real interaction.
4. Cooperative—two or more children discuss plans for play, assign roles or actions, and develop their play together. Cooperative play has its beginnings toward the end of the third year. Children make up their own rules, which may be in a continual state of change.
5. Games with rules—two or more children play a game, following superimposed rules.

A second scheme moves from: (1) functional—moves blocks, but does not build with them; to (2) manipulative—discovers that blocks can be used for building; to (3) symbolic—substitutes one object for another or depends upon imaginary objects.

Such schemes serve a purpose in helping us to understand the developmental progression. The stages should not be viewed as mutually exclusive. For example, it is generally accepted that games-with-rules is the most advanced stage in the development of play. Such games have their beginnings in the give-and-take interactions of caregiver and infant. Certainly rules are followed in the simple game of peek-a-boo (Garvey, 1977).

Two major types of activities have been selected to illustrate the relationship between play and motor skill development and coordination. Infants and toddlers are stimulated through self-initiated activities when they are provided with objects to look at, move toward, and interact with. The most traditional objects in early childhood education are blocks.

Block play

Blocks teach best when the children are allowed to explore, discover, and manipulate on their own. Playing with blocks will enhance all areas of a child's development.

Throughout the early years the child should be exposed to a variety of types of blocks, each providing a different sensory input. Blocks of foam, cloth, rigid plastic, cardboard, and wood all send different messages to the child, and ask for somewhat different handling. Not only should the block materials differ, but blocks should also differ in size, shape, color, texture, weight, sound, and perhaps even smell.

As is true with all learning and development, block behaviors progress through a developmental sequence. The findings of two early studies (Johnson, 1933; Bates and Learned, 1954) and more recent descriptive accounts

(Rudolph, 1973; Hirsch, 1974; Bjorklund, 1978) agree on the following sequence:

1. Blocks are carried from place to place.
2. Blocks are used for building rows (either horizontal or vertical, with much repetitious building).
3. "Buildings" are expanded by bridging (two blocks with a space between them, connected by a third block over the top of the space).
4. Blocks are used to enclose space.
5. Beginning symmetry and balance.
6. Naming of structures for dramatic play. Earlier structures may have been named, but the names were at random.
7. Buildings are recognizable as models of actual structures. Dramatic play rapidly increases around the block structures.

The sequence will come to life in the following episodes.

Episode 17. Shelly, almost 18 months old, has never been in the block corner before. She is getting acquainted with the unit blocks. There are other children present in the corner, but she is oblivious of anyone as she bangs the blocks on the floor, shakes them, moves them from one hand to the other, and carries four of them, one by one, to another part of the room. She returns to the block corner to watch the other children play.

Shelly is learning the properties of the wooden blocks and their relationship to her. They are an appropriate size to handle and carry, and their shape and solidity appear to be unchanging. The next time she comes to the block corner, she may manipulate some more, and she also may start to line them up or stack them. She is not yet socially ready to interact with other children, but is interested in their activities.

Episode 18. Danny (2½ years) has been attending the center for only a week. Because he has had at-home experience with blocks, he spends much of his free time in the block corner as he gradually adjusts to being part of a group. He stacks blocks of two different sizes and builds horizontal roadways on the floor. He rebuilds these same structures many times. He is careful to place the blocks exactly on top of each other and is discovering that it works best when a larger block is on the bottom of the tower. He plays near, but not with, the other builders. Yesterday he labeled a single block "truck" and today he "parks" a block next to a larger one, which he labels "garage."

Episode 19. Three-year-old Carrie is busy with trial-and-error experimentation to get blocks to fit together without falling. She is able to build enclosures and bridges, imitating other children's structures. Marie joins Carrie, and they each build a house close to the other's. There is some verbalized planning "Now I need a roof," but there is little verbal conversation. However, the girls are sharing the blocks amiably.

Children between the ages of 2 and 3 years achieve much satisfaction from block play, whether it be carting them from one place to another or building with them. Blocks are satisfying because there is a tangible end product that is always "right."

Particular attention is given here to the values of hardwood unit blocks. Many programs are inclined to spend less money and purchase a playset of blocks. Playsets may represent a farm or a circus ring or a gas station, and therefore limit the kind of play they suggest. A set of unit blocks can be a farm today, a circus tomorrow, a gas station the next day, and a multitude of other things in the days and years to come. The initial investment is high, but it is worthwhile. An introductory set of unit blocks should be provided for children by the time they are 2 years of age. A beginner's set usually consists of eight basic shapes and 32 pieces. The shapes should be proportioned to the basic block unit, measuring 2¾″ by 5½″ by 1¾″. Additional blocks should be purchased periodically. They become

increasingly important throughout the early childhood years. Building with unit blocks incorporates both small and large muscles.

Other kinds of blocks are equally useful in an infant-toddler center. Hollow wooden blocks and large bricklike cardboard blocks suggest episodes of dramatic play. These blocks are especially suitable for very young children because they involve the use of large muscles. Large and small blocks can be homemade with a little time and effort. The first building blocks can be made from two half-gallon milk cartons, one inserted in the other. These are light in weight and fairly sturdy. They may be painted with one or two coats of acrylic paint or covered with contact paper. Satisfactory blocks of all sizes and shapes can be made from cardboard boxes with a little practice—and a great deal of compact stuffing. Even toothpaste, tissue, and cereal boxes can be made geometrically true and therefore stackable. They are light in weight, do not hurt little fingers or toes when they topple, and can be handled easily. Although not useful as building blocks, larger cardboard boxes or cartons serve as ready-made houses or private nooks, and are excellent for climbing in and out of. With opposite ends cut off, they make excellent tunnels to crawl, walk, run, or ride through, depending on their size.

Smaller wooden, plastic, or foam rubber cubes, attribute blocks, parquetry blocks, and Lego blocks all require fine motor coordination. Their use can be unstructured or structured. Some 3-year-olds are able to build structures using Lincoln logs, thereby making good use of their eye-hand coordination skills.

There can be no question regarding the benefits of block play for the development of coordinated motor movements. All block play requires manipulation of some kind. The picking up of small blocks with a pincer grasp and building a stack or tower develop fine motor control as well as eye-hand coordination. When children squat to pick up a large block, lift it, and stand to make a higher tower, they are utilizing

larger muscles. When block-roads are made for walking on, children learn to balance their entire bodies while moving. When pathways are delineated by lengths of parallel blocks with space in between two rows, children walking the path will learn control as well as spatial awareness. A large assortment of blocks is a necessary component in any infant-toddler center.

Sensorimotor manipulations are the dominant play activities during the first 12 to 18 months. Shelly's "getting-to-know-blocks" (Episode 17) is a good example. Sometime during the second year a new play form emerges: symbolic play. Simple block structures or enclosed spaces offer the environment for this new form of play.

Symbolic and dramatic play

The play focus shifts from random banging, waving, or pushing, to the use of things as objects with practical purposes. Fein (1979) describes the development of symbolic play in the following way:

> Initially, the play is self-directed, but soon it becomes other-directed; the child begins to feed a doll or another person, at times indicating that a social relationship between giver and receiver is being represented. At first the play requires objects similar to those actually used in real life, but soon increasingly dissimilar objects can be substituted, such a piece of wood for a doll, a stick for a horse. . . . And while symbolic play is initially solitary, by three years of age it becomes a collaborative social effort (p. 2).

In symbolic play, young children move in and out of the roles and events with which they are most familiar. Although they are pretending momentarily, they frequently need to touch base with reality and real objects. Symbolic play may be suggested by wooden or cardboard boxes of various sizes, by block structures or simple block enclosed spaces, or by a simple, child-sized housekeeping corner. Episode 14 in Chapter 8 offers a good example of solitary symbolic play. Young children go through the actions of familiar events, apparently hoping to understand them by imitating them. They are not yet pretending to be someone else in the true sense of the word. During the third year, children make up play stories and act them out, frequently engaging in self-talk. Two children may be engaged in similar or different activities in the same housekeeping corner at the same time, but there will be little evidence of playing together.

Early symbolic play episodes are primarily imitations of adult activities. Sweeping the floor, shoveling snow, raking leaves, unloading grocery bags and putting away the groceries, carrying out the trash, washing tables, preparing meals, and washing dishes all require the coordinated use of arms and hands. Finer co-ordinations are involved in caring for a baby doll: feeding, rocking, washing, spanking, and tucking into bed.

Role-playing is also important for learning about self and others. Observations of young children who severely punish their teddy bears after having been scolded by their parents are not unusual. Gordon (1975) maintains that these children are identifying with their parents by trying out parental behaviors while at the same time trying to handle their own feelings of powerlessness. Role-playing is also a precursor of sociodramatic play. According to Smilansky (1968), advantaged 3-year-old children:

. . . demonstrate in their play all the basic components of sociodramatic play. They undertake roles and imitate in action and verbally the role figures; they use make-believe to change the function of objects to evoke imaginary situations and to describe nonperformed activities; they interact with other children (mostly one or two only) whenever they have an opportunity, and cooperate in the elaboration of the theme; they are able to sustain the game for relatively long periods (p. 40).

All the children who attend an infant-toddler center should be "advantaged" by virtue of their experience with trained caregivers and teachers in an environment designed to guide and encourage their development and learning. In such circumstances, symbolic or pretend play will be well established by age 3 and the children will be moving toward socialized dramatic play.

The housekeeping corner may be as simple or as detailed as desired. However, crude play equipment will draw upon the imagination of the child. A cardboard or wooden carton suddenly becomes a stove when it is equipped with empty spools as knobs for turning on the heating elements. Recommended equipment for a beginning housekeeping corner includes a stove, refrigerator, cabinet, and table and chairs. Accessories that will enhance the child-initiated play include a mirror, child-size broom and dust pan, plastic pan for a sink, doll bed and dolls, a telephone, clothesline and clothespins, play iron and ironing board, and plastic or metal cups and plates of various sizes.

Sociodramatic play does not depend upon dress-up clothes, but even the youngest toddler likes to play dress-up. Any assortment of adult-sized clothes, with perhaps a tuck taken here and there, may lead to role-playing or just to prancing around. The assortment should not be limited to everyday clothes. Jewelry, high-heeled shoes, evening gowns or skirts, neckties, hard hats, and hiking boots will all add to the fun.

Concluding statement

At the beginning of this section on play, Arnold's (1971) statement that children become teachable through play was cited. The continuation of his statement is now appropriate.

But teaching must always follow, rather than precede a child's playful use of toys and materials. He can only become curious and receptive to information after play has given him partial insights into problems and processes, and into why things work or fail to work when used in a particular way (p. 29).

The most important teaching-and-learning responsibility of the teacher of infants and toddlers is to provide rich play experiences for each child. In conjunction with the play experiences, however, the teaching and learning of the self-help skills is an integral part of motor development.

SELF-HELP SKILLS

Self-help skills are those skills that are used daily, require repetitive actions, and lead toward independence from adults. They include the skills of dressing, grooming, toileting, and eating. The routines of learning and teaching these skills take up a large proportion of the awake hours of the infants, and a smaller but still important portion of the toddler's hours in a group center. Therefore good caregivers and teachers use these routine times for language, cognitive, social, and emotional development, in addition to motor development. Many of the adult-infant interactions described previously centered around the routines of diapering, dressing, and feeding. There is a striking change of emphasis as the baby enters the toddler stage and all kinds of investigative opportunities are available. It is during the toddler stage, also, that the foundation skills for independent dressing, grooming, eating, and toileting are taught. The developmental progression of the self-help skills and related routines is contained in Table 9-2. The information is taken from Caldwell's AID Chart (1980). It is not the intention here to present detailed tasks analyses of the self-help skills. Detailed descriptions of each skill can be found in any of a number of teaching guides for use with young handicapped children.

Typical infants and toddlers appear to develop the skills as a result of the combination of maturation, imitation, adult encouragement, and a few techniques that have proved to be helpful. Suggested techniques follow.

Independent dressing

Completely independent dressing and undressing should not be expected by the third birthday. However, many of the motions and activities during the first 3 years will give practice in the beginning skills. These predressing skills are encouraged by handling Nerf balls, beanbags, and sponges; by putting buttons in the slot of a coffee can lid or pennies in a bank; by unraveling yarn or crepe paper that has been wrapped around one's body; by stringing beads or Lifesavers; by dressing up (and down) in dress-up clothes; by dressing and undressing dolls; by tossing a ring onto someone's arms or legs; by removing clothespins clipped onto the edge of a carton or one's clothing; by putting a sack or puppet on one's hand; and by lowering a Hula Hoop or innertube over one's head and all the way down the body.

Children will begin to cooperate with their dressing sometime around their first birthday. They will duck their heads for a pullover shirt, start to put one arm through the sleeve, and put out both feet for one shoe. As teachers dress the baby, they should talk about what they are doing, labeling parts of the body as well as articles of clothing—"Now we'll put the shoe on your foot . . . Your arm goes in here . . ." If the shirt or dress is a pullover, baby can put hands into the armholes so that the teacher can pull it on, fitting the neck opening over and down under the head. Pants with elastic waists are best; wide hooks are easier than snaps; and a wide belt with a single-prong buckle is best. Iron-on appliques or some other mark should be applied to the fronts of the garments. The easiest way to introduce pulling on pants is to sit the toddler on a low chair, gather the pant legs into "doughnuts," and lay them on the floor just in front of the child's feet. His job is to step into the holes; yours is to ease the doughnuts around his toes and ankles. Both of you grasp the top of the pants and pull up together.

Socks are fun because they have heels. Again make a doughnut, with the child stepping into the holes, and the teacher bringing the sock to and over the heel. The toddler can pull the sock up the leg. Tube socks (socks without heels) might be used when the toddler is first ready to do it himself. Midway between the first and

TABLE 9-2   Developmental objectives for self-help skills and routines*

Age	Objectives	Age	Objectives
By 1 year	1. Eats cereal and other mashed food. 2. Accepts clean-up activities without a struggle (diaper changing, hand and face washing, etc.). 3. Eats table food without choking. 4. Finger feeds self. 5. Eats a variety of food. 6. Helps hold bottle. 7. Helps in dressing (tenses arm or leg, does not resist or fight). 8. Settles down for nap after a little rocking or patting. 9. Gets in and out of chair at table without help. 10. Helps when washed. 11. Eats most of meal with spoon. 12. Holds own cup or glass for drinking and can set it down without spilling. 13. Pulls off shoes and socks. 14. Takes off coat or jacket without help. 15. Can unzip or zip (if tab inserted) jacket or coat. 16. Can take off all outer clothing by self. 17. Will pick up toys with help and encouragement and will place them where requested. 18. Gets outer clothing from cubby, closet, or locker and tries to put it on. 19. Holds cup or glass with only one hand. 20. Eats most of meal with spoon (unaided) and without spilling or messing. 21. Will sit briefly on potty or toilet seat. 22. Produces bowel movement on toilet or potty if placed when "signals" are being given at a regular time.		32. Can pour milk from small pitcher into cup or glass. 33. Uses napkin to wipe hands and face. 34. Helps clean up after meal (carries dish, sponges table, etc.). 35. Waits patiently (or finds something to do) as adults talk to one another or to another child. 36. Is wary of traffic when outside. 37. Blows nose when aided.
By 2 years	23. Does not have bowel movement in diaper or clothing when awake. 24. Is toilet trained (i.e., has only rare accidents while awake or asleep). 25. Goes to toilet by self (pulling down own clothing) requesting help only for clean-up. 26. Can take off all clothing, possibly requiring help with stubborn shirt and shoes. 27. Puts outer clothing in cubby, closet, or locker. 28. Returns toys or books to a routinely used container, shelf, or cupboard. 29. Washes and dries hands before meals with little or no supervision. 30. Can carry out two linked instructions. 31. Feeds self completely with fork, spoon, and cup (some spilling is allowed).	By 3 years By 4 years	38. Knows way around house or center (does not get lost). 39. Hangs up coat in specified place. 40. Can put on all clothing, possibly requiring help with stubborn shirts and shoes. 41. Puts shoes on correctly. 42. Can unbutton coat or shirt. 43. Can zip up jacket when aided. 44. Washes hands after using toilet unaided when reminded. 45. Takes care of self at toilet unaided (arrangement of clothing, attempt at cleaning self, flushing toilet). 46. Uses lavatory properly. 47. Will put toys away upon request. 48. Puts toys away when finished with them without being requested to do so. 49. Remembers routines with minimum of reminder. 50. In general, conforms to center rules. 51. Eats a good part of meal with spoon or fork though fingers may be used occasionally. 52. Follows local customs with regard to disposal of dishes. 53. Lies down to rest without prolonged protest. 54. Will run errands for teacher or do other chores within his/her capability. 55. Blows nose unaided and disposes of used tissues. 56. Can zip coat unaided. 57. Can button coat or shirt. 58. Completely dresses self. 59. Laces shoes. 60. Ties shoes. 61. Takes care of self at toilet. 62. Washes hands unaided after using toilet. 63. Puts toys or instructional equipment away after using. 64. Holds eating utensils properly. 65. Can properly open half-pint milk carton.

*Adapted from Caldwell, 1980.

second birthday, children will imitate others by pulling off hats or shoes. Even double knots are not childproof. The adult can untie the laces, but let the toddler loosen them (good eye-hand training). The parents might supply an extra set of laces, which will be needed before the shoes are outgrown or worn out. White glue will help stiffen frayed ends that have lost their tips. By the second birthday, children can remove shoes (if untied), socks, and pants independently. They will still put two feet into one pant leg and hats on backwards. They can put shoes on (not always on the correct feet) and can put socks on (sometimes the heel will be on top). Shoes can be color-coded with a dot of paint, or with different colored shoelaces. Only one shoe need be marked with a color. At this stage children will also help pulling up and pushing down pants.

Children do not usually conquer buttoning by their third birthday, but they may be able to manipulate a sturdy zipper if it has a large tab, or if a large paper clip or metal ring has been fastened onto the original tab.

Clothes one or two sizes too large help immensely when the child is trying to conquer the skills of independent dressing.

Grooming

Toothbrushing and handwashing are two essential grooming (and health) aids in the daily lives of very young children. Unfortunately they are sometimes overlooked.

Until toddlers have developed the coordination needed for purposefully using a soft toothbrush, their teeth and gums should be wiped clean with a damp cloth. Baby teeth arrive before the baby is able to understand "swish out your mouth," but a drink of water after each meal or snack will help remove food particles from between the teeth. At about 18 months, children should be provided with their own toothbrushes, but teachers will need to do much of the actual brushing for several months to come.

Handwashing, or at least handwashing by the caregiver, should be part of the daily routine from the very beginning. Hands should be washed before each snack and meal, as well as when the children come in from outdoor play. Prewashing skills are involved in every instance of water play: washing dolls, play dishes, and tables; finger-painting with soap suds, and playing with water or snow. Handwashing can be made special by having a dot of fragrant hand lotion to rub in after hands are dried. Liquid soap in a dispenser is easier to handle and more hygienic than a loose cake of soap.

Eating

Spoon-feeding. There is no need to introduce pureed or semisolid foods before 5 or 6 months, in spite of our apparent desires to rush baby into adulthood. A 5- or 6-month-old will suck pureed foods from a spoon and can swallow them without choking. The caregiver should use a spoon with a small, shallow bowl. It should be placed in baby's mouth from either side, with a slight downward pressure to counteract a tongue thrust. Baby will "chew" between 6 to 8 months if given soft foods such as banana pieces, mashed potatoes, or cottage cheese. By the first birthday, baby will lick food off a spoon, or lick an ice cream cone. Baby will learn to lick crumbs off the corners of his mouth if a bit of peanutbutter is placed on the corner. Sometimes watching himself in a mirror will help him find the food with his tongue.

After the baby can self-feed with fingers, it is time to introduce eating with a spoon. Before then, while an adult is feeding her, there may be less interference if she has a spoon to hold during the process. When teaching baby to use a spoon, the adult and baby can work through the motions together at first. A dish with a suction cup on the bottom will make it easier for the child to scoop with a spoon. Foods that stick to the spoon (mashed potatoes, applesauce) are easiest in the beginning stages. Loose foods such as peas or corn present additional challenges, and should be delayed for awhile. A fork should not be introduced until baby can chew solid foods, which should be cut into small pieces before serving.

Drinking. Between 6 to 8 months, baby will be able to hold the formula bottle, but this is no reason not to hold him during feeding times. A small cup can be introduced now. Some babies like two-handled cups, and some do not want any handles at all. A small cup with a spouted cover is the best first cup. The cover may be removed at 10 to 12 months.

Feeding problems. There are probably fewer feeding problems in a group setting than there are in the individual homes. Meals should definitely not become battles in either place. During the second year, eating gets mixed up with the self-assertion drive, and a child may refuse whole meals or refuse any but the most familiar foods. This becomes a feeding problem only if the adults turn it into one. An environment that accepts temporary refusals to eat and in which other children are eating will diminish the child's protests very shortly. According to Brazelton (1974), "one good meal a day in the second year is about par for the course" (p. 62). Teachers and parents together can ensure the child's getting the equivalent of one good meal without much fuss.

Toileting

Toilet training is a simple and normal developmental process in all children. Problems arise when training is started too early or too late, or when the adults are pressuring for success. Most children do not have the neuromuscular maturation to control their bowel and bladder until they are roughly 2 years old, although they may indicate by motions or words their need to go to the toilet before that time.

Signs of readiness include: (1) regularity; (2) awareness of self as the source; (3) the ability to communicate; and (4) a dry diaper for more than

an hour. When the child shows these indications of readiness, walking will have been established long enough so that the child will sit still for a few minutes, and voluntary sphincter control has developed. The toddler should feel comfortable in the bathroom before training begins, and can even try out sitting on the potty chair or child-sized toilet with clothes on, just to get the feel of it. Whether a potty chair or toilet is used, the child should be able to sit with his feet on the floor, so that there is no fear of falling.

Just as teachers comment on any performance, the simple statement that "Eddie is having a BM in his diapers" will call his attention to the process. Because Eddie knows the teacher is interested in what he is doing, he will start to tell the teacher when he is feeling the sensation, and he can be taken to the toilet. It is recommended that at first the toilet not be flushed until Eddie leaves. Control of the bowel is achieved first. BMs are less frequent than urination and cause more internal pressure. The same matter-of-fact approach can be used for bladder training: "Jean is wet . . . Jean is wetting now." When children are made aware that they are the source of a puddle, they may point to it or even get a cloth to wipe it up. They should be placed on the toilet right after a nap or a meal when success might be anticipated. Putting children in training pants when they are ready for bladder training will help psychologically. In the beginning stages, however, diapers are best during nap time.

Children are not intrinsically motivated to be toilet trained. They submit to it primarily to gain the love and attention of persons who are significant in their lives. Toilet training should be handled in the same way as "walking training" or "kicking-the-ball training." When children are seated on the toilet or potty chair, no distractions should be offered—no books to look at or stories to listen to and no food to eat.

Cooperation between home and center is

very important. Parents and teachers should agree on the initial starting time and on the words to be used in the process. It might be suggested to the parents that the child might observe them in the bathroom, and also that the child come to the center in clothes that are easy to remove. Of course there should always be a spare set of clothes at the center; most centers keep extras on hand, also. There should be accurate exchanges of information about the progress being made in both places.

■ CHAPTER SUMMARY ■

Motor skill development can be divided into six phases: reflexive, prelocomotor, locomotor, fundamental movement, specific abilities, and specialized abilities. By the age of 3 years, most children are in the fundamental movement phase, having acquired some abilities in throwing, catching, and kicking skills.

There are three key principles in the teaching of motor skills:

1. A wide variety of movement experiences will lead children to better learning of more movement responses.
2. Movement tasks should be developmentally appropriate.
3. Movement tasks should be staged so that children can solve them without adult help.

Before babies are able to move independently and intentionally, teachers can move them through increasingly complex actions that develop muscle strength, laterality, directionality, and a sense of balance. After babies can move independently, judicious provision of equipment and encouragement will further enhance the development of motor skills.

The teaching of gross and fine motor skills is an important part of the developmental-educational curriculum. We should not allow Topsy to "just grow." Suggestions for teaching gross motor skills include walking the tracks, following the path, walking the plank, crossing the river, walking the dots, tiptoeing through the tulips, the merry-go-round, squatter's rights, the giraffe walk, the leg swing, and moving day. The fundamental movements of walking and running, climbing and jump-

ing, and throwing and catching were described in some detail.

Action games and circle activities contribute to motor coordination and perception, both of which are forerunners of academic readiness. Suggestions to improve eye-hand coordination include scribbling on paper or chalkboard, using pegboards, and catching and tapping balloons.

Play brings together all kinds of motor skills and is the vehicle used in infant-toddler teaching and learning. Play is a valuable contributor to all areas of the total child. Play with blocks and symbolic or dramatic play are two types of play involving much learning of several kinds.

Self-help skills are also a part of motor skill development. They are best taught in an accepting environment by persons who are significant in the lives of the children.

SUGGESTED ACTIVITIES/POINTS TO PONDER

1. If you have not yet started a picture collection, now is the time to do so. Include in it mounted pictures that illustrate various kinds of movements. (The pictures are to be used with the children.)
2. List the steps involved in handwashing in order to increase your awareness of what the young child must learn to accomplish this routine.
3. Foxx and Azrin (1973) have demonstrated that basic toilet training skills can be taught in less than one day. Read this research summary. It is included in the References and Suggested Readings for this chapter.

REFERENCES AND SUGGESTED READINGS

Alexander, C.C., and Kotlus, E., editors: What do we do today? Modules for Training Caregivers of Young Children, City/Community EPSDT Day Care Project, 1980, University of Michigan.

Ames, L.B., and Learned, J.: Individual differences in child kaleidoblock responses, Journal of Genetic Psychology **85** (1st half):3-38, 1954.

Andrews, G.: Creative rhythmic movement for children, Englewood Cliffs, N.J., 1954, Prentice-Hall, Inc.

Arnheim, D.D., and Sinclair, W.A.: The clumsy child: a program of motor therapy, ed 2, St. Louis, 1979, The C.V. Mosby Co.

Arnold, A.: Teaching your child to learn, Englewood Cliffs, N.J., 1971, Prentice-Hall, Inc.

Bayley, N.: The development of motor abilities during the first three years, Monographs of the Society for Research in Child Development **1**:1-26, 1935.

Bjorklund, G.: Planning for play, Columbus, Ohio, 1978, Charles E. Merrill Publishing Co.

Bower, T.G.R.: A primer of infant development, San Francisco, 1977, W.A. Freeman & Co.

Brazelton, T.B.: Toddlers and parents, New York, 1974, Delacorte Press/Seymour Laurence.

Butler, A.L., Gotts, E.E., and Quisenberry, N.L.: Play as development, Columbus, Ohio, 1978, Charles E. Merrill Publishing Co.

Caldwell, B.: AID Chart (working draft), Little Rock, Ark., 1980, Center for Child Development and Education, University of Arkansas.

Caplan, F., editor: The first twelve months of life, New York, 1973, Grosset & Dunlap, Inc.

Chamberlain, D.: Hypnotized children recall birth experiences, Brain/Mind Bulletin, 6:4, Jan. 26, 1981.

Cherry, C.: Creative play for the developing child, Belmont, Calif., 1976, Fearon Publishers, Inc.

Clark, J.E.: Movement experiences for the young child. Della Ward Presentation, Iowa City, IA, 1978, The University of Iowa. (Unpublished.)

Cratty, B.J.: Perceptual and motor development in infants and children, Englewood Cliffs, N.J., 1979, Prentice-Hall, Inc.

Diem, L.: Children learn physical skills, Vol 1 (birth to 3 years), Washington, D.C., 1974, American Alliance for Health, Physical Education, and Recreation.

Dodson, F.: How to parent, New York, 1971, The New American Library.

Engstrom, G., editor: The significance of the young child's motor development, Washington, D.C., 1971, National Association for the Education of Young Children.

Evans, E.B., and Saia, G.E.: Day care for infants, Boston, 1972, Beacon Press.

Fein, G.G.: A transformational analysis of pretending, Developmental Psychology 11:291-296, 1975.

Fein, G.G.: Echoes from the nursery: Piaget, Vygostky, and the relationship between language and play, New Directions for Child Development (6):1-14, 1979.

Flinchum, B.: Motor development in early childhood: a guide for movement education with ages 2-6, St. Louis, 1975, The C.V. Mosby Co.

Fowler, W.: Infant and child care: a guide to education in group settings, Boston, 1980, Allyn & Bacon, Inc.

Foxx, R.M., and Azrin, N.H.: Dry pants: a rapid method of toilet training children, Behavior Research and Therapy 11:435-442, 1973.

Garvey, C.: Play, Cambridge, Mass., 1977, Harvard University Press.

Gordon, I.J.: The infant experience, Columbus, Ohio, 1975, Charles E. Merrill Publishing Co.

Hackett, L.C.: Movement exploration and games for the mentally retarded, Palo Alto, Calif., 1970, Peek Publications.

Highberger, R., and Schramm, C.: Child development for day care workers, Boston, 1976, Houghton Mifflin Co.

Hirsch, E.S., editor: The block book, Washington, D.C., 1974, National Association for the Education of Young Children.

Jenkins, G.G., and Shacter, H.S.: These are your children, ed 4, Glenview, Ill., 1975, Scott, Foresman and Co.

Johnson, H.: The art of block building, New York, 1933, The John Day Co.

Kaban, B.: Choosing toys for children: from birth to five, New York, 1979, Schocken Books, Inc.

Kaplan, F., and Kaplan, T.: The power of play, Garden City, N.Y., 1973, Doubleday & Co., Inc.

Kline, J.: Children learn to move: a guide to planning gross motor activities, Tucson, Ariz., 1977, Communication Skill Builders.

Kravitz, T.J.: Peter Pan in coach's gear, Day Care and Early Education 5(3):12-15, 1978.

Langenbach, M., and Neskora, T.W.: Day care: curriculum considerations, Columbus, Ohio, 1977, Charles E. Merrill Publishing Co.

Levy, J.: The baby exercise book, New York, 1975, Random House, Inc.

Lowe, M.: Trends in the development of representational play in infants from one to three years: an observational study, Journal of Child Psychology 16:33-48, 1975.

Marzollo, J., and Loyd, J.: Learning through play, New York, 1972, Harper & Row Publishers, Inc.

Marzollo, J., and Trivas, I.: Creative learning activities for children from one to three and sympathetic advice for their parents, New York, 1977, Harper & Row Publishers, Inc.

Matterson, E.M.: Play and playthings for the preschool child, Baltimore, 1967, Penguin Books, Inc.

McGraw, M.: Maturation of behavior. In Carmichael, L., editor: Manual of child psychology, New York, 1954, John Wiley & Sons, Inc.

McGraw, M.: The neuromuscular maturation of the human infant, New York, 1969, Hafner Press.

Piers, M.W., editor: Play and development, New York, 1972, W.W. Norton & Co.

Prudden, B.: How to keep your child fit from birth to six, New York, 1964, Harper & Row Publishers Inc.

Prudden, S., and Sussman J.: Suzy Prudden's creative fitness for baby and child, New York, 1972, William Morrow & Co., Inc.

Quick, A.D., and Campbell, A.A.: Lesson plans for enhancing preschool developmental progress: Project Memphis, Dubuque, Ia., 1976, Kendall/Hunt Publishing Co.

Rudolph, M.: From hand to head, New York, 1973, McGraw-Hill Book Co.

Shirley, M.: The first two years, a study of twenty-five babies, postural and locomotor development, Vol. I, Minneapolis, 1938, University of Minnesota Press.

Sinclair, C.B.: Movement of the young child ages two to six, Columbus, Ohio, 1978, Charles E. Merrill Publishing Co.

Smart, M.S., and Smart, R.C.: Infants, ed. 2, New York, 1978, Macmillian, Inc.

Smilansky, S.: The effects of sociodiamatic play on disadvantaged pre-school children, New York, 1968, John Wiley & Sons, Inc.

Stewart, M.L.: A child's first steps: some speculations, Childhood Education 47(6):290-295, 1971.

Sutton-Smith, B., and Sutton-Smith, S.: How to play with your children, New York, 1974, Hawthorn Books, Inc.

Uzgiris, I.C., and Hunt, J.M.: Assessment in infancy: ordinal scales of psychological development, Urbana, 1975, University of Illinois Press.

White, B.L.: The first three years of life, Englewood Cliffs, N.J., 1975, Prentice-Hall, Inc.

White, B.L., Kaban, B., Marmor, J., and Sapiro, B.: Patterns of experience during the second and third years of life. In White, B., and Watts, J., editors: Experience and environment, Englewood Cliffs, N.J., 1973, Prentice-Hall, Inc.

Whitehurst, K.E.: The young child: what movement means to him. In National Association for the Education of Young Children, editors: The significance of the young child's motor development, Washington, D.C., 1971, the Association.

Zaporozhets, A.V., and Elkonin, D.B., editors: The psychology of preschool children, Cambridge, Mass., 1971, MIT Press.

SECTION FOUR

From theory to practice

Theories of child development and infant-toddler care and education have been intermingled with their related practice throughout the preceding chapters. Characteristics of high quality group care for infants and toddlers have also been stated or implied. Selected characteristics may be listed as follows.

A high quality program will:

- Attend to the health, safety, and physical well-being of children and adults
- Provide an orderly pattern of activities, including the routines of child care
- Accommodate the uniqueness of young children and their physiological and psychological needs
- Provide time, space, and opportunity for exploration, learning, and using developed and developing skills
- Establish reasonable limits that are consistently enforced

The caregivers/teachers are adults who:

- Are sensitive and responsive to the needs of children
- Enjoy being with young children and delight in their well-being
- Play with and talk to and with children
- Teach new behaviors and skills in developmentally appropriate ways
- Enjoy their caregiving and teaching activities and responsibilities

These characteristics have focused on the day-to-day living in a group setting. They will come to life as you read the three typical days presented in Chapter 10. The descriptions were written by Jane Dunlap Petersen, former head teacher of the infant-toddler group at the Early Childhood Education Center, University of Iowa. Not only do they contain concrete examples of the theory and practices presented in preceding chapters, but also they introduce two additional components of a care and education program: the adults involved in the program, primarily caregivers/teachers and parents, and the physical setting of a program. These topics are discussed in some detail in Chapter 11. The concluding section of the chapter suggests steps to follow in becoming an advocate for children.

CHAPTER 10

LEARNING, TEACHING, AND LIVING IN AN INFANT-TODDLER CENTER

A DAY IN THE LIFE OF LUTHER
(3½-month-old boy)

A baby is an inestimable blessing and a bother.
Mark Twain

SETTING: A day care center for 84 children from 2 months to 60 months of age. The infant-toddler group serves children from 2 months to 3 years. It has two large playrooms connected by a nap room, and a bathroom. The infant room serves as the play and care center for twelve infants and young toddlers, with a staff of five. The room looks inviting. Its cheerfully painted walls are lined with colorful pictures. It has a feeling of spaciousness. At child's eye level, the space is broken up with a variety of shelving indicating areas of different uses. The shelves hold rattles, musical toys, dolls, cube blocks, and other age-appropriate materials. They also serve as supports for Busy Boxes, Cradle Gyms, and mobiles. The lower sections of two walls are lined with long metal mirrors, mounted so that sitting infants can enjoy their images.

The floor is covered with indoor/outdoor carpet, with different spots temporarily covered with a soft blanket for the infants when they are placed on the floor. One area is covered with a patchwork of carpet samples of different colors and textures. The area under and around the tables used for eating and messy play is covered with a large, heavy-duty piece of plastic, securely taped to the carpet. Another strip of plastic on the floor is marked with the outlines of selected toys that are kept in the area, to encourage shape-matching activities.

A wooden platform fills a large bay window area. Its closely railed sides make it a safe, out-of-the-way spot for infants to observe the sights and sounds of the activities of the others without being underfoot. It is about 1½ feet off the floor, and the steps leading to it offer a practice spot for beginning stair climbers.

Adult-sized rocking chairs are in constant use, as a relaxing or comfort zone for adults and children. Two broad-based scooter chairs are available to provide mobility to beginning walkers.

Essential equipment, such as the large Plexiglas recordkeeping board, cases of diapers, a mountain of bibs, shelves of baby food and formula, a refrigerator, and a hotplate, are placed for easy access. Most important of all is the warm but animated atmosphere created by caring, knowledgeable adult staff members.

The center is open from 7:30 AM to 5:30 PM 5 days a week. Luther's day takes place on a Monday during the month of January.

7:25 AM: Luther arrives, warmly enveloped in his plaid bunting, in his daddy's arms.

Phil: His mama say he can eat rice cereal today.

Caregiver: Good morning, Phil. So, Luther gets a little treat—I bet he will like that!

Phil: Harriet gave some to him over the weekend, but she say he don't use the spoon too good, and most of the food was all over his face.

Caregiver: He will catch on to that spoon in no time. Does this mean that Luther will be getting other foods too?

Phil: Yeah, doctor say he can try one new food each week once his stomach gets used to the stuff. He say he should start with fruits and then try yellow vegetables, then mix in green vegetables and meats.

Caregiver: That's great! Did you find that Luther was satisfied longer after feedings this weekend?

Phil: Harriet say that the solid food will fill him up better.

Caregiver: Does he need less to drink? Will we be needing to think about changing the amount of formula?

Phil: For now he not eating enough to make a difference, he only getting a teaspoon down, but when he's eating more, he'll probably take less milk.

Caregiver: That's great! I'll make a note on the daily chart (which hangs on the wall) that Luther will be starting on solid foods, and let the cook know so she'll be prepared. Just let us know what you'd like him to try next.

Phil: Oh yeah, Harriet say she thinks he'll eat better if you give him the cereal before his bottle.

Caregiver: Sounds good, thanks.

Luther, who has slept through all this, is passed from his dad's arms to the caregiver's. With a gentle stroke on his cheek, the caregiver says good morning to the baby.

Caregiver: I'll go unwrap him in his crib while you sign him in.

The caregiver takes Luther to his crib in the nap room, lays him down, and unzips his bunting. She gently takes out each arm and then each leg; she makes a diaper check. He's damp. She raises the side of the crib and goes for the bucket of changing supplies.

Luther doesn't notice the quick exchange of diapers. He is rolled over on his tummy. The crib side is checked to be sure it is securely latched in the top position, even though Luther is only rolling from side to side in his sleep. The caregiver takes the bunting and wet diaper with

her and replaces the supply bucket on the shelf.

7:35 AM: Rejoining Phil in the playroom, she puts Luther's bunting in his own cubby. The diaper goes into a closed container in the bathroom. She washes her hands, and then records the diaper change and nap time on the daily board. Phil's check-in information says that Luther woke up at 5:45, when he had an 8-ounce bottle of formula.

Caregiver: I see Luther slept late this morning.

Phil: Yeah, a big weekend, I guess.

Caregiver: Phil, what about feeding times? And how much do you want him to have?

Phil: Harriet say Luther will get cereal two times a day for now. You can give it to him at lunch time, and she'll give it to him when he gets home. Let him have whatever he'll take.

Caregiver: Sounds great, Phil. Thanks for the information. It really helps us when Harriet and you make this change for Luther over the weekend. We'll watch for any tummy troubles, but it sounds like he's doing fine. Thanks, Phil. Have a great day.

Phil: It's my day on the road, so if Luther has any problem you'll have to call Harriet at school.

Caregiver: O.K. Bye.

7:40 AM: A quick peek at Luther shows he hasn't moved a muscle. He is checked periodically. He rests soundly, even though there are the sounds of other arrivals in the area.

10:00 AM: Luther is starting to be active in his sleep. He has rolled on his side and is sleeping with his head against the bumper; he turns his head from side to side and then is still. Another child cries, and Luther's eyes pop open but close again. The caregiver gives him a reassuring pat and pulls the blanket up around his body. He sleep is not as settled now. His lower lip quivers and his hand moves.

10:15 AM: Luther's eyes open slowly, but then fall closed. A deep sigh, he rubs his face on the sheet, and then they open again. He stares, and then begins to focus. A big yawn, and then he pushes his head off the sheet, looking.

Caregiver: Hey there, Luther, are you ready to get going? (She maintains eye and voice contact as she walks over to the shelf for the diaper changing supplies.) Have a good rest? (She offers her finger, which he grips in his palm. She lowers the crib side with her free hand.) I'll bet your diapers are soaked. You took such a long nap. Let's take care of that right now.

She snuggles close to his face, humming a snatch of song. They touch nose to nose; she moves back a little; he makes a gurgling sound, which she imitates. They "talk" face to face. Luther is still gripping her hand. With the other, the caregiver taps his nose, says "Boop"; then she runs her finger around his ear, down his neck, under his chin, and down to his tummy. She gives his tummy a rub.

Caregiver: Okay, let's change those diapers . . . One snap, boop, boop, boop . . . There's that tummy. (She rubs his bare skin. Luther laughs.) Where are those feet? (She pulls his legs out of his sleeper.) There they are. (She runs her hand down one leg to the ankle, then holds both legs at the ankles and moves them in a running motion.) Look at those legs go! (She smiles, and lifts his trunk to remove the wet diaper, immediately slipping a dry one under him, with one end over his tummy. She cleans the diaper area with a moist towelette, and replaces the diaper end over him so he can air dry. She fastens the diaper.) In go those toes, and snap, snap, snap, you're ready to go. (She wipes her hands on a towelette, picks up Luther, slipping one hand under his shoulder blade and extending her fingers up to his neck and head. The other hand is under his bottom.) Up we go! (When he is secure on her shoulder, she picks up the supply bucket and the soiled diaper.) Let's go find all your friends.

The bucket is returned to its shelf and the diaper thrown in the container. Luther is set down on a blanket on the floor, while the caregiver washes her hands and records the diaper change and wake-up time on the daily chart. She reviews the information already recorded: Up at 5:45, bottle at 5:50, nap from 7:30 to 10:15. She returns to Luther, and picks him up.

Caregiver: Let's get something going for you—I bet you're going to be hungry real soon. (They go to the room refrigerator, take out the bottle with Luther's name on it, and put it in the bottle warmer.) Let's go visit for awhile until the milk is warm. (They walk over to a sunny corner of the room. Colorful posters are on the lower part of the walls, and two mobiles are hanging from the ceiling within the babies' visual range.)

10:25 AM: The caregiver sits down on the floor with Luther on her lap facing her. She brings up her knees to form a V, and places the baby in the valley formed by her bent legs. They are joined by 16-month-old Melissa, who is carrying a teddy bear.

Caregiver: Melissa, I think Luther would like to see your friend, Mr. Bear. Can you put him on Luther's tummy so he can see Mr. Bear's red tongue? Show me your red tongue, too. . . . There it is, just like Mr. Bear's. (The caregiver draws Melissa close, with one arm around her waist. Melissa touches Luther's ear.) I like the way you are careful when you touch Luther. That's just the way I do it too, Melissa. Did that tickle? (Luther smiles and gazes at Melissa. His eyes turn back to the caregiver when she begins to talk again.) Melissa, can you show Luther what you like to do with Mr. Bear? (Melissa firmly hugs the bear.) Oh, Melissa, I like hugs too. Will Bear hug me? (Melissa offers her furry friend, which the caregiver places close to her heart.) Your bear is a good hugger, Melissa. Let's see what Luther thinks of his hugs. (Bear is snuggled face to face with Luther, who laughs as its soft body rubs his face and tummy.) So soft . . . Luther likes the way he feels when Bear hugs him too. Thanks for sharing Bear with Luther. You are a good sharing friend, Melissa.

10:40 AM: Luther is getting hungry.

Caregiver: Melissa, thanks for talking to him while he had to wait. You helped him learn how to be a happy waiter. Do you think Bear would like something to eat too? (Melissa trots off to the play kitchen area, finds a Tyke Bike, and wheels off looking for some new excitement, leaving Bear and all thoughts of food.)

The caregiver makes a quick diaper check (dry), picks up Luther, and together they go to the daily chart. She records "dry at 10:40" and re-reads the feeding information. Another caregiver is there, and reaches over to take Luther, so that the first caregiver can wash her hands.

10:45 AM: Luther's caregiver and he go to the shelf holding small bowls, feeding spoons, and a box of dry baby cereal. Luther is pacified by the caregiver's tone of voice as she tells him what she is doing.

Caregiver: Two tablespoons of cereal in the bowl . . . and let's get your bottle. (They settle down again on the floor, with Luther in the V of the caregiver's legs, facing her. The caregiver tests the temperature of the formula, and pours a little into the bowl.) Ooo, you're going to love this cereal, Luther. (She takes his right hand in her left, strokes it, and guides it away from the cereal bowl. She puts a small bit of cereal in the spoon, and her mouth opens involuntarily as she brings the spoon toward Luther. His mouth forms a puckering circle as his tongue comes forward to suck. The caregiver carefully guides the spoon to the back of his tongue and lays the cereal down the back of his throat.) Good stuff, huh? (He wrinkles his face in uncertainty. Food runs out of his mouth as he

tries to work the corners of his mouth and chin with the edge of the spoon, and back in it goes.) Not too bad, old boy. (Several more small bites are eaten with the scoop and rescoop action. As another staff member passes by, Luther's caregiver asks her to get a warmed washcloth for them.)

11:10 AM: Luther takes two tablespoons of cereal and pushes the last bit out and gurgles.

Caregiver: That all you want for now? (She cleans his face as best she can with the spoon and talks to him in low tones as they wait for the washcloth. Carefully she wipes his face with the warm cloth.) There you go. You look so nice. (She draws him near and nuzzles face to clean face. They pick up the bowl and towel and go to get the bottle. Luther gives a bubble as he is moved to her shoulder.) Feel better? (The still warm bottle is retrieved and is taken to a rocking chair where caregiver and baby make themselves comfortable.)

Luther is placed low in the crook of her arm, next to her heart. They make eye contact as she smiles to him and begins a rhythmic rock in the chair. Comfortable and secure, she offers the bottle to Luther by gently sliding it along his lower lip until he takes it. His mouth opens reflexively and he sucks contentedly. With a big sigh his whole body heaves and he works intently on his bottle of formula.

His caregiver watches as he drinks. Stroking his hand she sings quietly to him. He answers occasionally with a hum of contentment. A dribble of milk runs out of the corner of his mouth. The caregiver moves the edge of his bib to catch the drip without disrupting his activity. Intent on sucking, Luther is still and relaxed. He and the caregiver enjoy the peaceful time together. She rocks and sings to enhance his concentration on sucking.

11:20 AM: Luther arches his back and wriggles, pushing the nipple away. He fusses as he wrinkles his face into a cry.

Caregiver: What seems to be the problem?

(She holds his bottle to see how many ounces he's taken. The bottle is two thirds empty.) Are you all done? (She moves him to her shoulder as she flips his bib so it is between him and her. She gently rocks as she pats from the base of his back up to his shoulders over and over again. He quiets as soon as she starts to rock. They rock as she pats—over and over again. She wonders if maybe he is finished. They rock some more . . . up comes the bubble. She offers the bottle once again to be sure he's satisfied, and he settles in for the rest of the formula.)

11:35 AM: Once again the familiar rock, but he's now more attentive to the caregiver's face. She smiles and strokes his hand. The end of the bottle comes as he sucks out the last drop. He stops sucking. His caregiver moves him onto her lap so that he is facing her. She wipes around his mouth and checks his diaper.

Caregiver: Let's see if you have another bubble. (She puts him to her shoulder. He burps and spits up a bit as she is putting him in position.) Hey, a good one—you got us both that time. (She gets up from the chair, puts the bottle and bib away and goes to the information board.) She writes:

11:00 2 T rice cereal
11:15 6 oz. formula
11:40 diaper change

11:40 AM: They go to his cubby for a fresh set of clothes, an 18″ by 18″ piece of white butcher paper, and the diaper-changing bucket. They settle down on the floor.

Caregiver: You'll feel better as soon as we get those wet diapers off. (She centers him on the paper.) We'll make this quick since you just ate. (She quickly removes his sour-smelling suit while telling him all about what a good eater he had been, and how big he was going to be if he eats that well all the time. She replaces the soiled suit with a fresh one.) First one arm and then the other . . . (She puts on only the top half.)

Now these diapers . . . (As she opens his diaper she finds him to be not only wet but soiled. She wipes him off as best she can with the diaper edges and rolls it into a ball. She then uses a towelette from the bucket to remove the rest.) There you go, and now a clean diaper. One, two, three. (The diaper is rolled up into the butcher paper, and the bucket goes back on the shelf. Luther is scooped up, along with the diaper and his soiled sleeper.)

11:45 AM: As they go across the room his caregiver plans a place for him to play. She sees an infant seat and sits Luther in it. She angles it at a 60 degree angle so that his lunch will settle and he can play with the mobile that she will set him next to. With the seat belt fastened between his legs and around his waist she taps the mobile to catch his eye and helps him to get involved in it. Luther is full, clean, and happy, and is able to play on his own in a quiet prepared area while his caregiver puts the soiled diaper in a plastic bag, seals it, and throws it away. She rinses out the soiled outfit and puts it in a bag in the baby's cubby. She washes her hands with soap and water, and goes back to the information board.

11:50 AM: She changes the notation on the chart to read: "10:40 BM." Out of the corner of her eye she is watching Luther. The mirror lining the wall that he is sitting next to has captivated him. He stares expressionlessly at the baby in the mirror. The breeze moves the mobile and Luther is involved with it again, watching the colors and shapes move.

12:00 PM: A clean flannel blanket is spread out on the carpet, and is prepared with rattles and rocking toys. Luther's caregiver sits next to his seat and loosens the strap. She lays him down on the blanket on his tummy moving the infant seat out of the way. She places the toys within his view and reach. Luther is so excited. His arms and legs fly as he arches his back to lift his head off the blanket. Back down . . . that's hard work, but up again they go for a second, over and over again.

While Luther is exercising, Travis brings a book over to the caregiver. He backs his way into her lap and gets comfortable. Luther gurgles to himself as he plays.

Luther is flinging his arms. He swipes his right ear again and again. The next time, much to his surprise, he finds a rattle. He startles at its sound. With a wild fling of his arm he knocks the rattle under his cheek.

Caregiver: Better move the rattle for Luther, Travis. We wouldn't want him to fall on it. (The caregiver reaches over and moves the rattle into Luther's hand. She then initiates a roll by laying her arm behind his back and tipping him into her arm.) Over you go. (Once on his back Luther rediscovers the mobile with a squeal.) Travis, listen to the story that Luther is telling. Let's see if we can say it back to him.

Caregiver and Travis: Ae, Ah, Ae, Ah (Luther quickly looks in their direction, and responds, "ah, ah, ah." The caregiver puts Luther on her legs in the V sit.)

Caregiver: Ah, Ah, Ah. (Luther responds. They exchange sounds, Luther waiting and watching his caregiver wide-eyed to see what will be next.) I've got your fingers. (She strokes her thumb against his fingers.) Let's take a walk up your arm. (As she walks her fingers up his arm, Luther begins to laugh.) Here's your neck and here's your chin, we'll skip right over that mouth . . . and there's that *nose.* (As she says "nose" she gathers him near and rubs noses and nuzzles with him. He giggles and laughs out loud.) Hey, did you hear that, Luther? (The caregiver shakes the hand still gripping the rattle. He looks at the rattle. She reaches for another rattle and shakes it on the other side.) What a surprise. (He looks around to find it.) Let's try that again.

12:15 PM: Luther drops his rattle as he stretches and makes a large yawn. He wrinkles his face and fusses as he bats at his right ear.

Caregiver: Are you getting tired? (She once again checks his diapers. They are dry.)

The caregiver moves Luther to her shoulder, picks up the blanket and rattles, and stands up. She puts the toys in the "toys to be washed" bucket, the blanket in a laundry basket, and marks the information chart that Luther's diapers were checked and found to be dry at 12:15. They find a rocking chair and sit.

Caregiver: Hey, Luther, let's rock for a minute. (With Luther on her shoulder, she begins the slow rhythmic rock and gentle "heartbeat" pat on his back. She hums quietly to him. He is very tired. With a great sigh, his body quivers and he molds to her arms. They rock.)

12:25 PM: Sound asleep, Luther is placed in his crib. Again the caregiver carefully lays him down on his tummy. "Sweet dreams," she whispers as she covers him with his blanket. She raises the crib side to the top and checks it, and goes to record his nap time on the information board. As she writes down the time, she anticipates another 2-hour rest for Luther. She checks on him frequently.

1:10 PM: Luther's sleep is less settled. He has kicked his blanket away. His arms and legs thrash as he seeks a comfortable position. The caregiver replaces his blanket quietly and strokes his back gently to relax him.

1:15 PM: Luther whimpers as he rubs his nose back and forth on the sheet. Again he kicks away his blanket. A few more pats help Luther to relax again.

1:25 PM: Luther is just not comfortable. He whimpers again. His glassy eyes open unwillingly as he gathers a mournful cry. The caregiver goes to his crib. Her voice is low and reassuring as she lowers the side of his crib to take him to a rocking chair to comfort him. He settles to her voice. Snuggled on her shoulder, they begin to rock. The caregiver notices how warm Luther's body feels next to hers. She presses her lips to his forehead . . . yes, he is warm. The caregiver decides that the nurse had better check him to see just how warm he is. A quick diaper check finds that Luther is still dry.

1:35 PM: The caregiver looks over the information chart and records the newest information about Luther's nap and diaper. Luther, wrapped in his blanket, and his caregiver are off to the nurse's office. Luther is very drowsy, and is relaxed on his caregiver's shoulder as they reach the office.

Nurse: What nice bundle do you have there?

Caregiver: Luther seems to be restless in his sleep and I thought he might have a temperature. He feels so warm. (The nurse takes Luther.)

Nurse: He does seem warm, doesn't he! Let's just check to see. (They disappear into a supply closet and return with a thermometer, jar of Vaseline, gauze pad, and fresh diaper. She takes Luther to the crib and lays him on his back. He stares blankly as she chats with him and loosens his sleeper.)

Caregiver: His diaper was still dry when I got him up, and his last change was at 11:40.

Nurse: He looks like he's just getting up. (The nurse carefully holds his ankles to lift his bare bottom and insert the thermometer.) Has he been lying on his right ear? It looks a little red. (She continues to talk with him while she listens to the caregiver's report.)

Caregiver: He was fussing with it a little while he was playing, but nothing much. His dad said that he slept late this morning, but he fell asleep as usual on his ride to the Center. He slept about an hour longer than he would ordinarily this morning, but was just great while he was awake to play. Did you notice on the information board that he started getting solids over the weekend?"

Nurse: The way this is rising, there's no doubt. It's to 102° already. We will call for his dad to pick him up. (The caregiver goes to the nurse's desk to locate her emergency numbers card file for Phil's number.)

Caregiver: Phil said that he was going to be

on the road today, so we'll have to call Harriet at school. (She lays Luther's card on the desk. Luther is fussing and begins to whimper.)

Nurse: Well, he's up to 103.5°. I won't make him wait any longer. (She chats with him and reassures him all the while. The caregiver moves to Luther's side and puts his diaper back on. The nurse gathers her equipment and goes to wash her hands.) He doesn't need to be sponged down, but he may like a bottle of water while he's waiting. (The caregiver quickly dresses Luther, blowing on his tummy and nestling with him as she fastens the last snap. Luther musters a smile, but drops to a tired stare immediately.)

2:00 PM: The nurse returns and places him on her shoulder.

Nurse: We'll give his mom a call. (The caregiver goes to the kitchen for a bottle of water, while Luther rests in the nurse's arms. When she returns Luther is watching the rattle in the nurse's hand while they rock.) His mom says that either she or Phil will be right here. She didn't leave a signed permission slip for Tylenol, so we'll just keep him cool and give him some water.

Caregiver: He looks so comfortable with you, I'll go get his things together from the room. (The nurse offers Luther the bottle in the same comfortable way that his caregiver does. Rocking slow and close, Luther sucks eagerly in a sleepy, stary state.)

2:15 PM: After 4 oz. of water, Luther is finding it very hard to keep his eyes open and has been lulled to sleep. The nurse moves him back to the crib to lay him down, but as she does he startles and whimpers. They rock again. His lips begin sucking action, so the nurse offers the bottle again. She strokes his brow and studies her docile patient, as they continue to rock. His sucking slows and stops . . . he hesitates . . . sucks again . . . he stops. His jaw quivers as he sighs and drops the bottle from his mouth. Luther is asleep. Again, the nurse takes him to the crib, but once more he fusses as he's lowered to the bed. They rock.

2:45 PM: Luther's dad appears at the door with the caregiver. He has the bunting and a plastic bag with Luther's soiled suit. They have been discussing Luther's day.

Phil: She tellin' me here that Luther got a temp, and he not feelin' too good. Maybe he got that bug his big sister had last week.

Nurse: Thanks for coming, Phil. The girls were saying that he was fussing with that right ear, and it does look a little red. That may be some place for the doctor to start.

Phil: His sister had those ear troubles 'til she was three. Sure hope he don't get those. Harriet told the Doc we'd be there at 3:00, so we'd better get packed up. (While the nurse was chatting with Phil she had guided Luther into his bunting without arousing him.)

Nurse: There you go. We'll be anxious to hear what the doctor thinks. Hope that your evening goes well. Bye. (Luther, still sleeping, has ended his day at the day care center.)

A DAY IN THE LIFE OF TRAVIS
(18-month-old boy)

The important thing is not so much that every child should be taught as that every child should be given the wish to learn.

John Lubbock

SETTING: The same infant–young toddler room described in Luther's day. It also contains equipment and materials appropriate for beginning walkers. The colors, sights, and sounds suggest more "mature" uses of the same equipment; the variety of shelves that house toys also make play corners for dress-up and housekeeping play. There are also a water table for sensory exploration and two three-step slides for climbing, sliding and imaginative play. Carpet samples are taped to a wall for texture and color discrimination. There are Velcro-covered balls for tossing. A shape-matching board is on another wall, which offers a vertical lotto game to be played with Velcro-backed matching shapes. There are milk carton blocks for stacking, diaper cartons for climbing in and out, and a small workbench holding large wooden nuts, bolts, and screws. A 3' × 5' chalkboard is mounted on one side of a room divider. Tape "highways" on the carpet suggest traffic patterns for cars and trucks. The platform area in the bay window overlooks a river, a parking lot, and an athletic field. A bookshelf containing cardboard and laminated picture books is readily accessible. Other shelves contain matching, sorting, stringing, building, and manipulating materials. There are both the security of familiar playthings and the adventure of the new.

Travis' day occurred during the springtime.

8:00 AM: Travis is delivered to the Center by his mother, Connie. As they enter the playroom, they are both greeted.

Teacher: Good morning, Connie. Hey, Travis, what a nice smile you're wearing this morning! I'm glad to see you too!

Information is shared about Travis' evening that the caregivers may need to know to help him through the day: a new word to reinforce, a scarey thing to avoid, a rash to watch for, and a doctor's appointment to be made ready for. Routine information is noted for all the staff to share in a notebook, and the amount of sleep, meals, and any health problems are recorded on a Plexiglas chart mounted on the room wall in plain view for everyone.

Travis shares his adventures in coming to the Center as his mother loosens the zipper tab so that he can unzip his jacket and hang it up. Mother shows her approval of his actions and also her positive feelings toward the Center.

Connie: Thanks for helping. Looks like you're ready to play with your friends. (Connie picks him up for a kiss good-bye.) Have a nice day. (She smiles and puts him in the arms of the greeter who gives him a good morning squeeze and smile as they wave bye.)

8:05 AM: Across the room another teacher greets him, "Good morning, Travis, I'm glad to see you here today." Together he and his greeter survey the room.

Teacher: Well, what looks like fun today, Travis? I see Jimmy cooking in the kitchen, Betty is looking at books with Ann, Carol is drawing on the chalkboard, Bobby is playing with the Busy Box, Mike is riding in a wheelie chair, and I see Mary watching the buses outside. (The teacher lets Travis down.) No one is using the slide or balls right now. Would you like to roll a ball to me or help Tom in the house?

Travis: House.

Together they walk to the housekeeping corner. The teacher picks up the receiver of the phone and sits down. After a brief conversation she says good-bye and hangs up. She then makes the phone ring, answers it, and hands it to Travis. "It's for you!" Travis excitedly says, "Hi" and hangs up. He laughs and rings the dial bell, calling over and over again. He continues exploring the phone and its bell, and even has a short chat with his mother. The teacher moves away unobtrusively. Travis remains captivated by his play, speaking in low tones, mostly to his mom, and dialing carefully over and again. After a time he takes the phone to a chair and sits down to continue his chat.

8:20 AM: Travis looks up as he hears the music of Ann's wind-up radio, and walks toward her with a smile on his face. He stops and looks at her, expecting her to give the toy to him. He then leans over and tries to take the toy out of her hands.

Teacher: Travis, Ann is using that radio; let's use our eyes and find another. (He continues to reach for the toy. The teacher then tells him to look near the doll for another toy just like the one Ann is using. The teacher tells him that Ann is playing with the toy to make him aware that he would either have to wait till she was through with it or look for another. Travis picks up the other radio. The teacher shows her approval.) Now you both have radios! Let's listen to their music.

Travis carefully holds the knob and twists the radio round and round to wind it up. He looks up contentedly as the music starts, and carries it to the chalkboard where Carol (13 mo.) is drawing. He drops the radio by his side as he grasps the dangling string to the fat chunk of white chalk, and finds a drawing space on the board. He draws with large sweeping motions until his marks meet Carol's and they both laugh. Travis drops his chalk over the top of the board and runs behind it to retrieve it. Delighted to find it, he runs back. Carol, charmed by his reappearance, laughs at his return. He continues ducking behind the divider and popping out in a peek-a-boo game with Carol, forgetting all about his vanished chalk.

As a teacher walks across the classroom she notices Tony (14 mo.) about to lose his balance. She scoops him up just in time in a dropseat position with her hands under his bottom and the child's knees over her arm. She begins swinging him, singing, "Ding dong bell, kitty in the well." Immediately Mike, Travis, and Carol move to her. Tony is set down, safely rescued. The teacher gestures to the others to move to a place where they won't bump Mark, who was watching nearby. Each child has a turn singing "Ding dong bell, Travis in the well; ding dong bell, Tony in the well" until everyone has had enough turns.

Travis loves it, and requests over and over again, "Ding dong, ding dong, Travis' turn."

9:20 AM: After several turns the teacher notices that Travis' bottom seems warm. As he sits down at the end of a turn, she unobtrusively slips her finger down the waist of his diaper. It is wet.

Teacher: Hey, let's change those wet diapers, Travis, that will feel much better! (Together they walk to get the diaper bucket and a piece of butcher paper, then walk to an unoccupied place in the room. She lays the piece of paper on the floor and Travis lays himself on it. While she takes his pants off and changes him, she is still singing the Ding-dong song and he is singing his part too. She blows on his tummy as she pulls his pants up and they laugh.) All done! Thanks Travis. Let's go wash our hands. It's almost time for snack! You may carry the bucket if you like. It's nice to have you for a helper, Travis. Thanks. (They walk across the room to the bathroom area. Travis steps up to the sink.)

Teacher: Who's that fellow in the mirror? (She brushes his hair to one side with her hand.) Nice smile, huh? I see Travis!

Travis: See Janie. (He points in the mirror and turns to smile to Janie in person.)

Teacher: Hey, you can see me in the mirror, too, can't you! Neat! This is the way Travis washes, Travis washes, Travis washes . . . This is the way that Travis washes, *now* he's shiny clean! (The caregiver leans over to mark the diaper change on the Plexiglas board.) You can dry your hands on the towel while I wash mine. Meet you at the snack table.

9:50 AM: The cook brings snack into the room and places it on the counter. As soon as the children see the cook, they know it's time to go to the bathroom to wash their hands and then go to sit at the table. One teacher takes the food to the table and passes it out. She tears off a paper towel placemat for each child and places a cracker spread with ham salad on each towel. Meanwhile other teachers are putting bibs on each of the children as they are helped into child-sized cube chairs. After the children and teachers are settled, juice is poured for all. During the whole process there is much conversation: "I see Jim is sitting next to Ann today. Mike, there is a chair by Freddie that no one is using, if you need a place to sit. Hey, you found it! I can tell you're ready for more crackers by the way you are showing me your empty hands, Carol."

Travis: Mo', mo' juice!

Teacher: Thanks for asking so nicely for more juice, Travis. I like that!

A plane flies overhead outside. Paul (21 mo.) screams, "Plane!"

Teacher: Did you hear a plane? Let's all listen, Paul hears something. (There is much giggling and excitement.) I can tell lots of us hear the plane. Thanks for telling us you heard the plane, Paul. You are a good listener! Planes go in the sky, not on the road like cars.

Paul: Mom plane.

Teacher: I remember when your mom went on the plane, Paul!

Travis: Mom.

Teacher: Oh, your mom has gone on a plane too, Travis?

Paul: Plane (He points upward. The teacher gestures with her arms and eyes to listen again.)

Teacher: I don't hear it this time, it must be gone. (Paul drops the idea and continues eating.) I like the way Mike holds his cup with two hands. It really helps him hold on so he won't spill.

When the children are satisfied, they individually leave the table and find their way to the

sink where there is an adult to help them clean up.

10:10 AM: In a quiet corner one of the teachers is gathering a group of four children. A large piece of posterboard is on the floor in front of them. It contains pictures of a candy cane, a bottle of baby lotion, a cup of coffee, a lemon, a flower, and a jar of peanutbutter. Travis joins the group as the teacher begins to speak.

Teacher: You're just in time to help us match some smells. Come and join us. (She offers each child a sealed canister with holes in the top.) We are going to discover what is inside the can without using our eyes. How can we do that? (Two children bring up their cans to their noses.) That's right, we're going to use our noses. (She sniffs her can.) Tami, would you show us the picture of what is inside your can? We'll watch. (Tami leans over and places her can on the picture of the baby lotion bottle.) Tami thinks her can smells like baby lotion. Will you give each of us a smell too? (Tami holds her can out to the others and they agree.) Thanks, Tami. Let's see if Travis can show us which picture shows the smell in his can. (Travis puts his canister on the picture of the peppermint stick, and runs off to play. He goes back to the snack table and watches the teacher who is washing it off.)

Teacher: Oh, would you like to wash too?

Travis: Wash too.

Teacher: Okay, I'll get a cloth for you too, Travis. I like to have a helper. (The teacher wets several cloths knowing there will be more volunteers.) There you go, I want you to wash off this red chair, Travis. Mike, you do the blue one over there. Thanks guys! (The washcloths and helpers scatter to other areas. The cover of *Early Bird* catches Travis' eye as he washes the bookshelf. He drops the washcloth and takes the book to a teacher sitting nearby. He backs up and lands in her lap.)

Teacher: Thanks for sharing this book with me, Travis. I like this one too. Oh, look Travis, show me where Early Bird is . . . yes, he's just waking up from a good rest, isn't he? Can you stretch like Early Bird? Let's do it. (Travis stretches, but reaches up for the teacher's arm and quickly pulls it back down to hold the book.) And look! What is he doing in this picture?

Travis: Eat.

Teacher: Yes, he's eating his breakfast with his mom and dad—just like you do! (Paul comes over to show them a truck he's using.) Travis, look at the truck Paul is using. What kind of truck are you driving, Paul?

Paul: Milk. (Paul answers after a glance at the book, which shows a milkman. Travis meanwhile is making himself more comfortable lying back in the nest he has made of the teacher's lap.)

Teacher: Hey, Early Bird likes milk for his breakfast, doesn't he, Travis? There's a spot right here next to me if you'd like to see this book with us, Paul. Neat, now we can all see the book. (A squeeze for Travis reassures him of his safe place.) Let's see what happens next. (The two boys laugh as they point to the pictures.)

10:40 AM: When Paul and Travis notice some children getting sweaters on, they jump up and run to their cubbies.

Travis: 'Side, 'side.

Teacher: Sure, I'll get your sweater so *you* can go outside too, Travis. (One teacher has moved to the door and is singing, "If you're ready and you know it, clap your hands . . .," while the others are getting ready to go.)

A teacher has prepared the playground with Tyke Bikes, wagons, balls, and trucks for the sandbox. One teacher leads the five children out and another follows.

Travis heads straight for the stationary climbers. He climbs to the top of one of the two pieces of climbing apparatus. The teacher is very attentive, standing next to him and talking with him about his actions directly. The teacher comments to Travis, using his name, about how high he is and how he had managed to climb up unassisted. The tone of the teacher's voice is very warm and enthusiastic; her physical proximity seems also to lend security (although at no time does she actually touch or move to support him while he is at the top of the climber).

When Travis is ready to climb down, he looks to the teacher for assistance. While talking with him about the action as it takes place, the teacher helps Travis by guiding his foot to the next lowest rung. At no time does the teacher take major control of the child's movement, but acts merely as a guide to assure him of his actions. Although not at all verbal during the activity, he never appears to be apprehensive and seems to enjoy the climbing and interacting with the adult.

He runs across the playground where three or four children have gathered in a loose circle to play with several rubber and textured balls. The teacher talks with Jimmy and Ann about the ball she has, describing its shape, color, size (relative to a smaller textured ball), and its bouncing action. She then encourages Jimmy to roll the ball to Ann and back again, talking about their actions and the movement of the ball all the while. When Travis joins the group, he proceeds to roll over in an awkward but complete somersault. The teacher is delighted with this action, and, encouraging him to tumble again, says, "Travis can roll just like a ball." Ann and Jimmy continue to roll the ball back and forth, with occasional bounces in between. Travis rolls over and over until time to go inside.

11:20 AM: One teacher takes three children inside, but Travis and Mike stay out a few minutes longer, in order to give the inside teacher a chance to help each of her children take their sweaters off and put them away, get a drink, wash their hands and have their diapers changed. Travis, Mike, and their teacher come in.

Another teacher is sitting on the floor waiting for them with colored shape blocks and cards with one or two corresponding shapes. Those interested move to her quiet corner. At one point, Travis picks up all the cards and starts to leave the area with them. The teacher says quietly that he should leave the cards there. After a slight hesitation, he gives the cards to her, and she puts them in the box.

Teacher: Thanks, Travis, now the other kids can use them too. (Jimmy reaches for the box of cards and Travis becomes very excited. He repeats "No" to Jimmy several times and moves the box away from him. The teacher suggests to Travis that he could share them with his friends. Her tone is calm and nonthreatening. He doesn't appear to understand. After about a minute, he leaves the area and the cards behind, appearing to forget his original interest.)

Another teacher, seeing that Travis was having problems finding something to do, focuses her attention on him for awhile. The teacher picks out a hat from some play clothes and puts it on.

Teacher: Travis, can you see a hat to wear?

Travis: No.

Teacher: Come here, Travis. Show me what you have there? Hey, that's a frog!

Travis: Yep.

Teacher: What does he say?

Travis: Ribbet! (Travis has fun repeating "ribbet," and during the conversation the teacher picks him up and sits with him on her lap, rocking in a chair. After talking about the frog the teacher begins singing a song to which there are hand motions. She shows him the motions so that he can follow along, which he does on several parts.)

11:40 AM: After a few minutes he is relaxed and ready for a rest.

Teacher: You feel so relaxed, Travis, I bet you're ready for a nap. Can you say goodnight to your friends? (An adult sitting close by says goodnight to Travis. His diaper is checked (dry) as he is carried into the nap room. He reaches for his blanket as he sits on his crib.)

Teacher: Do you want your shoes off or on? (Travis rolls over with his shoes on and his blanket is tucked around him. The caregiver pats him on the back and kisses him.)

Teacher: Night-night, Travis. Have a good rest. See you after your sleep. (His crib side is raised and the caregiver leaves.)

The teacher checks frequently to be sure he has fallen asleep quickly and to be there when he wakes up. Travis usually sleeps for two hours at this time (late morning).

1:10 PM: Travis wakes and is brought back into the big room from his nap. He is still sleepy, and stands in one spot by the door. The teacher in the room gets up from her chair and goes over to welcome him with a hug.

Teacher: Hi, Travis, how are you today? Oh, oh. We need to change your diaper before we have our lunch. (He stands still while the teacher gets the white butcher paper and the pail full of clean diapers and changing supplies, then lies down by himself on the paper on the floor. The teacher kneels down to begin changing him. She bends over very close to his face.)

Teacher: I'll bet those dirty diapers are uncomfortable, aren't they? We will get rid of them and make you feel good. (She tickles Travis and he smiles.)

All the while she is changing his pants, the teacher talks to him constantly, giving him little pats and tickles during the process. She talks about what she is doing during the different steps of changing. Travis lies quietly, watching the teacher's face and smiling appropriately. He says nothing. When the process is completed and the teacher has washed her hands, together they straighten his clothes, comb his hair, and sit down in the rocking chair by the windows.

Teacher: It seems like you're still tired. Let's rock a minute. (He responds by smiling, hugging, and nodding his head. When the teacher finishes rocking him, he gives her another hug, and Travis runs off to play, wide awake.) I'm glad you're ready to play.

1:20 PM: Lunch had been kept warm for those children who were sleeping while the other older children had eaten. The plates of food had been set on the table with glasses of milk, and the late-risers came over to eat. Travis makes his way to the bathroom to wash his hands and seats himself at the table. Again a teacher helps put on bibs and sits with the children to keep them company while they eat.

There are four children seated around the table enjoying their lunch. Travis soon decides that he has had enough to eat. He leaves the table and goes to the bathroom to wash his hands.

Teacher: There's that guy in the mirror again!

1:35 PM: Travis notices a teacher taping together large diaper cartons for the children to play in. He wants to help, and the teacher is happy to have some help. He puts the tape randomly on the boxes.

Teacher: Hey, Travis, you are doing a nice job. (He appears pleased.) Will you please throw these scraps in the wastebasket? (He rushes over to the wastebasket to toss in the scraps and rushes back to her.) Thank you, Travis. You are a good helper. (Travis is truly interested in what she is doing.) I'm making a train for you and your friends to play in. (He is very anxious to have a part in every one of the teacher's movements. She comments positively about each of his movements. He continues to tape and

carry scraps to the wastebasket until the project is over. He then gets into the boxes, and the teacher sits down to watch and talk with him.) All aboard, here you go! Cho-cho-choo. (Travis choo-choo's along. The teacher sings "Down by the station" and Travis laughs.)

Travis quickly busies himself. He leaves the boxes and disappears into the housekeeping corner. After a few minutes he returns with an armful of cans, puts them in the box train and returns to the kitchen. He works silently until he has filled the large box with smaller boxes, dolls, and toys. Other children walk by and help themselves to the refound treasures, without bothering him. He continues to fill the car. When the car is filled to his satisfaction, he sits down in the next car and chooses a purse to open, close, and study.

1:55 PM: The playroom door opens and the nurse, dressed in a white lab coat, walks in carrying a glass containing several labeled vials of medication. She walks over to Travis, smiling, and stands watching his play for a minute or two. She bends down and tells him that it is time for his medicine. He opens his mouth as she pours the pink liquid in. He takes it readily.

Nurse: Thanks. Travis, you drank it down to the last drop! (She picks up a plate.) Where are you doing with all your cargo? (He smiles and goes back to his work. The nurse pauses for a few more minutes on her knees as the children play.)

From the collection of toys Travis pulls out a duck puppet. Gary, 22 months, sees it and comes over. He stands and looks until he finds a puppet, too. Gary puts his hand in his puppet. "Cock-a-doodle-do!" he says to the duck. Travis picks up his puppet, puts it on his hand, and tries a "quack." A teacher nearby enhances their interaction by singing "Old *McGary* had a rooster . . ." and "old *McTravis* had a duck . . ." letting Gary and Travis do the animal sounds. The boys look at each other, laugh, and run to the window.

Travis (pointing to the river): Ish—wa—wa. (Gary laughs.)

2:15 PM: The boys spot the masking tape circle on the rug. Travis goes over to stamp on it. He runs around and around the circle until he falls, but gets up laughing. Around some more and down again!

A teacher turns a record on and invites the children to come listen to the music: to move fast when the music makes them feel like going fast, and slowly when it makes them feel like going slowly. The music begins and each child moves in his own way. Everyone smiles and enjoys feeling the music. They jump, roll, twirl, and just stand still; one by one they leave the group until only the teacher remains.

2:30 PM: Travis has slipped away to the infants' corner. He is sitting and studying the Busy Box, silently showing the nearby infant how each activity works. The caregiver thanks him for showing Mark (4 mo.) how it moves, and reassures him that soon Mark will be doing it for himself now that he has shown him how. The teacher explains that she is getting ready to give the baby a bottle of formula.

Teacher: If you'd like to help, you could come over and sit in the rocking chair with us. (Travis makes his way into the chair with a helping hand, and careully holds the baby's bottle, studying the baby's fingers.) You used to be tiny like Mark, didn't you, Travis? And I'll bet you drank from a bottle too! I like the way you are careful with his fingers, Travis. You are a good helper. Mark is smiling. He likes you too!

2:45 PM: Travis soon loses interest and crawls down to explore other parts of the room. He sits for a moment. A teacher sitting by a large mat of pictures catches his eye.

Teacher: Travis, can you find the picture that shows how you came to the center today?

(Travis jumps to his feet and runs to the picture board. He sorts through the pile of 3″ × 5″ laminated cardboard matching pieces and picks out the picture of a bus and of red sneakers.) Hey, Travis. Okay! I rode a yellow bus today. We both rode on the bus.

Travis sits down and matches the pictures of the sneakers, a teddy bear, and a book. The teacher slips away, and sets a large ball of play dough on the table. Travis looks up, drops the picture cards, and goes off to investigate. Other children notice the play dough, and a few join Travis and the teacher at the table. As each one sits down, the teacher gives out a glob of dough to manipulate.

Teacher: My dough feels cold. How does yours feel? My dough feels soft now. I'm going to pat it. (As she pats it she sings a pat-a-cake song. Some of the children imitate her, others feel, tear, and squeeze the dough. Now that they are started, the teacher comments on what they are doing.) Travis, I like the way you are patting yours so softly. (He smiles, looks up and says "cake," and looks over to see what the other children are doing. As Ann begins to put the play dough in her mouth the teacher quickly intervenes, asking Ann to show her how she can pound the play dough. As children lose interest they leave and go to the bathroom to wash their hands.)

2:55 PM: The snack that usually is served at the play dough table has been taken out to the playground since it was such a nice day. After the children wash their hands they are taken outside. A blanket has been spread under a tree for a picnic. Bananas and a thermos of milk are enjoyed along with the breeze.

Teacher: I'll start to open your banana, and *you* can peel it down. Here you go. If you need some help let me know. I like the way you are holding the bottom of yours, Travis. As soon as you are finished, put the peel part in this trash can and I'll give you a towel for your fingers and mouth. You are good helpers. Thank you.

Travis trots over to the rabbit hutch. He squats down to look at the bunny, his fingers entwined in the mesh cage. Suddenly he dashes to the corner of the playground, grabs a handful of grass, and rushes back to the cage. He throws the grass against the cage. Some of it goes in, and he dashes back for more.

3:10 PM: Meanwhile, Travis' mother has come to the playroom to pick him up for his doctor appointment. She reads the daily information on the Plexiglas chart. A teacher approaches as she is gathering Travis' belongings in his cubby.

Teacher: Hi, Connie. How did your day go? Travis really got involved putting toys in the cardboard train. You'll have to ask him about it tonight. He's just had a snack, so he should be in good spirits for the doctor. Hope all goes well. See you tomorrow.

A DAY IN THE LIFE OF VICTORIA
(30-month-old girl)

The world is so full of a number of things, I'm sure we should all be as happy as kings.
Robert Louis Stevenson

SETTING: The toddler playroom is colorful and includes components that appeal to sight, touch, and sounds. The large windows are low enough for the children to look out at the world. They are dressed with muslin curtains that have been handprinted by the children. The walls are lined with artwork from the day before. Each child has a cubby for personal belongings. The shelves of free choice materials are low and open, and invite curious hands and eyes with well-arranged toys.

The room is divided into active and less active play areas. Today the large motor area contains the postman's Tyke Bike "delivery cars" and a large portable climber with an attached slide. The quieter area contains a drawing station, a bookcase filled with picture books, a toy mailbox, action posters of the postman sorting and delivering mail and other related tasks. There is also a housekeeping corner with empty food containers, pots and pans, doll babies, cribs, and table and chairs. Another corner of the room has clothes racks holding child-sized costumes of many varieties, as well as dress-up hats, shoes, dresses, pants, and shirts. A full-length mirror is hung on the wall. A chalkboard the length of one side of the room is mounted just off the floor and is equipped with white chalk fastened to long strings. A privacy cave lines the other wall, made by removing cupboard doors and replacing them with flannel blankets hanging down over the openings for easy entrance and exit. An adult-sized rocking chair completes the list of furnishings. There are 12 children enrolled in the group, with usual attendance of about 9 or 10. There are four teachers.

The time of the year is early fall.

8:15 AM: Victoria appears at the open playroom door. She is greeted by her teacher.

Teacher: Good morning! You must have fast feet today, Victoria. I don't see your dad. Is he taking Sissy to her room first?

Victoria seems eager to join the other eleven children who are already busy. She surveys the situation as she waits for her dad. She spots two boys sitting in an $8' \times 10' \times 15''$ box filled with rice that is permanently placed on the floor. The inner sides of the box are lined with action posters of farm life and animals. Ben, wearing a railroad engineer's cap, is busy scooping a tractor and wagon full of rice. Ron is intent on setting up a fence around a barn for rubber animals. Sam, Allan, and Susie scoot by the doorway, "double-footing" their Tyke Bikes in an aimless rush. Victoria reaches down to pick up Sam's hard hat, which had fallen off as he made a wide turn in front of her.

8:20 AM: Victoria's dad has now arrived, and Victoria points out her vegetable print from yesterday, hanging on the wall.

Victoria: See, Daddy? I used a carrot.

Father: I like the red color, Victoria. It will look real nice on the wall of your room at home. (She and her dad go to her cubby, where she takes off her sweater and hangs it on the hook. Her dad puts a record on the cubby shelf.) Victoria would like to share her new disco record if she could.

Teacher: Sure, Victoria, I'll bet the kids would like to boogie while we get ready for lunch. We'll keep the record in your cubby until we need it. You help me remember, Okay? (Victoria smiles.)

8:25 AM: Carol and Janelle spot Victoria and her dad and race over, squealing, to the new arrival. The three laugh and grab each other happily.

Janelle: We both have stripes, don't we? (She points out their striped turtleneck shirts.)

Victoria: Yeah-a-ah. (She is pleased at this bond of friendship. Carol offers Victoria a doll like the one she is holding.)

Carol: Here's yours. (Victoria accepts the doll. Victoria hugs her dad's leg, says goodbye, and scampers off with Carol and Janelle to the housekeeping corner.)

Father: Sissy has an ear infection and has to

go to the doctor at 11:00. I'll stop in to see Victoria then.

Teacher: Could you have lunch with us? We'll be eating around 11:50.

Father: Thanks. Sounds good. I'll try to, if we are back from Sissy's appointment.

8:35 AM: Victoria has already started "cooking" in the kitchen with Carol and Janelle. They giggle together as they noisily empty the cupboard of cans with picture labels, dishes, pots and pans, realistic plastic food, wooden spoons, and food containers. Trisha, a teacher's aide, approaches the noisy area and finds no direction in the dumping.

Tricia: What a messy kitchen you ladies keep! I'd never be able to find my way around in here. It's time to get these things put away. Victoria, you use your bright eyes and pick out all the things that go in the refrigerator and put them there. Carol, you look for all the pans and put them on a convenient shelf. Janelle, you can put away the cans, and I'll help with the plates and spoons. (Victoria and Carol get busy putting their things away.)

Carol: I found a can with a picture of a tomato on the front.

Tricia: What do you suppose was in it?

Janelle: Tomato juice!

Tricia: You know, my tomato juice comes in a can like that too. It looks like the tallest can to me. I'll put it on the back of the shelf. Can you find another one the same size?

Janelle: This one is fat like that one. (She places a pear can on the shelf.) I found one that looks the same—we found two alike! (The two cans have the same diameter as the juice can, but are shorter. Trisha continues to motivate Janelle.)

Tricia: Let's find a can that had corn in it. (Janelle finishes putting the cans away, and the aide stacks the plates away.) What great picker-uppers we are! The kitchen looks so clean. Look, Victoria put the yogurt in the refrigerator with the milk and eggs. What a good idea to keep the ice cream hard in the freezer. Carol, you put all the pans in the oven! That's where I put mine too, sometimes. But what's in that big pot on top of the stove?"

Victoria: Stew. (Everyone has an imaginary taste.)

Janelle: Ick! I don't like stew!

Trisha: What do you like to eat?

Janelle: I like spaghetti!

Carol: Fried chicken!

Victoria: Hot dogs.

Trisha: I looked at the lunch menu and it says we'll be having something long, skinny, and white, with red sauce and brown meat, and Janelle really really loves it!

Victoria: Sgetti!

Carol: I can cook it. (She reaches for a can of corn. Janelle sits down at the table to help a doll.)

Janelle: She's messy. (She wipes the doll's face with a cloth. The other two girls continue preparing dinner.)

9:35 AM: Victoria looks around and announces that she needs to go potty.

Trisha: Thanks for reminding me, Victoria. Ben, Ron, do you need to go to the bathroom too? (Ben, Ron, and Victoria scoot to the door.)

Teacher: Let's pretend we're helicopters. (She sings as they walk together down the hallway.) Propellers on the helicopters go around and around. (The children chime in.) Not up front and not behind, but right on top of the plane you'll find. Propellers on a helicopter go around and around. (They go into the bathroom, a large open space with a row of child-sized toilets and sinks. Ron and Ben stand in front of the same toilet; Victoria tries to unfasten her belt.)

Teacher: Have a new belt on your jeans today, Victoria?

Victoria: Ya. My mom said I could undo it myself. (After several futile attempts, she looks up.)

Teacher: How about a helping hand? (She loosens the fastener by taking it out of the hole and making the belt into a large loop in the buckle.) Now you try. (Victoria pulls it out with satisfaction.) There you go, it just needed to be looser. (The boys are finished, and Ron is trying to pull up his jeans with his underwear still at his knees.) Remember to pull up those white underpants, Ron. There you go . . . now your jeans will fit right over them. Good job! (Ben flushes the toilet and goes to the sink to wash his hands. He turns on the water in both sinks full force. Ron giggles.) You two will not be comfortable in wet shirts. (The teacher turns down the water and hands them the soap. She sings as the boys wash their hands.) Over and under, inside and out, look how they're shiny clean. (As they towel their hands dry, the teacher notices that Victoria is working on a bowel movement.) Look at those guys in the mirror. (Ben is still wearing the engineer's cap and smiles at his image.)

Ben: I see you too. (He turns to look at the teacher's face.)

Teacher: You know, Ben, with that hat on you look a lot like the farmer in the picture in the rice box. He has something else on his face. Kinda black, right above his lip.

Ron: A moustache! Like my dad.

Teacher: Ben, do you know anyone who wears a moustache?

Ben: Uncle Bill. (He gazes at himself in the mirror.)

Teacher: Where would one look good on you? (Ron and Ben both point to their upper lips. They turn and head for the door.) You'll need to wait for Victoria and me.

Victoria is working on her belt, having wiped herself, flushed the toilet, and gotten her clothes in place.)

Teacher: Did your mom say you should buckle it too?

Victoria: Yeah, she showed me. (Victoria slowly manages to thread the strap through the buckle and latches the prong on the first hole. With a smile of accomplishment, she goes to the sink, with belt sagging, to wash her hands. Four more children with another teacher appear at the door, and Victoria's group trots down the hall to their room.)

9:40 AM: While they were in the bathroom, the cook had delivered the morning snack. An assistant teacher had prepared the table, with Carol placing a napkin and a cup at each place. The remaining children go to the playroom sink to wash their hands and sit down at the table.

Teacher: I see Jon is ready for snack. (She initiates conversation while waiting for the others to be seated.) Today we're going to have something that is yellow and long and grows on trees, and monkeys like to eat them. (Several children yell "Bananas!" Sam is trying to sit in the same chair that Susie is settled into.) Sam, you need to look for a chair no one is using. Susie is sitting in that one. Can you find the yellow one next to Jim? Thanks, that works better. Today these bananas are going to have a special taste, if you like. (The teacher holds up six small plastic bags, each half filled. Two contain graham cracker crumbs, two granola, and two coconut.) When you finish peeling your banana, you can shake it up in one of these bags, and give your banana a new taste. The teacher puts a pinch of crumbs on each napkin.) How do you think it will taste if you use this bag?

Janelle: It tastes like crackers.

Teacher: Mmmm, it does taste like graham crackers. If you like that taste, you may want to shake your banana in this bag. Let's use our noses to guess what is this white stuff. (She passes around the opened bag of coconut. Victoria says she likes the way it smells. All the children are given a pinch to taste.) This grows on a tree in a large brown nut. It's coconut.

The teacher continues in the same manner with the granola. She then gives each child a banana half to peel, and asks which taste they want on their banana. Another teacher passes a bowl of milk for banana-dipping, and then zips up the seal as each child puts in the banana. Each one shakes his or her own. Half glasses of milk are poured after the children finish shaking. A third teacher records the bathroom information while the children concentrate on their snack. Victoria asks for, and is given, another banana half.

10:10 AM: As soon as the individual children finish, they leave the table. Victoria starts to get up.

Teacher: Victoria, you need to stay in your chair until you are finished chewing. It's not a good idea to play while you are chewing. Thanks. (Victoria is now finished. She puts her milk glass in the dish tub, and scoops her banana peelings and napkin into the wastebasket. She then goes to the sink to wash her hands and wipe her mouth.)

10:15 AM: She surveys the room looking for the "bathroom" teacher, who is making impromptu paper moustaches for Ben and a few others. Victoria joins them. "Me, too," she says as she waits for her moustache. She puts it on her lip and crowds for a spot at the long mirror. Satisfied, she turns to see some children watching the fish in the aquarium, some children in dress-up clothes, and some looking at books in the book corner. She discovers Janelle and Carol pretending to sleep in the bottom of the climbing apparatus. They giggle as Victoria wedges her way between them. The three stretch and lie still. Carol makes a snoring sound. They pop up, giggling. Down again, and silence. Carol snores and they shriek with delight, again and again. Victoria reaches out to get a doll and tucks it close beside her. Allan decides to join them. He climbs up and stands

on the ledge above them, stamping his feet. The girls giggle, and he repeats his noise-making.

Victoria: Get down, Allan. (He refuses and stomps again. The girls protest, and a teacher's attention is attracted.)

Teacher: It looks like Allan is your alarm clock, girls. Allan, is that the way your mom wakes you up in the morning? (Alan smiles.)

Allan: No—she says "Wake up!"

Teacher: Those girls are sleeping now. How do you think they would like to be waked up?

Allan: R-r-ring wake up! (The girls sit up laughing; Allan laughs. The girls lie down again; the sequence is repeated over and over. Allan slides down the slide to get a moustache, and the girls continue to chatter in their private place.)

The table has been cleared and is being readied for an activity. Bottles of liquid starch and liquid soap, a stack of washcloths, a stack of paper squares, a dishpan of water, and a crayon are grouped at the teacher's place. The teacher places a paint shirt on the back of each chair and quietly announces, "If anyone would like to mix colors, come over and find a chair." Five children hurry over. Victoria leaves Carol and Janelle to take care of the doll baby and joins the group. The children put on their smocks. The teacher makes a puddle of the starch, soap, and powdered tempera paint in front of each artist. Victoria's eyes follow closely the whole procedure, and then she puts her right hand in the blue and her left hand in the yellow, and swirls them around.

Victoria: Hey, I'm two colors! (She holds up her hands.)

Teacher: You look as blue as the sky over here, and as yellow as our bananas over here! (Victoria laughs and claps her hands.)

Teacher: Let's see what happens when you put your blue hand in the yellow. It's green! (She stirs the two colors together. Then she "prints" on the table top with her hands, mixes some more, smoothes it, and even runs her fingers through it in a finger-painting motion.)

Teacher: Would you like another color? (Victoria nods and the teacher adds red tempera to the puddle. Victoria mixes it in.)

Victoria: Ooo, this is icky color. (The teacher adds some white tempera.)

Teacher: Does that make it a color you like better? Maybe you would like to start over. (Victoria smiles. The teacher and she wipe up the murky puddle from Victoria's spot on the table. Both rinse off their hands in the tub of water, and the procedure starts again. Victoria chooses yellow and white, and she is soon smoothing the two colors from side to side, and apparently is enjoying the smooth wetness of the mixture. The other children are making hand prints or paper prints [pressing a sheet of paper down on their puddles]; some are scaring each other with their gooey hands.)

10:40 AM: As the children tire of the activity, each one is given a washcloth to wipe their table area before washing their hands. Victoria is fascinated with her yellow hands and covers them back and front with the paint.

Victoria: I'm all yellow.

Teacher: Victoria, if you were all yellow, you'd be a . . .? ("Big Bird," volunteers the orange person in the next chair, "and I'm an orange bird!" Victoria and the "orange bird" laugh, and then Victoria hiccups.) Would you like a drink of water, Victoria? (She hiccups again, and they both laugh. Victoria dips her hands in the tub and wipes them on a washcloth. Another teacher offers her a cup of water.) That should get rid of those hiccups. (Victoria drinks it down in a large gulp, and gives a big sigh, which the teacher imitates. Victoria sighs again—they both laugh.) Hey, Victoria, you did it! You got rid of your hiccups! (Victoria announces "I'm done," and the

teacher gives her a cloth to wipe up the yellow puddle on the table.)

10:50 AM: Ron, who is looking out the window, spots a garden tractor mowing the field below. Victoria drops the cloth, wipes her hands on her pants, and runs to the window with some others. One of the boys proudly announces that his dad can drive a tractor. The group watches the methodical movements of the tractor, and they talk about where to drive a tractor, its uses, how it is different from, and like, a car, and places where they have seen a tractor. This lively discussion continues until the tractor disappears in a grove of trees. The sound is still audible, and Bob is certain another one is coming. The teacher sees that the art table has been cleared and cleaned, and silently communicates to another teacher, who moves to the cubby area.

Teacher: Maybe we could see the tractor better if we watch it from the playground. Go get your sweaters on and I'll meet you at the door. (All the children run to get their sweaters, and go to the door where the teacher is waiting.) She sings: If you're ready and you know it, clap your hands; if you're ready and you know it, clap your hands, if you're ready and you know it, your clapping will really show it; if you're ready and you know it, clap your hands. (She continues with "tap your head" and "jump up and down" until all the children and teachers are ready to go.)

Victoria holds onto Ron's hand, and they all go to the playground, with two teachers leading and one following the last child. The teachers remind the children to listen for the tractor sound as they approach the playground. The area had been prepared. Today the environment includes the open playhouse, tricycles, chalk for drawing, and crepe paper streamers tied to a tree. The children head for the sound of the tractor while they continue to share their own knowledge of tractors. Karen and Valerie choose a paper streamer, and run to the hiding place inside the concrete culvert. Victoria joins them and buzzes around the culvert, pretending to be an airplane. Soon there are three airplanes buzzing noisily around the yard, with streamers flying. They "land" by the playhouse and start to eat their sand cake and drink, which is passed out to them, drive-up style. "Hi, Sissy," Victoria shouts as she sees her sister in another part of the play yard. She rushes over for a quick hug, and then back to the drive-in for service. The tricyclists whiz by, some stopping for a pie, and then off again.

One teacher draws a hopscotch design with the chalk. Victoria notices it, goes over, and asks about it. The teacher looks around for a stone while she answers.

Teacher: It's hopscotch. I'll show you how, and then you can do it. (The teacher hops down the board.) One foot, two feet, one foot, two feet . . . Watch this! (She whizzes around at the end. They both laugh, and she starts back.) I don't want to step on a line . . . now you. (Victoria jumps on— bump, bump, bump down the board, using two feet each time. She goes straight on, back to her playhouse friends.)

11:30 AM: It's time to go inside. The group leaves the play yard a third at a time so that each child will have the chance to go to the bathroom and wash hands before lunch. Victoria is part of the last group.

Teacher: Need any help with your belt, Victoria?

Victoria: No, I can. (She works at it, needing just a little help. With clean hands, Victoria joins the others on the rug for group time. She wants to sit right next to the teacher and pushes her way to the front. The teacher already has two children on her right, two on her left, and one right in front of her.)

Teacher: It doesn't look like there's a space right here, Victoria. You'll need to find a place where no one is sitting. (Victoria turns and sits at the edge of the circle, im-

mediately saying "I can't see" even before she is seated. The teacher acknowledges her concern.) You'll need to move your body til you can . . . and I'll hold the book very high.

The book is a favorite one, *A Whistle for Willie.* The teacher begins by showing the cover to the children.

Teacher: What do you suppose this book is about? (The group answers, "A dog!") Does anyone know this dog's name?

Carol: "Willie."

Teacher: Do you remember this boy's name? (The teacher points to Peter.)

Carol: Peter.

Teacher: I guess Carol has read this book before! Do you know what Peter wanted to learn how to do?

Carol: Whistle.

The teacher asks if any of the children can whistle, and apparently no one can. She continues by saying that as they listen to the story, they can try, just like Peter did. The teacher opens the book and begins reading. She points out the pictures, and the children are engrossed. In the story, Peter tries and tries to whistle. Each time he tries, the teacher and the children try. She asks how they feel when they can't whistle, and the children respond with deep frowns. As the story continues, Victoria's sad expression brightens when Peter produces his whistle. The story ends.

Teacher: Wasn't that a good story? Let's try to whistle again. (There are no whistlers in the group.) Well, I guess we'll just have to try and try and try like Peter. And some day we'll be able to whistle too.

The children had been so attentive that the teacher asks if they would like to read the story to her, and there is a rousing "Yeah." She holds the book up high.

Teacher: This is a story called . . .

Children: Whistle for Willie. (She opens to the first page.)

Teacher: What's going on here? (She listens

to the many answers.) Yes, Peter is feeling sad because he can't whistle and he wants to learn. (She recaps each page, as the children tell her what is happening.)

When the story is almost finished, Victoria's special teacher hands the record jacket to Victoria, and signals to the group teacher that she has put the record on the player.

Teacher: You sure are good story readers. I like the way you remembered all about Peter and Willie. I can tell you like that story. We can read it again someday. But today, Victoria brought a surprise for us. Victoria, can you tell us? (Victoria stands up and shows the jacket to her disco record.)

Teacher: Can you tell us about your record? Look at the picture . . . do you think that is a Winnie-the-Pooh record? ("No!" is the group response, accompanied by giggles.) Well, what should we do to find out what kind of a record it is?

Victoria: We can hear it.

Teacher: Good idea. (She walks over to the record player and turns it on. Lively music fills the room, and everyone laughs.) Let's boogie. (She moves to the music. Victoria joins in, dancing wildly. Everyone jumps and runs and moves to the music with much joy. When the first song ends, the teacher picks up the needle.) Whew, I'm pooped! (The children stop too. She asks if they want to dance some more, and they all say "Yeah!" Again the room is filled with much activity and music.)

11:55 AM: Another teacher appears and indicates that lunch is ready. At the end of the next song, the group teacher stops the record and announces that lunch is ready, and that they can disco over to eat. The music starts again, and the children parade over to the lunch tables.

Teacher: Victoria, I'd like you to sit in this red chair today. (Victoria sits down in front of a plate containing spaghetti, tossed salad, French bread, and applesauce. Bibs are put on the children, and they all start to eat

eagerly.) You all look kinda warm . . . what have you been up to?

Allan: We were dancing!

Teacher: We dance all the time, but I never saw you look so warm before. Was there something different about the music?

Victoria: Yeah, it's disco!

Teacher: Oh, I love to disco. (The conversation continues about dancing, partners, and different kinds of dancing, and then shifts to remembering the tractor event of the morning.)

Victoria asks for more spaghetti and salad. Gradually the other children finish, and announce "All done." When Victoria finishes her lunch, she washes her hands and face, takes off the bib, and goes back to the play area. During the children's lunch, a teacher had brought the dress-up clothes—costumes, hats, shoes, long dresses, jackets and gloves—to the center of the rug. Many of the children are dressing. Victoria chooses her favorite apricot taffeta dress and yellow high-heeled shoes. She asks if they could dance some more. The teacher responds that she is all dressed up for dancing and asks what she would like to hear. She holds up four record jackets.

Victoria: Disco!

Teacher: Well, okay, but we'll need to keep it pretty low.

The music starts, and the music corner is soon filled with dressed-up disco dancers who are wiggling and giggling. The dancers soon slow down, and the teacher changes the record to a more quiet one. Victoria yawns a big yawn and sits down.

Teacher: Victoria, you look like you are ready for your rest. I'll get your record so you can put it back in your cubby while you put your beautiful dress back in the dress-up box. (Victoria undresses herself, puts the dress and shoes away, and goes to the bathroom. The teacher follows.) Good idea. I'm glad you remembered you might need to go. Would you like to put that special belt in your cubby with your record? It will feel better if you don't wear it while you rest. (Victoria and her teacher head toward her cubby. Victoria places the record and her belt in her cubby.)

Teacher: Now your daddy will know just where to find it when it's time to go home. Thanks. (Hand in hand, Victoria and her special teacher walk into the sleeping area and to the cot with Victoria's name on it. The teacher lowers it to the sleeping position and Victoria takes off her shoes and reaches for her blanket. She clambers onto the cot. The teacher spreads the blanket over her and gives her a special hug.)

Teacher: Sweet dreams, Victoria. (She rubs Victoria's back gently; Victoria closes her eyes momentarily and then opens them.)

Victoria: Can we play the record again?

Teacher: Sure, the kids will like that. (Victoria settles again and drops off to sleep. She sleeps soundly for 2 hours.)

3:20 PM: Victoria awakens and sits up on her cot. "Ready to wake up?" asks the teacher who is sitting in the rocker nearby. Victoria stretches and smiles sleepily. The teacher motions to her.

Teacher: Bring your shoes and I can help you put them on. (Victoria gathers her shoes and one sock . . . She looks around and finds the other one in a ball under her cot. The teacher smiles, and boosts Victoria onto her lap.) You look like you had a good rest . . . but your feet must have gotten too hot. Look at those toes! (Victoria smiles as the teacher rubs her feet to give a friendly wake-up squeeze.) Do you want me to help with your socks, or do you want to do it? (Victoria pulls out the toe of the balled sock. She gives two giant tugs, and the socks are on.) Good. Put your sneakers on and I'll tie them for you. (Victoria is ready to go.) Hey, we need to find your belt. Now where did we leave it?

Victoria: It's in my cubby.

Teacher: Oh, yes, I'll get your belt and meet you in the bathroom.

Victoria: Is Carol playing?

Teacher: No, she's still resting. But Ben and Joanna and Sam are ready to play.

Once in the bathroom, Victoria goes directly to the toilet and takes care of herself, including pulling up her pants. The teacher is waiting with the belt.

Teacher: "Here you go . . . round and round we go, one loop, two loops, three loops, four loops, five loops! (The teacher tucks in her shirt and buckles the belt.) There you are, ready to find your friends. (Victoria bounces into the playroom.)

3:40 PM: Valerie and Janelle are tearing pictures out of magazines and taping them to the mirror, with a teacher's help. Sam is looking at a picture book. Ben and Joanna are shelling soybean pods at the science table. Victoria spots a "beauty parlor," which was not there before. An area semienclosed with floor-length mirrors is decorated with pictures of beauticians, barbers, hairstyles, and other magazine pictures. A hair dryer is secured to a round table in the center, and a customer's chair is backed up to it, holding a doll ready for care. The counter is filled with the necessities: brushes, combs, empty shampoo bottles, hair bonnets, rollers, capes, faucet spray attachments, and wigs. Victoria puts on a blonde wig, inspects herself in a mirror, and goes over to the hair dryer chair.

Carol is up! Off goes Victoria to join her. With an exchange of hugs and excited chatter, Victoria leads Carol to the "surprise." She places Carol under the dryer, but Carol gets up to investigate the area for herself. Both girls put on hair bonnets, and they begin to rearrange the chairs and wash the doll's hair. More children arrive after their naps, and the beauty parlor is a busy place. The end of Allan's hair sprayer hits Victoria's arm.

Victoria: It isn't nice to hit. (Victoria is scowling: Allan appears surprised. He rubs up next to her arm, looking sympathetic.)

Victoria orders Carol: "Don't let Allan hit me again!" (The two girls turn away with disgust.)

In one corner children are lined up in front of a mirror where the teacher is offering shaving cream and tongue-depressor razors to bibbed customers. Victoria and Carol are intrigued by the fragrance.

Teacher: You two ready for a shave? (The girls laugh and run over to the window, where a teacher is sharing a book with Janelle. The book is all about feet. The girls wiggle their feet when the teacher asks, "Where are your feet?" and "Can you feel with your feet?")

Victoria: I feel wet grass with my feet.

Teacher: I like the way that feels too, Victoria. What can you feel, Janelle?

Janelle: I feel wet grass, too.

Teacher: Do you feel anything else?

Janelle: I feel my socks. I have one, two.

Victoria jumps up and starts to sing "Put your left foot in, put your left foot out." Carol and Janelle join in with "and you shake it all about. You do the hokey pokey and you turn yourself around—that's what it's all about—Hey!" The teacher is smiling and clapping to their music. The girls grin back, and go off together to the snack table. The other children join them. Placed on the table are six small bowls of peanut butter, with two spreaders for each bowl. The crackers are passed and the cranberry juice is poured. Conversation centers on the beauty parlor/barber shop. Snack is finished, and each child throws the napkin and paper cup away, and washes hands. The table is cleared of snack.

4:15 PM: A teacher sits at the table, and in front of her are a sweet potato, a white potato, and a carrot; a pitcher of water, paper towels, and a knife.

Teacher: Anyone who wants to help can come over and find a chair that no one else is sitting in. (Five children hurry over and sit down. The teacher holds up a potato.) What's this? Where do potatoes grow—on

a tree? (A chorus of "No!") On a bush? (Again no.) Well, where?

Sam: In the ground.

Teacher: Thanks, Sam. How do you get them? (Sam shrugs his shoulders.) You have to dig them with a shovel. Here's another kind of potato—a sweet potato. (She then holds up the carrot.) What's this? ("A carrot!") Where does it grow? ("In the ground.")

Victoria: You pull it.

Teacher: That's right. The potatoes and the carrot all grow in the ground, don't they? (The vegetables are passed around and each child touches and sniffs them.) What color is this potato? (A fast answer: "Brown.") What color is it inside? (No answer.) What color are mashed potatoes?

Janelle: White.

Teacher: Well, if we cut up this potato to make mashed potatoes, what color do you think the inside will be? Let's cut it open with our knife and look inside. (Silence while the teacher cuts.)

Janelle: It's white. (Victoria is watching quietly.)

Teacher: Would anyone like a taste? (The teacher offers a small piece to each child. Sam spits his out and says, "Ick!" Victoria makes a face, and Carol asks for more. They all volunteer how they fix potatoes at home, and which kind is their favorite.)

The teacher then holds up the carrot and follows the same procedure. She then holds up the sweet potato, asks the questions about the color inside, and asks how can they find out. "Cut it" is the answer. She does, and they are surprised to see that it is orange, just like the carrot. After samples of the sweet potato are passed around, the teacher says she would like to grow some plants, and asks if the children think they could grow a carrot or a potato plant. They say yes.

Teacher: What will we need? (No response.) What do you do at home to make plants grow?

Sam: Water 'em.

Teacher: Yes, so I think we can do an experiment with water. Let's put this potato half in the jar of water, and we'll look at it every day to see if anything happens. Would you like to grow a plant too? (The chorus of yeses is gratifying. Each child is given a small cup with his or her name printed on it, and carrot pieces are passed around. Victoria pops hers into her mouth.) That's for your cup, Victoria! (The teacher gives her another one. Water is poured into each cup.) Where should we put them so they will grow?

Janelle: Sun. (The children are directed to the window ledge, and each cup is set down so that the name labels are visible.)

Teacher: We will check each day to see if the plants are changing. We'll put them right next to our bean seeds. Can you guess how they will change?

Sam: It will grow.

Teacher: Yes, we need to watch the bottom part. We might see the little tiny hairs that make roots. We can watch our bean seeds and our carrot starts every day. Thanks for helping.

4:35 PM: The gardeners are taken to the bathroom to clean up and get ready to go outside to play. The yard offers the same playhouse and tricycles. In addition, there are bowls of soap bubbles and blowers, on a wooden bench. Several empty diaper cartons are on the ground, arranged in a train. A teacher is helping a few children cut out the doors and windows of the train cars. Victoria watches the train activities, but then goes to the bubble-blowing activity. She and Janelle blow bubbles and then chase after them. Janelle's mother appears at the playground gate. She and Janelle say good-bye to the group and go into the room for Janelle's things. Other moms and dads appear to pick up their children. Victoria is eying the gate frequently, as she and the remaining children pick

up the playground for another day. They tramp inside, and several get drinks of water. Victoria appears to be feeling unhappy, and her teacher notices.

Teacher: Would you like to sit on my lap for a minute? Can you choose a book to share? (Victoria brings a book and snuggles on the teacher's lap. The book is a favorite one, and the teacher asks Victoria to tell the story as the pages are turned. Instead, Victoria asks, "What's happening on this page?" They both laugh, and Victoria responds to her own questions with silly answers. In a minute, Victoria remembers her record, leaves the teacher's lap for the record player.)

Victoria: Can we hear my record? (Victoria gets the record from her cubby, and joins the teacher at the record player. She watches the teacher put the needle down, and soon the room is filled with music and enthusiastic dancers.)

5:10 PM: The door opens and Victoria's dad appears. Victoria runs over for a hug.

Father: Is that your record I hear?

Victoria: Yeah. (She begins to bounce. They are joined by a teacher.)

Teacher: The kids have really enjoyed Victoria's record today. We listened to it at lunch time, too.

Dad: Sorry I missed lunch, but Sissy's doctor's appointment took longer than I expected.

Teacher: No one mentioned it to Victoria, so maybe you can do it another day. (While this conversation is going on, another teacher has helped Susie choose a different record, and has given Victoria's to her.) Thanks for sharing this with us today.

Victoria and her dad clear her cubby, and dad notices the beauty shop equipment.

Father: That looks like fun. Did you play there? (Victoria and her dad leave to pick up Sissy, chatting about Victoria's day.)

CHAPTER 11

INFANT-TODDLER DAY CARE: THE PHYSICAL AND SOCIAL ENVIRONMENTS

"The time has come," the walrus said, "to talk of many things."

Lewis Carroll

The many components of group programs for the care and education of very young children have been presented in the preceding chapters, with two major exceptions: the physical and social (or human) environments necessary to bring it all together. The typical days described in Chapter 10 give examples of putting it together. They also reveal complete dependence upon well-designed, age-appropriate environments, upon well-trained, responsive caregivers/teachers, and upon mutually trusting relationships with parents. These components are discussed in the following pages.

The Office of Human Development Services (HDS) of the U.S. Department of Health and Human Services has produced a Parent's Guide to Day Care (1980), which lists suggestions of things to look for in day care centers or family day care homes. Those items applicable to day care in general, and to day care for infants and toddlers in particular, are incorporated in the following information. Where appropriate, the actual licensing standards of one state (Iowa) have been cited. These Licensing and Approval Standards for Child Care Centers of the State of Iowa (1976) are required of any center providing day care for seven or more children with the exception of: (1) instructional programs administered by a public or nonpublic school system approved by the state department of public instruction or the board of regents; (2) a church-related instructional program of not more than one day per week; and (3) short-term classes held between school terms.

Rules and regulations are often framed by persons whose chief motivation is to prevent things from happening. Therefore, after the regulations are specified, suggestions are included to make things happen.

The Human Development Services suggestions for parents are identified by the initials HDS. The licensing requirements are identified by the section number in the rules of the Iowa Department of Social Services. It is recommended that similar licensing rules from other states be investigated.

THE PHYSICAL ENVIRONMENT: RULES AND REGULATIONS

Physical space

HDS. Enough space indoors and out so all children can move freely and safely.

109.5(1). The minimum program room size shall be eighty square feet.

109.5(2). The child care center shall have thirty-five square feet per child in indoor area and seventy-five square feet in outdoor recreation area per child using the space at any given time. Kitchens, bathrooms, and halls may not be counted in the square footage.

Heat, light, and ventilation

HDS. Enough heat, light, and ventilation; strong screens or bars on windows above the first floor.

109.5(4). In all centers, the following minimum requirements must be met: ceiling height shall be a minimum of seven feet, six inches for rooms above ground level and a minimum of seven feet for rooms below ground level. Buildings not having air conditioners shall have a ratio of window area to floor area of eight percent or more and all openable windows and doors shall be screened with sixteen mesh wire. Areas used by the children shall be heated when the temperature falls below 68 degrees so a temperature of 68 degrees to 72 degrees is maintained at the floor level. Lighting with a capacity to produce a light intensity of twenty foot candles in the program area shall be provided. All rooms shall be ventilated, without drafts, by means of windows which can be opened or by an air-conditioning or ventilating system.

Furniture, equipment, and materials

HDS. Enough furniture, play things, and other equipment for all the children in care; equipment and materials that are suitable for the ages of the children in care; equipment that is safe and in good repair.

109.7(2). Play material and equipment for both indoor and outdoor play shall be in sufficient variety and quantity to meet the interests and needs of the children. Equipment and materials shall be suitable for the age range served and shall be selected according to the type of supervision required. All equipment shall be kept in good condition, free of sharp, loose, or pointed parts, and, if painted, only lead free paint shall be used. Permanent outdoor play equipment must be firmly anchored.

a. Materials and equipment shall be provided to encourage muscular activity, social and dramatic play, intellectual growth, creative expression, and shall be of safe construction and materials that are easily cleaned.
c. Highchairs shall be equipped with a safety strap and shall be constructed so the chair will not topple.
d. Washable toys, large enough so they cannot be swallowed, shall be provided. Toys shall have no sharp edges or removable parts.
f. When playpens are provided, no more than one child shall be placed in one at any time.

Provisions for caregiving: sleeping

HDS. Enough room and cots and cribs so the children can take naps; cribs with firm mattresses covered in heavy plastic; separate sheets for each baby in care.

109.7(3).e. A crib shall be provided for each infant (up to two years old)—older: a clean washable individual cot, bed, or crib and bedding to cover both cot, bed, or crib, and cover shall be provided for each child who naps. Each crib shall be of sturdy construction with bars closely spaced so a child's head cannot be caught, and have clean, individual bedding, including sheets and blankets. Each mattress shall be completely and securely covered with waterproof material. When plastic materials are used, they shall be heavy, durable and not dangerous to children. A child shall not be placed directly on the waterproof cover. A crib shall be provided for the number of children present at any one time and shall be kept in a clean and sanitary manner and always cleaned and changed upon the change of an occupant. There shall be no restraining devices of any type used in cribs. The minimum spacing between cribs shall be two feet on any side except that which is next to the wall.

Provisions for caregiving: toileting and feeding

HDS. Enough clean bathrooms for all the children in care; a potty chair or special toilet seat in the bathroom; a clean and safe place to change diapers.

109.5(7). One toilet and one lavatory for each fifteen children or fraction thereof, shall be provided in a room with natural or artificial ventilation. The facility shall be maintained in a clean and sanitary manner. Training seats or chairs should be allowed for children under two years of age. There shall be handwashing facilities for child care personnel in rooms where infants are housed.

109.7(3).b. Each infant's diaper shall be changed as frequently as needed in his own crib or on a surface which is cleaned and sanitized between each infant change. When changing diapers the infant shall be washed and dried, using his individual toilet accessories. There shall be a covered, waterproof container for the storage of soiled diapers and clothing.

HDS. Nutritious meals and snacks made with the kinds of food you want your child to eat.

109.6(1). Children at the center during regular meal times shall have available to them a full balanced meal which provides at least one-third of the child's daily nutritive allowances, except breakfast which shall provide at least one-fourth.

109.6(2). Menus shall be planned at least one week in advance. Such menus shall be dated, posted, and kept on file at the center. Notations shall be made for special dietary needs of the children.

a. Menu planning shall include a variety of foods and varying textures, flavors, and colors that will provide children with many different food experiences, and help stimulate their interest in food.

b. Each noon or evening meal menu shall include a bread or cereal type food, a meat or meat substitute, a vegetable, a salad, and milk. Children remaining at the center longer than two hours shall receive midmorning and midafternoon nourishment. Meals shall consist of a variety of foods each day based on the following: Breakfast—½ cup of milk; ¼ cup of juice or fruit; ½ slice of bread or ½ cup of cereal or equivalent.

Lunch or supper—½ cup of milk; 1 ounce (edible portion as served) of lean meat or an equivalent quantity of a protein food; ¼ cup of vegetable; ¼ cup of fruit; ½ slice of bread or equivalent; ½ teaspoon of butter or fortified margarine.

109.6(3). Feeding of children under two years of age.

a. All children under six months of age are to be held during feeding. No bottles are to be propped for children of any age.

b. Single service ready-to-feed formulas shall be used for children three months and younger unless otherwise ordered by a parent or physician.

c. Grade A pasteurized milk shall be used for children not on formula unless otherwise directed by a physician.

d. Special formulas prescribed by a physician shall be made available for the child who has a feeding problem.

e. Aseptic techniques shall be used in the preparation of all milk mixtures and other foods prepared in the center.

f. Spoon feeding shall be adapted to the developmental need of the child.

Safety regulations (indoors)

HDS. Safety caps on electrical outlets; a safety plan to follow in emergencies; an alternate exit in case of fire; fire extinguishers; smoke detectors; covered radiators and protected heaters; gates at tops and bottoms of stairs.

109.5(3). All stairways used by children shall be provided with hand rails within reach of the children and maintained free of all obstacles.

109.3(6). Disaster (such as tornado, flood, and fire) escape procedures shall be developed, posted, and practiced a minimum of quarterly. (Comment: The State Fire Marshal requires that fire drills be practiced a minimum of monthly. Drills should be recorded.)

Health regulations

HDS. A safe place to store medicines, household cleansers, poisons, matches, sharp instruments, and other dangerous items; a separate place to care for sick children where they can be watched.

109.3(2).b. Medications shall be kept in a locked cabinet. The medicine cabinet key shall be in the possession of the person designated to administer medications. Medications requiring refrigeration shall be kept in a refrigerator.

109.3(4). A quiet area under supervision shall be provided for a child who appears to be ill or injured. The parents or a designated person shall be notified of the child's health status.

The outdoor area

HDS. An outdoor play area that is safe, fenced, and free of litter.

109.5(5). Premises used for outdoor play by the center shall be maintained in good condition throughout the year; shall be kept free from litter, rubbish, and flammable material at all times; shall be fenced off when located on a busy thoroughfare or near a hazard which may be injurious to a child; and shall be free from contamination by drainage or ponding of sewage, household waste, or storm water.

109.5(6). An area shall be provided properly and safely equipped for the use of infants and free from the intrusion of children over two years of age.

PHYSICAL ENVIRONMENT: FROM THEORY INTO PRACTICE

A carefully designed environment frees the caregivers/teachers for relationships with children. Poorly designed environments place time-consuming burdens on staff and children alike. There are dimensions of the environment that are not included in either the HDS suggestions to parents or the state's licensing requirements. These, along with additional comments about the required components of the physical environment, are discussed below.

Acoustics

Noise level is seldom cited in state licensing standards, but it plays a definite role in the behaviors and the learnings of both children and adults. Realistically, a satisfactory acoustical environment differs for children and adults, but in general, steady familiar sounds do not distract attention. On the other hand, "extreme quiet does not provide an appropriate environment for many learning activities" (Environmental Criteria, 1971, p. 32). A day care facility, when possible, should be in an area with a low outside noise level. Sounds can be minimized with acoustical tile ceilings, carpeted floors, full drapes on large window spaces, fabric wall hangings, and fabric room dividers. Cork bulletin boards and some upholstered furnishings also help absorb sounds.

Density

Licensing requirements for space regulations range from 20 to 50 square feet per child. It would appear that the 35 square foot requirement is sufficient for an infant-toddler center, because the infants are not yet mobile! The rooms should be large enough for active play and a feeling of openness, but not so large that the toddlers feel lost or threatened. An open physical environment does not mean a big room with little in it besides children. It means open spaces, but also separations or delineations of activity centers. Even too-large rooms can be made visually comfortable by varying the floor surfaces (carpet and tile) or by using different colors on the floor surfaces. Light weight room dividers hanging from the ceiling and touching the floor serve as acoustical control devices, as well as space delineations and aesthetic addi-

tions (Bohlen et al., 1976). Raised platforms or balconies provide "watching" places, and add visual interest to the space of a large room.

In addition to the open spaces, small secluded or enclosed spaces give toddlers the opportunity to regain their energies for mingling with others, or simply to have a few quiet moments. Almost anything can be turned into a private nook: hollow block enclosures, large cardboard boxes or barrels, tables turned on one side with a blanket over the top, even large storage shelves with a curtain hanging over the front. A day care center is not a classroom; it is a living room, in the truest sense of the word.

Temperature and light control

Most regulations specify an optimal indoor temperature (68° to 72° F); some are more precise in requiring this temperature range from 1 to 3 feet from the floor. It is possible to have thermostats placed at these levels, but because they are not playthings, they should be encased in a manner that prevents manipulation by toddlers.

Windows admit light, which can be controlled by blinds, curtains, or shades when desirable. When possible, a window should be used to extend the child's visual environment; babies can be held so that they can see out, while the caregiver talks about what is seen. Toddlers will enjoy a wide window seat either as a resting place or to look at the world. In a one-story building more light can come through a skylight of plain or colored plastic.

Flooring

The floor in an infant-toddler center is really part of the furniture. It is the primary playing and learning surface. Wall-to-wall carpeting is excellent from the children's point of view: it is a nice warm surface to sit and play on. It also helps reduce the noise level when the blocks come tumbling down. Opinions vary as far as maintenance is concerned. The best of two worlds can be managed if sheets of heavy plastic are taped to the carpet under the messy spots: painting and eating areas. Some centers have effectively combined carpet with tiled spaces. Such a combination gives subtle directions to the flow of traffic, and also to delineation of activity centers.

Most centers arrange their playrooms with the center part unoccupied, and activity centers around the edges. Prescott and David (1976) suggest that a better arrangement is to provide several decentralized floor areas with at least one part of the floor elevated with one or two steps. Cohen (1974) notes:

> The shape of a room can affect the activities in it. For example, a long, narrow room encourages children to run and slide. Its tunnel-like appearance—if it is undesirable—can be minimized by placing interest areas at each end, by arranging equipment to break up straight pathways, and by conducting activities in the center of the room (pp. 58-59).

Color

Environmental Criteria (1971) suggest the most appropriate uses of color in day care environments from a psychological standpoint, as follows.

Red is best used on outdoor play equipment, indoor or outdoor gross motor equipment, and cognition activities that require stimulation.

Orange is suggested for the entrance to the center or to a playroom; also for gross motor equipment.

Green, blue, or white is suggested for reading or story corners, nap and eating areas, and the isolation room, if it is to be used as a "quiet room."

Yellow is suggested for gross motor equipment, and for the music and art corners.

Black and gray may be used as occasional accents or to complement other colors.

The response to color is highly individualized, and the above suggestions are based on the generally accepted responses to individual colors, and not on empirical findings. Environmental Criteria (1971) advise that:

> Color selection should be based on the children's responses to color, the purpose for which the area will be used, the nature of the children using the area, and the size, light exposure, and other physical characteristics of the area. Personal color preference should also be considered, especially in spaces that are occupied for long periods of time by one person. This is particularly applicable in offices or similar spaces. Color can be used as a means of identifying a child's personal property, e.g., his storage space, his chair, his glass, etc (p. 29).

Walls

Walls are a large part of the physical environment and should do much more than structurally define the room limits. In an infant-toddler center, they should be used as low bulletin boards, to display children's artwork or pictures, or as a writing and drawing space (if appropriately finished). A long, low, horizontal, unbreakable mirror is an interest center all by itself. An area of the wall surface may be used as a texture board or a color board. Tackboard walls or walls paneled with soft wood allow the display of light weight materials. Even large sheets of cardboard can serve as the children's bulletin board. Children and teachers seem to prefer low-stimulating colors on large areas of wall space, with perhaps one wall in a contrasting color. To be most pleasing to the eye, the bright colors should be used on the equipment and furnishings and not on the walls.

Sleeping areas

Wooden cribs are awkward and space consuming. Ideally, a crib room is separated from the general playroom(s) in an infant-toddler center, but this is not always possible. Perhaps, from the child's standpoint, it is not even necessary. Twardosz et al. (1975) investigated the effects of a closed off versus an open, unprotected area on the sleeping patterns of infants and toddlers. They found that the open environment did not have adverse effects on either infants or toddlers.

Outdoor play areas

Suggestions for equipment and safety have already been made. The one missing ingredient is the appropriate ground cover for an area used by infants and toddlers. Very young children need grassy areas, with a few strips or areas of hard surface for riding or pulling wheel toys. Part of the yard should be shaded by trees or an overhanging roof. A sandbox big enough for several to sit and play in is a must. It should be shaded for part of each day. Ideally, some provision can be made for water play, also.

Play equipment

Specifications for play equipment are rarely included in regulations for infant-toddler day care. Many examples have been mentioned in the chapters concerned with the developmental-educational curriculum and need not be repeated here. More appropriate here is a list of criteria for play equipment for infants and toddlers. Play materials and toys should encourage action and should respond to the child's action in a natural way (balls roll, blocks tumble). A variety of play materials should be available so that children have a choice based on their manipulative abilities, interest, and desire to play alone or with someone else. The play materials should give children opportunities to use their emerging skills, and should lend themselves to a variety of uses and modalities (Willis and Ricciuti, 1975).

In many cases the best play materials are natural parts of the environment: sand, water, mud, earth, growing plants and flowers, and various kinds of surfaces for walking, running, balancing, and climbing.

Dimensions of the physical environment (and program)

Which is more inviting to you as an adult, a straight-back wooden bench or an overstuffed

sofa with soft pillows? Jones and Prescott (1978) describe the environment in terms of five dimensions: (1) softness/hardness, (2) open/closed, (3) simple/complex, (4) intrusion/seclusion, and (5) high and low mobility. They define softness as "sensory responsiveness" (p. 1). Of course, the sofa with its pillows is both soft and responsive to your body as you sink in it. "The younger the children, the more essential softness becomes in an environment" (p. 13). Such items as water, sand, mud, play dough, finger paints, cuddly animals, and pillows can be rated as soft materials. (A caregiver's lap is the most important soft item of all!)

The open/closed dimension can be used to rate materials, storage spaces, programs, and even the day care center itself. Even the attitudes of the caregivers and teachers can be described as open or closed—open to exploration, open to the wonder of emerging skills, open and warm in their relationships with the children, parents, and other staff members. Open materials, of course, are those with a variety of uses or responses. Open storage describes an orderly arrangement of toys and materials on shelves within a child's reach. I also like to think of the whole center as being open to the world outside its walls. Infants are entranced by outside sights, smells, and sounds, and should be allowed to experience them as much as possible.

The simple/complex dimension relates primarily to materials, equipment, and activities. A simple object has one obvious purpose and reacts in one predictable way. A complex object has subparts and allows the child some exploration and manipulation. Cooking would be defined as a complex activity, with its measuring, combining, stirring, and pouring. Running or crawling through an obstacle course is much more complex than moving from one point to another. Jones and Prescott (1978) report that increasing complexity is directly correlated to length of attention span, and point out that "in the long day care day, this is a goal worth considering" (p. 18).

Intrusion/seclusion can be applied to the arrangement of space: are there places for getting away in a nook or for people-watching, in addition to places and equipment that are inviting to more than one person? It can be applied to the caregivers/teachers, also. Do they allow the time and opportunity for a child, or several children, to work out their own problems or play themes and to learn by trial-and-error without premature intrusion? Is the center itself secluded psychologically, or does it welcome visits from parents or resource persons?

The high and low mobility dimension is self-explanatory. It can be used to describe the activities, equipment, and space that require large muscle movements (running, climbing) and the small muscle movements (listening to a story, building towers with cube blocks).

An infant-toddler program, including its physical arrangement, is determined by and reflects the teachers' preferences and values at some point in each of the dimensions. In general terms it is recommended that the day care center and its components be more soft than hard and more open than closed. Materials and activities should range from simple to complex, to meet developmental levels. The equipment and activities should require many more large muscle actions than small. There should be times for active adult input, but more times for the child's direction and initiative.

It is inappropriate to state specific rules for programs and their environs, because the quality of any program is determined by its goodness-of-fit for each individual. "When there is a good fit, the adults in the program and the activities which they provide enable a child to experience himself as competent and likable and provide him with opportunities for enthusiastic and sustained involvement" (Jones and Prescott, 1978, p. 37). The environment, as well as the adults, should be nurturing as well as stimulating. Abilities to arrange an environment that is designed to meet the physical, emotional, social, and intellectual needs of children are vital.

They can be learned. Without a sound knowledge base of child development, however, techniques can become routine, mechanical, cold, and without lasting effect. Assuming the ability to organize an appropriate day care environment, the crucial variables seem to lie in the more intangible interpersonal relationships that sustain, foster, and nourish emotional growth and intellectual curiosity.

THE SOCIAL ENVIRONMENT: RULES AND REGULATIONS

The social environment is determined by the people in the physical environment, including the director, the head teachers, the social worker, and the families of the children enrolled. In family day care homes there may be just one or two persons. In large center programs there may be many persons who meet specific responsibilities, but who need to act as one in their attitudes and approaches to people. Regardless of the number of persons involved in the delivery of child care, the relationships with the parents are of prime importance.

The Parent's Guide to Day Care (HDS, 1980) and the state licensing standards for day care personnel are described below. The same kinds of information are not considered in the two documents; therefore they will be considered separately.

Office of Human Development Services

It is suggested that parents decide which of the following caregiver characteristics they consider to be important for their particular needs.

Does the caregiver:
• appear warm and friendly?
• seem calm and gentle?
• seem to have a sense of humor?
• seem to be someone with whom you can develop a relaxed, sharing relationship?
• seem to be someone your child will enjoy being with?
• seem to feel good about herself and her job?

- have child-rearing attitudes and methods that are similar to your own?
- treat each child as a special person?
- understand what children can and want to do at different stages of growth?
- have the right materials and equipment on hand to help them learn and grow mentally and physically?
- patiently help children solve their problems?
- provide activities that encourage children to think things through?
- encourage good health habits, such as washing hands before eating?
- talk to the children and encourage them to express themselves through words?
- encourage children to express themselves in creative ways?
- have art and music supplies suited to the ages of all children in care?
- seem to have enough time to look after all the children in her care?
- help your child to know, accept, and feel good about him- or herself?
- help your child become independent in ways you approve?
- help your child learn to get along with and to respect other people, no matter what their backgrounds are?
- provide a routine and rules the children can understand and follow?
- accept and respect your family's cultural values?
- take time to discuss your child with you regularly?
- have previous experience or training in working with children?
- have a yearly physical exam and TB [and hepatitis] test?
- seem to enjoy cuddling your baby?
- care for your baby's physical needs such as feeding and diapering?
- spend time holding, playing with, talking to your baby?
- provide stimulation by pointing out things to look at, touch, and listen to?
- provide care you can count on so your baby can learn to trust her and feel important?
- cooperate with your efforts to toilet train your toddler?
- "child-proof" the setting so your toddler can crawl or walk safely and freely?
- realize that toddlers want to do things for them-

selves and help your child to learn to feed and dress him- or herself, go to the bathroom, and pick up his or her own toys?
- help your child learn the language by talking with him or her, naming things, reading aloud, describing what she is doing, and responding to your child's words? (pp. 31-33)

State licensing requirements concerning personnel

The Iowa Licensing and Approval Standards, Chapter 109—Child Care Centers (1976) include the following requirements for day care personnel.

109.4(1). The director or administrator shall:
a. Have two years of administrative or program experience in a child care center, or be able to demonstrate an equivalent amount of other child development related experience, employment or educational experience.
b. Have completed high school or an equivalent program. Persons who do not meet this educational requirement, and who possess unusual qualifications or experience in the child age group with which they will be working, could be employed with the approval of the department of social services.
c. Be at least eighteen years of age.
109.4(2). Persons considered part of the staff ratio who have direct contact with the children shall meet the following requirements:
a. Demonstrate competence in working independently with children.
b. Be at least sixteen years of age.
c. At least one staff member on duty shall have a valid certificate in standard first aid or documentation of equivalent training.
109.4(3). Staff ratio shall be as follows:

Age of children	Minimum ratio of staff to children
Two weeks to two years	One to every four children
Two years	One to every six children
Three years	One to every eight children
Four years	One to every twelve children

a. Regardless of the staff ratio in rule 109.4(3), when seven or more children five years of age or younger are present, basic minimum qualified child care staff shall consist of two people on duty. Combinations of age grouping shall have staff determined on the age of the youngest child in a group.

b. Every child-occupied program and nap room shall have adult supervision present.

c. In transporting six or more preschool children, any child care vehicle shall have a minimum of two staff members or other adults present.

d. Any child care center sponsored preschool aged program activity conducted away from the licensed facility shall provide a minimum of one additional responsible person over the required staff ratio for the protection of the children.

SOCIAL ENVIRONMENT: FROM THEORY TO PRACTICE

The social environment is as, if not more, important as the physical environment. It is the presence, availability, and responsiveness of the familiar persons in the young child's life space that bring alive the physical environment. These familiar persons really bring alive the child, also.

The maternal deprivation syndrome, which caused concern in the 1950s, really was caused by the deprivation of significant persons (whether mother or someone else). A person is significant to an infant or toddler to the extent of the responsive interactions between the two. Persons who have been entrusted with the care and education of children for a substantial number of hours each day have the opportunity to become familiar persons to the children in their care. They should be required to do so. The problem of ensuring that each caregiver knows several children well can be adequately solved by initiating a plan for primary caregiving. It has been described well by the head teacher of the infant-toddler room at the Early Childhood Education Center at the University of Iowa (Rosenthal, 1979).

Under this plan each staff person functions as a primary care giver for one or two groups of children. These two groups were divided according to the ages and developmental levels of the children. Primary care givers make the primary attachment to the children in their group. They are available for comfort and the child and adult develop a close relationship. Parents can focus on the primary care givers for communication about their child. The children within each group are more likely to interact and to depend on each other as the group spends special times together during the day.

The responsibilities of the primary care givers are:
- To check the Plexiglas chart for children in the group and keep it up to date. (We use this chart to communicate with parents and other staff about children's eating, napping, and toileting activities throughout the day.)
- To communicate with parents on a daily basis either verbally or by writing in the diary.
- To check diapers and anticipate needs of the children (prepare bottles, baby food, any special diet or considerations).
- To put children in their group down for their naps.
- To plan individual and group activities for the children.
- To assess the children at various stages of their development.
- To redesign the environment when necessary.

Initially we were concerned that dividing the children and care givers into primary groups would segregate us during the day. We have avoided this problem by remaining flexible in implementing the primary care giving arrangement. We interact with all the children and the children are encouraged to interact with each other. Thus a child will feel comfortable in the presence of another care giver. This is important when one considers the staffing schedules for a ten hour day, children's eating and napping schedules, as well as those times when children from both groups are together.

Here are examples of how our system has worked:
- When Rachel was three months old she began coming to the center. She had developed a strong attachment to her parents and was unhappy with a variety of care givers—all so anxious to please her. By the second day we limited her interactions to a morning and afternoon care

giver. This helped Rachel adjust and offered her care givers the opportunity to "read" her signals and wants.
- Gena and Sy are the oldest children in the group. They enjoy doing things together during the day. We have made their nap a shared experience. The toddler care giver usually reads them a story or engages in a shared quiet-time activity with them just prior to nap. They both go into the sleeping room together. Gena walks with Sy to his crib and they say good-night. Then Gena is put to sleep in her crib. This consistency in their napping routine by their care giver has helped them develop an attachment to one another as well as to their care giver. It also offers security in knowing what to expect.
- After snack the children wash their hands and faces. Diapers need to be checked and changed before a teacher-directed activity begins for the toddlers. Some infants are being fed and a few infants and toddlers need to take their morning nap. The infant care givers are working together to coordinate their care-giving efforts and the toddler care givers are doing the same. When a care giver from one group is not busy with her children, she will help the other group's care givers complete their routines and responsibilities. Thus our transition time from snack to activity time is smooth, well organized, and personal. Children have learned what to expect and are comforted by the consistency of the routine and of their interactions with care givers.

We are always working on the organization of the room. The care givers need to keep lines of communication open so they can function well within care-giving groups as well as to learn how both groups can work together. Our satisfaction comes from observing positive changes in children. We feel that our program is a relaxed and warm environment and very homelike (pp 1-2).

The assignment of children to primary caregivers, instead of the assignment of tasks (one person in charge of diapering and toileting, etc.) is the best assurance that each child is known intimately by at least one caregiver/teacher and that each child has a familiar, and therefore significant, person at the center.

Of course, the social environment for any child

includes the other children in the group as well as the adults. Other infants and toddlers are both stimulators and receivers of stimulation through proximity to others, but the team of nurturing adults holds the keys to the dynamics of optimal growth, development, and learning.

If infants and toddlers are in the same room or rooms, the age range is approximately 3 years. This 3-year range offers opportunities for rich experiences among the children if there is ample provision made for individual and group space. Distribution of staff is essential, so that the toddlers and walkers receive their share of attention. It is too easy to become so immersed in the physical care routines of babies that the "independent" toddlers are left to their own devices too much of the time. The model for a multiaged group of children is more closely related to a commune than to a family. This statement is not political, but implies that each child is an individual with equal rights and privileges. The rights of each include the appropriate quantity and quality of care and education. Its daily delivery differs because of differing developmental stages and needs. If the caregiver insists on child-child interaction, when such is not developmentally appropriate, little is gained and much is lost. The 1- and 2-year-olds rarely approach others in a social mode on their own volition. They are engaged in the serious processes of self-identity (and learning to walk!). Even though the young children are members of a group by virtue of attending a day care center or home, there must always be an escape hatch for those children who wish or need it.

Having made the plea for an escape hatch, let me hasten to add that much learning results from one child watching another child or group of children. Mere watching is both stimulating and social, because it is a prerequisite for human interaction. When the little ones are ready to join in, they will do so on their own. This is one instance when teacher intrusion is not warranted.

Our society's custom is to have some space in the private home reserved for baby—either in a separate room or in a corner of an adult's room. Basically, this arrangement is to satisfy the American adults' need for privacy and individuality. Psychological and physical space between baby and primary caregiver is specific to the culture; it is not universally practiced. It is not an innate need of the child. Michael Lewis, professor of pediatrics at Columbia Medical Center and director of the Institute for Exceptional Children at the Educational Testing Service in Princeton, suggests that this "cultural view of privacy and individuality has influenced the way we have conditioned our children's spatial needs" (1981, p. 28). Baby learns from the periodic separation from caregivers that being alone is important. Although the physical environment is not the focus here, we need to understand that spatial arrangements can teach baby a pervasive concept, namely that being alone sometimes is desirable. This will not hinder baby's social development if the alone-times are balanced by together-times. Baby's innate curiosity need will also counterbalance the learned need for privacy.

The child's social environment in the family, and the variety of emotions and moods resulting from family living, are a necessary part of learning socialized behavior. The variety is unavoidable, and may be a plus, unless carried to extremes. To counterbalance the variety instead of adding to it, the center staff members should aim toward consistency and continuity in behaviors toward one another and toward the children. Individual personalities need not be sacrificed, but there should be a commitment to agreed-upon policies, methods, and approaches that further each area of growth and development. The very young child in day care literally has two homes—but not two families. The child retains primary family membership, regardless of the number of hours away from the family setting. The child's psychological adjustment to the two locations is sufficient challenge. It should not be compounded by either inconsistent behaviors by caregivers or undue intrusion in the child's life space.

Principles for establishing meaningful relationships and interactions with young chilren have been indirectly suggested throughout the preceding chapters. Perhaps a listing of them would be helpful. They are equally appropriate for parents and center personnel:

1. Invest time, and be totally available to the child during this time. Total availability determines quality and is more important than a quantity of time without total involvement.

2. Learn the child's system of communication (gestures, vocalization, cries, verbalizations). Respond to the child's communication attempts and teach her yours.

3. Involve the child in things that are of interest to him and that channel his emerging skills.

4. Respect the child as an individual.

5. Model the behavior you want to teach (language, socially acceptable behavior, approaches to learning).

6. Allow the child the opportunity to solve age-appropriate problems without interference.

7. Enhance the child's sense of trust by being trustworthy.

Caregiving and teaching infants and toddlers requires more than tender loving care. It takes basic knowledge about the principles of child development and learning. Although it is a temptation to use volunteers in the day care delivery, volunteers need more than willingness to help to qualify them. The incident described in Episode 20 is proof of the foregoing statement. If I had not seen it myself, I would find it hard to believe.

Episode 20. Chuck is in a highchair and has just finished his snack. The teacher comes over him with a damp washcloth, saying "All finished, Chuck? Let's wash our hands." She wipes one hand, and uses the cloth to hide it, saying "Where's Chuck's hand?" she removes the cloth, saying "There it is!" Chuck watches carefully, but gives no other observable re-

action. Teacher repeats the peek-a-boo game with the other hand. Then she hides just one finger, asking "Where's Chuckie's finger?" Chuck is very attentive. He laughs, grabs the washcloth and hides his own hand with it. He laughs again and whisks the cloth away when the teacher asks "Where's Chuckie's hand?" "There it is—you like to play, too." The teacher and the baby laugh together. She removes the highchair tray, unbuckles the safety strap, and lifts Chuck in her arms. "Let's go to the bathroom," and the teacher and Chuck laugh again as they leave the scene.

Meanwhile, two high chairs down from Chuck, a volunteer notices that Tina is finished with her snack. She gets a washcloth, wipes Tina's hands and chin, removes the tray and belt, and carries Tina to the bathroom. There was no play, no language, no smile, no real human contact.

One wonders if the volunteer did not enjoy babies or felt somewhat imposed upon or just was having a bad day. Frequent bad days like this one, however, can have disastrous effects on the babies and should not be repeated. Unfortunately, this center was a parent cooperative, and the volunteer was one of the mothers who was paying part of her child's tuition by helping with the routines.

The report of the National Day Care Study (1979) includes the frequencies of categories of caregiver behaviors for infants (6-18 months) and toddlers (19-30 months). The frequencies are presented in Table 11-1. Few other posi-

TABLE 11-1   Percentages of caregiver behaviors: infants and toddlers*

Behaviors	Infants (6-18 months)	Toddlers (19-30 months)
Child-directed		
Social interaction	26	25
Talks with children	24	25
Touches children	21	15
Cognitive-language stimulation	4	11
Management (of behavior)	2	4
Observes children	7	7
Non–child-directed		
Talks with adults	7	4
Administrative tasks	9	9

*Adapted from National Day Care Study (1979).

tions require such a high percentage of concentration on and with children. It was observed in a model infant-toddler day care center, which was the forerunner of the Early Childhood Education Center, that neither professional nor paraprofessional caregivers and teachers were able to function appropriately with children for an 8-hour stretch of time, even when allowed coffee breaks. Scheduling of 8-hour days should include no more than 6 hours contact with children. The other 2 hours can be spent profitably in record keeping, reviewing curriculum, relationships with parents, or even for mending a raggedy stuffed elephant! Until the child reaches about 2½ years, an alert, untired adult is necessary as the mediator who structures the learning environment and experiences for the child. Bettye Caldwell (1976) states this well: "An infant day care setting in which the adults are not animated, interactive, verbal, and loving

people will most likely be an under-stimulating environment for infants" (p. 61).

It is impossible to end this section on the desirable qualities and behaviors of caregivers/teachers without giving one bit of advice about children's table manners, found in *Perfect Behavior* (Stewart, 1922):

If you are a father and your boy Edward persists in bringing his pet tadpole to the table in a glass jar, you should not punish him or scold him; a much more effective and graphic method of correcting this habit would be for you to suddenly pick up the tadpole one day at luncheon and swallow it. No whipping or scolding would so impress upon the growing boy the importance of the fact that the dinner table is not the place for pets (p. 207).

With this bit of wisdom from the "good old days," we turn to the last major component of the care and education of infants and toddlers: the parents and families of the children.

PARENT-CENTER RELATIONSHIPS: RULES AND REGULATIONS

The Office of Human Development Services pays scant attention to the essential nature of the relationships between the child's home and the day care center or family day care home. The guidelines (1980) do suggest its importance in their list of desirable characteristics of the caregiver:

- Someone with whom the parent can develop a relaxed, sharing relationship
- Someone who has attitudes and methods about childrearing that are similar to the parents'
- Someone who will help each child become independent in ways approved of by the parents
- Someone who accepts and respects each family's cultural values
- Someone who will cooperate with the parents' efforts in toilet training.

The Iowa licensing standards state

109.8(1). Opportunity shall be provided for parents at times convenient to them to observe their children in the child care center and whenever possible to work with the program.

109.8(2). Whenever a non-profit child care center provides day care for forty or more children, there shall be a policy advisory committee or its equivalent. Committee membership shall include not less than fifty percent parents or parent representatives, selected by the parents themselves in a democratic fashion. The committee shall perform productive functions which may include, but are not limited to:

- a. Initiating suggestions and ideas for program improvements.
- b. Assisting in organizing activities for parents.
- c. Encouraging parental participation in the program.

The issues of parent involvement and participation in the day care program have received little systematic attention. Most recently parent involvement has emphasized parents as child advocates, as decision- or policy-makers at the center, or as students in parent education classes or home visits. These roles are important, but the focus here is on a relationship that protects and improves the well-being of the child. According to Fein (1976):

Disruptions in the continuity of care are likely to be stressful for the child. Since parents are the most viable sources of continuity for the child, the interface between the family and the surrogate caregiver must be broad, the overlap extensive, and the transition between home and institution as smooth as possible (p. 32).

We are just beginning to understand the nature and the importance of the relationships between the day care provider and the family. They should be based on a mutual sense of basic trust. If they are not, the young child will suffer. The center-home relationships have the potential of serving many of the functions formerly provided by the extended family. Most parents using infant-toddler group care are in some kind of a stress situation: single parenthood, teenage parenthood, lack of economic resources, lack of a responsive community.

PARENT-CENTER RELATIONSHIPS: FROM THEORY INTO PRACTICE

In general, the parents of infants and toddlers in group care are separated from their own families, are first-time parents, and have feelings of guilt about placing their very young children outside of the home for a substantial number of hours each day. Once their child is placed in a program, they are inclined to think that the day care providers know what is best for their child, and therefore do not question what is done at the center. Because it is the easier choice, some parents seem willing to shift their childrearing responsibilities to the professionals. Fein (1976) reminds us that "parents as individuals have responsibilities to their own children, responsibilities which are best exercised on a day-to-day basis" (p. 22). Day care staff members need to support the parents in their childrearing responsibilities, and must not assume these responsibilities themselves. The decisions about the timing of introducing solid foods or of initiating toilet training (and how to do it) or methods of discipline are in the parents' domain. Ideally, parents and caregivers can reach a mutual decision about these and other items.

Categories of parents

The state of the continuity and interface between families and child care programs has been investigated by Elardo and Caldwell (1973), Winetsky (1978), and Powell (1979). Powell (1977) has identified three major subgroups of day care parents: dependent, independent, and interdependent. The dependent parents view the center as a source of child development and childrearing advice, and attempt to put into practice "what the teacher says." They view the child care center as the authority, and thereby subtly shift their responsibility to others. They may share some child-related information with the center, but they do not assume much initiative in child-related decisions.

The independent parents, on the other hand, assume that all the responsibility for childrearing is theirs, and that the hours their children spend in a group center are benign, but have little important effect on the child. They assume that the providers do whatever they are supposed to do because they are in the business of caring for children. These parents scan the center's bulletin board for announcements of babysitting wanted or outgrown baby clothes or furnishings for sale; they see little reason for more than a hello and good-by as they deliver and pick up their children. Indeed, they are annoyed by the center's rule that they must personally deliver and pick up their child. It is much more convenient to use a carpool or center transportation.

Powell (1977) describes the interdependent parent as follows:

The interdependent parents reflect considerable intersection between family and day care centers; the two childrearing systems function in an interdependent manner. Interdependent parents have a high frequency of communication with caregivers, discuss parent/family related information, believe strongly that family information should be shared with caregivers, and believe that parents and caregivers should discuss childrearing values (p. 18).

Such interdependency should be the goal of every infant-toddler program. It is not easily reached because of differing philosophies about parental responsibility and about child development and education. It is also difficult to reach because both parents and day care providers are always pressed for time. It is a recognized fact that adults make time according to their priorities. Therefore, the center needs to help staff members and parents reorder their priorities when needed. The center is the initiator of the interdependent network.

Transition times

The highest frequency of communication between parents and caregivers occurs when the children are delivered and picked up. In spite of this, Powell (1977) found that more than one-fourth of the parents and caregivers in his sample of 212 parents and 89 caregivers had transition time contacts less frequently than once a week. The first step, therefore, in initiating an interdependent network, is to require personal delivery and pick-up of each child. Detailed examples are included in Chapter 10. Carpool transportation to the center should be discouraged, particularly for children under 3 years of age.

The second step is to provide mechanisms to increase the quality of the communication at the transition times. Without advance planning, even these daily contacts can easily become superficial. "How did things go?" and "Thanks, see you tomorrow" have little communication potential. A major problem, of course, is that centers operate on an extended day, and few caregivers work more than 8 hours a day, if that long. If the primary caregiver is present at the center's opening time, the 8-hour day is completed before many of the children have been picked up. Split-shifts for primary caregivers are one solution, although split-shifts are not usually looked upon with favor by the caregivers. Even if they agreed to be present at the beginning and ending of each session, the responsibilities for the children would rest on nonprimary caregivers for a major portion of the day. Any split-shift arrangement is undesirable from the adult's standpoint and is very inadequate from the child's standpoint. Rosenthal's (1980) suggestion of assigning one person in the morning (e.g., 6:30 AM to 2:30 PM) and another in the afternoon (10:30 AM to 6:30 PM) as primary caregivers is one good solution, as it provides an overlap of time in the middle of the day and the child is supplied continuity in care.

The organization of the transition time periods can facilitate meaningful communication, also. Is there a spot in the center where a parent and a staff member can talk freely without interruption? Can the parents come in time to wait for the child to settle in (e.g., the nap for Luther, the transfer from mother to caregiver for Travis, and the discussion about the disco record between Victoria's father and the caregiver)? A little extra time with the parent at the end of the day is advisable also.

The transition time communications can be made more meaningful and substantive by incorporating written messages. A Plexiglas wall chart serves two purposes. It provides a running diary of each child's eating, sleeping, and toileting for reference by the different caregivers. It also provides a quick summary of these items at the end of the day for the parent. It frees the few minutes of face-to-face contact for the discussion of other items. In addition to the wall chart, a notebook should be readily available for parents and caregivers alike. Parents sign in their children upon arrival and write any special news events (for example, Bob's grandmother arrived last night, and will visit the center this afternoon; Cindy had a restless night; I'd like to talk with you for a few minutes tonight when I pick up Ruth; or even Do you know any babysitters who could stay with us when the baby comes?) Caregivers' written messages might be: Johnie really loves carrots; Susie seems cranky—she may be coming down with something; or Ralph took his first step today! This last item raises an interesting question. Should a caregiver deprive the parents of the thrill of their child's first step? If you think not, perhaps a more appropriate notation would be: Ralph is so close to taking his first step. Maybe he'll do it tonight.

If parents are rushed at the end of the day, and they usually are, they can be updated about their child's day with these special messages. More information is available when the messages are written than when the caregiver(s) try to remember the newsworthy events. This message writing also minimizes the disadvantages of multiple caregivers for any one child. In addition, any announcement to all the parents (e.g., "Don't forget the potluck tomorrow night") can be written just once in bold letters at the top of the day's page. Announcements with more detail can be typed and duplicated, with a copy placed in each child's cubby for pick-up at the end of the day. The written messages in the notebook not only supply necessary information to all concerned adults, but are a major means in establishing the interdependence of family and center in reaching the goal of the well-being of each individual child.

Parent conferences and other events

Individual parent conferences should be scheduled periodically. They should he held at

least two times a year, and ideally more often because infants and toddlers change so rapidly. There are general rules that should be followed for all parent-teacher conferences, regardless of the age of the child. The most important rule is to always begin with the positives. When we help parents see their child's good points, we are reinforcing their self-images as parents. Ga-

linsky (1980) asserts that the images parents hold of themselves as parents play an important role in how they feel and what they do. Day care personnel must remember that their comments about a child are probably the first professional evaluation the parent has had. If the caregiver sees the child as a beautiful, developing person, the parent will begin to see the child in the same way and will take pride in the fact that this child is the result of good parenting.

A second important rule is to have the first conference before the child has started to attend the center's program. Not only is background information necessary (see Appendix B for a suggested form), but also this first conference sets the stage for mutual trust and respect, which then grows throughout the time of enrollment. Ideally, parents visit the center before enrolling their child to ascertain both the physical and psychological environments and to check out the items recommended by the Office of Human Development Services.

In addition to communications during transition times and the scheduled parent conferences, there are other ways of increasing parent-center interdependency. Many caregivers and parents become close friends and may see each other on a more social basis. Many centers schedule family potlucks for children and adults. These can provide both fun and another step in closer communication. If the potluck time is set very close to the center's closing time, there will be time after the meal for a "serious" parent meeting (if child care is provided and the meeting does not last too long). Parent meetings can be mutually beneficial—or mutually deadening. If the parents have been asked for suggested topics, there is a better chance of higher attendance when these topics are either presented or offered for discussion. Meetings that include a slide show of the children at the center are always well attended. They offer the center staff an opportunity to insert a few "words of wisdom" related to the activities shown in the slides. An excellent starter for a series of parent meetings can be drawn from parents' responses to the question "What do you expect from day care?"

Instead of center-to-parent meetings, some centers have initiated parent-to-parent meetings, which have proved successful. These include a brief presentation by one parent of a specific aspect of parenting, experience-sharing, discussion, and refreshments. If the traditional coffee and cookies seem a little tame to the fathers in the group, there is no reason why beer and pretzels can not be served!

Suggested topics for either staff- or parent-directed discussions include:

1. Nutrition—feeding and diets at different ages; vitamins; weaning and self-feeding; appetites of small children; suggested snacks.
2. Safety—accidents, accidental poisoning; car safety; water safety.
3. General health—immunizations, patterns of communicable diseases, sources of free or inexpensive health care, care of the teeth and gums.
4. Elimination—normal patterns, toilet training.
5. Behavior and development—curiosity, speech and language, attention span, temper tantrums, attempts at independence.
6. Interpersonal relations—sibling jealousy, sharing and taking turns, fear of strangers, discipline, courtesy, parent attitudes, attention getting, behavior management, need for affection and praise.
7. Any other problem or interest indicated by the parents.

A popular program for involving parents in groups is the Parent Effectiveness Training system (Gordon, 1970, 1976). It is designed to help parents better understand and deal with their children. There is also a series of audiotapes in the program titled Systematic Training for Effective Parenting (STEP) by Dinkmeyer and McKay (1976), which can be used as discussion starters. Both the PET and the STEP programs are designed to teach specific techniques to parents for meeting their own needs and for solving their problems with their children.

The parents of each center are unique. Their interests and needs are also somewhat unique. Centers have to find their own best methods of

TABLE 11-2   Ideas for center-parent contacts

New children	Initial meeting with director
	Meeting the related classroom staff
	Pre-enrollment visit by parent
	Parent stays with child on first day
	"New parent" meetings
Ongoing contacts	Daily contact at arrival and departure
	Parent-director face-to-face contact
	Periodic phone contact
	Notes sent home or included in the diary notebook
	Children's cubbies used as parent mailboxes
	Newsletter
	Scheduled conferences
	Home visits
	Parent meetings
	Parent bulletin board giving center news, daily reminders, suggested articles and books to read, community news, special announcements
	Parent manual
Participation	Open-house (child care provided)
	Observation during the day
	Father's lunch or breakfast
	Open house during parents' lunch hours
	Pot lucks and picnics
	Individual parents invited to lunch
	Trips or programs for whole families
	As helpers on field trips
	As substitutes
	As classroom volunteers
	As resource persons and class visitors: fire fighter, nurse, veterinarian, musician
	Workdays (to repair, repaint, etc.)
	Save "beautiful junk"
	Member of decision-making committee
	Center library for toys, children's books, and books on childrearing

encouraging parent involvement and partnership. But parents the world over have one thing in common. When asked "What do you want for your children?" they respond "a good life." The language may be different, the educational and economic backgrounds may be different, but the goal is unanimous. Good teachers share parents' goals and dreams, and work for them.

Day care personnel must commit their resources to strengthening the home experience as the primary and significant experience for the child. A listing of parent-contact ideas is given in Table 11-2. As yet there is little information on the specific effects of parent contact with the center upon the child's development, or ability to cope with the day care situation. However, strong parental involvement at the center nearly always results in better care for the children at the center, and perhaps in the home. One last comment, expressed by Honig (1979):

> Parenting skills come in all sizes and shapes and degrees in all families. Lots of us could use more of these skills. Parent involvement is not only for those with children in day care or school programs. All babies and preschoolers in or out of such programs can use that special early learning supplement that only parents can implement on a full scale, anytime anyplace basis (p. 80).

ADVOCACY FOR CHILDREN

Parents, caregivers/teachers, and responsible citizens must speak up for children. They should not limit their activities to in-center and in-home efforts, but should become involved in community affairs. Community decisions frequently have direct or indirect effects on young children. Proposed routes of main thoroughfares through the city, or choices between a new city park and a new government building, zoning regulations in residential or business areas, all affect young children in some way. Concerned adults can influence these decisions when they participate in community planning groups such as the United Way, the city's planning commission, the local school board, the "social concerns" committees of churches, the League of Women Voters, or local chapters of the political parties. Other opportunities present themselves in organizations such as the National Association for the Education of Young Children, the Day Care Council of America, the Children's Defense Fund, and the 4C's (Community Coordinated Child Care).

Teachers and caregivers should make themselves knowledgeable as resource persons in a special area of child care and education. Experts in child nutrition, current research, legislation, and state and national standards are always sought after as speakers at parent and professional meetings.

A professional child care worker will make a commitment to some degree of involvement at some level of the community. A concern for children is just one among many public issues that need the involvement of citizens who have the background for influencing decision-making. Many people are not specifically interested in concerns for children as their area of community participation. Some persons are more interested in saving old buildings, public transportation, politics, international relations, or planting petunias at the civic center. There are important decisions to be made in all areas and levels of our lives. The guide for decision-making for child care professionals is: Is it good for children?

Decisions are also made at the national level that have much impact on each child. There is a current trend toward diluting and even eliminating some state standards for child care. Therefore there is a need to build a strong care for protections at state and federal levels for children who are cared for outside their homes. A good case in point is the recent history of the federal day care regulations, which were years in the making, and may have completely disappeared by the time this book is published. The revised regulations were printed in the Federal Register of March 19, 1980. Implementation of the standards has been periodically postponed. I suspect the most recently publicized date for implementation has been bypassed in the move to block grants.

How to be a child advocate

At the state level. The citizens of each state can have influence in their state legislature. Legislators listen to their constituents, but the citizen's influence is dependent upon each person's initiative. There are three methods of contacting state legislators:

1. Letters and postcards mailed to an individual legislator at the state capitol. A state legislator can be swayed by as few as two or three letters, but ten or twenty are safer. Constituents' letters should not be written as though inspired by a group, but simply from an interested, concerned citizen. The letters should be short and state the position you hope the legislator will take and a sentence or two explaining why. If a legislator votes according to your requests, send a follow-up note expressing your appreciation.
2. Telephone calls to the legislator at his or her home on weekends. Legislators and their families expect to be interrupted in this way.
3. Telephone calls to the legislator while the House or Senate is in session. Ask that the legislator be brought to the phone and ask him or her to call you right back on the legislative Watts line. If the legislator is not available, ask the secretary to have your call returned.

When a senator or representative is appointed to chair a committee, he or she represents the state as a whole. Committee chairman, as well as district legislators, should know your views. It is important to be informed. If you are referring to a specific bill, know its Senate or House number. Also know why you support or oppose the bill or individual section. You can get a free copy of any bill by writing to the secretary of the senate or the chief clerk of the house at the state house in your state capitol.

Persistence is the most important single factor in keeping a bill moving. Legislators have hundreds of bills to consider and many reasons for their positions. Identify those who support the bills you favor, and keep in touch with them. Try to convince undecided members, and keep in touch with the chairman of the committee in which the bill is impending. If sufficient interest is not expressed, the bill may never be considered and will die in committee.

At the national level. Unfortunately, letters to congressmen are frequently less effective than they might be. A lengthy, verbose, or threatening letter will turn off anyone. But with a little forethought, you can avoid these shortcomings. Here are some pointers to keep in mind when writing:

1. Be brief. Confine your letter to one issue. State the purpose for writing in the first paragraph. Give the number of the bill, not just the subject. Include all facts at your disposal, briefly and concisely. Give your suggestions for improving the situation. Limit your remarks to one page. Thank the legislator for his or her consideration.
2. Be courteous. Do not threaten (e.g., "I won't vote for you next year"), demand, or apologize. Spell the legislator's name correctly; use the correct title and salutation; do not send carbon copies of letters; do not use a form letter or a postcard. Public officials should be addressed as follows:

PRESIDENT OF THE UNITED STATES
   Envelope: The President
     The White House
     Washington, D.C. 20500
   Salutation: Dear Mr. President
U.S. SENATOR
   Envelope: The Honorable _____
     United States Senate
     Washington, D.C. 20510
   Salutation: Dear Senator _____
U.S. REPRESENTATIVE
   Envelope: The Honorable _____
     House of Representatives
     Washington, D.C. 20515
   Salutation: Dear Sir (or Madam)

3. Be timely. The legislative process is a long, complicated one. After a bill is introduced, it is usually considered by a subcommittee and a full committee before going to the House or Senate floor. By the time it comes up for a final vote, your congressman may have already reached a decision. Therefore, the earlier you make your opinion known, the more influential it will be.

■ CHAPTER SUMMARY ■

The physical and social (human) environments of the day care center or family day care home are vital components of the group care and education of infants and toddlers. They enable the caregivers/teachers to provide a quality program.

There are state rules and regulations for licensed centers, which dictate many aspects of the physical environment. There are also federal rules and regulations. There are recommended guidelines for parents who are selecting a day care situation for their children. All of these are the results of professional judgment, research findings, and citizen input. Professional child care workers are those who get involved at the community, state, and national levels of legislation.

Parent-center relationships are a vital component of any day care center. They require concentrated efforts by the day care personnel to make them a positive force in ensuring the well-being of each child in day care. These relationships are enhanced when attention is paid to transition times, to parent conferences, and to parent meetings with a variety of topics and activities.

SUGGESTED ACTIVITIES/POINTS TO PONDER

1. Secure a copy of your state's licensing requirements for child care centers. Compare it with Iowa's requirements or the requirements of any other state.
2. Interview the parents of an infant or toddler who is in day care. Ask what they expect of day care.
3. Visit an infant-toddler day care center or family home. List the caregiver's characteristics using the suggestions from the Office of Human Development Services as guidelines.

REFERENCES AND SUGGESTED READINGS

Auerbach, S., editor: Creative centers and homes. Vol. III of Child Care: a comprehensive guide, New York, 1978, Human Sciences Press.

Bohlen, S., Digby, J., and Larson, B.: Just hanging around: ideas for creative use of a child's learning space, San Antonio, Texas, 1976, The San Antonio Association for the Education of Young Children.

Bronfenbrenner, U.: Toward a theoretical model for the analysis of parent-child relationships in a social context. In Glidewell, J., editor: Parental attitudes and child behavior, Springfield, Ill., 1961, Charles C Thomas, Publisher.

Bronfenbrenner, U.: Is early intervention effective? In Leichter, H.J. editor: The family as educator, New York, 1975, Teacher's College Press.

Bronfenbrenner, U.: The ecology of human development, Cambridge, Mass., 1979, Harvard University Press.

Bronfenbrenner, U.: Who needs parent education? Teachers College Record **79**(4):767-787, May 1978.

Caldwell, B.M.: Some precautions in establishing infant day care. In R. Elardo and B. Pagan, editors: Perspectives on infant day care, ed. 2, Little Rock, Ark., 1976, Southern Association on Children under Six.

Cochran, M.M.: A comparison of group day and family childrearing patterns in Sweden, Child Development **48**:702-707, 1977.

Cohen, D.: Serving preschool children, No. 3, Washington, D.C., 1974, U.S. Government Printing Office.

Dimond, E.: From trust to autonomy: planning day care space for infants and toddlers. In Jones, E., editor: Supporting the growth of infants, toddlers and parents, Pasadena, Calif., 1979, Pacific Oaks College and Children's School.

Dinkmeyer, D., and McKay, G.: Systematic training for effective parenting: parent's handbook, Circle Pines, Minn., 1976, American Guidance Service.

Drezek, W.: Infant teachers take cues from mothers, Dimensions **5**(3):74-76, 1977.

Elardo, R., and Caldwell, B.: Value imposition in early education: fact or fancy? Child Care Quarterly **2**(1):6-13, 1973.

Environmental criteria: mentally retarded preschool day care facilities, College Station, 1971, Texas A & M College of Architecture and Environmental Design.

Fein, G.G.: Infant day care and the family: regulatory strategies to ensure parent participation. Report prepared for the Office of the Assistant Secretary for Planning and Evaluation, Department of Health, Education, and Welfare, July, 1976.

Fein, G., and Clarke-Stewart, A.: Day care in context, New York, 1973, John Wiley & Sons, Inc.

Fogel, A.: Expressing affection and love to young children, Dimensions **8**(2):39-44, 1980.

Fowler, W.: Guides to early day care and teaching, Occasional paper no. 18, Ontario, 1978, The Ontario Institute for Studies in Education.

Galinsky, E.: Between generations: the six stages of parenthood, New York, 1980, Time-Life Books.

Golden, M., and others: The New York City infant day care study, New York, 1978, Medical and Health Research Association of New York City.

Gonzalez-Mena, J.: What is a good beginning? Young Children **34**(3):47-53, 1979.

Gordon, T.: Parent effectiveness training, New York, 1970, Wyden Press.

Gordon, T.: P.E.T. in action, New York, 1976, Bantam Books, Inc.

Herbert-Jackson, E., O'Brien, M., Porterfield, J., and Risley, T.R.: The infant center, Baltimore, 1977, University Park Press.

Honig, A.S.: Parent involvement in early childhood education, rev. ed., Washington, D.C., 1979, National Association for the Education of Young Children.

Honig, A.S., and Lally, J.R.: How good is your infant program? In Peters, D.L., editor: Day care: problems, processes, prospects, New York, 1975, Human Sciences Press.

Human Development Services: A parent's guide to day care, Washington, D.C., 1980, U.S. Government Printing Office.

Jacobson, A.L.: Infant day care: toward a more human environment, Young Children **33**(5):14-21, 1978.

Johnson, H.: Children in "the nursery school," New York, 1972, Agathon Press, Inc. (Originally published in 1928.)

Jones, E.: Dimensions of teaching—learning environments: a handbook for teachers, Pasadena, Calif., 1973, Pacific Oaks College.

Jones, E., editor: Supporting the growth of infants, toddlers and parents, Pasadena, Calif., 1979, Pacific Oaks College.

Jones, E., and Prescott, E.: Dimensions of teaching—learning environments. II. Focus on day care, Pasadena, Calif., 1978, Pacific Oaks College.

Kagen, J.: Family experience and the child's development, American Psychologist **34**(10):886-891, 1979.

Katz, L.G.: Contemporary perspectives on the roles of mothers and teachers. In Parenthood in a changing society, Washington, D.C., 1980, National Institute of Education.

Kritchevsky, S., Prescott, E.: Planning environments for young children: physical space, Washington, D.C., 1969, National Association for the Education of Young Children.

Lewis, M., and Harlan, E.: Space, Mother's Manual, Feb. 1981, pp. 28-30.

Licensing and Approval Standards, Chapter 109, Child Care Centers, Des Moines, Ia., 1976, Iowa Department of Social Services.

Mattick, I., and Perkins, F.J.: Guidelines for observation and assessment, Washington, D.C., 1973, The Day Care and Child Development Council of America.

National Day Care Study: Final report. Vol. I: Children at the center, Cambridge, Mass., 1979, Abt Associates, Inc.

Ostrom, G.: When adults communicate effectively, Dimensions 1(2):3-6, 1973.

Powell, D.R.: The interface between families and child care programs, Detroit, 1977, The Merrill-Palmer Institute.

Powell, D.R.: Day care-family transitions, Children in Contemporary Society IYC Series, Part 3, 13(1):11-13, 1979.

Prescott, E.: Is day care as good as a good home? Young Children 33(2):13-19, 1978.

Prescott, E., and others: Assessment of child-rearing environments Part I: Who thrives in group day care? Pasadena, Calif., 1975, Pacific Oaks College.

Prescott, E., and David, T.: The effects of the physical environment on day care. Report prepared for the Office of the Assistant Secretary for Planning and Evaluation, Department of Health, Education, and Welfare, 1976.

Provence, S., Naylor, A., and Patterson, J.: The challenge of day care, New Haven, 1977, Yale University Press.

Rosenthal, J.: Primary care giving: an important element of a quality infant-toddler program, Early Childhood Education Center Newsletter 2(1):1-2, 1979.

Schwarz, J.D.: Childhood origins of psychopathology, American Psychologist 34(10):879-885, 1979.

Somer, R.: Tight spaces, Englewood Cliffs, N.J., 1974, Prentice-Hall, Inc.

Stewart, D.O.: Perfect behavior, New York, 1922, George H. Doran Co.

Thomas, A., and Chess, A.: Temperament and development, New York, 1977, Brunner/Mazel.

Twardosz, S., Cataldo, M., and Risley, T.: Infant use of crib toys, Young Children 30:129-144, 1975.

Tyler, B., and Dittmann, L.: Meeting the toddler more than halfway, Young Children, 35(2):39-46, 1980.

Weissberg, G.M.: Designing stimulating environments for children. In Auerbach, S., editor: Creative centers and homes. Vol. III of Child care: a comprehensive guide, New York, 1978, Human sciences Press.

White, B.L., and Watts, J.C.: Experience and the environment: Major influences on the development of the young child. I. Englewood Cliffs, N.J., 1973, Prentice-Hall, Inc.

Willis, A., and Ricciuti, H.: A good beginning for babies: guidelines for group care, Washington, D.C., 1975, National Association for the Education of Young Children.

Winetsky, C.S.: Comparison of the expectations of parents and teachers for the behavior of preschool children, Child Development 49:1146-1154, 1978.

Yarrow, L.J., Rubenstein, J.L., and Pedersen, F.A.: Infant and environment: early cognitive and motivational development, Washington, D.C., 1975, Hemisphere.

Zigler, E.: Speech to the Education Commission of the States Meeting, Denver, Dec. 7, 1972.

Zigler, E., and Cascione, R.: On being a parent. In Parenthood in a changing society, Washington, D.C., 1980, National Institute of Education.

APPENDIX A

SOURCES FOR MATERIALS AND INFORMATION

SOURCES FOR FREE MATERIALS ABOUT POISONS

American Association of Poison Control
 Centers
c/o Anthony R. Temple, M.D.
McNeil Consumer Products Co.
Fort Washington, PA 19034

Council on Family Health
Dept. P
633 Third Ave.
New York, NY 10017

Human Action for Poison Prevention in Youth
2 Hardman Dr.
Bloomington, IL 61701

National Agricultural Chemicals Association
Safety Division
115 15th St. N.W.
Washington, DC 20005

Northeast Iowa Poison Information and Treatment
 Center
Allen Memorial Hospital
Waterloo, IA 50703

Poison Prevention Week Council
Secretary
PO Box 1543
Washington, DC 20013

Public Information Center
U.S. Environmental Protection Agency
401 M St. S.W.
Washington, DC 20460

Red Cross chapter (local)

The Soap and Detergent Association
475 Park Ave. S. at 32nd St.
New York NY 10016

SOURCES FOR FILMS, SLIDE TALKS, PUBLIC ADDRESSES, AND MEDIA AIDS ABOUT POISONS

American Association of Poison Control Centers
c/o Anthony R. Temple, M.D.
McNeil Consumer Products Co.
Fort Washington, PA 19034

Mar/Chuck Film Industries
PO Box 61
Mt. Prospect, IL 60056

Modern Talking Pictures
2323 New Hyde Park Rd.
New Hyde Park, NY 11040

National Safety Council
444 N. Michigan Ave.
Chicago, IL 60611

Superintendent of Documents
U.S. Government Printing Office
Washington, D.C. 20402

U.S. Consumer Product Safety Commission
5401 Westbard Ave.
Bethesda, MD 20207
Attn: OC

Visual Education, Inc.
Suite 424
1425 H St. N.W.
Washington, DC 20005

SOURCES OF ADDITIONAL INFORMATION ABOUT CHILD ABUSE AND NEGLECT
Associations

American Humane Association
Children's Division
PO Box 1266
Denver, CO 80201 (extensive publication available)

Child Abuse Listening Mediation (CALM)
PO Box 718
Santa Barbara, CA 93102 (volunteer program)

Child Welfare League of America
67 Irving Place
New York, NY 10003

Children's Bureau
Administration for Children, Youth and Families
PO Box 1182
Washington, DC 20013 (federal agency)

Day Care and Child Development Council of
America
1401 K St. N.W.
Washington, DC 20085

National Committee for Prevention of Child Abuse
Suite 510, 111 E. Wacker Dr.
Chicago, IL 60601

National Center for the Prevention and Treatment
of Child Abuse and Neglect
University of Colorado Medical Center
1001 Jasmine St.
Denver, CO 80220

Parents Anonymous
2801 Artesia Blvd.
Redondo Beach, CA 90278 (Parent self-help)

National Center for Comprehensive Emergency
Services to Children in Crisis
320 Metro Howard Office Building
25 Middleton St.
Nashville, TN 37210

Regional Child Abuse and Neglect Resource Center

Region I Child Abuse and Neglect Resource Center
Judge Baker Guidance Center
295 Longwood Ave.
Boston, MA 02115
617-232-8390
(CT, ME, MA, RI, VT, NH)

Region II Child Abuse and Neglect Resource Center
College of Human Ecology
Cornell University
MVR Hall
Ithaca, NY 14853
607-256-7794
(NJ, NY, PR, VI)

Region III Child Abuse and Neglect Resource Center
Howard University Institute for Urban Affairs
 and Research
2935 Upton St., N.W.
Washington, DC 20008
202-686-6770
(DC, DE, MD, PA, VA, WV)

Region IV Child Abuse and Neglect Resource Center
Regional Institute for Social Welfare Research
PO Box 152
Athens, GA 30601
404-542-7614
(AL, FL, GA, KY, MS, NC, SC, TN)

Region V Child Abuse and Neglect Resource Center
Graduate School of Social Work
University of Wisconsin-Milwaukee
Milwaukee, WI 53201
414-963-4184
(IL, IN, MI, MN, OH, WI)

Region VI Child Abuse and Neglect Resource Center
Graduate School of Social Work
University of Texas at Austin
Austin, TX 78712
512-471-4067
(AR, LA, NM, OK, TX)

Region VII Child Abuse and Neglect Resource
 Center
Institute of Child Behavior and Development
University of Iowa, Oakdale Campus
Oakdale, IA 53219
319-353-4825
(IA, KS, MO, NE)

Region VIII Child Abuse and Neglect Resource
 Center
National Center for the Prevention and Treatment of
 Child Abuse and Neglect
1205 Oneida St.
Denver, CO 80220
303-321-3963
(CO, MT, ND, SD, UT, WY)

Region IX Child Abuse and Neglect Resource Center
Department of Special Education
California State University
5151 State University Dr.
Los Angeles, CA 90032
213-224-3283
(AZ, CA, HI, NV, Guam, Trust Terr.)

Region X Child Abuse and Neglect Resource Center
Western Federation for Human Service
157 Yesler Way, #208
Seattle, WA 98104
206-624-5480
(AK, ID, OR, WA)

RESOURCES FOR FREE MATERIALS ABOUT FOOD AND NUTRITION

American Dental Association
Order Section CAT 77
211 E. Chicago Ave.
Chicago, IL 60611

American Dietetic Association
430 N. Michigan Ave.
Chicago, IL 60611

American Home Economics Association
2010 Massachusetts Ave., N.W.
Washington, DC 20036

American Institute of Baking
400 E. Ontario St.
Chicago, IL 60611

American Meat Institute
59 E. Van Buren
Chicago, IL 60605

American Sheep Producers Council
200 Clayton St.
Denver, CO 80206

Bureau of Dental Health Education
211 E. Chicago Ave.
Chicago, IL 60611

Bureau of Community Health Services
Program Services Branch
Room 12A33
5600 Fisher Lane
Rockville, MD 20852

California Fisheries Institute
300 S. Ferry St.
Room 2016
Terminal Island, CA 90731

Cereal Institute
135 South LaSalle St.
Chicago, IL 60603

County Extension Offices
(Check your local phone directory for number and
   address.)

Federal Extension Service
USDA
14th St. & Independence Ave., S.W.
Washington, DC 20250

Food and Nutrition Information and Educational
   Materials Center
National Agricultural Library
Beltsville, MD 20705

Idaho Potato Commission
Box 1068
Boise, ID 83701

Kansas Wheat Commission
1021 N. Main St.
Hutchinson, KS 67501

Manfacturing Chemists Assoc., Inc.
1825 Connecticut Ave., N.W.
Washington, DC 20036

Money Management Institute
Household Finance Corporation
Prudential Plaza
Chicago, IL 60601

National Dairy Council
6300 N. River Rd.
Rosemont, IL 60018

National Livestock and Meat Board
3650 Wabash Ave.
Chicago, IL 60603

National Turkey Federation
PO Box 69
Mount Morris, IL 61054

Nutrition, USA
Pueblo, CO 81009

Nutrition Foundation
99 Park Ave.
New York, NY 10016

Nutrition Information and Resource Center
Beecher-Dock House
Pennsylvania State University
University Park, PA 16803

Parents' Magazine Films, Inc.
52 Vanderbilt Ave.
New York, NY 10017

Poultry and Egg Association
National Board
18 S. Michigan Ave.
Chicago, IL 60603

Rice Council
Box 22802
Houston, TX 77027

Society for Nutrition Education
2140 Shattuck Ave.
Suite 110
Berkeley, CA 94704

Sperry-Hutchinson Co.
Consumer Relations Department
3303 E. Kemper Road
Cincinnati, OH 45241

Standard Brands Educational Services
Box 2695 Grand Central Station
New York, NY 10017

Sunkist Growers
Box 2706 Terminal Annex
Los Angeles, CA 90030

Superintendent of Documents
U.S. Government Printing Office
Washington, DC 20402

United Fresh Fruit and Vegetable Association
777 14th St., N.W.
Washington, DC 20010

U.S. Department of Agriculture
Food and Nutrition Service
14th St. & Independence Ave.
Washington, DC 20250

U.S. Department of Health and Human Services
200 Independence Ave., S.W.
Washington, DC 20201

Vitamin Information Bureau
383 Madison Ave.
New York, NY 10017

Western Growers Association
3091 Wilshire Blvd.
Los Angeles, CA 90010

Wheat Flour Institute
14 E. Jackson Blvd.
Chicago, IL 60604

RESOURCE MATERIALS FOR ADULT-CHILD FOOD EXPERIENCES

Childbirth Education Association: Feed me! I'm yours
Minneapolis–St. Paul Meadowbrook Press
16648 Meadowbrook Lane
Wayzata, MN 55391

Cooking and eating with children: A way to learn
Association for Childhood Education International
3615 Wisconsin Ave. N.W.
Washington, DC 20016

Croft, K.B.: The good for me cookbook
Rand E. Research Associates
4843 Mission St.
San Francisco, CA 94112

Ferreira, N.J.: The mother-child cookbook
4085 Campbell Ave.
Pacific Coast Publishers
Menlo Park, CA 94025

Good times with good foods: classroom activities for young children
Learning Institute of North Carolina, Leadership Development Program
1001 N. Elm Street
Greensboro, NC 27401

Goodwin, M.T., and Pollen, G.: Creative food experiences for children
Center for Science in the Public Interest,
1779 Church St.,
Washington, DC 20036

Harms, T.: Maximizing learning from cooking experiences: Teacher's manual for A child's cookbook
Frank Porter Graham Child Development Center
University of North Carolina
Chapel Hill, NC 27514

Harms, T., Veitch, B., Wallace, G., and Wallace, T.: A child's cookbook
Child's Cookbook
656 Terra California Drive No. 3
Walnut Creek, CA 94595

McClenahan, P., and Jaqua, I.: Cool cooking for kids
Fearon•Pitman Publishers, Inc., 6 Davis Dr.
Belmont, CA 94002

Miles, B.: The cooking book
Alfred A. Knopf, Inc.
201 E. 50 St.
New York, NY 10022

Moore, E.: The Seabury cookbook for boys and girls
The Seabury Press, Inc.
815 Second Ave.
New York, NY 10017

Stevens, H.A.: Fixing and eating
Campus Book Stores
Iowa Memorial Union
University of Iowa
Iowa City, IA 52242

Teaching the fun way with rice
Rice Council of America
PO Box 22803
Houston, TX 77027

Wanamakes, N., Hearn, K., and Richarz, S.: More
  than graham crackers
National Association for the Education of Young
  Children
1834 Connecticut Ave. NW
Washington, DC 20009

Wilms, B.: Crunchy bananas
Peregrine Smith, Inc.
1877 E. Gentile St.
Box 667
Layton, UT 84041

SOURCES OF ACTIVITIES FOR INFANTS AND TODDLERS

Adcock, D., and Segal, M.M.: Play and learning, two-years-old, Rolling Hills Estates, Calif., 1979, B.L. Winch and Associates.

Anselmo, S., and Petersen, J.D.: A manual for caregivers of infants and toddlers, San Francisco, 1978, R & E Research Associates, Inc.

Aston, A.: How to play with your baby, New York, 1971, The Learning Child, Inc.

Badger, E.: Infant/toddler learning program, Paoli, Pa., 1971, The Instructo Corp.

Bluma, S., Shearer, M.S., Frohman, A.H., and Hilliard, J.M.: Portage guide to early education rev. ed., Portage, Wisc., 1976, Cooperative Educational Service Agency.

Brown, S.L., and Donovan, C.M.: Stimulation activities. Vol 3 of Schafer, D.S., and Moersch, M.S., editors: Developmental programming for infants and young children, Ann Arbor, 1977, The University of Michigan Press.

Caplan, F.: The first twelve months of life, New York, 1975, Grosset & Dunlap, Inc.

Caplan, F., and Caplan, T.: The second twelve years of life: a kaleidoscope of growth, New York, 1977, Grossett & Dunlap, Inc.

Clare, C.: Creative movement for the developing child, rev. ed., Belmont, Calif., 1977, Fearon Publishers, Inc.

Cohen, M.D., editor: Developing programs for infants and toddlers, Washington, D.C., 1977, Association for Childhood Education International.

Cole, A., Haas, C., Busnell, F., and Weinberger, B.: I saw a purple cow and 100 other recipes for learning, Boston, 1972, Little, Brown & Co., Inc.

Cole, A., Haas, C., Heller, E., and Weinberger, B.: Recipes for fun, ed. 4, Northfield, Ill., 1974, PAR Project.

Diem, L.: Children learn physical skills. Part 1. Birth to 3 years, Washington, D.C., 1974, American Alliance for Health, Physical Education and Recreation.

Engel, R.C.: Language motivating experiences for young children, Van Nuys, Calif., 1968, DFA Publishers.

Gordon, I.J.: Baby learning through baby play; a parent's guide for the first two years, New York, 1970, St. Martin's Press, Inc.

Gordon, I.J.: The infant experience, Columbus, Ohio, 1975, Charles E. Merrill Publishing Co.

Gordon, I.J.: Baby to parent to baby; a guide to developing parent-child interaction in the first twelve months, New York, 1977, St. Martin's Press.

Gordon, I.J., Guinagh, B., and Jester, R.E.: Child learning through child play; learning activities for two and three year olds, New York, 1971, St. Martin's Press.

Hagstrom, J., and Morrill, J.: Games babies play, New York, 1979, A & W Visual Library.

Herbert-Jackson, E., O'Brien, M., Porterfield, J., and Risley, T.R.: The infant center; a complete guide to organizing and managing infant day care, Baltimore, 1977, University Park Press.

Huntington, D.S., Provence, S., and Parker, R.K.: Day care 2 Serving infants DHEW Publication (OCD) 73-14, Washington, D.C., 1973, U.S. Government Printing Office.

Huntington, D.S., Provence, S., and Parker, R.F.: Infant development program, 1976, Hicksville, N.Y., The Johnson, & Johnson Baby Products Co.

Jones, S.: Good things for babies, Boston, 1976, Houghton Mifflin Co.

Koontz, C.: Koontz child development program: training for the first 48 months, Los Angeles, 1974, Western Psychological Services.

Lambie, D., Bond, L., and Weikart, D.: Home teaching with mothers and infants, Ypsilanti, Mich., 1974, High/Scope Educational Research Foundation.

Lehane, S.: Help your baby learn, Englewood Cliffs, N.J., 1976, Prentice-Hall, Inc.

Levenstein, P.: Toy demonstrator's visit handbook, Freeport, N.Y., 1969, Family Service Association of Nassau County.

Levy, J.: The baby exercise book, New York, 1975, Random House, Inc.

Marzollo, J.: Supertot, New York, 1977, Harper & Row Publications, Inc.

Matterson, E.: Games for the very young, New York, 1969, American Heritage Press.

McDiarmid, N.J.: Loving and learning: interacting with your baby from birth to three, New York, 1975, Harcourt Brace Jovanovich, Inc.

Meier, J.H., and Malone, P.J.: Facilitating children's development, Vol. I: Infant and toddler learning episodes, Baltimore, 1979, University Park Press.

O'Brien, M., Porterfield, J., Herbert-Jackson, E., and Risley, T.R.: The toddler center, a practical guide to day care for one- and two-year-olds, Baltimore, Md., 1979, University Park Press.

Painter, G.: Teach your baby, New York, 1971, Simon and Schuster, Inc.

Prudden, S., and Sussman, J.: Suzy Prudden's creative fitness for baby and child, New York, 1972, William Morrow & Co., Inc.

Quick, A.D., and Campbell, A.A.: Lesson plans for enhancing preschool developmental progress: Project MEMPHIS, Dubuque, Ia., 1976, Kendall/Hunt Publishing Co.

Rosenthal, J.K., and Wichael, A.: Homemade playthings and activities for infants and toddlers, Iowa City, 1981, Early Childhood Education Center, University of Iowa.

Roufberg, R.B.: Today he can't tomorrow he can! Your child from two to five years, Vol. 2, New York, 1972, The Learning Child, Inc.

Roufberg, R.: Your child from two to five years, New York, 1977, Fountain Publishing Co.

Scott, L.B., and Thompson, J.J.: Rhymes for fingers and flannelboards, N.Y. 1960, McGraw-Hill Book Co.

Seaman, R.: Through their looking glass, Nashville, Tenn., 1979, Incentive Publications, Inc.

Segal, M.M.: From birth to one year, Rolling Hills Estates, Calif., 1974, B.L. Winch & Associates.

Segal, M.M., and Adcock, D.: From one to two years, Rolling Hills Estates, Calif., 1976, B.L. Winch & Associates.

Sparling, J., and Lewis, I.: Learning games for the first three years; a guide to parent-child play, New York, 1979, Walker and Co.

Streepey, S.: Today he can't tomorrow he can! Your child from birth to two years, Vol. 1, New York, 1971, The Learning Child, Inc.

Sutton-Smith, B., and Sutton-Smith, S.: How to play with your children (and when not to), New York, 1974, Hawthorn Books, Inc.

Tronick, E., and Marks, P.: Infant curriculum: the Bromley-Heath guide to the care of infants, New York, 1973, Media Projects, Inc.

Umansky, W., Oyler, D., and Smith, E.: Infant curriculum, Athens, Ga., 1978, University of Georgia.

Watrin, R., and Furfey, P.H.: Learning activities for the young preschool child, New York, 1978, D. Van Nostrand Co.

SOURCES OF TOYS, EQUIPMENT, AND MATERIALS

ABC Supply, Inc.
437 Armour Circle N.E.
Atlanta, GA 30324
A wide variety of early learning materials. Distributor of many popular name products.

John Ahlbin & Sons
Division of Scott & Fetzer Co.
184 Garden St.
Bridgeport, CN 06605
Scissors and shears of all types.

American Guidance Service
Publishers Building
Circle Pines, MN 55104
Tests and educational materials, including a wide range of educational kits for early learning experiences.

American Toy & Furniture Co.
6130 N. Clark St.
Chicago, IL 60660
Tool chests, magnetic puzzles, toys and doll furniture, preschool toys, bulletin boards.

Angeles Nursery Toys
4105 N. Fairfax Dr.
Arlington, VA 22203
Manufacturers of wagons, tricycles, carts, etc. Replacement parts available.

Beckley-Cardy Company
1900 N. Narragansett Ave.
Chicago, IL 60639
Distributor of many popular products of various manufacturers; very comprehensive listing of materials, supplies, and equipment.

Behavioral Publications
Subsidiary of Human Sciences
72 5th Ave.
New York, NY 10011
Day care and early education curriculum materials for professionals and parents.

Binney & Smith, Inc.
380 Madison Ave.
New York, NY 10017
Adhesives, brushes, chalks, crayons, modeling clays, Edu-Cards educational products.

Dick Blick
PO Box 1267
Galesburg, IL 61401
Vendor for early and special education enrichment aids including Montessori-type materials.

Louis A. Boettiger Co.
31 Franklin Ave.
Hewlett, NY 11557
Infant toys and accessories.

Bowmar Publishing Corp.
622 Rodier Dr.
Glendale, CA 91201
Manipulative books and toys; listening-singing-rhythm series.

Childcraft Educational Corp.
964 Third Ave.
New York, NY 10022
A wide range of early childhood materials and equipment, including toys and games.

Child Guidance Toys, Inc.
New York, NY 10472
Educational toys and activities, puzzles, sewing cards, cloth books.

Childhood/Alan Jay
180 W. Westfield Ave.
Roselle Park, NJ 07204
Preschool educational toys, crib and play pen toys, giant pounder.

Community Playthings
Rifton, NY 12471
Sturdy equipment, furnishings, and toys

Connor Forest Industries
PO Box 847
Wausau, WI 55401
Woodboard inlay puzzles, block sets, and infant and youth furniture.

Creative Playthings
Columbia Broadcasting System
Princeton, NJ 08540
Complete line of infant and early childhood toys, games, and activity sets, including furniture and equipment for physical development.

Developmental Learning Materials
7440 Natchez Ave.
Niles, IL 60648
Manufacturers of a wide variety of educational materials to enhance sensory and academic skills.

Elka Toys
269 37th St.
Brooklyn, NY 11323
Stuffed animals, infants' toys, puppets, musical toys.

Fisher-Price Toys
606 Girard Ave.
East Aurora, NY 14052
Pull and push toys, infant and musical toys, play family toys, puzzles, wood action toys.

Gund Manufacturing Co.
360 Suydam St.
Brooklyn, NY 11237
Hand puppets, beanbags, infant toys, musical animals.

Halsam Products Company
Division of Playskool
Chicago, IL 60645
Complete line of preschool toys, educational wood toys, infant toys, Tyke Byke, and other toys and games.

Hasbro Industries, Inc.
1027 Newport Ave.
Pawtucket, RI 02862
Doctor and nurse kits, sewing kits, wooden toys, Romper Room series, phono-viewer machines.

Ideal School Supply Co.
11000 S. Lavergne Ave.
Oak Lawn, IL 60453
Wide range of toys and games and other educational materials to promote preacademic skills; equipment and supplies.

Instructo Corporation
Cedar Hollow Rd.
Paoli, PA 19301
Flannel Boards and manipulatives, mobiles.

Judy Company
310 N. Second St.
Minneapolis, MN 55400
Puzzles, games, See-Quees, records

Kaplan School Supply Corp.
600 Jamestown Rd.
Winston-Salem, NC 27103
Outdoor and indoor play equipment, infant toys, diagnostic tests and programs (Learning Accomplishment Profile).

Kusan, Inc.
3206 Belmont Blvd.
Nashville, TN 37212
Push-pull toys, play sets, furniture, Disney characters and games.

Learning Products, Inc.
725 Fee Fee Rd.
Maryland Heights, MO 63043
Building blocks and puzzles, chairs and tables, ride toys.

Marlin Toy Products, Inc.
300 Ellison St.
Horicon, WI 53202
Infant and preschool toys.

Merwin Smith Company, Inc.
200 5th Ave.
New York, NY 10010
Infant toys, beach and sand toys.

Miner Industries, Inc.
200 5th Ave.
New York, NY 10010
Child-size household items, infant toys, dolls.

Montessori Toys, Inc.
15 Central Dr.
Farmingdale, NY 11735
Manipulative toys and activities to accompany Montessori-type programs.

Olympus Publishing Co.
1670 E. 13th S.
Salt Lake City, UT 84105
Toy lending library, audiovisual support system for parents and teachers, child development and career education materials.

Parents' Magazine Press
52 Vanderbilt Ave.
New York, NY 10017
Audiovisual support system for parents and teachers to gain understanding of the child.

Platt and Munk
Questor Education Products Co.
1055 Bronx River Ave.
Bronx, NY 10472
Child guidance toys and activities; Sesame Street materials, magnetic boards, Tinkertoy sets.

Milton Bradley Co.
3720 N. Kedzie Ave.
Chicago, IL 60618
Preschool toys, wooden toys, infant toys, tiles and bricks, activity kits.

Stahlwood Toy Manufacturing Co.
601 W. 50th Street
New York, NY 10019
Infant toys, cradle exercises, washable toys.

Tonka Corporation
Mound, MN 55364
Scale model vehicles for young children.

Toy Tinkers
A.G. Spalding & Bros.
807 Greenwood St.
Evanston, IL 60201
Wooden beads, geometric blocks, tools.

Tuco Work Shops
Div. of Munro Games
3901 Union Rd.
Buffalo, NY 14225
Wood puzzles (triple thick quality).

Tupperware Corp.
Orlando, FL 32802
Select group of toys appropriate for infants and young children.

Whitney Bros. Company
Water St.
Marlborough, NH 03544
Hardwood manipulative toys and furniture for young children.

APPENDIX B

BACKGROUND INFORMATION*

1. Child's name _____ _____
   last   first   middle   Name used
2. Sex _____ Date of birth _____ Birth place _____
3. Father's name _____ Occupation _____
   Business telephone _____
4. Mother's name _____ Occupation _____
   Business telephone _____
5. Home address _____ Telephone _____
6. What are your goals for your child's attendance at the center? (Include goals for your child and for
   yourself.) _____
   _____
   _____

Home relationships

7. Who resides with child in the home? (Please give birthdates of other children.)

   Name   **Birthdate**
   _____   _____
   _____   _____
   _____   _____

8. Describe the relationships of the child to others in the home.
   a. Responsibility for care of the child:
   b. Sibling relationships:
   c. Discipline used and child's reaction:
   d. Child's status in the family:
   Does your child have a pet?
9. What activities does your child particularly enjoy?
   What activities do you particularly enjoy doing with your child?
10. How self-sufficient is your child in dressing in indoor and outdoor clothes?

---

*Adapted from form used by the Early Childhood Education Center, University of Iowa.

Description of child

11. How would you describe your child's personality and temperament?
12. How does your child comfort himself/herself?
13. How does he/she react to anger or frustration?
14. Does your child have any particular fears? If so, please describe.
15. How has your child reacted to change or to separation from parents?

Social development

16. What group contacts has the child had? (Include description of the type of play, ages of children; also former day care experiences.)

Language development

17. Describe the sequence, rate of growth, vocabulary.

Additional information

18. Add any other information that would be of help in understanding your child (e.g., play patterns, behavior patterns, interests, handicaps.)
19. Describe meal times, food preferences, parental attitudes and methods, self-sufficiency of child, food allergies, etc.
    In case of special diets please describe completely.
    How self-sufficient is your child in eating?

Sleeping

20. Please describe regularity, amount, need for naps and usual schedule, specific problems and methods for handling.

Elimination

21. Please describe methods and timing of toilet training, parental attitudes, treatment of accidents, position, special words, responsibility.
    Describe any problems which the Center might have connected with elimination.

Filled out by _____

Date _____

APPENDIX C

SCREENING PHYSICAL EXAMINATION
Age 3 days to 7 months*

INSTRUCTIONS:
1. Select the column appropriate for the child's age.
2. Record examination results by circling or checking the letter (A) N for abnormal, A (N) for normal.
3. When the answer space contains an arrow and small letters (a← n), the item may be omitted from the examination if it was recorded at the last age indicated by uppercase letters.
4. Any abnormal findings should be completely described at the end of this form or on a separate note.

	3-7 days	1-4 mos.	5-7 mos.
General appearance, body shape, size and proportions	A N	a← n	A N
Facial features, head shape, ear shape, hands, feet	A N	a← n	A N
Skin—texture, rash, deformities, birthmarks	A N	A N	A N
Palpation of sutures and fontanelles	A N	A N	A N
Inspection of conjunctiva, cornea, iris, red reflex, pupillary reaction to light	A N	A N	A N
Eyes follow light or object and move conjugately	A N	A N	A N
Ophthalmoscopy of central retinas	A N	a← n	A N
Otoscopic exam of ear canals and drums	A N	a← n	A N
Inspection of palate, uvula, pharynx, dental ridge and oral membranes	A N	A N	A N
Palpation for submucous palatal cleft	A N	a← n	a← n
Both nasal airways patent	A N	a← n	a← n
Palpation of clavicles	A N	a← n	a← n
Inspection and palpation of neck and axilla	A N	A N	A N
Chest configuration and respiratory movements	A N	A N	A N
Auscultation of lungs	A N	A N	A N
Heart sounds—rate, rhythm, tone, murmurs	A N	A N	A N
Femoral pulses palpable and equal	A N	a← n	A N
Palpation of abdomen for musculature, organs, masses	A N	A N	A N
Genitalia including size, shape, masses in labia or spermatic cords	A N	A N	A N
Hips by abduction and Ortolani maneuver	A N	a← n	A N
Muscle tone, strength, and mobility of extremities, trunk, and neck by manipulation and inspection	A N	a← n	A N
Mother's attentiveness to child's comfort and safety during the examination	A N	A N	A N

*From Frankenburg, W.K., and North, A.F.: A guide to screening for the Early and Periodic Screening, Diagnosis and Treatment Program (EPSDT) under MEDICAID, Washington, D.C., 1974, U.S. Government Printing Office, pp. 87-89.

APPENDIX D

SCREENING PHYSICAL EXAMINATION
Age 7 months to 30 months*

INSTRUCTIONS:

1. Select the column appropriate for the child's age.
2. Record examination results by circling or checking the letter Ⓐ N for abnormal, A Ⓝ for normal.
3. When the answer space contains an arrow and small letters (a̅ n), the item may be omitted from the examination if it was recorded at the last age indicated by uppercase letters.
4. Any abnormal findings should be completely described at the end of this form or on a separate note.
5. Items marked with an asterisk (*) need not be repeated if they were recorded on the 3-day to 7-month Screening Physical Examination record.

*From Frankenburg, W.K., and North, A.F.: A guide to screening for the Early and Periodic Screening, Diagnosis and Treatment Program (EPSDT) under MEDICAID, Washington, D.C., 1974, U.S. Government Printing Office, pp. 90-92.

	8-10 mos.	12-14 mos.	17-19 mos.	23-30 mos.
Gait, posture, and body proportions	A N	A N	A N	A N
Vocalizations and speech appropriate for age	A N	A N	A N	A N
Facial features, head shape, hands, feet	A N	A N	A N	A N
Skin—texture, rash, deformities, birthmarks	A N	A N	A N	A N
Inspection of lids, conjunctiva, cornea, iris	A N	A N	A N	A N
Eyes follow light or object and move conjugately	*A N	A N	a←n	A N
Ophthalmoscopy of central retina, pupillary reactions to light	*A N	A N	a←n	A N
Otoscopic exam of ear canals and drums	*A N	A N	a←n	A N
Inspection of palate, uvula, pharynx, dental ridge, and oral membranes	A N	A N	A N	A N
Dental caries	- -	- -	A N	A N
Palpation for submucous cleft palate	*A N	a←n	a←n	a←n
Nasal mucous membranes	*A N	A N	a←n	A N
Inspection and palpation of neck and axilla	A N	A N	A N	A N
Chest configuration and respiratory movements	A N	A N	A N	A N
Auscultation of lungs	*A N	A N	a←n	A N
Auscultation of heart—rate, rhythm, tone, murmurs	*A N	A N	a←n	A N
Femoral pulses—palpable and equal	*A N	A N	a←n	a←n
Palpation of abdomen—musculature, organs, masses	*A N	A N	a←n	A N
Genitalia—size, shape, masses in labia or spermatic cords	*A N	A N	a←n	A N
Hips—abduction and Ortolani maneuver	*A N	a←n	a←n	a←n
Muscle tone, strength and mobility of extremities, trunk and neck by manipulations and inspection	*A N	A N	a←n	A N
Mother's attentiveness to child's comfort and safety during examination	A N	A N	A N	A N

APPENDIX E

SPEECH, LANGUAGE, AND HEARING COMMUNICATION CHART

Newborn to 3 years

Normal development expectancies: Responses to acoustic stimuli, the learning of language, and speech output*

Age	Activities responses	Parental observation	and	Office procedures	Interpretations and meaning
Newborn	Startle reflex to sound, more often to sudden sounds of moderate-to-loud intensity. Arousal responses. Investigators have demonstrated that relatively loud sound will arouse the newborn infant from accustomed sleep state.	Not pertinent		Not pertinent	Not ideal time to test auditory responses. Lack of expected responses bears little relationship to later communication problems. Conditions which apparently lead to auditory or other communicative problems may not become operative until several days after birth. In neurologic terms, clinical motor responses in the early months are relatively simple (gross). At this stage, more complex "apparatus" neurological pathways (ultimately used for communicative purposes) may or may not be intact.

*Committee on Standards of Child Health Care: Standards of child health care, ed. 3, Evanston, Ill., 1977, American Academy of Pediatrics, pp. 140-145.
Continued.

Normal development expectancies: Responses to acoustic stimuli, the learning of language, and speech output—cont'd

Age	Activities responses	Parental observation and	Office procedures	Interpretations and meaning
4 mo	Typically turns eyes and head in direction of sound sources. Awakens or quiets to mother's voice. May change expression or vocalize in response to sound (during babbling several speech sounds are used). May open eyes when sound is presented, or, when eyes are open, palpebral fissure size may increase. May be cessation of typical movement. May frown, smile, or search for sound. May jerk head toward sound source.*	What does he do when you talk to him? Does he react when he cannot see you? Do you see him turn toward sound of crib toys? How does he use his voice at home? If child actually has severely impaired hearing, previously noted babbling may cease or be diminished.	Tester should kneel or squat behind and to side of mother's chair. Baby is seated on mother's lap and held upright. Using quiet voice say baby's name; say s-s-s-s-s-s or k-k-k-k-k-k or use noisemaking toys. Keep sound source at ear level, but out of baby's peripheral vision. Be careful not to use a vowel (uh) after s or k.	With these procedures one is not measuring baby's hearing but indexing babies whose response seems abnormal. Lack of expected response to sound does not necessarily mean impaired hearing, but that baby's status and development need to be studied carefully. Premature or mentally retarded infants may be slow in developing expected responses to sound.
8 mo	1. Turns head and upper torso toward interesting sounds (at level of quiet conversational voice). 2. Vocalizes with variety of sounds and inflections. Done spontaneously when alone. Gives vocal responses when somebody talks to him, e.g., smiles, giggles, coos. 3. Usually responds to familiar sounds (his name, telephone bell, vacuum cleaner, barking dog) and quiets to mother's voice. 4. Usually awakens when mother talks to him.	1. Have you seen this? 2. What have you heard him say? What noises does he make? 3. What does he do if he hears father's footsteps, the vacuum cleaner, the telephone? 4. Does he respond to "no-no"? Does he jiggle to music?	Test at ear level. Baby should seek and find sound source. It is important to test from both sides out of baby's vision range. When baby does respond, reinforcement must be used to hold baby's attention. This is done by immediately repeating stimulus at a louder level while expressing approval of baby.	Response should be prompt. Delayed responses suggest possible hearing involvement. Persistent turning to one side or searching for sound but not identifying appropriate direction of its source suggests hearing problem. Failure to turn quickly in presence of other evidence of hearing suggests developmental lag and need for careful follow-up. Item 3 responses indicate baby's developing ability to "understand" everyday sounds around him (listening and discrimination).

5. Has babbling decreased?

	Behavior	Method	Significance
12 mo	1. Responds to a number of different sounds, often with different reactions, and seems to recognize them as different, e.g., jabbers in response to human voice, may cry when there is thunder, quiet when he hears mother nearby (vacuum cleaner), and frown when scolded.	1. Direct query and observation. What kinds of sounds and noises does he make when you talk to him? What does he do when he hears a loud noise?	1. Average behavior is similar to 8-mo period (Item 3), but responses should indicate more differentiation among speech sounds.
	2. Demonstrates understanding of some words by appropriate behavior, e.g., points or looks at familiar objects on request.	2. Try to test with appropriate objects by saying the word quietly without general conversation or instruction.	2. This behavior indicates early differentiation of speech sounds as symbolic meanings.
	3. Uses sounds. "Talks" to toys. This is an enjoyable experience for baby.	3. Direct query and observation. Does he "talk" to himself or make sounds as he plays with his toys?	3. One can look for changes in baby's "talking" as his attention and patterns of play change.
	4. Tries to imitate some simple words.	4. If possible, have mother demonstrate this; he is more used to her manner of speaking.	4. This is evidence of developmental maturation. Many children use a few words at this age. However, babies may not imitate words at 12 mo. Absence of verbal utterance indicates a need to inquire about verbal stimulation at home, parental attitudes, and expectancies, e.g., "Do you have time to sit and talk with him and let him jabber back?" "Does his father?"

*6 to 7 mo. is about the earliest developmental time a clear effect of orientation to sound in space can be expected.

Continued.

Normal development expectancies: Responses to acoustic stimuli, the learning of language, and speech output—cont'd

Age	Activities responses	Parental observation and Office procedures	Interpretations and meaning
18 mo	1. Expect some progressive increase in child's vocabulary (more definite words) from what was observable at 12 mo.	1. Query and demonstration. How many understandable words does he use? More or fewer than he used a few months ago?	1. Note any apparent loss of words that were previously used. With a child who has severely impaired hearing, one can expect cessation or regression of previously noted babbling.*
	2. Begins to identify parts of body, e.g., may point to nose on request.	2. Demonstration, if possible. The baby should be able to show you his nose or eyes.	2. This is clear evidence of verbal symbolic understanding.
	3. Begins to pay attention to, and identify, various sounds from considerable distance.	3. Note detail of parental anecdotes. It is important that auditory responses are identified without the use of visual cues. What does he do when refrigerator door opens in another room? When ice cream man's bell rings? When there is a fire siren? When you open a box of candy that he cannot see? Does he seem to react to music? With rhythm? Does he like to look at books with you, and turn the page?	3. Whereas at 8-12 mo. baby's auditory attention is limited to close environment, by 18 mo. he is responding to wider environment of sound, e.g., from another room or from outside the house. If hearing loss has been acquired, he probably will not do this and may show symptoms of regression in speech attempts previously made.
24 mo	1. Can follow verbal commands with two components without the aid of gestures, e.g., "Pick up the block and give it to mother."	Screening requires demonstration as well as parental reporting. Often it is easier and more economical to let mother do the demonstrating. The response should be observed and not simply accepted from parental statements. Mother can tell him to "Close the door and sit down." "Pick up the block and give it to me." "Get my purse and put it on that chair." Inquire whether he shows interest in musical introductions to regular television shows. Does he listen to music from a record player?	5. This is only one item in a battery of achievements for this age. If it can be demonstrated, this accomplishment represents a significant landmark. It is perhaps best to direct mother to undertake this. Failure to accomplish it on the part of a just 2 year old may be re-
	2. Can identify familiar objects when named.		
	3. Can spontaneously name familiar objects.		

4. Initiates "sentences" of two or more "words" which are meaningful to listener.
5. Learns new (simple) word with only one presentation.

...lated to various developmental states of affairs, any of which warrant careful investigation.

36 mo

1. Can identify objects or activities with the use of pictures, e.g., "Show me the one that is good to eat." "Show me the one you wear."
2. Identifies his or her own sex.
3. Understands some verbs, adjectives, pronouns, and prepositions.
4. Repeats a four-word sentence.
5. Uses some verbs, adjectives, pronouns, and prepositions.
6. May respond to pure tones from an audiometer, as well as to speech.
7. Names familiar objects.

1. Should be readily demonstrated.
2. "Are you a boy or a girl?" Put correct reference first.
3. Preferably, this should be demonstrated with the use of toys in a doll house or other appropriate objects: up, down, in, on, under, big, little, you, me, I. "Put the baby in the big bed." "Make the dog jump." "Push the car."
4. Actually, he should be able to repeat and use four-word sentences.
5. This requires observation, or acceptable reports, of the child's typical behavior.
6. To be determined in appropriate circumstances by qualified testers.
7. Should be readily demonstrated.

Child should be using speech socially. Deviations from normal development which may become apparent at this time and generally require extensive diagnostic evaluation include: "the retarded child," "delayed speech," "motor interference," "impaired hearing," and "emotional disturbance." If he does not quite readily demonstrate these verbal capacities, there is need for careful follow-up. If he uses jargon and gestures to try to control his environment instead of words, hearing involvement may be suspected. There always may be confusion between the dull child and the deaf child (frequently both conditions may be present). Further definitive measurement of hearing is readily available for the child of this age. Various kinds of audiometry can be done, but these require special equipment and experience. (Routine pure-tone audiometry can be carried out with confidence with about 50% of just 3 year olds.)

*This usually happens before 18 mo. if the child is, in fact, deaf.

INDEXES

AUTHOR INDEX

SUBJECT INDEX

A

AAP; *see* American Academy of Pediatrics

Abuse, child, types of, 66; *see also* Child abuse and neglect

Accidents, 47
  and emergencies, 121-124
  incidence of, 49, 54-56, 59-60
  management of, 101, 122, 124

Accidents, types of
  burns and fires, 60-61
  choking, 55-56
  falls, 54-55
  ingestion of toxic substances, 56-60
  motor vehicle, 47-54
    restraint systems for, 48-53
  strangulation, 56
  suffocation, 56

Acoustics, 271

Action and interaction, 170-175
  and learning, 170-173
  and objects, 167-168; *see also* Exploration and manipulation
  sequence, developmental, 173-174
  teacher, role of, 174-175

Admission to center
  information, background, 301-302
  policy, 99-100, 103

Advocacy for children
  local, 81, 286-287

Advocacy for children—cont'd
  national, 287-288
  state, 287-288

An Agenda for America's Children, 96

Aggression; *see also* Relations, child-child
  as exploration, 177
  as normal behavior, 192
  response to, Episode 8, 175
  suggestions for teaching, 195-197
  types, 194-195

AID charts; *see* Objectives, developmental

Allergens, 60

American Academy of Family Physicians, 104

American Academy of Pediatrics, 53, 96, 99, 102-104, 113-114, 118, 122-123

American Medical Association, 15, 104

American Nurses' Association, 96

American Red Cross, 55-56, 61

American Society for Dentistry, 79

Anemia, iron-deficient, 80-81

As You Like It, 23

Assessment, health, 99, 103, 113-115

Atherosclerosis, diet and, 76, 79

Attachment
  and detachment, 191
  importance of, 190
  and love, 25
  and need and need gratification, 25
  need for, 37

Attention
  influences on, 147-148
  problem of the match, 161

Italicized page numbers refer to illustrations.

319

Child abuse and neglect—cont'd
  procedures in cases of suspected, 67-69
  results of, 64
  sources of information, 292-293
Child Abuse Prevention and Treatment Act, 62-63
Child Care Food Program, 84
Child development; *see also* Development,
    theories of
  characteristics, developmental, 31*t*, 32*t*, 33*t*
  overview, 22-23
  principles of, 23, 28, 34
  sequence of, Gesell, 26-27
Child Development Associate, vii
Child Nutrition Act of 1972, 84
Childhood, as stage of life, 4, 6, 9, 10-11, 16
Childrearing, advice and customs of
  breastfeeding, 4, 11
  education, 8, 10, 11, 12-13, 15
  moral and character development, 4, 6, 8, 196
Children's Center at SUNY, 40
Children's Defense Fund, 286
Choking, recommended treatment for, 55-56
Church, influence on
  appearance, physical, 8
  attitudes toward children, 13, 15
  readiness, academic, 8
Cleaning, teeth, 80, 112, 234
Climbing; *see* Locomotion
Cognition, social
  definition, 181
  other-knowledge, 190-193
  self-knowledge, 184-190; *see also* Identity, sense
    of; Self, sense of
Color, environmental, 272
Committee on Standards of Child Health Care, 114
Communication
  and conversation, 201-204
    need for partner, 183, 199, 201, 204
    nonverbal, 183, 201-202
    singing, 140-141
    Speech, Language, and Hearing Communica-
      tion Chart, 306-311
    verbal, 203-204

Communication—cont'd
  parent-center, daily
    arrival at center, *111*, 241-242, 249, 257
    pickup at centers, *111*, 248, 256, 266
    pickup and delivery, policy, 53-54, 282-283
    and primary caregivers, 277
    written, 93, 283
Community Coordinated Child Care, 286
Competence
  development of, 163-164
  foundations of, 23, 37
  need for, 160
  presence or absence, 18
  representational, 167*t*, 170
  teaching for, 175
Competency, social
  components, 181
  landmarks, developmental, 182
  need for communication partner, 183
  objectives for involvement with people, 193*t*
  objectives for self-regulation, 188-189*t*
  processes, developmental, 181-182
  teachers of, 182
Component
  health, of group care, 95-126
    administration of, 99, 102, 112, 114
    policy, 99-101
    supervision of, 100, 110-115
  nutrition, of group care, 72-94
    coordinator, need for, 73
  safety, of group care, 47-71
    coordinator, need for, 68, 102, 123
Concept, self; *see also* Identity, sense of; Self,
    sense of
  and child abuse, 64
  goals for, 156, 181
  importance of, 158
  as indicator of reading readiness, 158
  and sense of self, 185
  teaching techniques for, Episodes 3, 4, 5; 158-159
Concepts, nutrition, 92-93
Conferences; *see* Relationships, parent-center
Conscience, beginnings of, 25

Mortality, infant, 9-11, 19
Mother Goose, 11
Mother-play and Nursery Songs, 13
Mothers, working, incidence of, 35
Motivation, 30, 157-164
  and basic needs, 159-160
  and curiosity, 146, 157
  and imitation, 175
  and self-concept, 158-159
  and stimulation, 160-164
Motor skill development; *see also* Development,
    motor; Physical fitness; Skills, motor
  objectives, developmental, 212*t*
  in play, 227-228
  principles of, underlying, 213
  sequence of, 143-146, 211-213
Motor vehicle accidents, 47-54; *see also* Restraint
    systems for motor vehicles
Movement; *see also* Motor skill development; Physi-
    cal fitness
  definition, 211
  education, 143-146
  values of, 210-211
Mumps, 106
Music in the curriculum, 139-141

N

Napping, 269, 272-273
National Association for the Education of Young Chil-
    dren, 286
National Center on Child Abuse and Neglect, 62
National Center for Health Statistics, 76-78
National Clearinghouse for Poison Control Centers,
    58
National Council of Jewish Women, 63-64
National Council of Organizations for Children and
    Youth, 19
National Day Care Study, 279-280
National Institute of Mental Health, 161
National School Lunch Act, 84
Needs, basic, 35, 159-160
  and group living, 37
  and growth and development, 36-37
  and role of teacher/caregiver, 41*t*-42*t*

Norms, age, 26-27
Nutrients, 83-84
Nutrition, 73-74, 92-93
  disorders, related, 75-81
  relation to intelligence and learning, 74-75

O

Obedience, 10
Obesity, prevention of, 75-76
Object permanence; *see also* Objects
  activities to teach, 134-135
  awareness of, beginning, 144
  development of, 165-166
  and self-knowledge, 185
Objectives, developmental, for
  imaginative and creative behavior, 149*t*
  involvement with people, 192*t*
  language, 200*t*
  motor development, 212*t*
  numerical concepts, 172*t*
  object manipulation, 172*t*
  reading, 171*t*
  self-help skills and routines, 233*t*
  self-regulation, 188*t*-189*t*
  writing, 171*t*
Objects; *see also* Exploration and manipulation;
    Object permanence
  criteria for selection, 167
  reading-related, 170
Obstacle courses, 218
Office of Child Development, vii, 97, 181
Office of Human Development Services, ACYF, 104;
    see also Parent's Guide to Day Care
Olfaction, 142-143
On the Origin of the Species, 12, 23
Origins of Intelligence in Children, 29
Otitis media, 116-117

P

Parallel Lives, 6-7
Parasites
  infectious, 118
  intestinal, 81
Parent Effectiveness Training System, 285